david beckham

KU-391-277

davidbeckham
MY SIDE

David Beckham
with Tom Watt

CollinsWillow
An Imprint of HarperCollins*Publishers*

Tom Watt, who collaborated with David Beckham on this book, is an established author, actor, sportswriter and broadcaster

First published in hardback 2003 by
CollinsWillow
an imprint of HarperCollins*Publishers*
London

First published in paperback 2004

© Footwork Productions Ltd 2004

1

All rights reserved. No part of this publication may be reproduced, stored in a retrieval system, or transmitted, in any form or by any means, electronic, mechanical, photocopying, recording or otherwise, without the prior written permission of the publishers

The Author asserts the moral right to be identified as the author of this work

A CIP catalogue record for this book is available from the British Library

ISBN 0 00 715733 9

Typeset by Rowland Phototypesetting Ltd,
Bury St Edmunds, Suffolk

Printed and bound in Great Britain by
Clays Ltd, St Ives plc

The HarperCollins website address is www.harpercollins.co.uk

To Victoria, Brooklyn and Romeo
The three people who always make me smile
My Babies Forever

Love David

Contents

Acknowledgements

To Mum and Dad: without your love and guidance there wouldn't be a story here for the telling.

Love to the family, especially Lynne and Joanne, Colin, Georgina and Freddie, Nan and Grandad, Tony and Jackie, Louise, Haydn, Liberty and Tululah, Christian and Lucy.

To my school friends, my pals from boyhood and my Ridgeway team-mates: I've not forgotten any of you.

To the friends I've been lucky enough to find during a career in professional football, including Gary, Phil, Ryan, Nicky and Scholesy. And special thanks to Dave, Terry and Steve for your company, advice and more in recent years.

To Andrew and Charles; Caroline and Jo.

To everyone at HarperCollins, including Michael, Tom, Jane and David, for their patience and support. Particular thanks to my co-writer Tom, for jogging my memory and helping me find the words I needed.

To the team at Footwork and 19. Thanks for all the hard graft.

Thanks to all the coaches and managers, particularly Stuart Underwood, Malcolm Fidgeon, Eric Harrison, Sir Alex Ferguson and Sven-Goran Eriksson, who've lit up my time in the game we love: you have my gratitude, respect and admiration.

Thanks, as well, to all the great players I've been privileged to play alongside for Manchester United, Real Madrid and England. Whatever I've done has only been possible because of the talent, commitment and inspiration of the other ten.

David Beckham
August 2004

The Back Garden, August 2004

*'What matters most in my life
I can see in front of me.'*

In Madrid, the evenings are perfect like this more often than not. It's just gone seven, the sun's down from the sky but it's still warming my heart and warming my bones. There's a glass of red wine on the table in front of me. And another in front of Victoria. Brooklyn's being some kind of superhero, plunging in and out of the little pool a few yards down the garden from this terrace where Mr and Mrs are sitting, feet up, cheering him on. Romeo's at the bottom of the steps that take you out onto the grass, being best friends with Carlos. That's the dog, not the left-back. It's a long way from Chingford but, just like the house I grew up in, it's not just a *casa*. It feels like a home, somewhere you belong. *Un hogar*, they call it in Spain.

Back from a summer away and Euro 2004, we've found a place to live together, the four of us, here in Madrid. We've taken a three-year lease – my contract at Real finishes in 2007 – on a house in La Moraleja, a residential area to the north of the city. We're twenty minutes from the training ground and from the Santiago Bernebeu; half an hour from the middle of town. And just a few minutes from where Brooklyn is going to start school next month. La Moraleja is green and quiet – *todo tranquillo* – and the trees spread shade across our garden, which I can see the end of from here, for most of every day.

I've got my first competitive game of a new season waiting for me in a week's time, after last season left Real Madrid needing to qualify for the group stage of the Champions League this time around. It's crossed my mind a couple of times recently that we had to do the same at United before going on to win the thing back in 1999. I don't know if you could ever have quite the same feeling ahead of a new season with any other club: here at Real our own sense of ambition in the dressing room is as tangible as the sense of expectation around the streets of the city. This is a football club, after all, where anything – anything at all – seems possible. Each fresh start feels like history waiting to be made. What's more, we know we owe the *madridistas* after what happened to us –and to them – last spring.

I've been in Madrid for twelve months now. A year ago, all of it was new, and as confusing as it was exciting. I was waiting to find out what was expected of me; what I could expect from life at a new club and in a new city. Now, I've found my way past most of those questions. I mean: I know now what I'm going to be asked. The answers, of course, will have to wait for kick-off. And a new manager at the Bernebeu, José Antonio Camacho, has already made sure we understand that we'll need to find the right ones.

To say a lot's happened since I left the club I grew up at, Manchester United, and came to Spain to start learning all over again, wouldn't be the half of it. Some of what's gone on I could perhaps have been half-expecting. Most of it, though, I had no idea at all about when I got here a season and a major international tournament ago. I can still remember the adrenalin rushing through my system the August morning I was introduced to Madrid as a Real player. At the Pabellon Raimundo Saporta, I'd been hurried through corridors and then ushered onto a stage alongside the President, Florentino Perez, and the greatest player ever to pull on the white shirt that I was going to wear for the next four years, Alfredo di Stefano.

Thinking back now, one thing nags me about that day. Especially after the shocks and challenges and lessons I've learnt over the months since. Amidst all that felt just right that morning, one thing jarred at the time and still does. Now, in August 2004, I'm grateful to put right a choice of words I made before my life was turned upside down during a year in Spain, back home in England and at Euro 2004. The last twelve months have reminded me – if I needed reminding – what's made the whole adventure worth the living so far.

When it came time for me to speak to the press and to the Real supporters, my voice trailing away across that hangar of a basketball court, I remember I said:

'I have always loved football. Of course I love my family and I have a wonderful life. But football is everything to me. To play for Real Madrid is a dream come true.'

Football and my family: know about them and you know most of what you need to about David Beckham. Back then, though, I had those things – the things that have made me the person I am – in the wrong order.

I probably knew then. And I definitely know it about myself now. Football's the best game in the world, the best career I could possibly have been lucky enough to enjoy. It's given me fulfilment and a lot more besides. But *everything to me*? No, I'm sitting here on a terrace at our new home in Moraleja and what matters most in my life – in anybody's life, surely – I can see in front of me. I can put my arms around them right now: my wife and my two sons. They're what I'm here for. I hope I'll never have to, but I'd sacrifice what I do for a living and everything it's brought my way without a second thought to have what I have having them. I met Victoria, fell in love with and married her and, together, we've made our family. Until you love your own children, you never realise quite how much your mum and dad loved you. I'm ready to do for my family what Mum and Dad did for me: everything. Doesn't matter how exciting, frantic or rewarding the rest of it is, it's Victoria and Brooklyn and Romeo who make sense of it all.

'To play for Real Madrid is a dream come true.'

That's right enough. And it keeps coming true every time I pull Real's white shirt over my head. But for us Beckhams, here together with the warm air wrapped round us, back in England or wherever else the future's going to take us: it's the *together* that counts: I could never have imagined how sweet it would be until it happened. And it has for me; and for my wife and for my children too. Our lives have come true: a family. Whatever lies ahead of us, I won't ever let them go.

Murdering the Flowerbeds

'Mrs Beckham? Can David come and have a game in the park?'

I'm sure Mum could dig it out of the pile: that first video of me in action. There I am, David Robert Joseph Beckham, aged three, wearing the new Manchester United kit Dad had bought me for Christmas, playing football in the front room of our house in Chingford. Twenty-five years on, and Victoria could have filmed me having a kickabout this morning with Brooklyn before I left for training. For all that so much has happened during my life – and the shirt I'm wearing now is a different colour – some things haven't really changed at all.

As a father watching my own sons growing up, I get an idea of what I must have been like as a boy; and reminders, as well, of what Dad was like with me. As soon as I could walk, he made sure I had a football to kick. Maybe I didn't even wait for a ball. I remember when Brooklyn had only just got the hang of standing up. We were messing around together one afternoon after training. For some reason there was a tin of baked beans on the floor of the kitchen and, before I realised it, he'd taken a couple of unsteady steps towards it and kicked the thing as hard as you like. Frightening really: you could fracture a metatarsal doing that.

Even as I was hugging him better, I couldn't help laughing. *That must have been me.*

It's just there, wired into the genes. Look at Brooklyn: he always wants to be playing football, running, kicking, diving about. And he's already listening, like he's ready to learn. By the time he was three and a half, if I rolled the football to him and told him to stop it, he'd trap it by putting his foot on it. Then he'd take a step back and line himself up before kicking it back to me. He's also got a great sense of balance. We were in New York when Brooklyn was about two and a half, and I remember us coming out of a restaurant and walking down some steps. He was standing, facing up towards Victoria and I, his toes on one step and his heels rocking back over the next. This guy must have been watching from inside the restaurant, because suddenly he came running out and asked us how old our son was. When I told him, he explained he was a child psychologist and that for Brooklyn to be able to balance himself over the step like that was amazing for a boy of his age.

It's a little too early to tell with Romeo, but Brooklyn has got a real confidence that comes from his energy, his strength, and his sense of coordination. He's been whizzing around on two-wheeled scooters – I mean flying – for years already. He's got a belief in himself, physically, that I know I had as well. When I was a boy, I only ever felt really sure of myself when I was playing football. In fact I'd still say that about me now, although Victoria has given me confidence in myself in all sorts of other ways. I know she'll do the same for Brooklyn and Romeo too.

For all that father and son have in common, Brooklyn and I are very different. By the time I was his age, I was already telling anyone who would listen: 'I'm going to play football for Manchester United.' He says he wants to be a footballer like Daddy, but United or Real? We haven't heard that out of him yet. Brooklyn's a really strong, well-built boy. Me, though, I was always skinny. However much I ate it never made any difference while I was growing up. When I was playing football, I must have seemed even smaller because, if I wasn't with my dad and his mates, I was over at Chase Lane Park, just round the corner from the house, playing with boys twice my age. I don't know if it was because I was good or because they could kick me up in the air and I'd come back for more, but they always turned up on the doorstep after school:

'Mrs Beckham? Can David come and have a game in the park?'

I spent a lot of time in Chase Lane Park. If I wasn't there with the bigger boys like Alan Smith, who lived two doors away on our road, I'd be there with my dad. We'd started by kicking a ball about in the back garden but I was murdering the flowerbeds so, after he got in from his job as a heating engineer, we'd go to the park together and just practise and practise for hours on end. All the strengths in my game are the ones Dad taught me in the park 20 years ago: we'd work on touch and striking the ball properly until it was too dark to see. He'd kick the ball up in the air as high as he could and get me to control it. Then it would be knocking it in with each foot, making sure I was doing it right. It was great, even if he did drive me mad sometimes. 'Why can't you just go in goal and let me take shots at you?' I'd be thinking. I suppose you could say he was pushing me along. You'd also have to say, though, that it was all I wanted to do and I was lucky Dad was so willing to do it with me.

My dad, Ted, played himself for a local team called Kingfisher in the Forest and District League, and I would go along with my mum Sandra, my older sister Lynne and baby Joanne to watch him play. He was a centre-forward; Mark Hughes, but rougher. He had trials for Leyton Orient and played semi-professional for a couple of years at Finchley Wingate. Dad was a good player, although he always used to get caught offside. It took me a long time to understand how that rule worked and I'm not sure Dad ever really got it sorted out. I loved watching him. I loved everything that went with the game, and I could tell how much playing meant to him as well. When he told me he was going to pack in playing regularly himself so he could concentrate on coaching me – I must have been eight or nine at the time – I knew exactly what that sacrifice meant even though he never talked about it in that way.

From the time I was seven, Dad was taking me to training with Kingfisher on midweek evenings down at a place called Wadham Lodge, just round the North Circular Road from us. I've got great memories of those nights, not just being with Dad and his mates, but of the ground itself. It was about ten minutes from the house in the car. We'd drive down this long street of terraced houses and pull in through a set of big, blue wooden gates, past the first car park and onto the second car park, which was right next to the training ground. The pitch was orange-coloured gravel and cinder, with proper goalposts and nets, and there was a little bar, the social club, that overlooked it. Beyond that pitch, there were three or four others, including the best one which was reserved for cup games and special occasions. It had a little wall all around it and two dugouts. It seemed like a massive stadium to me at the time. I dreamt about playing on that pitch one day.

Wadham Lodge wasn't very well looked after back then. I remember the changing rooms were pure Sunday League: mud on the floor, really dingy lighting and the water dribbling out of cold showers. Then there was the smell of the liniment that players used to rub on their legs. It would hit you as soon as you walked in. There were floodlights – just six lamps on top of poles – but at least once every session they'd go out and somebody would have to run in and put coins in a meter that was in a cupboard just inside the changing room door.

As well as training with Kingfisher during the football season, we'd be back at Wadham Lodge in the summer holidays. Dad used to run, and also play for, a team in the summer league, so I'd come to games with him. We'd practise together before and after and then, while his match was taking place on the big pitch, I'd find some other boys to play with on the cinder next door. I've had most of my professional career at clubs with the best facilities and where everything's taken care of, but I'm glad I had the experience of a place like Wadham Lodge when I was a boy. I mean, if I'd not been there with my dad, I might have grown up never knowing about Soap on a Rope. More to the point, it was where I started taking free-kicks. After everybody else had finished and was in the social club, I'd stand on the edge of the penalty area and chip a dead ball towards goal. Every time I hit the bar was worth 50p extra pocket money from my dad that week. And, just as important, a pat on the back.

The other dads might bring their boys along sometimes but, once I started, I was there week in and week out. I'd sit in the bar and watch the men training and then, towards the end of the session, they'd let me join in with the five-a-sides. I was so excited to be out there playing with the rest of them – these grown men – that I took whatever I had coming. I do remember an occasion when one of them came flying into me with a tackle and Dad wasn't happy about it at all but, usually, if I took a knock he'd just tell me to get up and get on with it. He warned me that I had to be prepared to get a bit roughed up now and again. If he'd been running around telling people not to tackle me all evening, it would have been pointless me being there in the first place. The fact that I always seemed to be playing football with players who were bigger and stronger than me when I was young, I'm sure, helped me later on in my career.

On the nights when I wasn't at Wadham Lodge, I'd be in Chase Lane Park. We had this secret cut-through to get there: across the road and then four or five houses down from my mum and dad's where there was a private alley. We'd wait around at the top of it until there was nobody about and then sprint fifty yards to the hedge, then through it and the hole in the fence. I still have one or two friends who I first met in Chase Lane. I went on to school with Simon Treglowen and his brother Matt, and I'm still in touch with Simon now. We decided we got on all right after one particular row about whether or not I'd scored past him in goal. That turned into a big fight, even though Simon's four years older than me. Fighting: it's a funny way boys have of making friends. Usually we'd just kick a ball around until it got dark, but there also used to be a youth club, in a little hut, run by a lady called Joan. My mum knew her and would phone up to say we were on our way over. You could play table tennis or pool and get a fizzy drink or some chocolate. There was an outdoor paddling pool at the back that got filled up in the summer. Some days, Joan would organise a minibus and we'd all head off down to Walthamstow baths. There was also a skate ramp by the side of the hut. I suppose my mum knows now that some of my cuts and bruises were from skateboarding, even though I wasn't allowed on a skateboard back then. The one bad knock I got happened one evening when I fell getting our ball back from the paddling pool after it had been closed up for the night. Joan was still there and she phoned home to tell my parents how I'd got the cut on my head. For about six or seven years, into my early teens, it was a whole world in that park. All those facilities have gone now. It's a shame. Times change and some kids started messing the place up until it had to be closed down.

My very first close friend was a boy called John Brown who lived just up the road. John and I went through both primary and secondary school together. He wasn't really a footballer so, when I couldn't talk him into a kickabout over at the park, we'd play Lego or Gameboy round at one of our houses, or ride our bikes or rollerskate up and down our road. Later on, when I started playing for Ridgeway Rovers, John used to come along to some of our games even though he didn't play. A few of us, especially me and another Ridgeway boy named Nicky Lockwood, were always up for the pictures and John used to come too; I remember Mum would drop us off at the cinema over in Walthamstow. When we were little, John Brown and I were best mates but I suppose my football took me in a very different direction. John went off and became a baker after we both left school.

Lucky for me, they loved their football at my first school, Chase Lane Primary. I can still remember Mr McGhee, the teacher who used to coach us: a Scotsman and passionate with it, a bit like Alex Ferguson in fact. Kids used to tell tales about Mr McGhee throwing teacups, cricket balls, anything really, at the wall when he was annoyed. I never witnessed that myself but we were all a bit scared of his reputation, anyway. We had a really good team and used to turn out in this all-green kit. I was playing football with the Cubs as well, which you could only do if you went to church on Sunday. So all the family – me, Mum and Dad and my sisters – made sure we were there every time, without fail.

My parents knew how much I loved football. If there was a way for me to get a game, they did everything they could to make it happen. Whether it was playing or getting coaching, I'd have my chance. I was at every soccer school going. The first one was the

Roger Morgan Soccer School, run by the former Spurs winger. I went there over and over again, doing all the badges until I got the gold. Dad was a lifelong United supporter and we started going to watch them when they played in London. My mum's dad was diehard Tottenham and he used to take me to White Hart Lane. Every Christmas, I'd end up with a United kit and a Tottenham kit, and maybe an England kit from my mum. If it was football – or anything to do with football – I was there.

Mum wasn't all that keen on football. Her dad was, though, which was one of the reasons I loved being with him as much as I did. Joe was employed in the print trade. For a long time he was over the road from home, at the Stationery Office in Islington. Then he moved down to Fleet Street. He and my grandmother, Peggy, lived on an estate just off City Road, down near Old Street. My dad went out to work early most Saturdays. The rest of us would get on the train at Walthamstow and go down to see my grandparents for the day. We had to get there before noon: Grandad would be off about 11.30 if he was going to watch Spurs. Before leaving, he'd come downstairs and watch me play football in the little park on the estate. I'm sure Grandad remembers those times: he definitely remembers me breaking his spectacles. I was only about six but I was already kicking a ball hard enough that his glasses didn't stand a chance the time I accidentally caught him full in the face.

Once Joe went off to White Hart Lane, Peggy would take us off to the shops. Sometimes we'd go to the West End but, more often, we'd get the bus up to the Angel and go to Chapel Market. I didn't mind at all. I had to follow Mum and Nan and my sisters around for a bit, but I always seemed to wangle a toy or something by the end of the afternoon. We sometimes had pie and mash for lunch in Chapel Street as well. Once we got back to the flat,

Joe would be getting in from football. Then he'd get ready to go out and do the night shift. Dad would pick us up in Wenlock Street after finishing work and we'd all drive home together.

Once I started to get serious about playing football, Joe and Peggy would come over to us on Sunday morning. Grandad came and watched all my games. I liked him being there: he was softer with me than Dad when it came to talking about the match and how I'd played. Mum wanted to come too, so Peggy would stay at our house. She'd look after Lynne and have Sunday dinner ready when we all came in. Then, Sunday afternoons, we often went down to Victoria Park in Hackney. There was plenty of open space to play football with Dad and Grandad, and there were lots of other things to do as well: a big playground, the boating lake and even a little zoo.

I couldn't have asked for anything more and I didn't, but along came Ridgeway Rovers anyway and took over my life. I was seven, so it's not surprising I'm not sure now how it all happened. My mum remembers me being spotted playing in the park and a bloke called Stuart Underwood knocking on our front door to ask about me. My dad, though, reckons there was an advert about a new boys' football team in the local paper and that afternoon over at Chase Lane was a sort of trial. Either way, I'm really grateful – and proud – that I was part of that first Ridgeway Rovers team. And the man who set up the team had a lot to do with me making a future for myself in the game.

Stuart Underwood's a massive bloke. About six feet four, with a big booming voice and this fantastic presence about him. He was a bit of a sergeant major type. I was scared of him at first. He could be pretty tough: no matter how young you were, if you weren't playing well, in a game or in training, he'd tell you that you were rubbish and needed to do better, instead of just jollying you along. Stuart was honest with you. But he wasn't one of those dads who stood on the touchline at kids' games, bawling and screaming. He had this softness about him as well. His own son Robert played in the team, but Stuart seemed like a father figure to all of us. And he had this dream about creating a really good team.

Every single boy just loved playing for Stuart and we had this fantastic team spirit. He'd organise for Ridgeway to play in competitions in Holland and Germany, so we gained the same sort of experience as a professional footballer playing in the Champions League or an international tournament. Other fathers got involved, too. My dad took on some of the coaching. So did a man called Steve Kirby, whose son Ryan played for Ridgeway and ended up playing against me ten years later in the League. Dad was always a fit man and he did running with us, as well as working on our technique. Steve was a bit of a tactician and he used to do positional play, runs off the ball and that kind of thing. A lot of the time, all three of them would be there and we'd split into smaller groups: there weren't many boys our age who got that much attention paid to their training. The three of them – Steve, Stuart and my dad – used to argue a lot, but it was all in the cause. They were honest people wanting to make the team as good as they could.

It worked. I don't know where Stuart found them, but we had some really good players: Ryan Kirby, Micah Hyde, who's now at Watford, Jason Brissett, who was at Bournemouth last I heard, and Chris Day, who was a lanky centre-forward for us but ended up playing in goal for QPR. It was all about the team, though. Stuart Underwood's son, Robert, was a perfect example. To be honest, he didn't have great ability to start with but because he worked so hard at his game, he made himself into a good team player. That was credit to him, but it was credit to Stuart and the rest of us too. We never once thought to ourselves: he's not good enough to be playing for Ridgeway.

Stuart had to have everything done properly. We always had a decent pitch on which to play our home games, like the one at Ainslie Wood Sports Ground, which was just a short walk from home. We trained twice a week. Stuart lived nearby, in Larkswood Road, and there was a park there, with decent facilities, that we used to use. One way or another, Stuart would make sure we had what we needed. When we had important games, like Cup finals, he'd insist on us eight and nine-year-olds wearing a collar and tie. One important rule was that if you didn't turn up for training in the week, then you didn't play at the weekend; it was as simple as that. It was a good habit to learn: I always made sure I was there and that I was there on time. I loved the training anyway. Lived for it. But it was also another reason we had such a good team: Ridgeway Rovers always went about things the right way.

With so many boys' sides, you notice the most talented players. They make a big fuss of the individuals in the team. That wasn't allowed with Ridgeway: any showing off and you'd be brought back down. It was all about the team. In no time, we were starting to win games ten and eleven-nil and people could see there was something special about us. Professional clubs started watching our players, and I think West Ham asked about me when I was eleven. But Stuart, Steve and my dad had decided that there should be no need for any of us to be involved with clubs until we were older. If you were training with a professional club, the rule was you couldn't be training with a Sunday League team at the same time. I knew I didn't want that, I wasn't ready for it. We all stuck with Ridgeway. I think, in the long run, those rules were why so many of us went on to make a success of ourselves. We learnt about commitment and dedication right from the start.

I had to learn about not playing football too. Because I was smaller than most, I used to get my share of knocks. Dad had drummed into me that, most of the time, the best thing to do was just get up and get on with it, like I'd had to with his mates over at Wadham Lodge. He taught me a lot about avoiding injury as well. As a winger – and because people were starting to hear about me a bit – I often had a defender trying to give me a kick. Dad worked with me on keeping the ball moving, releasing it quickly once it was under control. That still helps me keep out of scrapes as a professional player. And it's the best way to play. When I was about ten, I did have one layoff through injury: the kind that happens to lots of boys. Running and jumping all the time, especially on hard pitches, ends up jarring knees, shins and ankles. With me, it was my heels: pins and needles at first and then, later, aching during and after games. I tried putting bits of foam in my boots but eventually I had to have a complete break from football. I couldn't play, I couldn't train. Couldn't even have a kickabout over at the park. That was the longest five weeks of my life and, in a way, I've never got over it. Having to watch football instead of playing it still has me climbing up walls.

Ridgeway Rovers was a great time for all of us, not just the players. Our families got involved, whether it was washing kit, driving us about, coming on trips or raising funds. That team was together for six years, which meant our families were, too. And you can't spend that amount of time together without becoming pretty close. I remember Micah Hyde's dad, Ken, used to have dreadlocks: him and my dad – short back and sides – would be stood on the touchline together on a Sunday for the Ridgeway game. The parents used to organise dinners and Friday night dances to help raise money to pay for the team. Even though it was Dad who took us for training, my mum probably put in almost as many hours on me and my football, despite her job as a hairdresser. She was the only one of the mums who drove, so if there was a minibus run she always ended up with the job. When Dad was out working, Mum would be the one who got me to where I needed to be, when I needed to be there, with the right stuff ready in the right bag.

Looking back, it must have been quite hard for my sisters, with so much of our family time being tied up with my football. I've spoken to Lynne about it since and she says she did feel a bit left out by it all. She's three years older than me and had her own friends and just got on with her own life. Even so, when we were at school together Lynne would always stick up for me if there was any trouble. One lunchtime at Chingford High, I remember having an argument with an older boy in the dinner queue. He ended up whacking me out in the playground. It was Lynne who took me home. She made sure I was all right and that the teachers at school knew what had happened. Football, though, she didn't really like at all. We've both got our own families now: Lynne and her husband Colin have a girl and a boy, Georgina and Freddie. Even though we don't see that much of each other because of the kids, I'd say I feel closer to my older sister these days than I ever did when we were young.

It was different with Joanne. I was five when she came along. I can still remember standing in the kitchen at home and my dad coming in and telling me she'd been born and me bursting into tears. I really wanted a brother, of course. But we got on fine: if I wanted her to go in goal in the back garden, she never said no. She just trailed after me all the time: to football, the park, the shops, everywhere. Joanne's a hairdresser now, just like Mum, and it's only in the last couple of years, since she started working and I got married, that we've stopped being together so much like that. I suppose she had to grow up eventually; and so did I. Sometimes, though, I do miss having my little mate around. I'm sure Joanne misses running around with big brother as well.

Mum always tried to make sure we sat down together to dinner as a family. That was when she and Dad would try and get me to tell them about what I'd been doing at school. I do the same with Brooklyn now. If I ask him, I usually get the same response my parents got with me: nothing. It wasn't that it was a secret or anything. It's just how kids are, isn't it? When I was at primary school, I'd be around to help with meal times at home. I would take Joanne out in the garden or in the front room to play so Mum wouldn't be tripping over a toddler while she was cooking. When it came time to sit down, I used to have the job of laying the table. Then, at secondary school, I opted to do Home Economics – cooking, basically – because the alternative was a double period of Science. I enjoyed being in the kitchen when I was at home anyway. By the time I was thirteen, if Mum was working, she'd leave me to get dinner ready for all of us. If she was cutting hair at home, I'd make cups of tea and arrange little plates of biscuits for her clients while they were there at the house.

There must have been some kind of mistake, because when I moved on to secondary school – Chingford High in Nevin Drive – it turned out they played rugby instead of football. Lucky for me, our rugby teacher, John Bullock, was tough and disciplined but a lovely man. He was great with all of us and always seemed to have a lot of time for me. He was a fantastic teacher. He died a few years back, on the same night I got sent off against Argentina in Saint-Etienne, but he was the one teacher I stayed in touch with. Even after I first went up to Old Trafford, I used to write to

Mr Bullock, as well as go back to see him and the school, which I think meant a lot to him. People have told me since that he really adored me, and just talked about me all the time.

I don't think Mr Bullock was very interested in football, but there were that many of us boys going on at him, pestering him, that he agreed to give it a go. And everything changed. As soon as we had a school football team, we started winning leagues and cups, which was great for us. It was great for the school, as well. Maybe the football helped me to be happy there. I wasn't that interested in lessons. I was cross-country champion for the local borough and swam for Chingford High, but there was only one thing I ever wanted to do with my life. I was lucky that I had that drive from a really young age. Knowing what I wanted in the future, what would have been the point in messing about along the way? I got in trouble once or twice for being cheeky, like every school-boy does. But, most of the time, I kept my head down and did my homework: I used to pop into Alan Smith's house and his mum, Pat, would help me with some of it. She was really good at Maths, I remember, and Alan was too. He's in insurance now, working for Rothschild, and I run into him now and again: he's married and has moved away but he works from an office in his mum and dad's loft. The important thing was that I never missed a day's school, unless I was ill, at either Chase Lane Primary or at Chingford High.

If it hadn't been football, I don't know what I would have ended up doing when I grew up. I liked Music lessons and, at primary school, they thought I had a decent voice. I sang a solo in the school choir just before I left there. One subject I really enjoyed all through school was Art. Even before I went to Chingford High, I loved drawing and painting. As well as doing it at Chase Lane Primary, Joan had all the stuff we needed for painting inside the hut in the park. On a rainy day at home, I'd spend hours copying Disney cartoon figures out of comics. I seem to remember Donald Duck was my speciality. As I got older, I began drawing cartoon figures that I'd made up myself. Even the artwork ended up coming back to football, though. Once I started playing for Ridgeway Rovers, instead of Mickey and Donald, I started drawing cartoons of games and the other people involved with the team: great goals, complete with Stuart Underwood in the background, his speech bubble describing what was going on in the rest of the picture.

Playing for the school team was the way into representative football, of course, and I was able to play District for Waltham Forest and County for Essex. I've been lucky to have such good coaching ever since those evenings over in the park with Dad. Don Wiltshire and Martin Heather, were both great for me as a teenager, though they couldn't have been more different. Don, who managed the District side, was this solid, well-built man with a deep voice and a way about him that told you he knew exactly what he wanted for the team. When I first started playing for Waltham Forest, it felt like being selected to play for England.

People criticise schools football sometimes, saying it's all about getting the ball down the other end quickly, using kick and rush tactics, with the bigger kids always being the ones who get a game. All I can say is, it wasn't like that for me at school, at District or County level. All those teams tried to play. It took me a little while to get into the side because I was so much smaller than most of the other boys my age. But once I had a chance, Don and Martin both used to encourage me, and the rest of the team, to play to our strengths.

Martin Heather was the Essex manager and the exact opposite to Don – or Stuart Underwood, for that matter. All the boys loved him. Martin was also the sort of man that our mums would fancy:

quiet, always smart, very well-spoken. He was a very different kind of coach, too. He hardly ever shouted, which meant that when he did you knew he wasn't happy. He really looked after us. I remember he took us on a football tour to Texas when I was thirteen. I think all the parents had to help come up with the money for it, but Martin organised everything.

It didn't make any difference to me if I was on Hackney Marshes or at some tournament in a foreign country: either way, I was playing football. Because of that, most of those trips and the travelling just passed me by. For different reasons, it's still like that for me now: get on a plane, then on a coach, eat, sleep, play the game and then back on the plane and home again. I do, though, remember going with Essex to play in America.

I love the States. I love the patriotism, the way of life. For once, I didn't even feel homesick. That trip was different because instead of staying together, we lodged on our own with local families. The first people I stayed with were Mexican. Their house was just a couple of steps up from being a shack, to be honest, but they turned out to be really nice people. They had a son who was taking part in the competition. They were mad about football and couldn't do enough for me. All my Essex team-mates were staying in these huge houses and being driven around in huge cars. We'd just get in the pickup and drive down to McDonald's for breakfast every morning. I had such a great week with that family: I sometimes find myself thinking about them even now.

Happy at home and playing as much football as I was, there was only one worry in my life: I thought Manchester United were never going to notice me down in London. The Ridgeway policy of young boys not going off straight away to professional clubs didn't bother me. I was having a great time playing and training with the team and, because of my dad, there was only one professional club I ever wanted to play for. In the back of my mind I just had to trust that, if I got on and worked hard, United would hear about me. What else could I do?

Word got around about the success of Ridgeway Rovers and we got used to the scouts turning up at our games every week. I know my dad was approached by scouts from West Ham and Wimbledon, as well as from Arsenal and Spurs. When the time came to train with a professional club, I had to choose between the two North London clubs, as I couldn't have gone to United anyway, unless we'd moved up to Manchester. I chose Spurs. Maybe it had something to do with my grandad being Tottenham mad. I remember saying to Mum at the time:

'Grandad will be pleased, won't he?'

Tottenham seemed a friendly club; back then David Pleat was the manager. I just felt more at home there. The coaching was good and Spurs had some excellent players of my age: Nick Barmby was in the same group and so was Sol Campbell, who already had this great presence about him. I don't know what the coaches and the other lads thought about me turning up to train in my Manchester United kit. I wasn't going to hide the fact that I was a United fan, even though I enjoyed my time at White Hart Lane.

Despite the interest from London clubs, for me it was always Manchester United. I might have ended up being a supporter or playing for them anyway, but I'm sure Dad was the main factor. He was the original Cockney Red. And he was passing the passion on to me even before I knew he was doing it. Dad was ten years old at the time of the 1958 Munich Air Crash. He had already been following United but the disaster turned it into a lifelong obsession for him. I think it was the same for a lot of supporters of his generation. When I was young, we used to talk about the

United team of the time: Robson, Strachan, Hughes and the rest. But he used to tell me about the Busby Babes, about the European Cup at Wembley, about Best and Stiles and Law and Charlton. What other club could there have been for me? Here I was, almost a teenager, with people saying they thought I had half a chance of someday making it as a professional player. I don't know about United born; I was definitely United bred. And what kept me going was the idea that, eventually, I'd get the call I'd been waiting for ever since I'd first kicked a ball.

The Man in the Brown Sierra

'So, what have you got to tell me about this young lad?'

'What's the matter, Mum?'

'Lucky you had a good game today.'

'Why?'

I'd been playing for my District side, Waltham Forest, away to Redbridge. I must have been eleven. My dad had been working and couldn't come to watch, so Mum had taken me to the game. The 'good game' was probably one of the best I ever had for that team, and afterwards I remember coming out of the changing room with the rest of the boys. Mum was waiting for me. We got to the car park and I put my bag in the back of the car. It was only then that I noticed she had tears in her eyes.

'Just lucky you had a good game.'

'Yeah. But why?'

'That man over there: he's a Man United scout. They want to have a look at you.'

I can still remember the rush of joy and excitement. There was relief in there too. I burst into tears on the spot, just cried and cried. I couldn't believe how happy I felt. I'd wondered for such a long time if I'd ever hear those words. *He's a Man United scout.*

His name was Malcolm Fidgeon. He came back to the house and talked to my parents and explained the club wanted to give me a trial in Manchester. The next thing, a few days later, Malcolm was turning up in his brown Ford Sierra to drive me up north.

I owe Malcolm a lot. He was United's London scout and the person who took me up to the club and looked out for me until I moved there permanently. I went up that first time and then back for two or three other trials. I loved it, staying up in Manchester for days or a week at a time, playing football and talking about football from morning until night. I did everything I could to make the right impression and worked as hard as I could. Eventually, we were told they'd be interested in signing me. One evening at home, the phone rang and Dad answered it. A minute or two later, he came back in with this look on his face, like he couldn't believe what he'd just heard. Of course, this was his dream as well as mine beginning to happen.

'That was Alex Ferguson.'

Everything went quiet.

'He phoned to say they'd enjoyed meeting you, that you've got talent and that they think your character is a credit to you, and to me and Mum.'

And there was more.

'He said you're just the kind of boy Manchester United are looking for.'

That was the first contact I had with the man who became the driving force behind my career. Thinking back, for all my worrying about whether they would want me or not, maybe I wasn't surprised United came in when they did; or that the manager knew who I was. The summer before, I'd already had my chance to play in front of a capacity crowd at Old Trafford.

I was ten years old when I attended the Bobby Charlton Soccer

School for the first time. I had seen a feature about it on *Blue Peter*. Playing football in Manchester? With Bobby Charlton? I suppose Mum and Dad's only choice in the matter was how they were going to fund it: I think Grandad paid in the end. It was a residential soccer school for that first summer, with hundreds of kids from all over the world staying in the university halls of residence while the students were on holiday. It lasted the whole week and I played plenty of football, but the rest of the time I felt a bit lost. Mum and Dad came up and stayed with relatives near Liverpool, and I was on the phone to them every evening. I had toothache. I was homesick. And the week just passed me by a little.

I was desperate to have another go, so I went back the following summer. Things went a lot better. There were skills competitions on each of the courses, which used to run all through the summer, and the winners each week went through to a Grand Final back in Manchester in December. I made it through to that final and it turned out to be a fantastic weekend, for all of us. Mum and Dad stayed with me at the Portland Hotel in the city centre. I had my own room, twenty floors up, with this huge plate-glass window overlooking the city below. I think they were a bit nervous about that. On Saturday morning, we had to register and then go over to United's old training ground, the Cliff, for the first part of the competition which was held in the indoor sports hall: ball-juggling, target shooting and short passing. I think I was in the lead already by the time we broke off for lunch.

The second part of the competition was staged out on the pitch at Old Trafford. I was so nervous I don't think I'd eaten for a couple of days. Mum and Dad were there, probably feeling worse than me. That afternoon, United were playing Spurs, and by the end of the competition there must have been about 40,000 supporters in the ground. I was so excited to be out on that pitch, I wasn't even thinking about winning. They introduced each of us to the crowd before we did the dribbling and then the long passing. I can still remember when they announced 'David Beckham' and said I was from 'Leytonstone' – all the Tottenham fans started cheering. Then the guy on the tannoy said: 'And David is a massive United fan'. All the Spurs fans started jeering and the rest of the ground, the home supporters, began applauding. To be fair, I got a decent reception from both sets of fans when the announcement was made that I'd won.

We went up to the Europa Suite in the main stand where Bobby Charlton was doing the presentation. It was all quite an experience for an eleven-year-old. I know Mum and Dad were very proud; people were coming up to them saying how well they thought I'd done. Maybe, though, it didn't overwhelm me completely. I think the function was still going on, but I drifted away into a corner because the game had started and I wanted to watch it on one of the televisions. It had been some afternoon. It was some prize too: a fortnight's training with Barcelona at the Nou Camp in Spain.

I couldn't wait to get over there. Terry Venables was the Barcelona manager, while Mark Hughes and Gary Lineker were on the playing staff. Me and two other lads were joined by Ray Whelan from the Bobby Charlton Soccer School. The four of us were put up in what looked like a farmhouse – a pretty luxurious one – at the heart of the Nou Camp complex. I think that building had been there even before the football club was and you could sense the history of everything that had happened since: there were pennants and memorabilia on the walls, dating way back, alongside pictures of famous players from Barcelona's past. This was a place where legends had been born.

The farmhouse was right next to the first team's training ground, in the shadow of the stadium itself, and we stayed there with the boys from other parts of Spain who were with Barcelona's youth team. I was still only eleven and saw one or two things that I wasn't used to from life in Chingford: in the evenings, prostitutes would walk up and down outside, on the other side of the railings, and all the older Spanish boys would be leaning out of the windows whistling at them. We used to have this hot chocolate drink at night that I liked so much I drank two one evening and made myself sick. I went to the toilet, turned the light on and saw a cockroach crawl across the floor. What was I doing here? The football was an experience. And so was the rest of it.

We'd go out every day with Barca's youth teams and reserve players. The training was amazing. The only catch was that Ridgeway had a Cup Final against a team called Forest United, at White Hart Lane, at the weekend. I was devastated at the prospect of missing that game; there was also my grandad, who was such a big Spurs fan and wanted to see me play there. He ended up paying for me to fly home for the game and then back to Barcelona again. There wasn't a happy ending, though. Forest United had a young Daniele Dichio playing for them, aged twelve, already seven foot tall and growing a beard. They beat us 2–1 that afternoon. Then I was straight on the plane and back to Spain, on my own and not really sure if I fancied another week away from Chingford.

Barcelona, the football club, was really impressive. The training facilities were excellent, although the young kids trained on a gravel pitch, which I wasn't used to and didn't really enjoy. The first team had an immaculate surface to play on, and the reserve team had a 20,000-seater stadium all of their own. We were taken inside the Nou Camp one day. You come up from the dressing rooms, past the club chapel that's off to one side in the tunnel, and then up a flight of stairs onto the pitch. Sometimes you can't help yourself: with acres of grass and the stands towering above, I started running up and down, kicking an imaginary football and pretending to be Mark Hughes. What would it be like, to be out there actually playing a game?

All the boys who I was training with were probably sixteen and seventeen. The two lads who'd finished second and third at Old Trafford were fifteen and nineteen. Everybody was really friendly but, at first, it was like: *What's this child with the spiky hair and the funny accent doing here?* Once we got started, everything was fine. Obviously, none of the coaches or the other players spoke English but, if we were playing, we could make ourselves understood. It was the first time I'd been in a professional set-up, training with professional players. It opened my eyes. We'd watch the first team most days and, one time, we went out and were introduced to Mr Venables and the players. Of course, I'm quite good friends with Mark Hughes now. He often laughs about that time in Spain: the Barcelona players didn't have a clue who we were. I still have the photo of me, Mark, Terry Venables and Gary Lineker that was taken that afternoon.

It was an exciting time. I was training with Spurs, and United had let me know they were more than just interested. I went up to Manchester a few times in the holidays, always with Malcolm Fidgeon in that brown Sierra, and hooked up with the team when they came down to London to play. The club in general, and Alex Ferguson in particular, did their best to make me feel a part of it all. The older players, like Bryan Robson and Steve Bruce, gave me some stick about those times once I eventually joined the club. I was at pre-match meals and I'd be in the dressing room after games, helping clear away all the kit. One afternoon, when United were away to West Ham, they invited me to come along as the mascot. I was given a United tracksuit and there I was, at Upton

Park, warming up on the pitch with the likes of Bryan Robson and Gordon Strachan. Then they let me sit on the bench for the game. I even spotted myself on *Match of the Day* that evening.

United seemed pretty keen on me. Of course, I was so keen on United that it was almost embarrassing. I used to wear my hair spiky, wanting it to look like Gordon Strachan's, and the day of that West Ham game I took him a tub of hair gel as a present. He got some grief about that; and so did I a year or two later. Another time before a game in London, they invited me and Mum and Dad to have an evening meal with the squad at the team hotel at West Lodge Park. Never mind that I ordered a steak and then couldn't understand when a piece of tuna was put down in front of me. I was sat on the top table with the manager and the staff. They had a present for me: one of those big padded bench coats. It was about six sizes too big for me. You couldn't see my hands at the ends of the sleeves and it trailed round my ankles, but I didn't take the thing off for a week. Better still, I had a present for the boss: a pen. Alex Ferguson took it and looked at me:

'Thanks, David. I'll tell you what: I'll sign you for Manchester United using this pen'.

Remembering that, it might seem strange that there was ever any doubt about who I was going to sign schoolboy forms with before I turned thirteen. But I'd been really happy training at Spurs and got on well with their Youth Development Officer, John Moncur. It was also important that White Hart Lane was fifteen minutes down the road from home. Much as Dad might have dreamt about me playing for United, he put that to one side when we sat down to talk. It wasn't: this is what you should do. But: what do you want to do? We decided we should at least find out what Spurs had to say.

Maybe I knew all along that it had to be United. The meeting between me, my dad and Terry Venables, who'd come back from Spain and was then managing Spurs, left me feeling like I had more questions than answers. John Moncur took us along to Terry's office. I can picture the scene now: Terry had dropped something on the floor, either some crisps or peanuts, and was bent down in his chair, scrabbling on the carpet, trying to pick them up. He looked up at us:

'So, John, what have you got to tell me about this young lad?'

Never mind not remembering me from Barcelona: that must have seemed like ages ago. I got the impression that, although I'd been training at Spurs for a couple of years, the manager didn't really have any idea who I was. I couldn't help thinking about the times I'd been up to Manchester. Alex Ferguson knew all about me. He knew all about every single boy. He knew their parents, he knew their brothers and sisters. That seemed important to me, important for my future. It always felt like you were part of a family at United.

Spurs made us a really generous offer, which amounted to a six-year deal: two years as a schoolboy followed by two years as a Youth Training Scheme trainee and then two years as a professional. A thought flashed through my mind. *By the time I'm 18, I could be driving a Porsche.*

'So, David, would you like to sign for Tottenham?' Terry said eventually.

Dad looked at me. He'd never been one to make my decisions for me. I took a breath:

'I'd like to think about it, Mr Venables.'

In my head, though, I was shouting out: *United! It's got to be United!*

Of course, Mum and Dad and I talked about what we'd heard. I think Mum would have liked me to join Tottenham, because of

Grandad and because it would have meant me being able to stay at home, but she kept that to herself. Neither she nor Dad were going to put pressure on me one way or the other. We all knew that, if I ended up signing for Spurs, things would be fine. I'd be happy and well looked after at White Hart Lane. We had an appointment at Old Trafford to get to first, though.

I drove up with Mum and Dad and we had this conversation on the way up, pulled over in a motorway services of all places. We knew what Tottenham had offered, and Dad and I agreed that the actual amount of money involved wasn't the important thing. This wasn't some kind of auction. All I needed was a sense of security. I wanted to know I'd get a chance to prove myself. If United offered the same six-year commitment that Tottenham had, then my mind would be made up: the wages wouldn't come into it. If not, we'd drive back to London and I'd sign a contract with Spurs.

It was 2 May 1988, my thirteenth birthday. United were at home to Wimbledon and Alex Ferguson was waiting for us:

'Hello, David.'

This bloke knew me. I knew him. And I trusted him. So did my mum and dad. I'd had a special blazer bought for the occasion and United gave me a red club tie that I wore for the rest of the day. We went away to have lunch in the grill room where the first team had their pre-match meal: there was even a birthday cake. Not that I felt much like eating. At 5.30, after the game, we went up to Mr Ferguson's office. He was there with Les Kershaw, who was in charge of Youth Development at the club. Malcolm Fidgeon was there too. It was all pretty simple. United wanted me to sign and the boss set out the offer:

'We'd like to give you two, two and two.'

I looked over to Dad, who was in another world. He'd been

looking forward to this moment even longer than I had. I could see that he hadn't taken in what Alex had just said. I knew, though, I'd just heard what I'd been wanting to hear: *two, two and two*, equalling the six years I'd been offered at White Hart Lane. I didn't need to wait for the details.

'I want to sign.'

And out came that pen. How long had it taken? A minute? It didn't matter. I'd been ready, waiting to say those words, for the best part of ten years.

Home from Home

*'You may have signed for Man United,
but you haven't done anything yet.'*

'You know I'm Man United, but I don't want that to put pressure
on you. If you decide to sign for somebody else, I won't be upset.'

Dad had always made that clear to me. Of course, I'd always
known he was lying about the last bit. So the day I signed at Old
Trafford was as fantastic for him as it was for me. By the time we
left Mr Ferguson's office, Mum was in tears. She was happy for
me but she knew it meant that, sooner rather than later, I was
going to be leaving home. She'd put so much love and so many
hours into a kid who was mad about football; and the moment
we'd got to our destination was also the moment she was going
to have to get used to the idea of her boy heading north to start
a career.

She did a fair bit of crying in the months between me signing
up and starting my YTS at United. But I knew, deep down, she
was as proud of me as my dad was. Not letting my parents down
meant everything to me. They never made me feel like I owed
them for the support they'd given me, but I felt I had to do all I
could to make sure they didn't end up disappointed. Think about
it: if I let them down, it would mean I'd let myself down as well.
It's never been a case of me having to match up to their expectations. It's just that I've taken my parents' expectations of me

and made them the starting point for what I expect of myself. Even now, when my own family and career mean I don't see as much of them, I think I still judge myself by the standards I learnt from Mum and Dad.

What could have been more exciting than that day? Everybody shaking hands, me in my blazer and club tie, a United player; or, at least, a lad from Chingford who'd just taken the first step towards becoming a United player. Out in the corridor, Dad and I met up with the United captain, Bryan Robson. We'd spent hours in front of the television watching videos of this man, our absolute all-time hero. Dad had tried to hammer his qualities into me: courage, commitment, energy, vision and the ability to inspire players around him.

I'd met Bryan before, but this was the boss introducing me to him as United's latest signing:

'Congratulations, David. You'll find out for yourself but, I'd say, you couldn't be joining a better club.'

I don't remember us driving back to London at all. At least Dad didn't forget we were on a busy motorway. I couldn't have thought about anything else that evening, and I didn't want to. I'd just lived through the happiest day of my life.

Although I'd done the adding up in my head and got the answer I wanted, that first contract at Old Trafford wasn't actually for six years but for four. It was against regulations, anyway, for a boy signing schoolboy forms to have full professional terms set out there and then: I was only thirteen, after all, and so much could change before I turned eighteen. The rules were there to protect youngsters from getting trapped somewhere they didn't want to be; not that there was any chance of that happening to me. United told me that, if everything went well, I could expect to sign as a professional in four and a half years' time.

In a really important way, I think that bit of uncertainty was best for me and for all the other lads who joined the club at the same time. I knew I was wanted. But I also knew that I had to prove myself over the next four years. If I'd known all along that achieving the ambition of becoming a professional player at United was already settled – down on a piece of paper in black and white – who knows if it wouldn't have taken the edge off my determination to take the chance I'd been given? I think that extra hunger has had a lot to do with my success and the team's success in the years since: all the boys who've come through at the club will know what I mean. The day I signed didn't feel like the day I'd made it. The hard work was just starting. I wanted a challenge and Manchester United was the biggest challenge there was.

I knew I was in good hands. Even before I signed at United I had the feeling I was joining a family. It's about there being really good people everywhere at the club. I don't just mean the ones everybody would know about like the manager or the players, but people like Kath Phipps, who still works on Reception at Old Trafford. I can still remember, when I was just a boy, every time I went up to a United game she'd be there. She'd lean across her desk and give me a little kiss and the programme she'd saved for me. Later on, Kath used to help me with answering my mail. She's part of United and she was with me right through my career there.

Whenever I came up to Manchester to train or to be at a game, I'd be looked after by Joe and Connie Brown, who had an office at the ground. They would take me – and Mum and Dad, if they were with me – around Old Trafford, take us for a meal, show us down to the dressing rooms and introduce us to the players and staff. Joe and Connie made me feel really welcome. Joe was Youth Development Officer at United. He was responsible for young players' expenses and travel arrangements but that job stretched to him and Connie taking care of just about everything when youngsters from outside Manchester and their families spent time at the club.

Then, when it came to the football, there was Nobby Stiles. I worked with Nobby after I joined the club, too, but I first met him during the weeks when I came up to train in the school holidays. He was the coach I remember most clearly working with back then. Nobby was really hard, just like he was as a player, but I think he cared more about the youngsters he worked with than anything else in the world. Dad knew all about Nobby as a player, of course, for United and as a World Cup winner with England: he and Dad got on really well, even though every now and again Nobby would have to catch himself about his language when he was getting carried away during one of our games:

'Excuse me, Mr Beckham. Excuse me, Mrs Beckham.'

Not that Dad was too worried about that:

'No problem, Nobby. You carry on.'

Nobby was great with us and he was great with our parents as well. He knew mums and dads needed to be involved, not treated as if they were in the way. If you watched videos or heard stories about him as a player, you'd never believe how gentle he was with the boys, or how polite he was with the parents. No-one took liberties with Nobby, mind. For all that he didn't look a big man and used to wear these huge glasses when he was coaching, he still had something about him you respected straight away. Fifteen years later, he would still come straight up and give me a big hug like nothing's changed since. Kath, Joe and Connie, Nobby Stiles: they all had jobs to do but they also made United a place that felt like home.

I could have moved up the year after I signed schoolboy forms, in August 1989, and finished my last two years of school in Manchester but, in the end, we decided I'd stay in London until I started full-time as a YTS trainee at United. That meant I could be at home, with my friends and family, while I turned fourteen and fifteen. And I could keep playing for Ridgeway Rovers, which by then had become a team called Brimsdown: we were the same players more or less, just the name had changed. United were happy for boys to get on with their lives and play for their Sunday League teams until they moved to the city. Malcolm Fidgeon would come and watch me play for Brimsdown and, as long as I was enjoying my football and playing regularly, that was enough. The time for United to take all the responsibility was still a couple of years' away.

I used to go up to Manchester two or three times a year to train during the holidays. In the summer, I'd be up there for the whole six weeks. I loved it and didn't want to do anything else with my time off school but play and train and be at United. Those summers were fantastic. Boys could come up for a week or two weeks. Me, I wanted to be there for as long as they'd let me. There would be thirty or so of us together at a time, all looked after by Malcolm and the rest of the coaching staff, in halls of residence. I'd think about the place where I'd stayed in Barcelona; that lovely old house with the mountains rising up behind us. This was a bit different: a concrete block in Salford, stuck on top of a hill and freezing cold whatever the weather was like outside. You shared a room with another young player, the facilities were basic but at least there was a snooker table and a table tennis table for us to use in the evenings.

Not that where we were staying made much difference to me. We'd go to United's second training ground at Lyttleton Road every day and train morning and afternoon. Then, in the evenings, we'd live it up: trips to the pictures, fish and chip nights, all the glamorous stuff. I met other boys who had signed at the same time as me, like John O'Kane, who I spent a lot of time with back then. John was from Nottingham. He was a massive prospect at United all through our first years there together, a really good player. As a person, he was very relaxed. Maybe it was because he was so laid back that it didn't really work out for him at United. He ended up leaving to go to Everton, the season we went on to do the Treble, and is playing for Blackpool now.

Lads would come from everywhere for those holiday sessions. Keith Gillespie, who's now at Leicester, came over from Ireland. He was a lovely lad, and I used to get on really well with him. Colin Murdock, who's just moved from Preston to Hibs, came down from Scotland. We were all miles from home, in the same boat, and that made it easier for us all to get on, even if, in the back of our minds, we knew we were in competition with each other as well. The football was what mattered above everything and it was a new experience, training day in day out and being introduced to more technical coaching. It couldn't have been more different from Sunday League. All the time I was with Ridgeway, I'd tried to imagine what it would be like and this was it: football was my job. I didn't have to do anything else.

I had two years to get ready for moving up to Manchester permanently. I'd had plenty of trips away with Ridgeway and representative sides when I was younger, too. But neither of those things made it any easier when it came time to leave home. Of course I was excited and it was never a case of having second thoughts but, even so, it wasn't easy to go. I was very nervous about what lay ahead of me. Mum and Dad said they'd be up every weekend to see me play, that they wouldn't miss a game, and I knew they'd keep to their word. Promises count for a lot in the life of a family. Nowadays, I wouldn't dare forget if I've told

Brooklyn I'll get him something or do something for him: he'll remember even if I don't. Back then, I knew I could rely on my parents to be there when I needed them.

Being away for a week or a month is completely different to moving away from home for good: I was fifteen and a half. Where you end up staying in digs as a young player is so important, especially when you think about how much else you're going to have to find out about when you begin your working life, full-time, at a big club like Man United. Every club has a list of landladies they use and I've often wondered whether it's just chance who you end up with, or whether they try to fix boys up in places they know will be right for them. Looking back, I think I was pretty lucky although it was a while before I found myself somewhere that really felt like home.

My first digs were with a Scottish couple who lived in Bury New Road, next to the fire station. They were lovely people and very good to me and the other boys who were there. Being young lads away from home for the first time, there was a bit of backchat and mucking about that went on: late-night kitchen raids for snacks, that kind of thing. We had fun. When I left, it was because of a strange incident that was completely out of keeping with the rest of my time there. I'd gone down the road to the garage to get some chocolate and forgotten my key. I got back and knocked on the door, which was answered by the husband, Pete. He asked me where my key was and, when I said I thought I'd left it upstairs, he gave me a little clip round the ear. I wasn't too happy about it and I remember, that evening, my Dad was on the phone to him. I was on the other side of the room and I could hear Dad shouting down the line. That was the end of that arrangement.

I moved down to a place on Lower Broughton Road, with a landlady named Eve Cody. I got on really well with her son, Johnny, and was very happy there for almost a year. I shared a room with John O'Kane, who I already knew quite well from the holiday sessions at United when we'd still been living at home. I have to admit that, around that time, John and I used to struggle to get to training on time. It wasn't that we'd be out late at night; we were just both lads who loved our sleep. And we were lodging further away than some of the others like Keith Gillespie and Robbie Savage, who were almost next door to the Cliff. It's not surprising, I suppose, that early on there was a bond between us lads who were staying in digs, as opposed to the Manchester boys who were all still living at home.

After a while, the club changed us round and it was then that I moved in with Ann and Tommy Kay and, as friendly as the other places had been, I wished I could have been there from the start. It was made for me. I was still homesick but Annie and Tom were like a second mum and dad, so loving and caring. The food was great as well. The house was almost directly opposite the training ground, so I could roll out of bed and walk to work in a couple of minutes. Just what you need when you're a teenager who can't get up in the morning.

I shared a room with a lad named Craig Dean, who had to retire before he really got a chance to do anything, because of an injury to his spine. After a few months, Ann gave me Mark Hughes' old room, which looked out over the playing fields next door to the Cliff. I loved that room. It was the kind of size that meant, somehow, it felt like your mum and dad's room: big fitted wardrobes with a dressing table and mirror to match and a proper double bed pressed up to the wall in the far corner. I brought along the stereo my dad had bought me before I moved to Man-chester and went out and bought a nice television. I thought I had everything I could possibly need. I was really happy. The Kays made me feel like I was part of the family. Ann and Tom had one son of their own, Dave, and they made me feel like another. I know Ann has kept a box of old coins and things I left behind when I moved out and got a place of my own, and I've always tried to make sure I visit now and again.

I was lucky, as well, when I first moved up to Manchester that I met a girl named Deana who I went out with for the best part of three years. I wasn't chasing round like a lot of teenagers away from home for the first time. The romance with Deana was something that helped me feel settled: my first real relationship. We had a lot of fun together, whether it was going out or just being alone in each other's company. It was also a time for finding out the things that were trickier.

After training one afternoon, I went off to the snooker club with Gary Neville, Keith Gillespie and John O'Kane even though the original plan had been for Deana and I to meet up. I had my back to the door of the club and was leaning across the table to make my shot. Suddenly I glanced up and saw the colour draining out of John's cheeks. He was looking back over my head; I turned round to see Deana in the doorway behind me. The two of us went out into the car park so I could make my apologies, and that would have been that except, for some reason, I made the mistake of looking up at the first floor window of the club. Gary, Keith and John were standing there. I couldn't hear them but I could see their shoulders jigging up and down, the three of them giggling at the spot of bother I'd got myself in. I couldn't help myself: I started giggling too. I couldn't blame Deana at all for turning the rest of that day into a very long, very sorrowful one in the life of one teenage boy.

I have so many good memories of my times with Deana and also with her family. They were so welcoming: it was as if I just had to turn up on the doorstep and the next thing I knew we'd be in the kitchen; the kettle would be on, and there'd be something to eat on the way. It was very warm. Without making a big thing of it, Deana's mum and dad made me feel like I was part of the family. Her dad, Ray, was a Liverpool season ticket holder and I went to watch games at Anfield with him from time to time. Away from my own dad, I suppose I hooked onto Ray. He sometimes took me down to the pub. A couple of halves, of course, and I'd be rolling a bit. We'd wander back to the house together for some dinner. This was me really finding out about life as a man: out getting tipsy with my girlfriend's dad. It was a lovely time in my life and I'll always be grateful to Deana that she's never spoiled it. I know she's been offered money since by the papers to tell stories about me and always turned them down flat. I know that's because of the kind of person she is and I hope, as well, it's something to do with her getting a good feeling, like I do, when she remembers us being together.

Life in Manchester away from football was just part of what was totally new to me. There was this group of local lads for a start. Gary and Philip Neville, Nicky Butt and Paul Scholes were all from around Manchester, so they'd been training at United since they'd signed schoolboy forms, although they hadn't been at the holiday sessions I'd attended over the previous couple of years. I wasn't aware of it at the time but I think, to start with, they weren't sure about me at all: Gary says they had me down as a right flash little cockney. I can understand why. It wasn't because I was loud or anything but, when we were getting handed out our kit, I'd always end up with the nicest tracksuit and the best-fitting boots. I happened to get on really well with the kit man, Norman Davies, and he just looked after me. I'd known Norman for a long time already from going to the games as a kid and, maybe, this was my reward for helping him clear up dressing rooms for the first team at places like Upton Park all those years ago.

I was from London and the other boys were from the Manchester area but it was surprising how much we had in common. Apart from loving football and having the ambition to play for United, there were things in our backgrounds that brought us together as well. Gary and Phil's mum and dad, for example, were so much like my parents. They'd be at every game too. I think the Nevilles and the Beckhams had the same sort of values and saw life in much the same way. I know the four of them took to each other straight away and I'm sure the similarity in our upbringings had a lot to do with why Gary and I became such close friends.

Gary, Nicky Butt and Paul Scholes had all played together for the same Sunday League team. Boundary Park must have been a northern version of Ridgeway Rovers. Not only was the team successful, it had the same spirit and sense of loyalty that we'd had at Ridgeway. Those boys had been learning to approach football in the right way, picking up good habits, at the same time as we were. It was natural that a sense of togetherness grew pretty quickly at United. Quite soon after we started, we went off to Coleraine in Northern Ireland for a tournament called the Milk Cup. Teams came from all over the world to compete, and that was the first time we represented the club as a group.

We had a brilliant time. We were all about sixteen, on a tour together and getting to know each other, as players and as people. The Milk Cup competition is still going. As well as the games, there's quite a lot of ceremony: I remember us being paraded through the streets of the local town, trying to look sharp in our Manchester United tracksuits. Nobby Stiles was in charge of the trip, along with a physio named Jimmy Curran. Nobby knew me and trusted me, and he made me captain for the tournament. It was some team: as well as the players who are still at Old Trafford, there were plenty of others who went on to have good careers elsewhere. Ben Thornley was our best player on that trip and got the award for Player of the Tournament. He's done well since leaving United, despite some shocking injury trouble over the years. With Gary, Phil, Paul Scholes and Nicky Butt playing alongside the likes of Ben, Keith Gillespie, Robbie Savage and Colin Murdock, it's no wonder we won the cup. We stayed at a hotel owned by Harry Gregg, who was a United great himself. He survived the Munich Air Crash and he loved having the United youngsters around the place. The Milk Cup was the first silverware any of us ever won as United players.

Every single day was an exciting one back then. Before I'd left home to start as a trainee in Manchester, Dad had drummed one thing into my head.

'You may have signed for Man United, but you haven't done anything yet. When you've played for the first team, then we can talk about you having achieved something. Until then, don't start thinking you've made it.'

Did he need to tell me that? Well, it did no harm to know Dad would be around to keep my feet on the ground. But I hadn't been running around boasting, telling everybody that I had signed for United. I'd just been looking forward to going and couldn't wait to start work. Once I did, of course, I realised what Dad had meant. I'd been to United's old training ground, the Cliff, as a boy to watch the first team train. Now I had to be there for training each morning myself, along with the senior players. It dawned on me straight away that the most important thing wasn't being at United. It was working hard enough to make sure they'd let me stay there.

Come to think of it, there was never any chance of us not working hard; not with coach Eric Harrison in charge. If I think about the people who've really shaped my career, that has to mean my dad and Alex Ferguson – of course – but it'll also mean Eric. Even now, a dozen years on from first meeting him, I look to him for guidance and advice. He'll tell me what he thinks, not what he thinks I want to hear. And, like every other boy he worked with at United, I know he's always cared about me. Back then I was sure he had my best interests at heart. I still feel exactly the same.

Eric could be scary, though. We knew about his reputation and I was a bit anxious beforehand because of that. But I soon found out what a brilliant coach he was. Everything he did with us was spot on: the sessions he ran, how hard he made us work, how he understood how we were feeling and how much he made us believe in ourselves. Eric might have had a talented group of lads to work with, but the credit goes to him for turning us into footballers and, during the next three years, turning us into a team.

That fierce reputation, though, it's all true. When Eric was angry with you, he could dig you out worse than anybody I've ever known. We were younger then, obviously, but I'd say the volleys you got from Eric were even more terrifying than the manager in full flow. I remember when we had matches at the Cliff, Eric had an office with a big window that looked out over the pitch we used. If you made a mistake or did something you knew you shouldn't have done, you'd hear this furious banging on the glass. You didn't dare look up in that direction because you knew it would be Eric, not best pleased. But you'd have to have a quick glance. And if you couldn't actually see him shouting from behind the window, that's when you knew there was real trouble and it was time to disappear over to the other side of the pitch. It meant Eric was on his way down.

When Eric was pleased with you, it made you feel great. If I heard him say: 'Great ball, David' once in the morning, that would set me up for the rest of the day. Likewise, if he criticised something, you thought a long time before doing it again. I remember one session when, every time I got the ball, I was trying to pick someone out with a sixty-yard pass. Even when I was young, I was able to see what was going on ahead of me and could strike the ball a very long way. That particular day, though, nothing was coming off and Eric wasn't impressed.

'David. What are you playing at? Hitting those flippin' Hollywood passes all day?'

Hollywood passes? I'd never heard that before. I knew exactly what he meant, though. And I thought twice before I hit the next one. Truth is, I still love playing those long balls; they're a part of my game. But, even now, whenever one doesn't make it, I imagine Eric, shaking his head and grumbling: 'flippin' Hollywood passes'.

It's not always been true with Alex Ferguson or other coaches I've worked with, but with Eric you always knew exactly where you stood. If he lost his temper with you, he made sure you understood why and, somehow, he had the knack of shaking you up without ever abusing you or putting you down. We always knew, however hairy it got, Eric only ever wanted what we wanted too: to get the best out of ourselves and to achieve everything we could as individuals and as a team. No wonder he commanded the respect of every single one of us young players. Some young players nowadays who sign for a big club suddenly think they've hit the big time. There was none of that with our generation. And if there had been, Eric would soon have sorted us out.

I was lucky. I had good coaching all the time I was growing up but, of course, when I got to United and started work with Eric, I knew straight away that I'd moved up to another level. I remember hearing the argument a lot when I was young: that it would be best to start with a smaller club and work my way up to a bigger one like Manchester United. And I can see the sense in that. Once I began training at the Cliff, I realised that the only way from here, if things didn't work out, was going to be down. But my feeling then, and even more so now, is that if you're given the chance to be with the best, you should take it.

Everything at United was right: the facilities, the kit, the training and the other players in our group. Who wouldn't want to have Eric Harrison as a youth team coach? I couldn't get enough of it all. While we were trainees, Gary and I would go back to the Cliff in the evenings twice a week, when Eric was working with the schoolboys on the big indoor pitch, and join in the sessions just to get extra training under our belts. Phil Neville was in that age group – two years younger than me and Gary – and so was Dave Gardner. I don't know how you find your very best friends. Maybe they just find you. Dave and I just hit it off and we've been close ever since: I was best man at his wedding in the summer of 2003. He stayed on as an apprentice until he was eighteen, by which time I was playing regularly in the first team. Dave turned professional with Manchester City and he still plays non-League with Altrincham. Nowadays, for him, football's about staying fit and keeping his eye in: he's a full-time director of a sports management company.

During those first years at United, Eric used to make sure we went to every first-team game at Old Trafford. Not just to watch the game, but to watch individual players. I'd think back to Dad taking me to Cup Finals when I was a boy.

'Never mind the game, David. Just watch Bryan Robson. Watch what he does.'

Now Eric was telling us the same thing: 'Watch the man

playing in your position. One day, you're going to take his place.'

To hear something like that gave us so much confidence; not that we realised at the time how soon the manager was going to make us all part of his first-team plans.

Going to those games at Old Trafford was a chance, as well, for Eric to insist on the importance of having standards. He always made sure that we turned up in a blazer, with a collar and tie. It reminded me of Stuart Underwood wanting the Ridgeway players to be well turned out when we arrived for big games. I still think those things make a difference. Some teams might be seen arriving at a ground or walking through an airport in their tracksuits. The fact that a Manchester United team will always be wearing club blazers is part of having a professional attitude. That smartness said something about our respect for ourselves and for the club.

Our training sessions weren't all about technique and tactics and learning new tricks. If Eric spotted a weakness in your game, you could be sure he'd do his best to confront it. I don't know if 'Headers' was designed just to make me suffer, but some mornings it felt like it. As a forward player, you need to be strong enough to hold your own physically against bigger and tougher defenders. Heading and tackling weren't exactly my strong points, especially as I was smaller than most of the other lads. 'Headers' was Eric's way of toughening up young players like me. There were two teams: midfielders and forwards lined up against defenders. The ball was chipped up and you could only score with your head. That would have been fine, except it was an invitation to the likes of Gary Neville and Chris Casper to come crashing into you from behind in order to stop you. Gary was the worst. You'd end up bruised all over, wondering what you'd done to annoy him. I dreaded those sessions then but, four years later, by the time I was lining up in the Premiership against the likes of

Stuart Pearce and Julian Dicks, I was grateful that the first serious knocks I'd taken had been off my own team-mates.

It wasn't just when we were doing that particular routine that Gary and Chris Casper did their best to give me grief. Busy they were, the pair of them. Cas was very big and strong for his age. His dad, Frank, had been a player with Burnley when they were a top side in the sixties, and Chris had obviously picked up habits from him. He had this very grown up, professional attitude. And, when we were playing together, he talked non-stop through every single game. Sometimes Cas played at the back; he ended up playing centre-back as a professional. Other times he'd get a game in central midfield, which meant I'd be playing alongside him. He'd be geeing me up, telling me who to pass to. And not just me: he'd be telling anyone within earshot. He even used to talk to himself. After ninety minutes, I'd have a splitting headache and what made it worse was that Dad thought it was good to be like that.

'You should be like Cas, you know. You should be talking like him. More than him, even.'

I'd be thinking: I prefer silence. As I've got more experienced – and especially since I've been a captain – I've come to understand how important it is to communicate on the pitch. Obviously you have to let a team-mate know if someone's coming to close him down but, if someone can't see a pass for himself then, by the time you've told him, the moment's probably gone anyway. If you're playing for Man United or for England, do you need your mate telling you, minute by minute, if he thinks you're playing well? Of course you have to talk. Half the time, though, I thought Cas was talking just for the sake of it. It was like lining up alongside a commentator.

He used to get on my nerves when we played together, but

Cas and I were good mates too. He was one of a small group of us who went away on holiday together. My mum and dad were the first people to meet Joe Glanville: they'd always run into him at games. Joe was Maltese, and United mad. They got to know each other and, the next thing I knew, my parents were telling me we were going on holiday to Malta. Everything was being taken care of that end and we just had to get ourselves to the airport at the right time, with our bags packed.

We had a lovely time that summer. While we were out there, there was a United supporters' club function which Steve Bruce and Lee Sharpe were helping with. Joe and his friends put us up in a nice hotel. We'd wake up in the morning and someone would be there to take us wherever we wanted to go: down to the beach, into the village, or round the island. It was a great set-up and the Maltese loved their football. The next summer I went back with Cas, Gary and Ben Thornley. It was a lads' holiday; or, at least, as laddish as it was ever going to get with us – a couple of beers and a little holiday romance but nothing you'd need to keep a secret from your mum.

We'd told Joe beforehand not to book us a smart hotel or anything, although when we got to our apartment block we wished we hadn't mentioned anything. The place was terrible. There was no air-conditioning and Malta, in the summer, is stifling hot. Gary and Ben grabbed the one room that had a fan in it and Cas and I just sweated away, all day and all night. Those were really good times, though. I loved it so much I went back the next six summers on the trot. Gary even got himself his own place over there.

The four of us used to knock about in Manchester, too, along with Dave Gardner, who was younger than us but always knew the best places to go. Our regular night out together was on a Wednesday, usually to a place called Johnsons, which was in the centre of town but slightly tucked away. We were sensible lads – Ben, I suppose, was the most outgoing – and we knew when to stop; when to go home and when to get out of a place if it seemed dodgy. We also had Gary with us, who's one of the most paranoid people ever. He'd drive us mad sometimes. We'd all walk into a place, then turn round and see Gary, standing there bolt upright.

'No, lads. I'm not comfortable here. We've got to get out. Come on, we've got to get out.'

All it would take would be one funny look from someone. In a way it was good, because it meant we never had a whiff of trouble. Later, we'd all end up at Ben's to stay the night. He was still living with his parents and his room was right up at the top of the house: a big room but absolutely freezing. Ben, of course, would be tucked up cosy in his bed. Me, Gary and Cas would be lying on the floor, shivering. I miss those nights out: I couldn't do anything like that now, after all.

Like all young players, we had our jobs to do around the training ground. I remember Cas and I being put on the first-team dressing room, which meant we had to scrub the baths and showers and clean the changing room itself. I got in there first and got the easy half of it: got my shorts on and just sploshed around till the baths and showers were hosed down. Cas was too slow off the mark and got left with the mud and rubbish in the changing rooms. We had a bit of a row about that one, and almost 'got the ring out', which was when we'd wrap towels around our hands and have mock boxing matches to sort out an argument. To make it even worse for him, we changed over around Christmas. That meant I was on the changing rooms, looking busy cleaning boots, and ready to pick up the bonuses from the senior players at just the right time. Cas couldn't believe I'd got away with it.

It's one of the sad things about a life in football. You get really close to people and then, when they move to another club, you lose touch. I still see Ben Thornley now and again and I know Gary talks to Chris Casper sometimes. But I think back to when we were teenagers and the four of us were together all the time, and got on so well: once Ben and Cas moved on, that all finished. It's a shame but, perhaps, it just goes with the job: you have to focus on the players who are in the dressing room alongside you at the time.

Even though I was occasionally homesick, it was a fantastic life. Mum and Dad were great, coming up to watch me play every weekend without fail. And day to day at United was everything I'd imagined it would be. It hadn't taken long for me to become friendly with the lads I was training alongside all week; or for us to start winning football matches together five- or six-nil. Because I was smaller and, at first, Keith Gillespie used to play in my position on the right, I did worry that I wasn't getting in the team for some of the bigger games. That first season, most of the players we were playing against were a year older than us when it came to FA Youth Cup ties and, to start with, Eric used to leave me out of those games.

Eventually I got my chance. Keith Gillespie got moved to play up front so I could play wide right. I was competing with Robbie Savage for that position as well, but Robbie got injured during that season. I've found out since that United hadn't won the Youth Cup since 1964, when George Best was in the team, so what we achieved in 1992, with most of us in our first full year at the club, meant something special as far as history was concerned. At the time, though, none of us were really aware of that: it was just the excitement of playing and winning games for United.

I remember beating Spurs in the 1992 Youth Cup semi-final. Then, like the semi, the final was played over two legs. We beat

Crystal Palace 3–1 down in London. The game almost never happened: it had hammered down all day and the pitch was waterlogged but, just as they were deciding to call it off, the rain stopped and we went ahead. Nicky Butt scored two and I got the other – a volley, left foot, from the edge of the box after Ben Thornley cut the ball back – and then we won 3–2 back at our place. The bond in that team was amazing, with Ryan Giggs, who was a year older than most of us, as captain.

That second leg at Old Trafford was some night: there were 32,000 United fans there to watch, which made for a bigger atmosphere than any of us had ever experienced before. You always get supporters who want to see the local talent come through and so follow the Youth side. But 32,000 of them? Maybe the word was getting round that the club had found a particularly good group of young players. I think we were aware of what was going on, but we never really talked about it amongst ourselves. Over the two or three years we were coming through, Alex Ferguson said just once: 'If we don't get a first-team player out of this lot, we might as well all pack up and go home.' Other than that, nobody inside the club mentioned that there might be something special happening. The focus was always on that day's training session or on that afternoon's game.

We got to the Youth Cup Final the following year, too. I can still remember the semi-final against Millwall. We'd heard that they had something planned before the game. Sure enough, out they came on the night of the first leg at Old Trafford, and every single player had his head shaved. I don't know if that was what threw us out of our stride, but we lost 2–1. For the second leg we had to go down to the old Den – which, being nearly full, had a pretty intimidating atmosphere even for a Youth game – and we won 2–0 to go through to the final, where we played Leeds United.

People have said since that it was strange how we had so many future first-team players in our side and yet hardly any of the Leeds boys came through. In those two games, though, they played very well and were really fired up. We lost 2–0 at Old Trafford and then went to Elland Road for the second leg. There, it wasn't just the players who were up for it. We'd had a 30,000 crowd again in Manchester. When they announced that Leeds' home crowd was even bigger on the night, you'd have thought a goal had been scored. Their fans really got behind them and they beat us again, this time 2–1.

We'd played a lot of games that season and I remember being very tired, but losing that final wasn't such a bad thing. For most of us, it was the first big disappointment of our footballing lives and perhaps it made us stronger, having to experience it together. You want to make sure you don't feel that down again in the future. And you certainly don't ever want Eric Harrison going mad at you again like he did in the dressing room after we'd lost at Elland Road.

By then, the 1992/93 season, the players in our age group were starting to get involved, and to get games, with the first team. As early as September, I got called into training with the senior players and, a couple of days later, the manager told me that I would be travelling to Brighton for a League Cup tie. Gary, Nicky Butt and Paul Scholes were coming as well. We flew down on this little seventeen-seater plane. It was a horrible flight: the noise, the bumping, the cramped seats, and it seemed to go on forever. Maybe that was why I got such a great night's sleep once we'd finally arrived. I woke up to the news that I was going to be one of the substitutes.

About twenty minutes from the end, the gaffer told me I was going on in place of Andrei Kanchelskis. I was so excited I jumped off the bench and cracked my head on the roof of the dugout: a great start to a first-team career. The boss wanted to have a look at me and I think I did all right. Mum and Dad were at the Goldstone and they were as surprised as I was that I actually got a game. Seventeen minutes as a United player, but I still felt really young. What was I? Just seventeen? More like the boy who'd been on the bench at West Ham as a mascot than a man ready to be in United's first team. The manager had a little go at me in the dressing room afterwards. I don't remember having done anything wrong. He was probably just trying to make sure I didn't get ahead of myself: a sign of one or two difficult times, maybe, that lay ahead for the two of us further down the line.

It was a long time before I got another chance. The Youth Cup side had all moved up to reserve team football: we'd won the 'A' League and then the Central League, the first time the club had done that in over twenty years. I played in some League Cup games again early on in the 1994/95 season, when the gaffer rested his first-choice players. Back in the early 1990s, United struggled a bit in Europe because of the Overseas Players Rule, which meant you could only play three foreigners in the European Cup. It wasn't that we didn't have a strong squad, but the changes the boss had to make would disrupt the rhythm of the side. That particular season, we were already as good as out of the competition but had a home game against Galatasaray still to play. It was early December.

The first I knew about the possibility of me being involved was an article in the *Manchester Evening News* saying the gaffer was thinking about giving some youngsters a chance to try European football. On the day, he told a few of us we'd actually start the game that night. I don't know about the others, but I went into it not having a clue what to expect. About half an hour in, I scored my first senior goal for United. The ball rolled out to me, in front of the Stretford End, and I remember thinking: if I catch this right, something could happen. Even though I didn't really connect properly, the ball bobbled in somehow and I turned and ran away to celebrate. Eric Cantona was the first player to get to me. I was buzzing that much, he was having to fight me off in the end. I just wouldn't let go of him. *I've scored a goal and I'm celebrating with Eric Cantona.*

I really enjoyed myself. I think Galatasaray had left out some senior players, too, and the game wasn't as difficult as it might have been. We played well, and the fact that there were so many of the younger boys in the team made it even better. Starting the game had made a difference, too. I felt a lot more at home at Old Trafford that night than I had during my seventeen minutes down at Brighton, two years before. For us boys, it felt like the European Cup Final, never mind that United were going out whatever the result. As it was, we won 4–0, which is a decent score in a European game whatever the circumstances. The manager didn't say anything afterwards. He was disappointed to be out of Europe, but seemed happy enough with how the young lads had played.

That first start in a big European fixture was an exception for me. I still had work – and filling out – to do. The thing that has kept United and the players at the club driving on is the knowledge that if your standards slip, there's someone waiting to take your place. As a teenager, the doubts about whether you'd still be there in a week, a month, or even a year's time, were even more intense. It was back to the reserves after my start in the Galatasaray game. Back to wondering whether I was good enough to take the next big step: establishing myself in the first team by getting games in the Premier League. Sometimes in a career, even if you think you know what you need next, you have to be ready to make the best of what comes along.

It wasn't every day I got called in after training to see the manager in his office:

'Preston North End have asked if they could take you on loan for a month. I think it's a good idea.'

Straight away, I put two and two together and made five. I was nineteen. Nicky Butt and Gary Neville were already getting games on a fairly regular basis. I'd been involved with the first team, but I wasn't progressing as quickly as them. Had United decided I wasn't going to be strong enough to make it? Was this a way of easing me out? I couldn't get the thought out of my head. *They don't rate me. They want to get rid of me.*

It might have been an overreaction, but that's how I felt. Of course, the first person I spoke to was Eric Harrison and, because of the conversation I had with him, the boss had me back in to explain.

'This isn't about anything else but you getting first-team experience, in a different team, in a different league.'

I'm glad I had that chance to talk to him because it meant I went to Preston in the right frame of mind. I could have stayed in Manchester to train and just gone to Deepdale to play in the games but, because I knew now it was something United saw as part of me developing as a player, I decided to join up with Preston full-time for the month. If I was going to do it, then I should do it properly.

When I turned up at their training ground for the first time, I was pretty nervous. I went into the dressing room and all the Preston players were sitting there, as if they'd been waiting for me. I don't know if they were thinking it, or I just imagined they were. *Here's this big-time Charlie from United, and he's a cockney as well.* Either way, it was a really awkward morning. Preston were in Division Three. It was a world away from the life I'd got used to at a club where everything was taken care of for you, where only the best facilities were good enough. At the end of the first training session, I threw my kit down in the dressing room before taking a shower.

'Not on the floor. You take it home and wash it yourself for tomorrow.'

It didn't bother me. I just wasn't prepared for how things were done at Deepdale. The manager, Gary Peters, didn't waste any time by way of introductions. On that first day, he got all the players and me together in a circle:

'This is David Beckham. He's joining us for a month from Manchester United. He can play. And he'll take all the free-kicks and all the corners, which means you're off them and you're off them.'

He pointed to the lads who were usually on dead balls and didn't even wait for an answer. What a start. It must have annoyed some of the other players. It would have annoyed me. Things were a bit embarrassing to start with, but once we were working together and got to know each other, I had a great time with all the lads at Preston. We had a few nights out the month I was there. It made a real difference that I wasn't just turning up for the games. They knew I'd chosen to be at Preston every day for the month of the loan.

Amongst the players, David Moyes, who's now the Everton manager, was the top man. He was a centre-half, the kind of player who'd throw himself into any tackle possible. Even into some that weren't possible. He'd be shouting, geeing people up, and was passionate about winning games. He was club captain and he talked to me, got me involved, right from the off. It's not just hindsight: you could tell then that David was going to make a manager. He knew straight away what I was about, that I'd be quiet, keep myself to myself and just talk when I needed to. He put himself out to bring me into the group, to look after me, and I really appreciated that.

Gary Peters, the manager, was brilliant as well. It probably helped that he was a Londoner too. He made it clear what he needed me to do and gave me the confidence to do it. He seemed to really believe in me. He must have watched me playing for the reserves at United and I found out later that he'd asked about taking me on loan almost as a joke, not thinking the club would agree. He couldn't believe it when the gaffer said yes. I understand Preston even put a bid in for me after the loan spell, but Gary knew that really would have been pushing their luck.

It all happened very quickly. I trained with them on the Monday then Gary put me into the reserves on the Wednesday, which felt quite strange. Preston played in the Central League, like United's reserves, and beforehand it almost seemed like I'd fallen on hard times. But once you're out there playing you forget all that. I did all right, set up a goal and scored one myself. So, come the Saturday, I was on the bench for the first team against Doncaster at Deepdale.

It was a bit of a surprise when Ryan Kirby, who I'd played alongside for so many years with Ridgeway, lined up for Doncaster. My dad was up for the game, of course. And so was Ryan's dad, Steve, who'd also done some of the coaching when we were kids. For me and Ryan, though, it was more of a quick hello and then we had to get on with it.

One thing I wasn't really looking forward to was the tackling. I'm sure that's part of the reason the boss sent me to Preston in the first place, to harden me up a bit. I was a lot more fragile then than I am now. That first game, I sat on the bench for the first half and, every time a tackle flew in, I was cringing. I wasn't exactly looking forward to getting on. When I did, though, almost straight away we got a corner. It was a really blowy afternoon, with the wind behind us, and I remember thinking I'd just whip the ball in to see what happened. A goal. Not a bad way to start. We ended up coming from behind to draw 2–2.

The next game was against Fulham, who had Terry Hurlock playing for them. Now, I knew Terry by reputation and I'd watched him play: here was a bloke who liked a tackle and I was worried about getting a whack off him. As it turned out, I didn't and got a few challenges in myself. You soon realise that, if you're playing for Preston in Division Three and they need the points, you can't afford to be ducking out of the physical side.

We won 3–2 and it was during that game I scored my first-ever free-kick at first-team level. It was just outside the area and I fancied it. Gary Peters had put me on the free-kicks, and this one couldn't have gone better. I don't remember the goal so much as the celebration. I ran away with my arm in the air and one of the Preston players grabbed my head and started pulling my hair so hard I thought he was going to pull a handful out. Absolutely killed me. It might seem obvious, but I think a lot of people don't realise just how much goals and results matter to players. For the lads at a club like Preston, back then anyway, it was about playing and trying to pay your mortgage and keep up with the bills like anybody else. It gave the football the sort of edge I'd never experienced. The looks in the other players' eyes just told me how strong their desire was, how badly they wanted, and needed, to win the game. It was the same with the crowd at Deepdale. The club was the heart of the town; it had this long, proud history and people absolutely lived for Saturday afternoons and the match. I was lucky. They were great and took to me right from the off.

I've had some amazing experiences since but, truthfully, that month at Preston was one of the most exciting times in my whole career. I remember thinking then that if the boss had been looking to let me go, I could have been happy playing for Preston North End. When it came time, at the end of the loan, to go back to United, I didn't want to leave. How worried had I been before-hand? How nervous had I been when I got to Deepdale? Just four weeks later and here I was, asking Mr Ferguson if I could go and stay on with them for another month.

The answer was: 'No'. No explanation or anything. By the end of that same week, I understood why the gaffer wanted me back. There was an injury crisis at Old Trafford and the teamsheet for Saturday's Leeds game had my name on it: I was about to make my League debut for Manchester United at Old Trafford. After five really competitive – and physical – first-team games for Preston, I felt ready for the next step forward. More to the point, the boss thought I was, too. I was more prepared than I had been for those games against Brighton and Galatasaray, for sure. For an afternoon, at least, I could put any doubts to one side. It seemed like United and Mr Ferguson thought I did have a chance after all.

I knew that, for all the excitement of winning an FA Youth Cup and the thrill of playing those games for United in the Cups and Preston in Division Three, I hadn't achieved anything yet. But maybe this was my time to show that, one day, I might. It wasn't just me, of course. It wasn't just my generation, come to that. It's still true now: just ask Wes Brown or John O'Shea or Kieran Richardson. The gaffer has always had faith in the players who have been produced at the club. One of the best things about coming through the ranks at Old Trafford is that the boss involves the younger players in training – and gives them a game, too – as soon as he feels they're up to it. He believes in the lads who have grown up at the club and, above everything else, that's something for which my generation will always feel grateful to Alex Ferguson. The future isn't a responsibility he hands over to someone else. When I was a boy, he knew who David Beckham was. Once I'd signed for United, he was following my progress the whole time: coming to games, watching training, talking to Eric and the other coaches about how I was getting on.

When it comes to making a League debut, or even getting a start in a Cup game for United, you already feel like you're part of the first-team set-up. That makes it easier for any young player to relax and do his best when he's given his chance. With me, it seemed like I'd been involved at least since I was a kid, warming up alongside my heroes at Upton Park as club mascot for the afternoon. By the time I was ready for United's first team, I already got on well with the senior players. It wasn't a case of: who's this young so and so, coming in and thinking he can take our place? I knew them all and, just as important, they knew me.

As it turned out, my first Premier League game was a bit of an anticlimax. There's always a big atmosphere for Man United vs Leeds, whether we're playing at Old Trafford or at Elland Road, and the ground was buzzing beforehand. It was an incredibly hot afternoon, though, and the match was stifled because of that. It finished 0–0. I must have done all right because I played a few more League games before the end of that season and, by the summer, it felt as if, slowly but surely, things were starting to happen. What I didn't realise, and none of us did, was that the gaffer had already seen enough and was ready to take one of the biggest managerial gambles of all time. The season 1995/96 was the making of me. It was the making of all of us, thanks to a boss who believed in us even before we believed in ourselves.

DB on the Tarmac 4

'What if we go out and prove the lot of you wrong?'

There weren't many better players in their positions anywhere in Europe; but Mark Hughes, Paul Ince and Andrei Kanchelskis were leaving Old Trafford. During the summer of 1995, we read about it in the papers like everyone else: Alex Ferguson had decided to sell three of United's biggest stars. Andrei was a fantastic player but there'd been a problem between him and the boss. Stories on the back pages claimed that Paul had started acting as if he was bigger than the club itself. I know the gaffer wouldn't have stood for it, but I never saw Incey like that: he was a big personality who drove the team on, like Roy Keane does now. Incey was as good a player at that time, as well.

He might have been in his early thirties but, to this day, I think it was a mistake letting Mark Hughes go. Just ask Chelsea supporters. Mark went to Stamford Bridge and they'll tell you what a great player he was for them. I have to admit that I'm biased. I was a fan back then and I'm a fan now that he's manager of Wales. If it was up to me, Mark Hughes would probably still be playing for Manchester United. After Bryan Robson, he was my big hero when I was a teenager and that was still true when I had a chance to play alongside him. I was really disappointed he left: how were we going to win anything without Sparky in the team?

I still remember how upset I was when I found out that Mark, in particular, was leaving. I was surprised, too: like most United supporters my first reaction was to wonder what the manager was doing. You knew there had to be something going on for him to be letting such important senior players go. But the boss wasn't saying anything. Then the penny dropped: Andrei Kanchelskis was a right-sided attacking player. And so was David Beckham. What had Eric Harrison always told the young players before we sat down at Old Trafford to watch the first team play? *Watch the man playing in your position. One day, you're going to take his place.* When Andrei left Old Trafford, I couldn't help wondering, could I?

When we joined up for pre-season training, most of the younger players were waiting to see who the boss would sign to replace the big names who'd left. A couple of months later, with us all in the side, we were still assuming he'd have to bring in new players. How could he stick with just us young boys? Manchester United are a massive club, and you can understand that the fans expect success straight away. At the back of our minds, though, there was the hope that we'd get the chance to prove ourselves. Nowadays young players are different: they're more confident in themselves. In the situation we were in, you'd expect someone to say it straight out: 'Are we going to get a game here, or what?' Myself, the Neville brothers, Nicky Butt and Paul Scholes weren't like that. None of us asked and the boss didn't tell us. He just went ahead and started the new season with the youngest United side anybody could remember since the Busby Babes.

First game of the season, away to Aston Villa, we got hammered. I was on the bench and by the time I got on in the second half we were already 3–0 down. I scored: Denis Irwin chipped the ball forward for me. I got a good first touch on my instep, let the ball run forwards a little and then shot from the edge of the box. A slight deflection took it past Mark Bosnich, who was in goal for them. I remember celebrating almost on my own. We were still a couple of goals down, of course, and John O'Kane, who'd also come on as a sub, was about the only player who came over and hugged me.

For the remainder of the game I ran around all over the place trying to make a difference. I was quite pleased with myself afterwards. But the gaffer wasn't. I was devastated. He had a right go at me in the dressing room, telling me how important it was for the team that I stay in my position. After that defeat at Villa Park, the media were ready to write off United's season. The manager seemed to be putting his faith in a group of youngsters and the pundits weren't having any of it. They were all saying the same thing. Unluckily for him, Alan Hansen was the one who said it on *Match of the Day*:

'You'll win nothing with kids.'

I was sitting in front of the television that night. I'm sure the other lads were, too. Coming back from Birmingham there might have been doubts in some minds. As a group, we had risen to any challenge put in front of us. But on the coach that evening I think there were a few of us wondering if this was too big a step up and too soon. There were probably a few thousand United supporters headed back from the game who'd been wondering the same thing. But by the time we'd all got home and were hearing the experts write us off, I'm sure I wasn't the only one getting riled by the criticism. It had just been one game, after all. *What if we go out and prove the lot of you wrong?*

The next game was at home to West Ham and, for all that he'd criticised me after the Villa match, the gaffer named me in the team. Plenty of things rushed through my head, especially the

realisation that starting the game meant I would be lining up opposite Julian Dicks. I don't know why but I found myself remembering
a boy I'd been friendly with at Chingford High, Danny Fisher, who
was a mad, mad West Ham fan. I'd always looked out for their
results, too, even though I was a Manchester United supporter,
and the two of us talked and argued about football all the time.
What would Danny be thinking now when he saw me lining up
against West Ham and against Julian Dicks? I knew what I was
thinking: this bloke's a really hard player.

In my early United career, I think there were doubts about
whether I'd ever be physically tough enough to cope with first-
team football. As an eight-year-old playing Sunday League football, I believed I was good enough then to have been playing for
United. I know other people were concerned that, even at seventeen and eighteen, I hadn't really grown: It was talked about at
the club and I also remember talking about it with Dad. I worked
with weights to make me stronger but the spurt that took me up
to six foot didn't happen until much later. But, whatever anyone
else said, I wasn't worried about my size. I was determined it
wouldn't hold me back, anyway. I'd always played football against
people who were bigger and stronger than me. Julian Dicks,
though? The manager had a word with me in the dressing room
before kick off:

'When you get your chance, run at him or get your cross in.
But watch yourself. If he can whack you, he will.'

And he did early on, down by the corner flag. But Dicks could
play, too, and I knew I needed to keep going because, if he got
the better of me, he was the best passer of the ball in West Ham's
team. The United fans were fantastic that night. They might have
been nervous about the stars who'd left in the summer. But I think
they loved watching homegrown talent doing well for the club.

Gary and Phil Neville, Paul Scholes and Nicky Butt were all Manchester boys, which gave the fans an extra sense of pride. I still wonder now whether the Old Trafford crowd had the same feeling towards me, a Londoner rather than a local lad like the others. I'd like to think they did. Against West Ham, and all that season, it certainly felt like it. And that made a big difference. We won our first home game of the season 2–1; and I don't think I lost my own battle with West Ham's left-back.

For a young team, every game meant that we would find out more about ourselves, about what we could and couldn't do. We believed in our own ability but that didn't mean we didn't have a lot to learn from week to week. Ten days after the West Ham game, we went up to Ewood Park for one of the biggest fixtures of the season. Three months earlier, Blackburn had won their first Premiership title, finishing one point ahead of us despite losing at Anfield on the last day of the season. If we had won at Upton Park instead of drawing that day, we would have been champions. It had been that close. They had a strong, experienced team, with Chris Sutton and Alan Shearer up front. Going there, so early in the season, made it a very big night: the boss didn't say it, but I think it was a match we thought we couldn't afford to lose.

I remember two incidents really clearly. Early on, I tried a long ball that didn't come off – a Hollywood pass, probably – and Roy Keane had a go at me about it; in fact he absolutely ripped me apart. Before I knew it, I was having a go back at him. Sometimes the passion of the moment can take you by surprise. Roy does it to his team-mates all the time. It's part of his game and what people need to understand is that there's nothing personal about it. It doesn't matter to Roy if you've been playing for United for ten years or just ten games; if he thinks he needs to, he'll hammer you. It's all about wanting to win. That night at Ewood Park was the first time I'd been on the end of one of those volleys. It worked. It always works: Keano having a go fires you up because you know he's doing it for a reason, not just for the sake of losing his rag. Whether he's right or wrong, he always gets a reaction.

Later on, with the score at 1–1, I remember Lee Sharpe went into a challenge on the edge of their penalty area. The ball rolled out towards me and I swivelled to line myself up and then curled a shot into the top right-hand corner. That goal was the winner. To do something like that, in a game as important as that, was a really big thing for me. And the goal and the result were just as big for the club. That game was in the middle of a run of five straight wins that followed us getting beaten at Villa. Win nothing with kids? I think United supporters, at least, were starting to wonder if maybe we could.

Not that anyone got carried away by my goal up at Blackburn, or by anything else. Personally, I still couldn't quite believe I was playing for the first team. I was just as excited by that as I was by scoring. As a group of young players, we weren't the kind of characters to go round shouting the odds. In fact, the dressing room during that season was probably as quiet as a United dressing room has ever been. Aside from Gary Neville, none of us young lads were great talkers before and after a game. The older players weren't shouters even when they were saying what they needed to say. It was just the gaffer who, every now and again, would make us all sit up and listen. The atmosphere did change, though, as the season wore on and our confidence grew.

As well as the manager, the senior players kept us going. The likes of Steve Bruce and Gary Pallister had been through all this before. Peter Schmeichel was a huge influence, quite apart from the fact that he was the best goalkeeper in the world back then. Peter was the kind of person you could talk to any time, about your game, about opponents or about what was going on in your life. And he was merciless in training. Score past him and you could score past anyone. You could only improve. At the end of every training session, we used to practise crossing, which meant Gary Neville and I would be out on the right, Ryan Giggs and Denis Irwin would be out on the left. Peter used to give Gary a really hard time. His crossing wasn't as good then as it is now and some of the improvement, at least, must have been down to those sessions. Peter would knock Gary and then knock him again. Gary would get his head down, work harder and fight back. And when he did send over a decent cross, Peter's praise really counted for something.

Every good team needs a strong leader. We'd had Bryan Robson at United in the past. More recently we had Roy Keane. That season, though, the man who made us tick didn't come back into the side until early October. Eric Cantona had been signed from Leeds in November 1992 after he'd won the championship with them the previous season. I'd watched him play a couple of times and you could see he was a good player then but, once he arrived at Old Trafford, something more started to happen. In no time at all, Eric had become this player that the rest of us wanted to be. As a person, he had an aura about him: when Eric walked into a room, everything stopped. He was a presence. And he brought that same quality to being a Manchester United player.

In all the time we played together and trained together, I don't think I ever had a conversation with Eric about football. To be honest, beyond a few words here and there, I never had a conversation with him about anything. I don't think many people did, he was that private about his life. After training, and after games, he'd just disappear. We accepted that he had his own life and his own way of doing things. He'd turn up for training, driving this little Vauxhall Nova, and lever all six foot four of himself out from behind the steering wheel. He'd do his work. Then, when we'd finished, he'd squeeze himself back into the thing and be gone. Amazing, really, when you think about the impact he had not just on me and the rest of the players but on the whole club. We didn't talk to him but we talked about him almost all the time..

Eric could do no wrong in my eyes. And I think the gaffer was a bit in awe of him as well. One evening we were at a premiere of one of the *Batman* films. It was a club invitation so we were all supposed to turn up in black tie. Eric arrived wearing a white suit and his bright red Nike trainers. I laugh about it now, after the ear bashings I used to get from the boss about the clothes I chose to wear. Eric was special, though. The gaffer knew that and so did all the players. We never begrudged him being treated differently to the rest of us.

Eric was a class apart. If anyone tried it on, he made sure you knew that. Not that people risked it very often. There was one evening, after a game, when we'd arranged a 'team meeting': it was just a night out with the lads but calling it that meant you knew everybody had to be there. We'd planned to meet at a place in Manchester called the Four Seasons at 6.45 and then go on from there. By 7 o'clock, only Eric was missing. He eventually strolled up and Giggsy pointed to his watch:

'Seven o'clock, Eric.'

Ryan was doing his best to sound like the gaffer if you were late for training. Eric looked over:

'Six forty-five.'

Giggsy looked at his watch but, before he could say another word, Eric hitched up his sleeve and showed us the face of the most beautiful Rolex watch any of us had ever seen:

'Six forty-five,' he smiled.

End of argument. How could that watch, or the bloke wearing it, possibly be wrong about the time?

Watching Eric was a football education, especially in the way he used to practise. Every day, after training, he would be out there on a pitch at the Cliff, working on his own. He'd be taking free-kicks, doing his turns and little tricks, just as you might expect. But most of the time he'd be practising the simplest things. He'd kick the ball up in the air as high as he could and then bring it under control as it dropped. He'd kick the ball against a wall, right foot then left foot. Eric was one of the best players in Europe and he was doing the same stuff I'd done with Dad in Chase Lane Park when I was seven years old.

Once you're playing football as a professional, you have to spend most of your time preparing for two games a week. It doesn't leave much opportunity for the basics: controlling and striking the ball. My dad had always tried to make sure I understood that control was the most important skill of all. It didn't matter what else you learnt, a good first touch was the key. Which was why Eric, an established international, always made sure he found time to work on that. If you're comfortable receiving the ball, it gives you the room in your game to see what you need to do next. The gaffer has told this story about Eric on the eve of the 1994 FA Cup Final. He saw him outside in the hotel grounds, just practising on his own, and realised then that Eric was a player who set his own standards higher than anybody else could set them for him. He was an example to all of us, the boss included.

It wasn't that he set himself up as a leader. Before he came to England and while he was at Leeds, I don't think that part of Eric's character particularly stood out. Once he got to United, everything changed. It was as if he'd found the place he belonged and the stage he thought he deserved. In a United shirt, what he did was amazing right from the start. It was Eric's arrival three months into the season that was the key to United winning the League in 1992/93, putting an end to all those years of waiting for the club. Then the following season, he helped United to our first Double.

I didn't play in the first team during those two seasons, but when we did eventually play together, I could tell Eric must have been the spark that made it all happen. He led. The rest of us followed. It's a rare quality: a born captain, who hardly needed to say anything, to us or anybody else. You didn't hear Eric leading the team. Just seeing him on the pitch, standing there with his collar turned up, ready to take on the world, was enough.

When people talk about Eric, they'll always refer to the sendings off, and worse, during his career. The way I see it, though, all great players have an edge to their character and to their football. That edge is what makes them more than the ordinary. And if you go through a whole career with that quality, you're bound to have trouble with the authorities sooner or later. It may sound strange but despite the bookings, sendings off, bans or whatever, it would never have occurred to me to criticise Eric. We played football together and that was what my relationship with him was all about. I'd think about him, about what he brought to the dressing room and the team: his ability, his passion and his commitment. Nothing else bothered me. He played the game and lived his life the way he was driven to and he made things special for the rest of us by doing that. How could I have even started to think badly of Eric Cantona or anything he did? David Beckham owed him a lot and Manchester United owed him even more.

I was at Selhurst Park that night in 1995 when Eric jumped into the crowd. I wasn't on the bench but was in the stands, with a couple of the other lads, watching the game. I don't remember much about the game itself against Crystal Palace, but I remember the incident. Eric got sent off after a tackle on Richard Shaw and, as he was walking along the touchline, you could see this bloke force his way down to the front of the crowd. He was goading Eric, shouting things at him. And next thing, Eric was in the crowd, kicking and punching: the whole thing flashed by in a couple of seconds and then Eric was being hurried towards the dressing room. I think it was just an instinctive reaction, a natural thing to do. Anybody getting that sort of abuse in the street would have reacted in the same way. Just because Eric was a professional footballer, in the spotlight, didn't stop him behaving like anybody else might have done. I'm not saying what Eric did was right but you have to remember that, in any other circumstances, if someone was screaming that stuff at another person, you'd be surprised if there wasn't trouble.

There was no big fuss about what had happened in the dressing room after the game. It was quiet and the boss was really calm about it all. He just said that none of us should speak to the press. Obviously, nobody realised then what the consequences would be: Eric was banned from football for the best part of eight months. We ended up not winning anything that season; others can probably decide what effect losing Eric had on the team. As a player, you just had to get on with your job. Eric went home to France for a few weeks but then came back to Old Trafford and we would work and train with him every day, although he couldn't be involved in the games. He was still very much part of everything at the club but we wanted him playing. After the community service and the FA suspension, he was back in the side a month and a half into the 1995/96 season. From that October onwards, you couldn't quite say that Eric Cantona went on and did the Double on his own. But I'm absolutely certain the rest of us felt that we wouldn't have done it without him.

Talking about that season, it's almost a cliché to say that, during it, we grew up as players. When I think back, though, what I really remember is how much growing up as a person I was doing at the same time. For a start, after sixteen years with Mum, Dad, Lynne and Joanne and then three years in digs that were family homes in their own way, I got my own place. Ryan Giggs had already moved into a house in Worsley, North Manchester, and he told me there was another three-storey townhouse nearby that was coming up for sale. It was perfect. Worsley was a nice, quiet village, the house was brand new and barely ten minutes from the training ground: now I'd never have an excuse for arriving late for work.

I'd grown up in a suburban semi on the outskirts of London, in a house just about big enough for the five of us. Now here I was, collecting the keys to a proper bachelor pad and making it my own: a den with a pool table, a leather suite in the front room, a Bang & Olufsen television and music system, and a great big fireplace. The top floor was just one huge room, my bedroom. I had wardrobes made for it and, when the joiners put them in, I got them to build a cabinet at the bottom of my bed. You pressed a button and the television would come up out of it. When we first started going out together, Victoria used to rip me apart about that. And I had my mate, Giggsy, living next door, as well: what more could any boy ask for?

Even then, Ryan was a legend at United. He was only a year older than me and we'd played in the same Youth Cup winning side, but it seemed as if he was already a star when I got to Manchester. Giggsy was a first-team regular by the time he was eighteen. He was a hero to the younger lads and he was also great to work alongside. Once I moved in next door, I got to know him really well. And that meant getting to know all his mates at the same time: the so-called Worsley Crew. We'd all meet up at the local pub, the Barton Arms, for lunch. I felt like I was keeping Manchester's coolest company.

Giggsy and I have stayed close ever since. He's still someone who can win a game on his own, still a player every opposing defender will tell you they hate playing against. Think back to the 'New George Best' tag he grew up with. Giggsy's had his ups and downs at United like any other player but, over the past twelve years, he's had the ability and strength of character to live up to all the expectations people had of him. I hope Wales make it to Germany for the World Cup in 2006: it would be great to see Giggsy on that international stage. Whatever happens, by the time he packs it in – and there's not much chance of that for a long while – he'll go down as one of United's all-time greats.

I suppose lots of young lads in my situation would have been living on takeaways and looking for a phone number for a good cleaner. I've always been what you might call domesticated, though. Even when I was a boy, living at home, I can remember getting up early on a Sunday morning and cooking a full breakfast for my mum and dad. Not because I had to but because I wanted to: cooking was something I'd always enjoyed. Don't get me wrong. I'm no Gary Rhodes or Jamie Oliver. Mum will tell you that when I was at home I'd cook the same thing every time for an evening meal. Chicken stir-fry. When Mum and Dad came up to the new house and I cooked for them in my own home for the first time, I don't think they were all that surprised at what I'd made: chicken stir-fry. Not that what we were eating was all that important. I was really proud, being able to take my parents to my own place on a Saturday night after the game. I think they were pretty proud too.

What's more, I could drive Mum and Dad home in my own

motor. As a boy, when I wasn't thinking about football, it was because I was thinking about cars. I got a Scalectrix one Christmas and drove the thing into the ground through into my teens. As well as imagining myself playing for Manchester United, I'd spent plenty of rainy afternoons thinking about the car I might turn up at Old Trafford driving one day: how about a Porsche? When I passed my test, though, that kind of fantasy car was a long way out of my range. Instead, I bought Giggsy's old club car, a red Ford Escort Mexico. Three doors, one previous owner and a full service history – that first car set me back about £6,000.

A little later, when I was going out with Deana, I needed something a bit less laddish so I bought a brand new VW Golf. I used to get slaughtered by the other United players because of the number plate M13 EKS – which, with the letters bunched up, I had looking like M BECKS. Most of the lads have probably forgotten that. The one they never left me alone about was my first sponsored club car. At the time, United had a deal with Honda to supply the young players with a new Prelude once they'd played twenty first-team games. Gary and Phil and the rest all got theirs before I did, having been involved with the senior squad more often over the previous couple of seasons. By the time I was ready to pick up mine, I'd worked out exactly what I wanted to do.

I chose one in a very dark grey. Then I paid extra to have them fit a leather interior, a new CD player and big alloy wheels. That was money I didn't really have to throw around at the time and – because the cars would go back to Honda, eventually – it was money that I was never going to see again either. Of course, my new Prelude looked completely different to everyone else's. And I loved it because it was just how I wanted it. We'd often take it in turns to give each other lifts into training. That particular model was pretty cramped in the rear seats, which is probably why Gary

– an old man, you see, even then – changed his for a four-door Accord. One day at the Cliff, after we'd finished training for the day, I was getting ready to drive out of the car park and I already had someone in the front passenger seat. David May came running over and asked if he could jump in the back. Well, I'd just got this beautiful new car and I said no. David swears to this day that what I actually said was: 'No chance. I don't want you to scuff the leather.'

It took about half an hour for everyone at the club to hear about it; and then several years for me to stop hearing about it. I don't remember saying it but – if I'm really honest with myself – I can imagine I did. I am particular about looking after the things I like and, in a football club dressing room, whether it's on Hackney Marshes or at Old Trafford, that can get you into trouble. Footballers will always find each other's weak spots and, once they do, they'll never leave it alone.

I've always had a streak in me, which might seem flash if you don't know me, of being particular about the things I want and of valuing individuality, even if I get stick because of it. When I was about six years old I remember a family wedding where I'd been invited to be a pageboy. We all went along to get fitted for our outfits and I got my heart set on a particular look: maroon knickerbockers, white stockings up to the knee, a frilly white shirt, a maroon waistcoat and a pair of ballet shoes. My dad told me I looked stupid in it. Mum said she needed to warn me that people were going to laugh at me. I didn't care. I loved that outfit and I just wanted to wear it. Never mind at the wedding: I wanted it on all the time. I think I'd have worn it to school if they'd let me.

Along with being very particular about what I like, I'm very careful about looking after what I've got. My mum will tell you how, when I was at school, I used to come in and change but would only go out to play football after I'd folded up my dirty clothes. I'm still tidier than almost anyone else I know. When I first arrived at United, the other boys of my age weren't convinced about me, and maybe put some of my character, as they saw it, down to fancying myself a bit too much. The truth is, though – whether you're talking about a pageboy outfit, a club car with leather seats or a tattoo or a sarong, come to that – it's got nothing to do with one-upmanship or with making a point. My friends and my team-mates know that now, just as my family always have: I've got my own tastes and if I can indulge them I will, whatever other people might say. I've always been the same: knowing what I like is just part of who I am.

Everything that was happening away from football just added to the excitement at Old Trafford during my first season as a regular. I'd wake up every morning hardly able to believe what was going on around me. I'd drive into training, thinking to myself: *I'm a first-team player. I'm doing my work on the main pitch at the Cliff. I've got my own spot in the car park, with my initials there in white paint.* When I went to the training ground for the first time as a boy, those white lines marked out with the initials of the United players I idolised seemed to represent everything I dreamt of achieving for myself. Now, I belonged and it might have been easy to get swept away with it all. People at the club, though, and the manager in particular, didn't let that happen. They didn't suddenly start behaving differently towards me and the other young lads just because it said 'DB' on the tarmac and me, Gary and the rest were on the teamsheet every week.

I was excited every morning about going in to train with Eric Cantona, too. We'd made a good start without him during that 1995/96 season, but the captain being back at the club and back in the team counted for a lot. I don't know about the other players but, if Eric was in the dressing room, I'd find myself watching him: checking what he was doing, trying to work out exactly how he prepared for a game. If he was there, I hardly seemed to notice anything else that was going on. I've always been a fan: a Manchester United fan. And I still am. When I had my first chance to go into the dressing rooms at Old Trafford as a boy, I asked where Bryan Robson sat and then walked across to sit there myself. I was the same about Eric and couldn't quite get over the fact that I was sitting alongside him in the build-up to games, never mind that we'd be playing together later that afternoon.

We played some great football that season. I remember one night at Old Trafford when we played Bolton and won 3–0. It could have been ten. Paul Scholes scored twice, Giggsy got the other and we absolutely battered them. When the team was flying, Eric Cantona was usually at the heart of it. The difficult games, though, were the ones in which he really left his mark. After Christmas, we had a run of 1–0 wins. United supporters didn't even need to check: it was always Eric who scored. I remember one game against QPR down at Loftus Road. We were terrible and they were winning 1–0. I'd actually been substituted and the injury time at the end just dragged on and on. The home fans were going mad and then Eric arrived in the penalty area right on cue to equalise. Goals like that – results like that – turn a whole season.

We spent month after month chasing Newcastle United, who were twelve points ahead of us going into 1996. We went up to St James' Park in the spring and Eric – who else? – scored the only goal. From then on, we knew that we could do it. The penultimate game that season, at home to Nottingham Forest, was the night I realised we actually would. We beat Forest 5–0. I still remember the two goals I scored. Eric hit a volley which skewed off target and I headed in as the ball came across me. Then, I received a ball just inside the area which I turned on and hit under the keeper. In the end, we had to win our final game at Middlesbrough to be absolutely sure of the title, but everyone – players and supporters – at Old Trafford that night just knew we were going to be champions.

We'd just kept coming in for training, turning up for games and were all on the kind of high which has you half-expecting things to go wrong at any minute. In the United first team? Winning the Premiership? There had to be a catch. But there wasn't. Instead, it got better and better. We weren't just on our way to winning the League. How many FA Cup Finals had I been to at Wembley with Dad? Every time, both of us imagining what it would be like for me to play in one? And now, March 1996, here were United at Villa Park for a semi-final against Chelsea, who had Mark Hughes in their side. I didn't know if I'd ever have a better chance.

I couldn't wait, although I promised myself I'd stay well out of Sparky's way when the day came. I'm really friendly with Mark now. We see quite a lot of him, his wife Gill and their three children, who are the nicest, politest kids you'll ever meet. I always used to say to Victoria that they were how I hoped our children would be. I knew back then, though, that it didn't matter how well I knew Mark or how close we were off the pitch; on it – if he had to – he'd smash me as soon as he'd smash anybody else. He was one of those players whose character changes when they go out to play. Mark Hughes would fight for the ball, and fight anyone for it, all day long, which is why supporters and team-mates loved him like they did. I've seen games where he didn't just bully the centre-half he was playing against, he'd bully the entire opposing team.

Chelsea took the lead on the afternoon, Ruud Gullit scoring with a header. Then Andy Cole equalised for us. Well into the second half, one of their defenders, Craig Burley, misplaced a pass. Steve Bruce, who was on the bench, shouted: 'Go on, Becks!' As the ball came towards me, I took a touch and it bounced away a bit off my shin. That took me wider of the goal than I would have wanted. But the keeper came out – we actually caught each other's eyes for a split second – and I slotted it past him into the corner. I ran off to celebrate: I jumped up in the air, threw my fist up and, I swear, at that moment I felt like I could have reached out to touch the roof of the stand, like I could have hung there till the final whistle went. I remember being desperate, as we played out time, for that goal – my goal – to be the one that took us to Wembley.

My mum and dad were sitting up in the stand and, at full-time, I looked up towards them and felt the tears welling up inside of me. Wembley held so many memories for us, going back as far as the first time Dad took me. I can still remember going to a schoolboy international one Saturday afternoon when I was only seven and having to stand on my seat to be able to see. Dad kept telling me to get down. I kept getting back up. Eventually, the seat gave way and I fell and knocked out my two front teeth. There was blood everywhere and Dad had to take me home.

Wembley always meant the Cup Final, too: we were there for that amazing 3–3 draw between United and Palace in 1990, which had every bit of drama you could hope for, with Ian Wright coming on as a substitute and almost winning them the game. I remember not being able to go to the replay because it was a school night and going mad at home, jumping off the settee and dancing round the front room, when Lee Martin scored the winner. Every time United got to a final, I'd hang a flag in my bedroom window, with a picture of Bryan Robson stuck next to it, so everybody could see from the street who I supported. I don't know who said it first, but it's true: kids don't dream about playing for a team that wins the League. Every schoolboy's dream is about playing in the Cup Final. As we celebrated at Villa Park, I knew – and my parents knew – that dream was about to come true.

Wembley was six weeks away and we had Premiership games we had to win but, in the back of my mind, was the thought that I had to stay fit and keep playing well enough to make sure I was in the team against Liverpool. As it turned out, it was close. Steve Bruce told me later that the manager had been thinking, just before the final, about leaving me out. Liverpool played with three centre-halves and the boss and Steve and the coaching staff met to talk about matching their shape – playing with wing-backs – which would have meant I'd have been on the bench. At the time, and I'm glad about it, I didn't know any of that. All I had to think about was beating Liverpool and doing the Double.

For me, the FA Cup Final had always seemed like a very special occasion. It was for the club I was playing for, too. Manchester United have been in more finals – and won more of them – than anyone else. The club and the gaffer knew how to do it in style. We travelled down to London a couple of days before the game, all fitted out in new suits, and stayed at a lovely hotel down by the Thames, near Windsor. As well as training, there were things like clay-pigeon shooting organised, which obviously weren't part of the regular routine before an away game. It was all about building us up to the game but making sure we were relaxed as well. I think us young lads were just wandering around with big grins on our faces the whole time. Playing for United in the Cup Final? We were pinching ourselves.

It's amazing how often it's sunny on Cup Final day. In 1996, I remember being surprised how hot it was, even before we got started. I was sweating during the walkabout on the pitch an hour or so before kick-off. The Liverpool players were strolling around Wembley like it was their own front room: they'd been fitted out in white Armani suits. Some of them were just wearing trainers. Michael Thomas was filming it all on a camcorder. I looked up towards where my mum and dad were going to be sitting. I knew, even then, that the day was going to mean as much to them as it meant to me.

The game was really tough. Tiring, too: the pitch was very sticky because the grass had been left quite long. Things might have been different if someone had been able to get a goal early on. That might have opened up the game. I had a chance in the first five minutes but David James saved my shot and it went out for a corner. Liverpool tried to stop us playing. We tried to stop them playing. And, well into the second half, it looked like neither team was going to score.

I'd almost missed out on a place in the starting line-up. And I was almost taken off just before the moment that won the game. The boss told me later that he had been about to make a substitution. He'd not been pleased with my corners all afternoon: 'crap corners' he called them. But before the board went up for the change, we won another. I ran over to take it and, as I turned my back on the crowd to put the ball down, I was somehow able to hear this one United supporter's voice above the din:

'Come on, David! Come on!'

I swung it into just the right area, a yard or two outside the six-yard box, towards the penalty spot. David James came out, didn't hold it, and when the ball fell to Eric, a few feet outside the Liverpool area, he volleyed it straight back past James and into the goal. That moment was up there with any I've ever experienced, as intense as the feeling the night the goals went in to win the Treble in Barcelona. A surge of joy and adrenalin just rips through you when you see the ball settle in the back of the net. I think the whole team got to Eric inside a split second and it seemed like he lifted the lot of us off the ground and carried us back to the halfway line. It was the story of that whole fantastic season, right there.

When it came to walking up the steps to get the Cup, I made sure I was just in front of Gary Neville in the line. Eric held the trophy above his head, the roar went up from the United end, and I turned round and looked at Gary:

'Can you believe this is happening to us?'

It was chaos in the dressing room afterwards. We'd won the Cup and, even better, we'd beaten Liverpool to do it. I don't know if the boss or Brian Kidd or any of the players tried to say anything, either congratulations or summing the whole day up. You wouldn't have heard a word of it anyway. The elation just took over. People were spraying bottles of champagne everywhere, diving into the huge Wembley bath, screaming, singing and laughing like lunatics.

We stayed over at the hotel that night, before going back to Manchester on the train in the morning. A big celebration dinner had been organised for everybody, win or lose. That whole week-end, the club had made sure our families had been involved. My girlfriend at the time, Helen, and my mum and dad were with us. It made the occasion even sweeter, if that was possible. Early in the evening, the wives and girlfriends were upstairs getting changed and the players had arranged to meet in the bar for a drink before we ate. I remember, just before leaving my room, the adrenalin of the afternoon wearing off and the heaviness creeping into my legs. It had been some day. Some season. By the time I got down, Dad was already there in the thick of it. He was absolutely in his element, sitting at a table, chatting with Eric Cantona and Steve Bruce. It was probably why he'd pushed me

Above: The Beckham family home in Chingford, London.

Left: The boy must have been watching Starsky and Hutch.

Below left to right: Minder. Sister Lynne makes me sit still for a moment.

Oh, yeah. Swimming pool in the back garden. Me, Lynne and Joanne in the lap of luxury.

The water's lovely. A Beckham family day-trip to Southend.

Previous page: Larging it with Ridgeway Rovers.

This page: They were right all along. He can't tackle …

… he can't beat a man …

… and he's too small to ever make a player.

Right: Property of Ridgeway Rovers.

The trophy bears the following inscription:

PRESENTED BY
A.Y. HILTON
IN AID OF
FIELDS OF SMITHFIELD

1973-74	St MATTHEWS
1974-75	SOUTHBURY RANGERS
1975-76	PUMA F.C.
1976-77	AJAX F.C.
1977-78	AJAX F.C.
1978-79	LANFRANC LIONS
1979-80	LANFRANC LIONS
1980-81	ENFIELD UNITED
1981-82	LEA VALLEY
1982-83	ENFIELD RANGERS
1983-84	CHASE LODGE
1984-85	ENFIELD RANGERS

Above: At Chase Lane Park with the lads. Any chance of an Adidas contract?

Right: Playing for the District felt like playing for England.

Far right: Ridgeway Rovers Awards night. Coach Stuart Underwood made sure we looked our best. Maybe he should have had a word with Clive Allen.

Top: Flash cockney? Did they mean me? My first Manchester digs.

Above: Do it like Robbo. United's latest signing stands alongside his all-time United hero.

Left: 'I'll sign you with this pen.' The gaffer points me to the dotted line, 2 May 1988.

Congratulations from the man himself after I won the Bobby Charlton Soccer Skills competition in 1986.

'You'll never guess what I saw last night, Mum.'

so hard, and towards Man United, through so many years. He'd wanted the chance to be doing exactly what he was doing right at that moment. I laughed out loud I was so happy. Dad told me later that Eric thought I was a good player and a good listener. Every time Dad tried to talk to me that evening he seemed like he was about to get overwhelmed by it all. It felt like I was giving him – and Mum – something back at long last.

In my time at United, there was never a moment for stopping and thinking back on what was happening. We were always pushing on towards the next game or a new season. And, as time passed, I came to realise that there was always something else, even more amazing, waiting round the corner to happen. After that first Double season I had a wonderful summer. I was a United player and it felt as if, in my eyes, in my mum and dad's eyes and in the eyes of United supporters, we really had achieved something. Gary, Phil, Nicky, Scholesy and myself all had the first medals of a professional career to prove it. I went off on holiday to Sardinia and, to be honest, forgot all about football for a couple of weeks. There wasn't a television in the bedroom and so I didn't even see most of the Euro 96 tournament that everybody was glued to back home. I just swam, lay in the sun and ate pasta until it was coming out of my ears.

If any manager is going to make sure players don't get distracted by dwelling on the past, it's Alex Ferguson. We were back for training in what seemed like no time. And, all of a sudden, a new season was about to get underway. It was at Selhurst Park in 1996. We were playing Wimbledon and there was a real sense of anticipation in the dressing room and around the ground, which was absolutely packed with United supporters. Before the game, I was getting stick in the dressing room about my new boots. Over the summer, my sponsors adidas had sent me a pair of

Predator boots for the first time, but unfortunately this particular pair had been made for Charlie Miller, a young Scottish player at Glasgow Rangers. The word 'Charlie' was stitched on the tongues of the boots and the other players spotted that straight away.

Once the game kicked off, it soon felt like we were picking up where we'd left off the previous May. The team played really well and the game was as good as over by half-time. Eric Cantona was substituted, so he was sitting, watching on the bench. Jordi Cruyff tried to chip the Wimbledon keeper, Neil Sullivan, from outside the box. And I'm sure I heard someone say that, if the shot had been on target, Jordi might have scored. A couple of minutes after that, Brian McClair rolled the ball in front of me just inside our own half, and I thought: why not? *Shoot.* I hit it and I remember looking up at the ball, which seemed to be heading out towards somewhere between the goal and the corner flag. The swerve I'd put on the shot, though, started to bring it back in and the thought flashed through my mind. *This has got a chance here.*

The ball was in the air for what seemed like ages, sailing towards the goal, before it dropped over Sullivan and into the net. The next moment, Brian McClair was jumping all over me. He'd been standing there, almost beside me, and along with everybody else in the ground had just watched the ball drift downfield.

Back in the dressing room after the game, someone told me what the manager had growled when I shot:

'What does he think he's trying now?'

Eric Cantona came up to me while I was getting changed and shook my hand:

'What a goal,' he said.

Believe me, that felt even better than scoring it. Someone from *Match Of the Day* wanted to speak to me but the boss said he didn't want me talking to anyone. So I went straight out to get on the coach. Because the game was in London, Mum, Dad and Joanne were waiting for me. I've got a photo of the goal at home, of the ball just hanging against the clear, blue sky, and I can actually see my mum and dad in the crowd. I got to the steps of the coach and Dad hugged me:

'I can't believe you've just done that!'

That evening, I talked on the phone to Helen, who was at college down in Bristol:

'Did you score a goal today? Everybody here's talking about it, saying you've scored this great goal.'

People were coming up to me in the street all weekend and saying the same thing. I couldn't have known it then, but that moment was the start of it all: the attention, the press coverage, the fame, that whole side of what's happened to me since. It changed forever that afternoon in South London, with one swing of a new boot. The thrill I get playing football, my love of the game: those things will always be there. But there's hardly anything else – for better or worse – that has been the same since. When my foot struck that ball, it kicked open the door to the rest of my life at the same time. In the game, it eventually dropped down out of the air and into the net. In the life of David Beckham, it feels like the ball is still up there. And I'm still watching it swerve and dip through a perfect, clear afternoon sky: watching and waiting to see where it's going to come down to land.

The One with the Legs

'I'm in Manchester but I'll drive down. We could go out.'

My wife picked me out of a football sticker book. And I chose her off the telly.

Considering I grew up in Chingford and Victoria lived in Goff's Oak – fifteen minutes' drive away – it seems we travelled a very long way round before finding one another. We'd been to the same shops, eaten in the same restaurants, danced in the same clubs but never actually come face to face during twenty-odd North-east London years. Once we finally met, we had all that catching up to do. It felt straight away like we'd always been meant to be together. Maybe everything that had gone before was just about us getting ready for the real thing to happen.

It's November 1996. I'm sitting in a hotel bedroom in Tbilisi, the night before a World Cup qualifier against Georgia. Gary Neville, my room-mate, is lying on the other bed in the room. Aside from the matches themselves, overseas trips, whether it's with my club or with England, aren't my favourite part of being a professional player. What do you see? What do you do? Eat, sleep and train; sit in rooms that all look the same as the last one. That particular hotel in Georgia, the only one up to international standards after the break-up of the old Soviet Union, was built in a square, with balconies piled up on each side overlooking an open area containing the lobby, bars and restaurant. All the bedroom doors faced across at each other, there was steel and glass everywhere. This place felt even more like a prison than most. Looking out of the window, I could see a half-built dual carriageway and a grey river oozing along beside it. It wasn't the kind of view that made you think about going out for an evening stroll.

So Gary and I are just chatting. The television's on in the corner, tuned to a music channel. On comes the new Spice Girls' video, 'Say You'll Be There'. They're dancing in the desert and Posh is wearing this black cat suit and looks like just about the most amazing woman I've ever set eyes on. I'd seen the Spice Girls before – who hadn't – and whenever that blokes' conversation came up about which one do you fancy, I always said:

'The posh one. The one with the bob. The one with the legs.'

But that evening, in that claustrophobic hotel room, it dawned on me for the first time. Posh Spice was fantastic and I had to find a way to be with her. Where was my Lawrence of Arabia outfit? Who was going to lend me a camel?

'She's so beautiful. I just love everything about that girl, Gaz. You know, I've got to meet her.'

Gary probably thought I was getting a bit stir-crazy. We'd been through quite a lot together but that hadn't included me falling in love with a pop star on the television. That's what was going on: right at that moment, my heart was set on Victoria. I had to be with her. How could I make it happen, though? I was a young guy, with a career as a footballer that was just starting to go quite well. This beautiful, sexy woman who I was desperate to meet was a Spice Girl. At the time, Victoria and the Girls were everywhere: number one in the pop charts, on the cover of every magazine and on the front page of every newspaper, jetting all over the world. They were the biggest thing on the planet. There were pop stars and pop stars. And then there were the Spice Girls. Here was I, deciding I really needed to go out with one of them.

What was I supposed to do? Write to her?

'Dear Posh Spice. You don't know me but I have this very strong feeling that, if we could meet somehow, I think we'd get on really well. I don't know what your schedule's like but you can find me at Old Trafford every other Saturday.'

You hear stories about A-list celebrities who know how to arrange this sort of thing. Not me. I couldn't exactly get My People to speak to Her People. I'm sure I wasn't the only bloke in the world who was carrying a torch for 'The One With The Bob' at the time. It might have sounded crazy, but I was absolutely certain that meeting Posh Spice was something that simply had to happen, even though I didn't have a clue as to how or where. I got my sister Joanne to dig out a copy of *Smash Hits* so I could at least find out a bit more about Victoria: her surname, for a start.

Just a month or so later, we were down in London to play Chelsea and, before the game, someone in the dressing room said that a couple of the Spice Girls were at Stamford Bridge.

Which ones? Is Posh here? Where are they sitting? Somehow or other, I kept the excitement to myself. Maybe this was the chance I'd been waiting for. Later, I found out that it was Victoria, along with Melanie Chisholm, who'd come to the game. As I went up to the Players' Lounge, I was praying she would be there.

I met up with Mum and Dad. Victoria and Melanie were chatting in one corner. Their manager walked over and introduced himself:

'Hello, David. I'm Simon Fuller. I look after the Spice Girls. I'd like you to meet Victoria.'

I could feel little beads of sweat starting to roll down my forehead. Suddenly it was very hot indeed in that lounge. She came over. I didn't have a speech ready, so all I could manage was:

'Hello, I'm David.'

Victoria seemed pretty relaxed. I think she and Mel had had a glass of wine or two. In the game I'd scored with a volley, which I hoped might have impressed her, until I found out she hadn't been wearing her glasses. The truth was Victoria didn't really have a clue what had been going on during the match. She was looking at me and, I guessed, didn't have the faintest idea who I was. Man United? Chelsea? Were you even playing today? Later, someone reminded her that she'd picked my picture out of an album of football stickers when the Girls had been doing a photo shoot in team strips a few days before. Knowing nothing about football, she'd been the only one who hadn't made up her mind whose kit to wear. Looking at those pictures had been part of trying to decide which team she was going to pretend to support. Right then, though, that picture wasn't doing me any good at all.

'I'm Victoria.'

And that was that. I couldn't think what to say next. Simon Fuller rattled on for a bit about the game: I can't say I remember a word of it. She went back into her corner with Melanie. I went back to where my mum and dad were standing. I looked across the room at Victoria. Stared, in fact: I couldn't take my eyes off her. And I could see Victoria was looking back at me. *I should be trying to get her number, at least trying to say something else to her.* But I didn't. She left. I left. That was it; I'd blown my big chance. I got back on the coach and it was all I could do not to start banging my head against the back of the seat in front in frustration.

During the course of the following week, once I'd got over feeling sorry for myself, I found out a little more about the Girl of my dreams. Despite the missed opportunity, meeting her had only made me more certain about her. I saw the piece in *90 Minutes* magazine featuring the Spice Girls in their football kit, Victoria in a United strip and a caption saying she liked the look of David Beckham. I didn't know how these things worked; that the quote from her might have just been made up. No: made up was what I was. And for the next home game, there she was at Old Trafford.

This time, it had been the full works. Victoria had been wined and dined before the match by Martin Edwards, the United Chairman. She and Melanie had gone out on the pitch to do the half-time scores. And now she was in the players' lounge after the game, in the middle of another glass of champagne. I walked in and went over to say hello to Mum and Dad. And, because we'd met before – briefly, nervously – it was easier this time to say hello to Victoria. She looked fantastic in tight combat trousers and a little khaki top, cut quite low; an unbelievable figure. I remember hoping she wouldn't get the wrong idea about me and her cleavage: there was a tiny blemish, like a freckle, at the top of her breastbone that I just couldn't stop staring at.

Deciding what to say next wasn't exactly obvious. *This is it. You're the one.* That was in my head. But you can't really make that sort of declaration to someone you've only ever said three words to, especially with your mum and dad and your team-mates within earshot. Joanne was there and she and Victoria seemed to be doing better on the small talk than I was. My sister, at least, had some idea of how I was feeling. I did the bloke thing and went off to the bar to get in a round of drinks. The next moment, Victoria was there beside me. It wasn't like we knew what we wanted to say. How do you start? What's it like being a pop star? What's it like playing football for a living? But I think we both knew that we needed to be speaking to each other and once we started talking – at last – neither of us wanted to stop. Next time I was aware of where I was, I was looking around the room and thinking: *Where's everybody gone?*

Mum and Dad were still there. *Oh, no. Not a Spice Girl* they were probably muttering to themselves. And one or two other people were just sort of lingering, as if they were waiting to see what was going to happen. I remember Victoria going off to the ladies and me having this big now-or-never moment with myself. When she came back, I gabbled out an invitation to dinner. I didn't have any sort of plan. I hadn't thought about where we might go. It was just instinctive: I didn't want her to leave. Victoria said she had to go back to London, as the Spice Girls were flying off to America on the Monday. But she asked me for my phone number. Without missing a beat, I did the reckoning up. *What? So you can forget you've got it? Or lose it? Or decide not to call?*

'No, Victoria. I'll take your number.'

She scrabbled around in her bag and pulled out her boarding card from the flight up to Manchester that morning. She wrote down her mobile number, then scratched that out and gave me her number at home at her parents' instead. I still have that precious little slip of card. It was like treasure and I was never likely to lose it. But as soon as I got home, I wrote the number down on about half a dozen other bits of paper and left them in different rooms, just in case.

It usually takes me ages to get off to sleep the night after a game: the adrenalin's still pumping five or six hours later. That particular night, I was buzzing with having met Victoria properly too. I must have slept because I remember waking up late. At about eleven, I picked up The Number and dialled. The voice at the other end sounded just like her but, because I couldn't be sure, I decided to be polite as I could:

'Is Victoria there?'

Just as well I hadn't ploughed straight in. It was her sister, Louise.

'No. She's at the gym. Who is this? I'll get her to give you a call.'

Everybody's been a teenager. A teenager in love. And I'm sure there are plenty of people, like me, who were still getting a bit melodramatic about it all well into their twenties. *She's out at the gym? Well, that's it then: that's the brush off, isn't it? Getting her sister to answer the phone and say she's out.* I didn't actually go and lie down and beat the floor with my fists, but that's what it felt like. I knew Victoria and me had to happen. But maybe she didn't and now it wasn't going to. I just sat on the bed, staring at the phone. Half an hour? An hour? It felt like a week. And then the thing rang.

'David? It's Victoria.'

We picked up where we'd left off at Old Trafford the evening before. I got the feeling we were both talking away, trying to find the nerve to actually say what we meant. I'd already asked once, in Manchester, and eventually I got round to asking again:

'What are you doing later?'

'Nothing.'

'I'm in Manchester but I'll drive down. We could go out.'

Five hours later I was at the car wash in Chingford. First things first: the car had to look its best. I wasn't to know whether Victoria would be impressed with the new one, a blue BMW M3 convertible, but I wasn't taking any chances. I scrubbed it, hoovered it and by the time I got to my mum's I was looking in worse nick than the car had after the drive down. Mum knew I'd got Victoria's number at Old Trafford and I think she knew what was going on when I turned up on the doorstep. She wasn't too sure about the whole Spice Girls thing at all but she knew me better than to try talking me out of it: I'm as soft as she is but, when I get my heart set on something, I'm as stubborn as my dad.

'All right, David. It's up to you.'

She knew perfectly well she'd have no chance of changing my mind. On went clean clothes: a white t-shirt, a beige jacket, Timberlands and a pair of Versace jeans. It was like putting on my costume for the most important show ever. I rang the co-star and we arranged to meet – very swish setting – at a bus stop outside the Castle, a pub we both knew in Woodford. We worked out later that we'd been in that pub at exactly the same time as each other in the past but without realising it.

She pulled up in her car, a purple-coloured MG, and I went over. I climbed in the passenger seat. I was so nervous. *What should I do? Kiss her on the cheek? Shake hands?* With a little wobble in my voice, I mumbled:

'All right?'

I'd sorted out my car. I'd sorted out my wardrobe. I can't say I'd sorted out a plan for the evening.

'Where do you want to go?' Victoria smiled.

'Um. Where would you like to go?'

We pulled out into the road, neither of us having a clue where we were heading but both of us sure we wanted to go there together. I knew her manager, Simon, was really nervous about the Girls and their boys. Anything that was going on in Spiceworld was all over the papers almost before it had happened in those days. I didn't want to be sharing her company with anybody anyway, to be honest. So we drove around looking for somewhere that would be private enough.

The other reason for wanting to be out of the way was that she had a boyfriend, Stuart, who she was still seeing. He was off skiing in France with her dad at the time. Victoria was straight with me about it from the off; like me, she tries to be completely honest with people. We'd only just met. She didn't want us to muck each other around, or anyone else for that matter. There was just one difficult moment and that was that night: Stuart called Victoria on her mobile while we were driving around together. I was single, of course, but I told Victoria all about the important girlfriends in my past: Deana, who I'd been with for three years when I first moved up to Manchester and who had been so important to me as a teenager away from home for the first time; and Helen, who I'd been seeing for eighteen months more recently and who'd stepped away when people started making a fuss about this young lad from London making a name for himself at United.

Victoria told me about Stuart, and about a lot else besides, as we drove past crowded pub after crowded pub around North-east London. When you meet The One, there's a lot of catching up to do. We made a good start that night and, an hour or so later, I had my good idea:

'I know this little Chinese.'

There was a restaurant in Chingford that I'd visited with Mum and Dad. Nothing spectacular but it had one big thing to recommend it: there was never anyone else in the place whenever I'd eaten there. I gave Victoria directions; we parked up and went in. Perfect: it was absolutely deserted. We sat down and I ordered:

'Could we have a Coke and a Diet Coke, please?'

The lady who ran the restaurant looked at us. *Oh, the last of the big spenders.* She didn't have a clue who we were. I could understand her not recognising me, but Victoria? It was a little world of its own, that Chinese.

'You can't have drink unless you eat meal.'

I said we just wanted a quiet drink. She wasn't having any of it:

'This is an exclusive restaurant, you know.'

We were getting chucked out. I offered to pay for a full meal if we could just have our drinks but it was too late for that and, suddenly, at eleven o'clock at night, we were standing back out in the street. It was time for Victoria to have her good idea:

'We could go round to my friend's house.'

My luck: the friend was Melanie Chisholm. What had I got myself into? I was out with one Spice Girl and now we were going round to another one's house. How much more nervous could a lad get on a first date?

When we arrived, Melanie was in her pyjamas and had got out of bed to answer the door. The moment we walked in, my heart sank. There was this big Liverpool FC poster up on the door. *I'm not ready for this.*

I sat down and Victoria and Melanie went missing for ten minutes. I think they were in the kitchen chatting while I was left on my own on the sofa in the lounge like a complete lemon. By the time they came back, I'd wound myself up all over again. It was like being at a really awkward tea party. Victoria was nervous too, I think. We sat at the two ends of the sofa as if we hadn't been properly introduced. They chatted. I sat and listened. I'm not sure I actually said a word the whole time we were there.

An hour or two later we were back in Victoria's MG, continuing our tour of the M25's beauty spots. I remember she drove us past her parents' house at one point, maybe just so that I'd know where to find her. Eventually, in the early hours of the morning, we were back at the Castle. The Spice Girls were off to the States the following day and we had to say our goodbyes. I got back in my car and waved. Victoria promised to call when she got to New York. Not exactly the most romantic of first dates, but I felt like it couldn't have been better. I'd known that all we needed was to meet. Love at first sight? No, it was happening quicker than that.

So was everything else. That 1996/97 season United won the League again and got closer than we ever had before to what I think had become the gaffer's real ambition: winning the European Cup again for the club. It's a bit like learning football all over again, getting to grips with playing the best teams in Europe. There have been one or two teams that United seem to have played over and over again in the last ten years. I'm thinking of Barcelona, Juventus and Bayern Munich, in particular. It's almost as if you have to meet those teams in the Champions League just to find out what kind of progress you've made on the European stage.

In the autumn of 1996, I remember we got turned over twice by Juve, 1–0 both home and away. However much of the ball we had, we just couldn't work out how to beat them. We still qualified from the first group stage, though, and it felt for a while like we were on our way. There was one amazing night at Old Trafford when we beat Porto 4–0 in the quarter-finals. That was the start, I think, of people taking United seriously as a team that could win the competition. That year, we went into the semi-finals against Borussia Dortmund believing we had a real chance. Instead, they mugged us: like so many German teams, they were very organised and knew exactly what they were doing. They defended really well; I remember their left-back, Jorg Heinrich, was about as difficult to play against over those two games as any player I've ever faced. After they beat us 1–0 in the first leg in Dortmund, we fancied our chances, but they repeated that score line at Old Trafford and then went on to beat Juventus in the final.

Those games against Dortmund were real killers but, otherwise, things couldn't have gone much better for me that season. I found myself wearing the number 10 shirt, playing almost every game, and scoring the kind of goals I used to when playing for Ridgeway

Rovers: like the one from beyond the halfway line at Selhurst Park against Wimbledon, or the volley against Chelsea at Stamford Bridge on the day I first met Victoria. To top it all off, I was voted PFA Young Player of the Year. When the opponents you're up against in the Premiership every week give you that kind of recognition, you can't help but feel like you're doing something right.

It was a great time to be a United player. We had the best manager in the country, and it definitely felt like we had the best number two as well. I know the gaffer said some uncomplimentary things about Brian Kidd after he left Old Trafford to take the manager's job at Blackburn Rovers, but I thought they made a great team. Kiddo's a fantastic coach – just ask anybody who's ever worked with him – and I think, at United especially, he did a great job working between the boss and the players. Everybody in the dressing room thought that Brian was 'one of us'. After training or after a game, no one needed to watch what they were saying or doing. Kiddo would be having a laugh along with the rest.

He knew when it was time to be serious too. We worked really hard in training but you never noticed it with Kiddo because he made sure every session was different: it stopped us ever getting bored and the new routines kept players fresh. Scholesy and Nicky Butt and the Nevilles had known Brian even longer than I had: he was United through and through. I think that's part of the reason he handled relationships between people at the club so well. I know I'm not the only one who, at some point during his time at Old Trafford, had to thank him for defusing a confrontation with the gaffer. He never went against the manager, or tried to undermine him in any way, but I always felt like he looked out for us players. It made for a really happy dressing room.

It was also a pretty successful dressing room. We were disappointed to miss out in Europe but, in May 1997, winning the Premiership for the second year running was a big achievement in itself. In the end, we finished seven points clear, but it was more than just a one- or two-horse race. Liverpool, Newcastle and Arsenal all had a go at different times in the season. We won the title with a couple of weeks to spare; it was a bit strange becoming champions thanks to another team losing. On the Monday night we drew 3–3 with Middlesbrough at Old Trafford. You don't forget any game where Gary Neville scores a goal. Then on the Tuesday, Liverpool, the only team who could beat us to the title, had a televised match at Selhurst Park. I was round at Ben Thornley's house with Gary to see it. I don't like watching football on television at the best of times and, with what was at stake, I couldn't stand the tension. Gary and I ended up going out for a walk and missing the whole of the second half.

By the time we got back, Wimbledon had won and that meant we were champions. Normally at the end of a game in which you win a trophy, you can let some of the adrenalin out, on the pitch and back in the dressing room. That evening in 1997, though, we were sitting in Ben Thornley's lounge. We broke the club curfew that night; the only time I ever did. We had a game against Newcastle coming up on the Thursday and so we should have been at home, getting an early night. I'm not a drinker or a clubber anyway, as a general rule. But that evening was different. We'd won the League, hadn't we? It didn't feel like an occasion to be sitting indoors, so the three of us went out on the town in Manchester and had a beer or two more than we should have done. I'm sure the gaffer knew – he knows everything about everybody – but we got away with it. And there was no harm done because we drew against Newcastle two evenings later.

I think the really big winner that season was probably my mobile phone company. I knew straight away I was crazy about Victoria. I found myself thinking about how and when I could be with her during most of every day we were apart. No sooner had we met, she'd had to jet off to America with the Spice Girls. We spent hour after hour talking and the bills got scarier and scarier. But they were the best investment I've ever made. The couple of times we'd actually been face to face, I'd felt so nervous it took my breath away. It's strange how different it was on the phone. It seemed to be the most natural thing in the world to be telling this amazing woman all about my life – and my feelings – and listening to her do the same. By the time she got back to England, it felt like we really knew each other. We started to find out, as well, what we were going to mean to each other. Whatever the phone company had made out of it seemed like a bargain.

The florists didn't do too badly out of me, either. I sent flowers to each new hotel Victoria booked into and a single red rose every day for the best part of a month. I couldn't wait for her to come home. I think perhaps people have this idea that our life together must always have been about glamorous parties: stars, luxuries, photo opportunities. That couldn't be further from the truth. Having the time together was all that mattered. The first date had been about driving around, getting thrown out of a Chinese, and sitting on a friend's sofa. Our second evening out was just as low-key as the first. We arranged to meet up in another pub car park – that's how stylish we were – this one called City Limits. A strange thing happened on the way there. I stopped at a petrol station and went in to buy some chewing gum. Just as I was pulling out of the forecourt, I saw Victoria arrive, jump out and do the same thing. Fresh breath, or something to steady the nerves? Both probably. I drove on to City Limits and parked.

When Victoria arrived, I jumped out, went over to her MG and got in beside her. For such a little car, I remember there was a big gap between the driver's and front passenger's seats. We didn't go anywhere. We talked. And we kissed, for the first time. I had a cut on my finger from training. Victoria reached across me to the glove compartment and pulled out this sprig of a plant, Aloe Vera.

'It'll heal you.'

She rubbed it on the cut and then gave it to me. I must have told her about getting hurt on the phone and she'd brought it along. I remember, a week or two later, looking in my fridge and seeing this Aloe Vera plant, starting to decompose in a bag on the shelf. By then, whatever magic it contained had already done its job. At the end of that evening in the car park at City Limits, I felt like at least a year's worth of dreams had come true.

I went mad the next day and had roses and a Prada handbag delivered to Victoria at her mum's house. It's amazing what you find out in a *Smash Hits* 'Likes and Dislikes' feature. I still try and send gifts like that now: it's a natural thing to me. If you love someone, you want to treat them, surprise them, remind them how you feel, whether that means a weekend away somewhere, or a bowl of fruit in the morning laid out in the shape of a heart. I know Victoria thinks I'm romantic like that. Some people reading about it might call it soft. But that's me. I get a good feeling now, when I see Brooklyn with his baby brother or with other children at school, looking after them, being gentle, making sure they're okay. I think I know the parts of my character that I've inherited from my mum. Some of what a person grows up to be comes from what they see and learn. There are other things, deeper things, that are already with you and all you have to do is pass them on.

The next time Victoria and I met, we decided I would do the

driving. Not that we had any better idea as to where we were going to go. Victoria's mum and her brother, Christian, dropped her off at our favourite dodgy rendezvous, the City Limits car park. As she got out of her mum's BMW, Christian leant over and whispered to his mum:

'Well, at least he's got a decent car.'

I read somewhere that Victoria liked Aston Martins, so I managed to borrow this brand new silver DB7 from a showroom, telling the salesman that I was thinking about buying one. Of course, if it was going to make a difference with Victoria, I would have done just that. After a minute or two of our 'I don't know, where do you want to go?' routine, we settled on a run down to Southend: I'd gone to the seaside there so often with Mum and Dad and Lynne and Joanne when I was a kid. Who cared about the state of the beach or the sea back then? We'd always splashed straight in and loved every minute of it. Now, as we headed off round the North Circular, I suddenly realised this spanking new car didn't have a map in it. Worse still, I couldn't remember the way: Dad had always driven us down there and I'd probably been too busy messing about in the back with Joanne to take much notice of where we were going.

I couldn't tell Victoria I was already lost before we'd even left London, could I? So I just drove: all the way to Cambridge, as it turned out. We stopped and had a pizza in a restaurant in the middle of town, never mind that one or two of the other people in there were turning round and having to take a second look. It felt to me like Victoria and I had the place to ourselves. We drove back to London and I dropped her home at her mum and dad's. Not before time, it had been like a proper date: dinner for two, even if we had ended up about seventy miles north of where we'd been planning to go.

Next time out was lovely, too: the back row at the pictures down in Chelsea. We saw Tom Cruise in *Jerry Maguire*, but all I cared about was whose hand I was holding. The big deal that evening was going back to Victoria's parents' house afterwards and meeting Tony and Jackie for the first time. We walked in and I was so embarrassed. I remember sitting down on the settee, a big brown leather thing, the material gathered and pinned down with those little buttons, worrying about what noise I might make if I moved on it to get comfortable.

Victoria's mum came down and introduced herself. When you first meet Jackie, she can seem a little prickly. Or, at least, that's what it felt like that evening. It was probably as much to do with me, jumping to a new boyfriend's conclusion and imagining that the mother was being a bit sharp with me even though she wasn't meaning to be:

'You're the footballer then, are you?'

Victoria's mum and dad weren't interested in football, but living in Goff's Oak, an area where many footballers live too, meant they knew some older players socially. After the opener from Jackie, it was Tony's turn:

'What team do you play for?'

For whatever reason, I don't think they liked the idea of their daughter going out with a footballer. Maybe I got stuck with someone else's reputation at first, at least until we met and they could judge for themselves. I don't know if they thought footballers were all loud and cocky but I just sat there on their sofa and was too nervous to say more than a couple of words. At least they didn't kick me out of the house and, after a while, they said goodnight and disappeared upstairs. I'm sure every mum and dad feels that no boyfriend is ever good enough for their little girl. That, as well as me being a footballer, might have had something to do with

Tony and Jackie being wary of me at first. They knew Victoria, though, and that meant they were willing to get to know me. I'm glad they were. When you marry a woman, you become part of her family too. However frosty I might have imagined they were that first night, Tony and Jackie have welcomed me in ever since.

I think Victoria and I were so happy to have found each other that we wouldn't have minded telling complete strangers about it. That's how it is, being in love: you want the rest of the world to know about it. But our relationship was this big secret. Simon Fuller wanted it that way and I think Victoria understood why, early on at least. Who was I to argue? To be honest, all the ducking and diving, sneaking around and keeping ourselves out of sight, was exciting in a way as well. There was one night when Victoria was in Manchester for a Spice Girls concert. United had a party that same evening to celebrate winning the Premiership. Victoria had travelled up the night before and come to stay with me at the house in Worsley. We arranged that I would try and get to the hotel where she was staying after the club function wound down. All the Girls were around. She couldn't really have disappeared off to North Manchester after her gig.

I left our party around one in the morning, so it was already late. Victoria was staying at the Midland Hotel and I took a cab across town, and rang on the way to let her know I was coming. I was wearing this mac, probably looking like a character in a detective movie, and, sticking to the part, I sneaked into the hotel and up the back stairs to the leading lady's room. Victoria answered the door, half asleep, and then I kept her up half the night talking. At one point, very early the next morning, someone knocked at the door. I dashed into the bathroom to hide: well, I'd seen that particular move in plenty of films too. I crept out of the Midland the same way I'd crept in, and hailed a cab to take me back to Worsley. It wasn't until we were on our way that I realised all I had on me was a pocket full of loose change. I had to watch the meter and got out about 200 yards from my front door, which was as far as my money would take me.

I'd never felt this way about anyone before. As soon as I met Victoria, I knew I wanted to marry her, to have children, to be together always. I could have said it to her on that first date, as we drove round the M25 in her MG. I was that sure that quickly. After we first met, Victoria and I spent a lot of time apart: she was on tour, I was in the middle of an amazing season with United. We got used to each other, found out about one another and learned to trust each other during those four-hour telephone conversations. I'm not the world's best talker, not at least until I know someone well. Maybe being on opposite sides of the world wasn't the worst thing for us in those early days. When we had our chances to be together, it seemed like we'd already grown close very quickly. And for all that I was shy and would sometimes get a bit embarrassed in company, when it came to telling Victoria how I was feeling, I couldn't let nerves stop me saying what I needed to. I remember us lying side by side at her mum and dad's house one evening. It was the simplest, most beautiful conversation two people can ever have with each other:

'I think I'm in love with you, Victoria.'

'I think I'm in love with you, too.'

Keeping it all to ourselves wasn't exactly my choice but I respected the way things had to be for Victoria. I'd stepped into Spiceworld and understood how important the Girls and their management team felt it was to keep everything under control. I didn't talk to anyone about what was happening between us. My parents were aware something was going on but, at United, I wasn't going to be a lad who came into the dressing room one morning boasting that he was going out with a pop star. That wasn't me. I remember turning up for training one Monday after a lovely weekend with Victoria and Ben Thornley asking me why I was in such a good mood.

'I've met this lovely girl.'

'Who?'

'Oh, just this lovely girl who lives down in London.'

Rumours started anyway. I suppose that was bound to happen. And rumours are something we've lived with ever since. It wasn't long after our relationship became public that Victoria was getting phone calls to say the papers had pictures of me kissing another girl in my car. Those kinds of stories – completely untrue – still turn up now and again. Of course, proving something's not true is a lot harder than proving it is. We've got used to rumours, though, and how and why they happen. We had to almost from the start. Victoria and I trusted each other then, just as we do now. If you're with someone you love, you know anyway, deep down, what's real and what isn't.

With all the gossip doing the rounds, it got to the point where I had half a dozen photographers camped outside my house in Worsley every day, just waiting for Victoria to turn up. I'd never experienced anything like this before, whereas Victoria had, of course. I think she made the decision, really. She phoned to say she was coming up to see me and that she was happy enough to stop all the secrecy. We knew what we meant to each other, didn't we? It was better that we decided where and when the public found out for sure that we were together. People imagine ours has been a glitzy, showbiz romance. Just remember: the first photos of us together were taken when we were walking down my road to go to the newsagents on the corner.

Once the story was out officially, I couldn't believe the fuss:

flashbulbs popping everywhere we went, stories all over the papers almost every day and everyone having an opinion on us and our lives. I think the attention was as intense as it was because of Victoria; after all, the Spice Girls were making headlines every time they blinked in those days. If I'm honest, all that side of it made being with Victoria even more exciting. It was a daily reminder of just how good she was at what she did. I loved the whole package: her looks, her personality, her energy. Those legs. But I was really turned on, too, by her talent and the recognition in the public eye that came her way because of it. I knew I wasn't the only person out there who thought she was a star.

I realised what was going to happen. I think Victoria did, too. Before long, we'd started talking about getting engaged. I'd even asked her what sort of ring she might like and, being a woman with a pretty clear idea about her taste in things, Victoria had talked straight away about a particular shape of diamond, the stone longer and thinner at one end than the other, almost like the sail on a boat. She was busy with the Spice Girls, and so we didn't settle anything at first, but about six months after we'd begun seeing each other, I arranged a weekend away at a lovely old hotel in Cheshire. It was just down the M6 from Manchester and we checked in early one evening after a United home game.

Somehow I knew this was the right time. A week later, Victoria and the Girls would be off on tour; it would be a year before they were back in England for more than a few days at a time. We had a bedroom overlooking a lake and the fields beyond. It was August, so we had dinner in the room while the sun set in the distance. We were both wearing towelling robes, which wasn't exactly the obvious costume for the drama but, after we'd eaten, Victoria sat on the bed and I got down on one knee in front of her and asked her to marry me. I'd always wanted to marry and to have children and now I'd found the woman I wanted to spend the rest of my life with. Lucky for me, that night in Cheshire, the woman said yes. For all that I'd hoped she would, it's difficult to describe the thrill for me when she said that word. It was like an electric charge running up my spine.

I really believe in the traditional way of doing these things, which meant that proposing to Victoria was the easy bit. I had a pretty good idea that she felt the same way as I did. The really hard part was asking Victoria's dad for his daughter's hand in marriage. I was nervous before I took the penalty against Argentina at the 2002 World Cup but, for tension, building myself up to ask Tony the big question wasn't too far off. I knew I had to do it. I just didn't know how or where or when. We were at their house in Goff's Oak and no-one was giving me an inch. When I asked Jackie if she'd get Tony to come and talk to me, she wasn't having any of it:

'No, David. You have to do it yourself.'

I eventually cornered the prospective father-in-law in the pro-spective brother-in-law's old room. I'd asked Tony if we could have a quick word in private and we trudged up the stairs together, me feeling like I was off to an execution. I walked into Christian's old bedroom and tripped on the leg of the bed and stubbed my toe. At least Tony was behind me and so he didn't see it happen. I looked at him. He looked at me. I wasn't doing too well on breathing, never mind getting the words out and the pain in my foot didn't help.

'Tony. I'm asking Victoria to marry me. Is that okay?'

Not the best speech a would-be son-in-law ever made. He answered as if I'd just asked him if egg and chips would be all right for tea:

'Yeah. No problem.'

I suppose I'd been getting wound up about it enough for both of us. I know how much Tony and Jackie love Victoria, so I realised his relaxed attitude about us getting engaged meant they'd decided I wasn't the worst sort in the world. In fact, they'd already made me feel part of the family: this was just the next step for us all. Maybe I could have saved myself from a potential heart attack by not posing the big question, but asking Tony – like going down on one knee to Victoria – wasn't just for show. I was only going to do these things once in my life, which meant they were incredibly important to me: I wanted to make sure I went about them the right way.

I'd like to say that it was because those were the months when I fell in love with Victoria and proposed to her that I don't remember much of United's season in 1997/98. The truth is, I've probably done my best to forget reaching that May and not having any kind of winners' medal to show for it. It was new to all of us, the generation who had grown up together during the 1990s. We'd won Youth Cups and Reserve leagues and then, when we stepped up to the United first team, we'd just carried on where we'd left off as kids. The season ended up being a painful one, learning what it felt like to lose. Suddenly, here were Arsenal, doing what we expected to do ourselves: winning the Double. Without wanting to be disrespectful about that Arsenal team, the disappointment didn't ever undermine our belief in ourselves. They won their games but at United we felt we lost the Premiership by not winning ours. Confidence was still high but maybe our standards had slipped along the way.

We badly missed Roy Keane, who had ruptured his cruciate ligaments in October, and was out for almost the whole season. No team is quite the same without its best players but, when Roy's not in the United side, there's something more than just his ability as a player that the rest have to do without. He was and still is a huge influence. For leadership and drive there's absolutely no one to touch him: he's a great footballer, of course, but he also brings out the best in the players around him. Whoever he's getting at out on the park during games, his passion and determination always get that player, and the rest of the team, going. People can come in and cover for him but nobody replaces that strength United get from Roy. We didn't talk about it during the season. The supporters did, the papers did, but we just got on with our games. Maybe it's only looking back now that I realise how much we missed Keano.

I was lucky, though. So were Nicky Butt, Paul Scholes and the Nevilles. We were finding out what it was like to miss out with United, but we were getting the chance to be part of an England team together. And a successful England team at that. When it came to the end of the season in May 1998, we were hurting from losing out to Arsenal, of course, but there wasn't the time to sit down and feel sorry for ourselves. Almost as soon as the last League game had been played, I was packing my bags for La Manga in Spain, and joining up with the other United lads and the rest of a 27-man England squad to prepare for the biggest summer any of us had ever known. I might have felt a little weary after a long English season, and maybe we all did, but that wasn't important. I was about to experience a World Cup for the first time. France 98 meant new dreams and new expectations: as if being a husband-to-be didn't already have me buzzing every day. I couldn't wait for the tournament – and another chapter – to start.

Don't Cry for Me

'Oh, you're the soccer player, aren't you?'

There are plenty of football supporters in England who would rather see their club win the League than see the national team win the World Cup. I can understand that. You follow your club 365 days of every year; you're thinking and talking about it far more than the England side. Everybody gets involved when England are playing in the major tournaments and big games, but your passion for the team you support is there all the time. When I was younger, maybe I was a bit like that. Even though I thought about representing my country, all my focus was on making it at United. Playing for England didn't really begin to matter to me, and didn't begin to seem like a realistic ambition, until after I'd found my feet at Old Trafford.

When I was a boy, Dad used to take me to watch schoolboy internationals involving players who were my age or just a little older, but I don't think we ever went to see the full England side play. In my early teens, I played Representative football for my District and my County but I never got a sniff of a chance beyond that. Once I'd started at United, I did get invited for trials at the FA National School, which was based at Lilleshall in Shropshire in those days. I went along knowing full well that, even if I'd been offered a place, I wouldn't have taken it up. As it turned out, I never had to think twice about the decision: the coaches at Lilleshall thought I was too small for a sixteen-year-old. I do know players – current England team-mates like Michael Owen and Sol Campbell – who went there and had a really good time. But it wasn't for me. There was only one school where I wanted to be learning my game: Old Trafford. Who could be better teachers for me than the likes of Nobby Stiles, Eric Harrison and Alex Ferguson?

It's an honour for any player to represent his country. But you can't make it happen for yourself. All you can do is concentrate on playing for your club and hope that you catch the eye of the right person. As a teenager, I had enough on my plate trying to establish myself at United. That first Double-winning season, though, brought all of us into the limelight – and into the reckoning as far as England was concerned. When it happened for me, it all came quicker than I could have imagined, and was a bigger thrill than I'd ever let myself dream it might be. Almost overnight, it seemed I went from being a promising player at my club to being a regular part of the England team challenging for a place in the 1998 World Cup finals in France.

Terry Venables had left the England coaching job straight after Euro 96. I'd already met his replacement, Glenn Hoddle, during the Under-21 Toulon Tournament at the end of the 1995/96 season. We knew Glenn was going to be the next England manager, so it was quite exciting that he came out to France to watch a couple of games and introduce himself to us. As a player, Glenn had been a hero of mine. I'd always admired not just his technical ability – he really was a man who could hit a Hollywood pass – but also his whole approach to the game. I even got him to sign my England shirt after one of the matches. I'm not sure if the Toulon tournament was the first time he'd watched me, but I had a good game the night he showed up. He didn't say anything to me but, going into the new season, the possibility of playing for the full England side was in the back of my mind for the first time.

There aren't many players who get an England call-up completely out of the blue. New caps very rarely come as a complete surprise. I was lucky: I was playing in a successful United team and, at Selhurst Park, had scored the kind of goal that brings you to people's attention. Obviously, an England coach knows all about you anyway, but my start to the season meant there was a lot of speculation in the press, talking about me as a future England player who might be ready for his chance. There was a World Cup qualifier, away to Moldova, in September. I should have spoken to Gary Neville about it, but I think there was a bit of rivalry there: he was already in the England team and I wasn't. Most players have a story about a dramatic phone call or their club manager pulling them aside at the training ground to tell them the news. I found out I'd made the England squad while sitting on the sofa at my mum and dad's. Mum and I had been flicking through teletext, when the details came up. As soon as I saw the name Beckham on the list of players Glenn Hoddle had chosen for his first game in charge, I jumped off the sofa. I surprised myself how excited I was. Mum and I hugged, laughing out loud, and then I was on the phone to my dad who was at work. For once, I think he was completely lost for words. He was proud, though. As proud as I was to be given my chance.

Whenever a new challenge has come along during my career, my first instinctive reaction is to suddenly find myself feeling like a schoolboy again. That was definitely true as I prepared to join up with a full England squad for the first time. I was going to be working alongside big-name senior players like Paul Gascoigne, David Seaman and Alan Shearer. I was just twenty, but at that moment I felt even younger, like a kid who'd been given the chance to meet his heroes. These were the players I'd grown up watching on television and, all of a sudden, I had to get ready to train with them ahead of a World Cup qualifier.

At United, Alex Ferguson was great. He was genuinely pleased for me, and told me just to go down and enjoy myself:

'If you get the chance, play well. Just play like you have been doing for us at United.'

I took him at his word. I met up with the rest of the squad at Bisham Abbey and my first session with Glenn and with England was the best I'd ever trained in my life. I was beating players, getting my crosses in, every single pass reached its man. I even stuck a couple of shots away past David Seaman into the top corner. It was the kind of training session you'd have in a dream; it was a little bit weird just how perfect it was.

I don't know how much it had to do with impressing him in training but for his first game in charge as England manager, Glenn Hoddle put me in the starting line-up for my first cap. Of course, it helped that there were players around me who I knew well, like Gary Neville, Gary Pallister and Paul Ince. And we made a great start: Gary Nev and I were both involved in the build-up to the first goal, which was scored by Nicky Barmby. A few minutes later, Gazza had got a second and we weren't going to lose it from there. In the second half, Alan Shearer got a third. As debuts go, it wasn't spectacular but I felt as if I belonged straight away. I'd helped set up that third goal for the skipper as well. Perhaps because I hadn't had years of looking forward to international football, nerves weren't a problem and I'd just got on with playing my game, like the gaffer had told me to. On 1 September 1996, on a Sunday afternoon in a city called Kishinev, on a bumpy pitch in front of about 10,000 people, I became an international footballer.

Glenn Hoddle must have been pretty pleased, too. I played in every game of the qualifying campaign for France 98 that, thirteen months later, found us needing a draw in Rome against Italy to go through as group winners. After we'd lost 1–0 to Italy at Wembley, everybody had assumed we would have to win a two-legged play-off to qualify. And before the return game most people still thought that was what would happen. Italy had won their last fifteen fixtures at the Stadio Olimpico and we had our captain, Alan Shearer, out injured, with Ian Wright coming in for him on the night. Even the England fans who made the trip, believing we could do it, had a surprise coming: nobody expected us to play as well as we did. It turned into a fantastic night for England.

There were over 80,000 inside the stadium and there was quite a lot of trouble in the crowd before the game but, by the time we came out, the atmosphere was just amazing. We had a team full of young players but we gave a really professional performance. I thought we beat the Italians at their own game: we were disciplined, everybody knew what they were supposed to be doing and we passed and kept the ball brilliantly all game. Everybody played well but, early on especially, Paul Gascoigne set the tone for the whole team. Every time he got the ball – and he went looking for it all over the pitch – he kept possession and refused to be hurried. He was doing step-overs, nicking the ball through an opponent's legs for a pass, as if he was challenging them: *We're as good as you are with the football, you know.* It was just what the rest of us needed.

We kept our heads, even though the Italians were flying into their tackles, wanting the win just as much as we did. Then they had Angelo Di Livio sent off late in the second half. In the stands and watching at home on television, people must have thought we'd done it. In fact, it was only in the time left between then and the end of the match that I started getting nervous. Ian Wright was clean through, went round the goalkeeper, but then hit the post with his shot. *Is it going to be one of those nights? We're that close. Are they going to run up the other end now and score?*

The Italians broke upfield and Christian Vieri had a free header in the last minute and put it over the bar. Seconds later, the whistle went. Everybody charged off the bench and we were celebrating together out on the pitch. Glenn and his number two, John Gorman, were jumping up and down: they'd done a fantastic job preparing us for that game. Paul Ince looked like the hero of the hour, with his head all bandaged up after he'd caught an elbow during the game. Wrighty was dancing around, hugging everybody he could lay his hands on. The supporters up in the stand behind the dugouts were dancing, too, singing the tune from *The Great Escape.* I looked around me, trying to take all this in. I'd been an England player for just over a year and here we were, going mad, on our way to France for the World Cup the following summer. I was so proud to be part of it all.

It must have been an amazing night for Paul Gascoigne. He was back at Lazio's home ground with England and he was the one celebrating. People back home had been wondering if he was past his best and here he'd turned in the kind of performance you'd never forget. The way Gazza played that night – his ability, his nerve and the passion – I still wonder if that wasn't what we were missing at France 98. I know Glenn Hoddle had his reasons for not including Paul in the squad, but I think we'd have been better with Gazza there. Even if it was just him coming off the bench for twenty minutes, Paul could bring something to the team nobody else could. He could change a game on his own. And I know we'd all have liked him to be around as part of the squad.

What made it worse was the way Paul and the others found out they weren't going to be in the final 22 for the tournament. It was a bit like a meat market: 'You're in. You're out.' It was the wrong way to go about doing it. We were in La Manga in southern Spain, 27 of us in all, to prepare for the World Cup together before the manager made his decision about the final squad. Everybody was nervous, thinking about who wouldn't be going to France. *It could be someone from my club, a mate. It could be me.* One afternoon, after training, we were given timed appointments at the hotel: five-minute slots to go in and see Glenn, to find out what was going to happen to us. Almost from the start, the schedule wasn't working. I remember, at one point, sitting on the floor in a corridor with five other lads while we waited our turn. It was a ridiculous way to treat the players.

When eventually it came to my turn, the meeting didn't last long. Looking back, it makes it seem even more unlikely that things turned out for me the way they did once the World Cup began. I walked into the room and Glenn's first words were:

'Well, David, it goes without saying that you're in the squad.'

And that was it. At least I didn't hold up the next appointment. I was in the 22; but what about everyone else? Rumours had been flying around all day, not surprising when everybody was just waiting to find out what would happen to them. There was a leak somewhere in the camp, too: stories kept on turning up in the papers that could only have come from inside the England set-up. People were saying there was going to be one big story coming out of all this, that one high-profile name would be left out of the squad. The suggestion seemed to be that it would be Gazza. But nobody knew for sure, neither the press nor the players.

We were down by the pool earlier in the day and I was sat next to Paul. Suddenly, he turned over on his sun bed.

'Do you know something, David? I love you. You're a great young player and you're a great lad. I love playing football with you.'

I looked at him. This was me, listening to one of England's greatest-ever players.

'I really want to go to this World Cup, David. I want to play in this World Cup with you.'

He said that more than once. He must have heard the rumour that he might be left out. It wasn't until later that we all found out what had happened, that the manager had told him he wasn't in the 22 and that Paul had gone mad. Gary Neville was in the room next door to Gazza's and heard the shouting and the furniture flying. I must admit that by the time that news came through I was more concerned about a couple of my United team-mates.

The fact that Gary and Phil Neville, Paul Scholes, Nicky Butt and I were so close made it even worse when Phil and Butty missed out. A couple of days before, one of the staff had even given Phil a wink, as if to say he was going to be in the squad. That only made his disappointment harder to take. I went up to see them as soon as I found out. Their flight home was in an hour's time and they were standing in their room, bags packed. I gave Phil Neville a big hug. The five of us had grown up together and now two of them were on their way home. It must have hurt Gary even more, saying goodbye to his brother. Thinking about it now, of course, Butty and Phil had plenty of time ahead of them in international football. Paul Gascoigne had just missed out on his last chance of representing his country.

I wasn't the only one upset about the boys who'd been left out and the way they'd had to find out about it. We had a training session the next morning that was just about as bad as any I can remember. The atmosphere was eerie. We were just expected to get straight on with it. I realised the World Cup was only days away, but I felt there needed to be a time to relax, to take stock of things as a group. With Glenn, the intensity never dropped. Even when we had an evening off, we'd find ourselves all in a room with a bar, downstairs at the hotel, with the doors shut and the curtains drawn, so nobody could get near us. What we really needed was something different occasionally: perhaps just to sit in reception for an hour or two, sign some autographs for the kids and chat with England supporters. Everybody felt really low but nothing was said about the situation. The other lads had gone and Glenn just expected us to forget about the emotional side of it and act as if nothing had happened. It all felt very strange and, as far as the training went, it seemed to me that most of the players' minds were on other things that day.

Through my early months as an England player, Glenn Hoddle had always been really good to me. I enjoyed his coaching – all of us did, I think – and I was proud of what we'd achieved in qualifying for the tournament with him as manager. Why everything changed, and so suddenly, I'll never know. The first time I got any idea that things weren't going to turn out like I'd dreamt they might at the World Cup was after a friendly that had been arranged at our training camp in La Baule against a local scratch side, a few days before the start of the tournament. It was all very low key. We lost the game and I'd be the first to admit I didn't play very well. Then again, nobody did. Nothing was said but I felt then that the manager was being a bit stand-offish towards me. You get that sense, sometimes, from a boss: he's got the hump with you and you feel uneasy, almost as if you're being given the cold shoulder. That's how it felt after that practice game, without it making me think for a moment that I wouldn't play in our first match of the tournament. I'd played in every game leading up to the World Cup, after all.

I was wrong. Completely wrong. A couple of days before our opening fixture against Tunisia in Marseille, the manager sat us down, in a circle out on the training ground, to talk about the starting line-up. It seemed strange at the time that he started by saying that he expected players who weren't picked to still turn up for the press conferences and behave as if the team hadn't been announced. In a way, that part of Glenn's approach wasn't a surprise. He liked playing these guessing games. Before the match against Italy in Rome, I'd been sniffling a bit with a cold. He told the media I was struggling and even got me to leave training ten minutes early to make it seem I was worse than I was. I didn't want to miss any of the session but he insisted. He thought we'd have an advantage if the Italians weren't sure who'd be playing. Here in La Baule, though, two days before the start of our World Cup, it was different. I've realised since, of course, that the game Glenn was playing this time wasn't just about keeping the press or the Tunisians guessing. It was about him testing a young player, which definitely made things more difficult for me than they needed to be.

He announced the team to play against Tunisia: just read the players off a list written down on a piece of paper. I suppose I must have known, deep down, that it was going to happen. Things hadn't been right for a couple of days. Even so, when my name wasn't in the eleven, it felt like somebody had hit me in the stomach. I thought I was going to be sick. I even hoped for a split second that I'd just not heard Glenn saying 'Beckham'. I looked across at Gary Neville. He was looking back at me. Was he surprised, too? Or just watching to see how I might react? Of course it was a blow to my pride and that would always be something you have to be mature enough to overcome. What really knocked me sideways, though, was not having any real understanding of why the manager had made his decision.

I've always tried to have a professional attitude to training. I love it almost as much as I love playing. That morning, though, was a complete waste of time. I felt so low. I was so angry I couldn't force myself to work properly. Glenn must have been able to see that I wasn't coping with what I'd been told. I suppose I should have known what would happen next: as soon as we finished the session, he announced who would be taking questions from the press that afternoon. That list, of course, included my name. It was horrible. I've never been that good at hiding my emotions. If I'm unhappy or down, people just know. I did that press conference and didn't say anything out of turn, but it must have been pretty obvious something wasn't right. A couple of the other players got calls straight afterwards from journalists who were helping them do World Cup diaries for the papers. 'What's wrong with David?' they were asking. 'Has he been left out of the team?'

Lots of managers play mind games with the press and with opposing teams. Here, it seemed to me the England manager was playing mind games with one of his own players. That's what upset me the most. I didn't realise it there and then, but I wasn't going to enjoy France 98 from that press conference onwards. I didn't know which way to turn. I couldn't even decide who to speak to for support or advice. I called Victoria first. She was shocked and I think, instinctively, she would have told me to leave and come to America straight away, where the Spice Girls were on tour. She didn't say that, which is probably just as well; I felt so low I might almost have been tempted. Then I talked to Dad. He couldn't believe it, either, and at least reassured me that I wasn't over-reacting. He told me it was understandable that I was so upset.

I realised I had to speak to Glenn. I can still remember standing in the hotel reception, oblivious to everything and everybody around me. Then I saw the manager coming through, on his way out to play golf.

'I have to talk to you about this. Why have you dropped me? I need to know the reason.'

Glenn looked at me: 'I don't think you're focused.'

It took me a moment to understand what he'd said.

'How can you think that? How can you think I'm not focused for the biggest football competition in the world? I'm not thinking about anything else. How could I be?'

It wasn't until later that I found out what was probably behind it all. The previous week, we'd had a day off to relax, play golf, see our families, and do whatever we wanted. Most of the lads had gone out on the course. I'm not much of a golfer and, anyway, any chance I get I want to be with my family. Victoria flew out to France for the day and the two of us spent our time around the apartment complex swimming, sunbathing and catching up. Glenn didn't like that. The other players were on the golf course. And I wasn't. So that meant I wasn't concentrating on England, as far as he was concerned. *They're all playing golf and he's with his girlfriend: that can't be good for team spirit.*

It made no sense to me at all and I still don't really understand it. If he wanted us all to be together and thought that was so important, then why give us the choice? Maybe it was another chance to test a player, a chance to test me in particular. But why play those mind games with a 23-year-old – or anybody else in the squad, for that matter – especially if the spirit in the camp was something you thought was important?

As I stood there in the hotel reception, I felt like I'd been cut adrift. I couldn't let it go.

'Do you know what? I don't agree with you at all. I've not had a very long career but it feels like it's all been building towards this tournament. How can you think I'd be coming here worrying about anything else? This is the World Cup. That's how I feel, anyway. I suppose you'll do what you want.'

And Glenn did just that. He was leaving me out of the team and, now, he was hurrying off to play golf. He obviously wasn't interested in anything I had to say. He didn't care and, I suppose, didn't need to. It was a cold, cold moment.

'Well, I just don't think you're focused. It's as simple as that.'

We travelled to Marseille for that opening game and I found myself not wanting to be there. Of course, the supporter in me wanted to see England do well and I don't want to sound like I was just being selfish about it all. I can't pretend, though, that I wasn't completely devastated about being left out. I have a picture at home of me standing next to the dugout during the Tunisia game and the look on my face says it all: as if I'm about to throw up. I was that disappointed. And embarrassed, too: I felt like I'd failed somehow, and that I'd been shamed by the situation. The World Cup is the biggest thing any footballer can ever be involved in and I found myself wishing that I wasn't there at all.

Not being in the team was bad enough. What really killed me was the supposed reason for me being dropped. Was I missing out here because I'd wanted to spend that day with Victoria? As if it was Glenn's, or anybody else's, business? Even people who might criticise the way I live my life away from football can see that, once I'm out there playing, nothing gets in the way of my concentration on the game. How could the manager have misjudged me so completely?

Our next match was against Romania and, because we'd beaten Tunisia, it would have been a surprise to be selected for it. I'd talked to Gary, to my dad and to Alex Ferguson about what had been happening and they'd all been supportive. All of them felt I hadn't been treated well. I also got the impression from back home that supporters wanted to see the younger players, like me and Michael Owen, given their chance. It gave me a real boost, when the two of us were warming up on the touchline against Romania, to hear the England fans chanting my name. As it happened, Paul Ince got injured after about half an hour and I went on in his place and played pretty well. So did Michael: he scored, even though we lost 2–1 to a goal right at the end.

I was happy to have got my World Cup started, proud that the supporters had cheered so loudly when I came on in that second game. But nothing was clear-cut at France 98. No sooner did I have the feeling that things were starting to go my way, I took another knock. Glenn Hoddle told the press that he had been planning for Michael Owen and I to play the third game, against Colombia, all along. He'd hoped we'd have qualified for the next round by then. It was like being told that you were a squad member who'd get a run out when the manager wanted to rest his first-choice players. Knowing I was going to play was great. Glenn's explanation as to why just left a bitter taste again.

At our base in La Baule, we had a small training pitch which didn't get used all that much. It was somewhere you could go out with a ball and practise on your own. The day before the Colombia game, I bought some batteries and took this big portable stereo unit out with me. I borrowed two bags of balls. It was a boiling hot afternoon, so I was just in shorts and a vest. I stuck the stereo down, put on Tupac, the American rap singer, turned it up full blast and then spent a couple of hours on my own, practising free-kicks: putting a ball down and then bending it in to the corner of the goal, over and over again.

The day of the game was my mum's birthday and, before going into the stadium, we spoke on the phone:

'Score a goal for me.'

The free-kick against Colombia was my first goal for England. I suppose I should remember everything about it: the foul, the wall, the angle. But somehow, even at the moment itself, what it meant to me was more important than the goal itself. I knew it had a chance as soon as I struck it and I raced off towards the corner flag to celebrate. Graeme Le Saux tried to grab me round the waist and then Sol Campbell jumped on my back. I'd known Sol since we were twelve years old, training together at Tottenham. Right then, he knew as well as anybody how important this was for me. Even scoring, though, I couldn't just enjoy plain and simple. Part of me wanted to run over to the bench to Glenn Hoddle. *There you go. What did you make of that?*

It was a pity I didn't, because on the way to the dugout I might have remembered to do what I'd promised before the game: to go and hug Terry Byrne and Steve Slattery, the England masseurs, if I scored. Terry and Slatts had talked to me – and listened to me – through all the highs and lows so far. They'd been great company. The right company: they'd say what they thought, not just what they thought I wanted to hear. And they'd listen for as long as I had something to say. Terry has become a really close friend over the years. After the game, I was on the phone to everybody. I was so pleased at my own performance, that we'd won and that we were through to the next round. With that free-kick, I felt I'd proved a point as far as the manager was concerned.

But would I be in the team for the game against Argentina in the second round? I was still pretty confused about the manager's attitude towards me. We had another awkward episode before we left for Saint-Etienne. Sometimes Glenn wanted us to take a walk to loosen up in the afternoon, just in tracksuits and trainers. This time, though, we got down to the training pitch and he suddenly announced he wanted to work on a new free-kick routine that involved someone flicking the ball up and me volleying it over the wall and in. I was worried about a tight hamstring; in fact none of us had warmed up. So when he told me to do it, I just lobbed the ball over the wall rather than hitting it with full power. Glenn got really angry:

'Can't you do it? Well, if you can't do it, we'll forget it.'

I hadn't done what he wanted me to, because the last thing I needed was to injure myself. The atmosphere between us was strained afterwards, even though Glenn didn't mention it again. It was the kind of clash that players remember: not just the ones directly involved but their team-mates, too, who were standing watching it happen. Despite that, I felt I was worth my place in the next game and just kept my fingers crossed.

England vs Argentina is always a huge game, for all sorts of reasons; not all of them to do with football. It's one of the oldest and greatest rivalries in football. In Argentina, what we call 'derbies' they call 'classicos': not just games between neighbours, like United vs City or England vs Scotland, but fixtures with a history, like United vs Liverpool or England vs Germany. They reckon there's only one 'classico' between teams from two different continents: and that's Us against Them. No wonder it gets a big build up and that the game in Saint-Etienne in 1998 was no different. I was really excited and looking forward to it. I'd been made to feel insecure and had suffered emotional knocks since the start of the tournament. But I didn't, for a moment, feel anything but ready for Argentina. I certainly didn't have any idea what lay in store for me, during the game and after.

The evening started so well: a great game and us more than a match for them. After Argentina had taken the lead after only five minutes through a Batistuta penalty, Alan Shearer equalised, also from the spot. Over a year had gone by since his last penalty for England, but we all knew he'd lash it in. Then, five minutes later, I put the ball through for Michael Owen to score that fantastic second goal. They got one back and it was 2–2 at half-time. In the dressing room, there were a few words said about the defending at the free-kick from which Zanetti scored their second goal. Otherwise, we just couldn't wait to go out and get started again: the game was there to be won. How could I have known that, for me, disaster was waiting to happen?

I think Diego Simeone is a good player. Good, but really annoying to play against: always round you, tapping your ankles, niggling away at you. It gets to opposition players and he knows it. Maybe, too, he was aware that Glenn Hoddle had said before the tournament that he was worried about my temperament in pressure situations. I'd not really had any trouble with him during the game until then but, just after half-time, he clattered into me from behind. Then, while I was down on the ground, he made as if to ruffle my hair. And gave it a tug. I flicked my leg up backwards towards him. It was instinctive, but the wrong thing to do. You just can't allow yourself to retaliate. I was provoked but, almost at the same moment I reacted, I knew I shouldn't have done. Of course, Simeone went down as if he'd been shot.

I've made a big mistake here. I'm going to be off. Gary Neville came up behind me, put his arm around my shoulder and then slapped me on the back.

'What have you done? Why did you do that?'

He wasn't having a go at me. Gary just wanted to know why I'd kicked out at Simeone. At that moment – and to this day – I don't know the answer to that. The referee, Kim Nielsen, didn't say a word to me. He just pulled the red card out of his pocket. I'll never forget the sight of it as long as I live. Look at the video now: Simeone acting like he's in intensive care; Veron telling the ref what he thought should happen; the ref with the card; Batistuta nodding, like he thought justice had been done; and me, just walking away, eyes already focused down the tunnel. It wasn't as if I was angry. The look on my face tells you: I was in a different world. Simeone had laid his trap and I'd jumped straight into it. Whatever else happens to me, those sixty seconds will always be with me.

Even before I got to the touchline, Terry Byrne had run over from the bench. He put an arm round my shoulder and walked down to the dressing room with me. As soon as we got there, I phoned Victoria in the States. Obviously I hadn't seen the replays on television and wanted to know what had happened. She was watching the game in a bar in New York. There was something not real about it she said. No-one could make sense of the fact that I'd been sent off. Why had it happened? There wasn't much more to say.

Terry stayed with me. I went in and had a shower. A long shower, like it was going to somehow wash all this away. Suddenly, Steve Slattery came running in and was shouting:

'We've scored! Sol's scored!'

I jumped out of the shower, but a moment later, he was back and telling us the goal had been disallowed. I put on my tracksuit and a French guy, a FIFA official, came and told me I had to go through to the drug-testing room. At least they had a television in there so I could watch the game. At the end of ninety minutes, they told me I could leave and I went and watched extra-time from the tunnel leading out to the pitch. I couldn't take in what was unfolding in front of me: it was as if the sending-off wiped away any other memories I might have of the game. But the moment David Batty missed his penalty, and the Argentinians went rushing towards their goalkeeper to celebrate, it sank in. *I'll be going home tomorrow.*

That night was the worst of my life but I did have one miraculous thing to hang onto: I'd soon be with Victoria, who was pregnant with our first child. The day the England party had arrived in Saint-Etienne ahead of the Argentina game, we'd got off the plane and there'd been a message on my mobile.

'David. It's Victoria. Please call me as quick as you can.'

I'd got on the coach and rang her back.

'I've got some news for you,' she said.

'What is it?'

'We're pregnant.'

I couldn't believe it. I wanted to stand up in my seat and scream it out to everybody. It was mad. I couldn't believe what I'd just been told. I went into the tiny toilet on the team coach and just jumped up and down, hugging myself. I was so happy. It's the sort of news you want to share with people but, of course, I couldn't tell a soul.

There are particular things about that evening in Saint-Etienne that stand out clearly, as if they've been lit up by the flashbulbs that go off around a stadium at night: the sending-off itself, talking on the phone to Victoria, remembering I was going to be a father and, then, seeing my dad in the car park after the game. But the rest of it? Probably for my own sanity, it's a blur: the game's going on, but it's like I'm watching it through the wrong end of a telescope; the anger, the frustration and the shame; and the disbelief that this could all be happening to me.

When it was over, the England players went to the end where our supporters were massed. I didn't feel like I could be any part of that, so I turned and went back to the dressing room. At the time, Glenn Hoddle was doing the television interview in which he said that, if it had been eleven against eleven, England would have won. The papers and everybody else, of course, turned that into him saying it was my fault England had lost to Argentina.

The players came back into the dressing room and it was deathly quiet. Alan Shearer sat down next to me. 'Sorry Al,' was all I could think of to say. Alan just stared at the floor in front of him. What could anybody say? Only each individual player knows what was in his mind after that game. I won't ever forget that Tony Adams was the one man who came and found me. The first time I'd been in an England squad with him, Tony had scared me to death. Away to Georgia in a qualifier, just a couple of minutes before we went out for the game, he'd stood up in the dressing room. 'Right, lads! This is ours. We deserve this. We've come out here to win it!' It wasn't just that Tony was loud, it was the passion and the determination in his voice. I couldn't believe the ferocity of it. It was one of those moments when you're shocked into a new level of commitment. Not that you didn't care before: but being in that changing room, witnessing how much it mattered to Tony, was inspiring to someone who was just starting out as an international player. England losing in Saint-Etienne hurt him as much as it hurt anybody, especially as he thought he might not play for his country again. It was awful in the dressing room that night. There could be no disappointment like it. But Tony came over and put a hand on my shoulder.

'Whatever's happened here, I think you're a great young lad and an excellent young player. I'm proud to have played for England with you. You can be stronger for this. You can be a better player after it.'

We left the ground and my mum and dad were waiting by the coach. I fell into Dad's arms and started sobbing. I couldn't stop. I'm a bit embarrassed thinking about it now but, at the time, I just couldn't help myself. Eventually, I calmed down and Dad pushed me onto the coach. I sat down and leant my head against the cool of the window. Gary Neville got on and sat in the seat next to me. He could see I'd been crying. He could see I might be about to start again.

'Don't let anyone see you like this. You shouldn't be like this. You haven't done anything wrong. What's happened has happened.'

I looked at him.

'Victoria's pregnant.'

Gary's eyes opened that bit wider.

'Well, there you are. Just get out there and be with her. That's the best news anybody could ever have. Just think about that. It was a football match. This is a new life.'

When Seba Veron joined United, I remember we talked about the reaction of the Argentinian players, or at least some of them, when they saw me with my dad that night. As their coach pulled away out of the car park, we could see them looking back at the England coach, bare-chested, laughing and swinging their shirts above their heads.

We went straight to the airport and then flew back to La Baule for our last night at France 98. Some of the players went straight to their rooms; others went for a drink. I found myself in the games room with Terry and Slatts and Steve McManaman. Usually, we'd have hot chocolates and get off to bed a little after midnight. That last night, though, Terry told me I had to have something to drink. I had a couple of beers. I don't usually drink but, that evening, the alcohol helped numb the pain a little. We hung around, the four of us, not saying all that much – there wasn't much to say by now – and I don't think I turned in until about four in the morning, even though we had to be up at nine for our Concorde flight back to England.

I made arrangements to travel to the States that same night. England were out of the World Cup. I wanted as much time with Victoria as possible before training for a new season started. My parents flew straight back to England from Saint-Etienne and were there to meet me at Heathrow the following day. By the time Concorde touched down, someone at the airport had been kind enough to offer us use of her office for the couple of hours before I got my connecting flight to the States. I found Mum and Dad, gave them my belongings and got changed for the onward flight. I knew I wouldn't see them for the best part of a fortnight and I had news that I wanted to give them face to face rather than over a phone. I told them Victoria was pregnant.

They seemed very surprised. And worried, too. Maybe it was because they'd already got an idea of the reaction I was going to get back home after my sending off. Joanne was with them and she hugged and kissed me, but Mum was quite quiet and I remember Dad just said:

'Are you sure it's not too soon?'

We had to say our goodbyes. I headed off to the departure lounge and got to where I had to check in my luggage without any fuss at all. I'd been warned that there would be press around looking for me but it seemed like everything was quiet. Once I was through, I thought I'd be fine, that nobody would be able to get that side of immigration and passport control. I was wrong. Out of the corner of my eye, I saw a group of photographers and a couple of camera crews heading towards me, together with this little guy who I recognised from previous times; he'd always be running alongside you, whispering things to you and trying to provoke a reaction.

'Do you think you've let the team down, David? Have you let the country down? Do you realise what you've done, David? Should you be leaving the country right now?'

I had about two hundred yards to walk to the lounge. I slung my bag over one shoulder, just stared in front of me and marched on, not saying a word. It must have looked mad, with all these people trailing after me. Maybe it looked bad in the newspapers or on television, like I was running away. But I knew I just had to keep going. I couldn't afford to react in the wrong way now. I didn't need people telling me how bad I should be feeling. I already felt all that and worse. I wanted to be able to shut my eyes and be with Victoria. What could I do but try and blank the cameras out?

I made that finishing line and, a few minutes later, I was on Concorde again. The flurry of snappers at Heathrow had given me an idea of what I could have expected had I stayed at home. As the plane took off, I assumed I was leaving all that behind: not my own disappointment about what had happened in Saint-Etienne, but having it stuck in my face by the media.

It was a little bit scary arriving at New York's JFK. I'd been to America before but this was the first time on my own. I walked up to the security checkpoint. There were these security staff, with guns and dark sunglasses, looking really serious, wanting to know what was in this bag and that one. I'd arranged for a driver to meet me. As I walked out through the doors into the arrivals hall, there was a crowd of photographers, camera crews, and press waiting for me. *This is New York. This shouldn't be happening.*

I jumped into the car and went to close the door but there were people holding it open so I couldn't. It was ridiculous. I was having a tug of war with whoever was on the other side of the door. Then, when I got that one shut, the door on the other side of the car was pulled open, and a female photographer started snapping away at me in the back seat. I couldn't believe what was going on. I thought that, once I'd reached America, I'd be all right. Instead, I was in the middle of a scene from a movie: I'd never experienced anything like this back at home.

When we finally got the doors shut and locked, we headed straight to Madison Square Garden and a Spice Girls concert. I hadn't really organised things properly, so I didn't even know how to get in to the place. We arrived outside and I was wandering around, looking for a stage door, until I spotted one of the tour managers. He took me inside and we set off down this corridor towards the Girls' dressing rooms.

Then the strangest thing happened: we were walking along and Victoria came the other way and walked straight past. She didn't recognise me: I had this big jacket on and a hat pulled low down on my head after the craziness at the airport. She hadn't been expecting me to get there so early and it was one of those moments when it takes a couple of beats to realise what has just happened. I turned round and she came running back. I just held onto her and didn't want to let go. We went through to the changing room and I said hello to the other girls. Then Victoria and I crept into this tiny shower room and she showed me the scan of our new baby. It was just amazing. It was like a little pea on the picture: the scan was taken much earlier than the ones you're allowed to see in England. I was tingling with excitement. Any father will tell you, you can't imagine that feeling until it happens.

We went back to see the Girls and suddenly they were hugging and kissing me. I could hardly take it all in.

'Oh, I meant to say. Someone's coming in to meet us all in a minute,' said Victoria.

And in walked Madonna. She sat down and started chatting to Victoria and the other girls, while I just kept quiet and tried to make sure my mouth wasn't hanging open. Then she turned to me:

'Oh, you're the soccer player, aren't you?'

How did Madonna know who I was? I can't say I wasn't a bit pleased about that. As far as replying was concerned, I was dumbstruck. Madonna's just spoken to me, like she knows me. It was one of those situations where you're sure that, whatever you say, it's going to come out sounding stupid.

'Yes.'

It was time for the Girls to go on stage. The concert was absolutely fantastic. The Spice Girls were always great on stage: the energy, the colour, the talent and the hard work, all of it shone through. Whether it's a football match or a pop concert, the people who've paid to be there deserve their money's worth. And the Spice Girls delivered every single time. I try to be professional about my game. Victoria and the girls were unbelievably professional about putting on their show. Over the next twelve days, I turned into the Spice Girls' number one groupie. It wasn't the most relaxing holiday I've ever had but I loved every minute of it: travelling around on the tour bus, hanging out with Victoria in luxurious hotel rooms and then, every night, going to watch one of those amazing concerts.

On that first night at Madison Square Garden, I remember watching Victoria up there on stage, in front of a packed audience at one of the world's great venues, looking and sounding so good and, at the same time – in the middle of all the lights and noise and thousands of people jumping up and down – there was a little quiet place, all mine, where I knew Victoria had our baby inside her. I had that first picture of Brooklyn in my mind all evening long.

Maybe I'd been leading a charmed life until that summer in 1998. What disappointments had I really had to face until then? I'd grown up dreaming about playing for Manchester United and the dream had come true. No sooner had I got to Old Trafford, I was in the first team with this inspired group of boys my own age and we were winning championships and cups. And then, almost overnight, I'd had the call to play football for England and been part of getting my country through to the finals of the most important tournament of all. In hindsight, perhaps luck had run for me. I hadn't had much practice dealing with the big knocks, the kind of blows I had to take that June. I know how disappointed the England players and fans were that night in Saint-Etienne. At the eye of the storm, I was crushed by what had happened too. What I wasn't ready for, at 23 years of age, was for all the blame for defeat against Argentina to be laid just on me.

My life, like anybody else's, has been full of lessons to be learnt. The difference that comes with a career as a high-profile foot-baller, with every move fixed in the public eye, is that I've had less margin for error and less time in which to come to terms with my mistakes. That isn't something I can complain about, because the same whirlwind that blew through my life as a result of me being sent off against Argentina, could also blow me across the Atlantic into the arms of the woman – the Girl – that I loved. Twenty-four hours after the worst moment I could ever have imagined, I was at Madison Square Garden, with a grainy hospital Polaroid in my pocket, as excited and as happy as any lad could ever be. One night, my life was falling to pieces on a football pitch in France. The next, despite that hurt, I was just letting the best feeling of all sink in: I was going to be a dad. I couldn't have known what was waiting for me back home in England, or how I'd have to deal with it all. But if I was going to be a father for that little speck of a new life in Victoria's scan, now had to be the time for me to learn to be a man.

Thanks for Standing By Me

7

'When we disembark, there'll be police waiting for you at the gate.'

Alex Ferguson has all sorts of great qualities as a manager. Remembering France 98, one stands out in particular: the boss sticks by his players and backs them, even through the very worst of times.

'Just get yourself back to Manchester,' he said to me. 'Don't worry about what anyone says. Get yourself back here, where people love you and support you. You can have your say back to the rest of them after the season begins.'

Some people have an idea that it's something to criticise, but I can tell you that the gaffer's loyalty to his players means they have cast iron respect for him as a man and absolute faith in him as a manager. One of the reasons I went to United in the first place was his attitude to young hopefuls: the boss made you feel like you were joining a family, not just a football club. And through thick and thin, beyond any disagreement or confrontation between us, it always felt like that at Old Trafford. The gaffer is the reason why. Knowing he was behind me really helped me get through that summer in 1998, and the early part of the season that followed.

While I was in America with Victoria, I had the chance to look at some of the English press coverage in the wake of what had happened in Saint-Etienne. Maybe I'd have been better off listening to the people who told me I shouldn't. Even thousands of miles away, some of the headlines like 'TEN HEROIC LIONS, ONE STUPID BOY' hit me hard. I realised what I'd done but, at the same time, it seemed to me that the media reaction was way over the top: it was a football match that had brought all this on, after all. A big football match, yes. But did that justify the way the papers seemed to be treating me? I'd expected a backlash but I was shocked by the intensity of it. I understood the disappointment of England being knocked out of the World Cup, but some of the stuff that was written – particularly that first morning after the Argentina game – lit a touchpaper with some people. For them, hatred seemed contagious.

Of course, I was away on the other side of the Atlantic but that didn't stop other people getting put under pressure instead of me. I talked to Mum and Dad: by the time they got back to London from Saint-Etienne, there were already more than thirty people camped outside the house. The phone was being bugged, they had camera crews in their faces every time they opened the front door. The press even set up a little table and chairs with coffee and tea for themselves on the pavement. They were there all the time I was with Victoria in the States. I'd already started to get used to that kind of attention from my life with Victoria. For my parents, it was something completely new and it wasn't as if it had been them who had been sent off at a World Cup. It was a real test for both of them but, because they were there for each other, they had the strength to see it through. Even now they haven't told me the half of what went on during those first few days after the Argentina game. Maybe they don't want me to know. Maybe they don't want to think about it themselves ever again. For all that I've put that time behind me now, some of it still haunts me: my face as a dart board, the effigy hanging from a lamp-post, the staged interviews with supporters.

'Beckham's a disgrace to his country. He should never play for England again.'

A lot of what was said and written about me appeared on the front pages, the news pages, and didn't come from football writers, although one or two of them were pretty vindictive too. I've got all of it filed away. It's not a black book or anything but, if you're saving stuff, you need to save it all. My parents' house was always full of clippings waiting to go into scrapbooks. We've collected them all since I was a boy. One or two people have come out since 1998 and said they regretted their part in what happened. The former Editor of the *Mirror*, Piers Morgan, whose paper ran the dart board thing, has been honest enough to admit they went too far. I remember the other things that really hurt at the time, and just hope the journalists who wrote them do as well. It's strange now, as England captain, when I stand up at press conferences. I think I've got a decent relationship with the guys who cover the national side and I'm proud to be there, talking to them on behalf of my team-mates. A lot of those same journalists were around during that summer six years ago, and I'm sure they remember, as I do, what it was like between the media and me back then. After I arrived back in England, I made a point of avoiding talking to the press completely for the best part of a year. That wasn't just a way of getting my own back for what was being said and written about me. I knew I was being watched like never before, and I didn't want to get into a situation where I might say something I'd later regret.

Even before I got off the plane after my time in the States, I got my own sense of what my family had been put through while I was away. The Chief Steward on the flight back to London came over to my seat an hour ahead of us landing at Heathrow.

'When we disembark, there'll be police waiting for you at the gate.'

I thought he was joking. *What were the police there for? To arrest me? To protect me?* Either way, this was going a bit far, wasn't it? Sure enough, there were half a dozen uniformed officers waiting to meet me. We walked through the terminal in a little cluster: me in the middle, them all around me. It was all I could do not to laugh out loud. *What was all this about?* I got my answer soon enough. When we came out through the arrivals area, a wave of camera crews, photographers and journalists broke towards us, shouting out for pictures, for me to say something, for any kind of reaction at all. The policemen just bundled me across the hall and into the back of the car that was waiting to pick me up. It was terrifying. And it was just the start.

A couple of days later, I was back at Old Trafford for pre-season training. For a few hours every day, at least, I could just concentrate on football and shut everything else out of my mind. There was a bit of light-hearted banter in the dressing room but my team-mates knew I was struggling with what was happening and, in that situation, players will always support each other. And I was happy being back with them and playing again. The distraction helped me put on a brave face for Mum and Dad, who were being put through it enough without having to see me really upset about things as well. They'd been advised by the police to come up to Manchester because it wasn't safe for me to be on my own in the house in Worsley. Dad used to drive me into training at the Cliff and then pick me up again after work. I wouldn't have asked them. In fact I offered to send them off on holiday for a break from it all. But I think my parents felt easier being there with me.

I think it might be hard for people to understand what it was like living my life in those first months after the World Cup. It was difficult enough for my friends to imagine it until they experienced it first hand. A couple of days after I got back from America, Dave Gardner and I met up after training to go and have some lunch in Manchester city centre. We went to a place we knew called The Living Room. Usually, it was friendly enough, and was some-where we went regularly because people knew us but left us to get on with our meal. That afternoon, though, Dave and I strolled in and it was like that scene in the Western where the guy walks into the wrong saloon in Deadwood Gulch. People turned round and stared daggers. It was pretty unnerving. We slunk over into a corner and just buried our heads in the menu.

'I'm not coming out with you again, mate,' Dave whispered. 'It's more than my life's worth.'

For the next few months, we used to joke about getting fitted up in bullet-proof vests and crash helmets before we left the house. You had to find a way of laughing about it just to keep the tension at arms' length.

On the football side, the gaffer didn't need to say much. He'd spent the summer signing new players: Jaap Stam, Dwight Yorke and Jesper Blomqvist, all big-name international footballers, arrived at the club. And we knew what we had to do: make up for the underachievement of the year before. That hadn't been good enough for us, for the club or for the supporters. We knew 1998/99 was going to have to be a big season. Even more so for me personally: I went into it with the feeling that, in the aftermath of the World Cup, this was make or break for me, at least as far as playing my football in England was concerned.

For the first Premiership game of the new season, we were at home to Leicester City. I don't think I've ever been as nervous before a football match as I was that afternoon. I'd always had a good relationship with the crowd at Old Trafford, but what reaction would I get now? I wasn't sure how I was going to react either. The last time I'd played a really competitive game had been in Saint-Etienne. There was this little nagging uncertainty in the back of my mind that morning: how did I know that what had happened against Argentina wouldn't happen again? It wasn't as if I understood exactly why I'd reacted to Simeone getting after me: I didn't know now, for sure, if I'd be able stop myself getting into the same situation again. I didn't have the experience back then to realise that I was a relatively immature person who, as a player, was just burning up with the desire to win games. I was desperate to kick off against Leicester but I was dreading those ninety minutes too.

There were more than the ninety to play, as it turned out. The home fans were fantastic to me that afternoon. Every time I went to take a corner, thousands of them stood up to cheer for me. They wanted me to know they were behind me. And that meant so much. It was an amazing feeling. With 60,000 United fans on your side, you're ready to take on the rest of the world. The game, though, had a twist: we were 2–0 down at half time. Teddy Sheringham pulled one back and then, in injury time at the end, we were awarded a free-kick just outside the Leicester penalty area. I stepped up and there was this hush around the ground: it was eerie, the silence. Anybody who was there, I'm sure, will remember it. The only voice I could hear was the one in my head. *Please go in. Please, please go in.*

Once I'd struck it with the inside of my right foot, the ball spun up over the wall and down into the corner of the goal, almost in slow motion, it seemed. The time it took for the shot to go past the keeper was enough for me to realise what a perfect moment this was. I ran to the corner flag with my arms stretched out and spun round in a sort of clumsy pirouette. I knew exactly what I wanted to say to the United supporters above the roar. *I didn't know what to expect. Thank you for standing by me. That goal's for you.*

I've always felt in control when I was out on the pitch. However difficult it was with away crowds, I could get on with playing. If I was kicking a ball, there was never a chance of anything else getting on top of me. Away from football, though, it got stranger and stranger. Victoria was on tour most of the time and Mum and Dad had gone back to London to work. I was on my own in the evenings at home. I remember one night in particular. The house in Worsley had an alarm system, so I wasn't worried about anybody breaking in. But, that night, a bang – sounding like it was coming from out in the garden – woke me up. I got a sinking feeling in the pit of my stomach, not knowing what was going on but fearing the worst. The police had given me an emergency number to ring in case anything happened but I decided to check for myself. I didn't want to call them out if it was just a cat trying to get into my bin.

I got out of bed and crept down the stairs. I leaned down and looked out of the landing window. Standing at the back fence was this bloke, arms crossed, looking back up at me. First thing I remembered was that I didn't have any clothes on. He just stared at me. It was like some weird kind of hypnotism. He wasn't moving and I couldn't either. Eventually, I pulled the window open and shouted at him.

'What do you want?'

He didn't move a muscle. He didn't reply. He just stood there, staring up at me, not caring at all that I'd seen him. I think those moments were the scariest of the lot. I don't know how long the pair of us were there, looking at one another. I didn't know what was going on, never mind knowing what I could do about it. I rang the police but, by the time they arrived, the man had disappeared. It gives me a shiver even now to think about it.

I'd been shaky before that Leicester game, even though it was at Old Trafford, in the heart of the United family. The first away fixture of the season was the one everybody had been looking ahead to: West Ham at Upton Park, where they'd already had plenty of practice, since the Paul Ince transfer, at giving a United player a hard time of it. That was where people were expecting me to really feel the pressure. In a strange way, though, I found myself looking forward to it. I had this sense that I needed to experience how bad the stick could be if I was going to get past it and put it behind me for the rest of the season. I knew it was going to be a challenge and I just wanted to get on with facing up to it.

I'll never forget arriving at Upton Park for the game. As I walked down the coach, trying to catch a glimpse of what was going on outside, there was this policeman standing at the door waiting for me. I thought he was standing on the steps at first. He was so huge he seemed to be blocking out the sun. It was almost as if the size of him was a warning about the scale of the hostility. They were waiting for me out in the car park: hundreds of people, anger all over their faces. It amazed me then. It amazes me even more, now that I'm a father myself: dads screaming abuse at me, calling me every name under the sun, with their sons – six- or seven-year-olds – standing beside them, looking up at that kind of example.

It was only some time later, when I saw pictures of the crowd, that I perhaps appreciated how intense it was at Upton Park that day. I've got one particular photo at home that still spooks me: I'm taking a corner and you can see the expressions on people's faces in the crowd behind me. You can almost feel the aggression; it's caught there in the picture. And it's not: you're a crap footballer who cost us the World Cup and who should never play for England again. It's way past that, way past anything to do with football. The looks on those faces said it all:

'If we could, we'd have you, Beckham.'

That hatred makes you wonder what football's worth, if it provokes those sorts of emotions. If you snapped out of your concentration on the game and became aware of moments like that, what would you do? Walk off the pitch? I just don't understand it at all. Lucky for me, I felt whatever was coming my way I could take on the chin. When we came off at the end of the match, after a 0– 0 draw, I felt a shudder of relief. I'd probably imagined far worse leading up to the day and it seemed the reality of it hadn't been that difficult to get through after all. The stick from the fans, in the wake of France 98, didn't stop after that afternoon at West Ham; but it being a problem for me as a Manchester United player probably did.

It started with me not sure about whether I'd make it through to the following May in one piece. It ended up being the most incredible season any of us – maybe any footballer playing in this country – will ever experience. I don't know if United will ever win the Treble again, or whether anybody else will. But, either way, it'll never be done the way we did it: whichever team comes after will have to write their own script because only that group of United players could have made the story unfold the way it did. And, for me, the adventures that season had their own personal twist, which took the events of the spring and summer of 1999 out there into make believe. Just when people were starting to imagine what might be possible for the football team, Brooklyn arrived in Victoria's life and mine. And just a couple of months after United's unbelievable night at the Nou Camp – the night the impossible happened – I, David Robert Joseph Beckham, took my vows and married the girl of my dreams.

Down the years, there are certain teams that Man United have learned to measure themselves against in European competition. We were in the same Champions League Group as two of them in 1998, and they were amazing games: we drew 3–3 twice with Barcelona and 1–1 and 2–2 with Bayern Munich before Christmas. Although we didn't win any of those games, it showed we could compete against the best around at the time. Outside Old Trafford, people started getting the idea that this might be United's year. We never thought about it, not that early on anyway. But self-belief isn't something that you need to be talking about for it to happen.

We played some great football in the Premiership that season. Dwight Yorke and Andy Cole couldn't stop scoring goals: they had an understanding between them right from the start. I remember beating Everton 4–1 at Goodison and Leicester 6–2 at Filbert Street. Then we went to the City Ground and hammered Forest 8–1; it was Steve McClaren's first game as team coach after Brian Kidd had moved on to take over as manager at Blackburn. That was some afternoon: Ole Gunnar Solskjaer came on as a sub and scored four goals in about ten minutes. Steve looked round the dressing room at us afterwards, new man in the job and not quite sure what to say. He got it about right:

'Not bad, lads. Is it like this every week?'

Obviously, things were going really well already when Steve came in to replace Kiddo. And in that first season with United, he did well not to disrupt what the boss and Brian already had in place. He just concentrated on keeping the momentum going. I think Steve is one of the very best coaches in the country; and maybe he had more to do with us finishing up with the Treble than people give him credit for. My generation had got to know the likes of Eric Harrison and Brian Kidd really well and we were worried about how the gaffer would find someone good enough to follow those two. There had been rumours about Steve coming from Derby to join us. In fact, I remember a game against them at Old Trafford just before he did: Steve was with Jim Smith on the Derby bench. He never stopped talking to his players; or to everybody else within earshot. I can still see him, perched on the edge of the visitor's dugout with his notebook. He was scribbling like mad at the same time as chattering away non-stop. I played wide on that side of the pitch for one half and could hear everything. *Blimey, mate. Do you ever shut up?*

A couple of days later, Steve was introduced to us as our new first-team coach. When you've had as much help with your game as I have, ever since the earliest days with Ridgeway Rovers, it's not right to talk about 'better coaching' or 'the best coach'. What I'd say for sure, though, is that Steve McClaren brought very different – and very much his own – qualities to the job. His technical ability, his organisation, his passing on of information on the training pitch, were all absolutely outstanding. He had a really open mind, too. If Steve heard about something new, he'd try it. If it worked, we'd use it. If not, nothing had been lost by having a go. When he arrived at Old Trafford in February 1999, he won the players' respect very quickly indeed.

United are a competitive team, even in training. Players have a go at each other, and at the coaching staff. We fly into tackles. Now and again, the gaffer will have to cut short a session because things are getting too heated. That's how it's always been at the club, from the youth team up. It's an edge: that desperation to win, never mind that it's only the five-a-sides at training on a Friday morning. Steve took that on and he understood, as well, that our style was all about possession of the ball and made sure that was what training focused on. He made us laugh, too. In his fantasy moments, Steve McClaren is a very stylish player indeed: back then, he thought he was Glenn Hoddle, spraying his passes around the training pitches at Carrington. We were already on a roll when Steve arrived but he kept the lads going all the way to the Nou Camp, even if it wasn't until the following season that he really made his own mark.

United have taken some criticism over the club's attitude to the FA Cup in recent seasons, particularly for not defending it in 2001 when we were asked to compete in FIFA's new World Club Championship out in Brazil. All I can say is that the gaffer along with every United player loves the competition, not least because it was so important the season we won the Treble. The third round tie against Liverpool was one of the biggest games of that 1998/99 season. Liverpool scored through Michael Owen almost from the kick-off and then we battered them for the next eighty minutes without making a really good goalscoring chance. The atmosphere was as good as I ever played in at Old Trafford. Maybe the fact that it was a cup game and Liverpool had more supporters there than they would for a Premiership fixture had something to do with it. Ole Gunnar Solskjaer came on as a sub. He always seemed to come on as a sub that season. And we equalised almost at once. Then Ole got the winner right on full-time and the place went berserk: for once the drama had been as intense as the rivalry. And United had won.

Cup football has an edge. The Champions League starts to get much more exciting, for the supporters and for the players, at the knockout stage. In 1999, we were drawn against Inter Milan in the quarter-finals. It would have been a big game anyway but, beforehand, all the hype was about the fact that it would be the first meeting between David Beckham and Diego Simeone, who played his club football for Inter, since the World Cup and Saint-Etienne. Never mind who was going to win, half the pre-match build-up seemed to be about who would and who wouldn't be shaking a particular opponent's hand before kick-off at Old Trafford in the first leg.

As far as I was concerned, all that really mattered was the game. The only thing I made up my mind about in advance was that I'd try to get Simeone's shirt afterwards. It's framed at home now, along with all the others from great players I've played against during my career. I had something else on my mind, too, that evening: the one thing in the world that might have seemed more important than the football match I was getting ready to play. Victoria was due to give birth to our baby any day. I was sitting in the players' lounge at Old Trafford, waiting to go into our team meeting, when the mobile rang. Victoria's number came up on the screen. *This is it. It's happening.* It turned out Victoria had called to tell me she'd had a twinge but that things were okay. She was fine and wished me good luck and I went into the team meeting with a clear head.

Before Champions League games, you go along the line of opposition players before kick-off, shaking hands. I still remember the explosion of flashbulbs that went off at the moment Simeone and I came face to face. During the match itself, we didn't see all that much of each other, bar a moment when we almost collided and he caught my ankle. I'll never know whether he meant it or not. The important thing was I didn't react. It turned into a great night for us. In the first half, I sent in two crosses that Dwight Yorke put away and the final score was 2–0. Inter were a really difficult team to play against and that result was just right. I was a happy man by the time I spoke to Victoria on the phone again.

She laughed when I told her I'd got Simeone's shirt and that he'd given me a peck on the cheek as we came off the pitch at the end. We agreed I'd head down to London after training the following day.

That win, a good night's sleep and a stretch in the morning – it suddenly felt like I was starting to move on from the sending off and everything that had come with it. Whether anybody else would, of course, wasn't up to me. It wouldn't be until the summer of 2002 that I'd be able, finally, to put what happened in Saint-Etienne behind me forever. But having played well against Inter – and with Simeone's shirt on the back seat of the car – I headed down the M6 at lunchtime without a care in the world. I'd be with the mum-to-be in a couple of hours.

I remember I was munching on a Lion bar when the phone call came. I nearly choked on the thing.

'David? It's Victoria. The doctor says he wants me to go into hospital and have the baby tonight.'

I've had a lot of things happen during my football career that not many other people have had the chance to experience. Every father, though, knows what I felt like the moment Victoria told me what was about to happen. The excitement, fear and happiness – this was the biggest thing that was ever going to take place in my life – left me feeling like I was going to be sick. I threw away the chocolate bar and held onto the steering wheel hard until I stopped shaking. I couldn't get down to London fast enough.

When I got to her parents' house in Goff's Oak, Victoria was in the bath. The pains had turned into something else. She knew what it meant. She looked up at me:

'David, I'm really nervous.'

You're not the only one. I didn't know what to say. We got everything ready and headed for the hospital, the Portland, in

London. Victoria was going to have an elective caesarean: the doctor had decided it was the safest thing for her and for the baby. Everything happened so quickly. We barely had time to put Victoria's bag down in her room before we were taken up to this small room beside the operating theatre where she got fitted up with a drip and had her epidural. I think those were the tensest few minutes of all. There was a little panic about getting me gowned up: I ended up wearing a pair of those blue hospital trousers that were at least five sizes too big. Maybe it was better to be worrying and giggling about that than thinking too hard about what was waiting on the other side of those double doors.

Victoria was rolled through on a trolley and then transferred to the bed in the operating theatre. I followed her through. I squeezed her hand and told her I loved her.

'What's going on?' she asked me. 'I can't feel anything, you know.'

Which was good because, by then, they'd already made the incision. I'd never been in an environment as weird and alien as that room: I just tried to concentrate on Victoria and put where I was out of my mind. She looked up:

'I'm really hungry. Do you think you'll be able to get me some smoked salmon?'

She'd been wolfing down the stuff all through the pregnancy – and I'm sure that's why Brooklyn has always preferred fish to red meat – but I hadn't expected her to get that kind of craving just then. I was waiting, watching. I could feel my heart beating away in my chest. And, all of a sudden, the mum was feeling peckish. The very next moment, our baby was there, held by a nurse in the air. I could see him; Victoria couldn't at first. Because it was a caesarean, they had to put Brooklyn on a table and run a little tube into his mouth and nose to clear his airways. The nurse bundled him up in a towel, as tight as you like, and passed him over to me. Because Victoria was still being stitched up at that point, I got to hold him first. I know it sounds selfish but it was such a privilege, such an amazing feeling. I've experienced it twice now, and nothing in my life, on a football pitch or anywhere else, comes close to the intensity of that moment: the thrill and the awe, holding your son in your arms for the very first time. I carried Brooklyn the few steps over to his mum and laid his head on the pillow next to hers: the two most precious people in the whole world, looking so much alike and so beautiful, too. That picture will be in my mind's eye forever.

I'd always wanted to have children. Maybe it was growing up with a baby sister in the house. Maybe I've just got that paternal thing from my mum and dad, I don't know. I can remember, when I broke into the United team, feeling jealous of the older players on the odd days during a season when they could bring their children in to training, to sit on the touchlines and watch Dad play. I wanted that really badly. And, I'll be honest, I always wanted a son. Two sons, in fact: as much as I loved Joanne, I know – and she knows, we laugh about it – I always wanted a baby brother, too. That afternoon at the Portland, gazing down at Victoria nuzzled up against our newborn son, I knew that, whatever else had happened or was going to happen in my life, I'd been blessed.

I remember Victoria turning to me as I cradled Brooklyn in my arms:

'Whatever you do, please don't leave him.'

We'd had threats made to us since the summer and, again, just before Brooklyn was born. We'd talked about it all beforehand, how we were going to handle the security, and I went with the nurse when she took Brooklyn to get him bathed and all cleaned up and ready, even though it meant leaving Victoria. All our family came round to the hospital that evening. It was like having all the people you love most wrapped around you. Then, that night, I stayed. There wasn't another bed in the room; Victoria was in the hospital bed, because she still had the pipes and monitors connected from the operation, and Brooklyn was in his cot. I slept on the floor with a towel for a cushion and my head pressed up against the door, so it couldn't be opened. Maybe we were a little nervous, but you can't ever know. All I was sure of was how happy I was: just me, Victoria and Brooklyn, breathing, sleeping together in that little room, through until morning.

Almost the first phone call I'd made was to Alex Ferguson, just to let him know there was another lad named Beckham about, and he was great. He's got sons of his own and I think he understood just how I was feeling. After the congratulations, he told me not to bother coming up to Manchester to train: just to stay with Brooklyn and Victoria and come back the day before the next game. I played against Chelsea on the Saturday and then drove back to London. At first, Brooklyn had trouble keeping his milk down. That evening, Victoria got him dressed up in this little green and white outfit and I arrived just in time to see his latest meal come up all over his clothes and the bed. It was like a special welcome for me, to the real fun of being a dad.

The day Victoria and Brooklyn came home was mad and, to be honest, I don't remember it as a good experience at all. We had an idea what things might be like outside the Portland. You looked out of the window and someone had hung this huge banner across the shops opposite, which said: 'BROOKLYN THIS WAY'. We made arrangements with the hospital and with the police, who both did everything they could to help: a back way in for the car, curtains hung in the windows all around the back seats, everything we could think of to make trying to get past this army of press and photographers and well-wishers a bit less scary and upsetting for a baby boy, just a couple of days old, and his very tired mum. It turned into something like a military operation and, of course, when it came to doing my bit, I was all over the place. I'd never strapped in a baby's car seat. Snarling the straps, putting the thing in the wrong way round, trying to line up the buckles: in the end, the midwife had to do it for me.

We got settled in the car and then had to draw the curtains, which meant that – apart from hundreds of flashes from the cameras – we didn't really see the fuss that was going on until we got home and watched it on television. We whizzed out the gate: left, then right, then right again onto the Marylebone Road. The press had positioned cars along the route, to hold us up so the snappers could get their pictures. The police, though, saw what was happening, which was dangerous for us and everybody else, and they closed off the main road to traffic for a couple of minutes so that we could get away. Frank, our driver, was great; he put his foot down and, about forty minutes later, we were where we wanted to be: snug, safe and having a cup of tea in Tony and Jackie's front room. We practically lived at the Adams' house until we bought our own place down south a few years ago. And where better for a new mum to rest up than her family home?

The grandparents were smooching over the baby and, for a few minutes, Victoria and I were alone, sipping our tea and looking at one another. I'm sure it's a moment that hits every new mum and dad. This is about as real as life gets, and nobody can tell you what you have to do. You take a deep breath. *Right. What happens now?*

Victoria breastfed for about a month. I'm really protective about my family anyway but, during those first days, watching my wife-to-be and our boy together – her feeding him milk and love – made those feelings more intense than I've ever known. But, fantastic as that was, after a couple of weeks I found myself starting to wonder. *You know what? I want to be able to help feed him too.*

Breastfeeding was really tiring for Victoria, just like it is for every mum, and so she let me go and raid the baby shelves at the chemists. I came back with the lot: bottles, warmers, pumps, sterilizers. I must have looked like some kind of mad scientist, setting it all up. I'm glad I did it, though. All the fiddling about to get a bit of Mum's milk into a bottle was worth it: I'll never forget Brooklyn with me on the bed that afternoon: there was my boy, cradled in my arms and glugging away like his life depended on it.

It was an amazing time. Things were so exciting at United and then, every time I could, I'd get down to London to see Victoria and Brooklyn. It was a while before they moved up to be with me at the new flat we'd bought in Alderley Edge. I didn't overdo the driving, although I've always found being behind the wheel more relaxing than tiring. It's time on my own, after all, and I don't get much of that. Even so, I never made the trip in the couple of days before we had a game. I think some people might have thought it would all be too much, but every time I saw the two most precious people in my life it gave me this amazing lift, like I'd been plugged in to recharge, and I'd go back to Old Trafford ready for more. If anything, what might have dragged me down would have been not being able to spend some time with them both.

Brooklyn's first few months were tough on Victoria. She'd worked so hard for so long with the Spice Girls and had put so much into a successful career, and then, all of a sudden, she had to stop and focus all her energy and attention instead on this tiny new baby who was completely dependent on her. I'm sure any mum must recognise those feelings. It's not like it wasn't what Victoria wanted to be doing but it was a giant shock to the system. Her life, and everything about it, changed almost overnight and in ways that nothing could ever have prepared her for. If anything, it was even worse when she moved up to Manchester, away from her family and friends.

Tony and Jackie's house is like the set of *Neighbours*: people are always dropping by, and there's always something going on. It was completely different in Alderley Edge. We hardly went out anywhere; hardly ever had people round unless it had been arranged in advance. I'd go off to training and Victoria would be left on her own, feeling trapped in the apartment. Even the gardens weren't private. Photographers would suddenly turn up with their lenses pointed in over the back gate. I think Victoria got pretty down. She stuck it out, though, and I'm grateful and proud of her that she did: we'd both decided that what was best for Brooklyn would be for the three of us – our little family – to be together as much as we could.

From April 1999 onwards, I was playing two games a week, which made trips to London pretty difficult to squeeze in. That was part of the reason Victoria decided to bring Brooklyn north when she did. It meant so much to me, having them there while the season flew by, getting more and more intense as each match came and went. I'd rush home afterwards and there would be my boy and his mum, waiting for me.

There were so many big games that Spring but one stands out above the rest: the one that made everything else possible. Ask any United player, any United fan, and they'll tell you which one I mean: the Wednesday night, 14 April 1999, at Villa Park. The FA Cup semi-final replay against Arsenal. We'd been disappointed not to win the first time, on the Sunday afternoon, when it finished

0–0, but as soon as we got to the ground on the evening of the replay, you could tell it was going to turn out to be something special.

Semi-finals are always exciting to play in; an evening kick-off, under floodlights, just made it seem even more dramatic. Arsenal were the closest team to United in the Premiership and here we were, extra-time and penalties if necessary, to decide who'd be going to Wembley for the Cup Final. It felt like we were playing for the Double, that there was that much at stake; the game meant that much to both clubs. I remember sitting in the dressing room forty minutes ahead of kick-off. *I've never scored against them. What would it feel like to get a goal against Arsenal tonight?*

Villa Park has always been a lucky ground for me: I'd scored the winner in our last semi-final there against Chelsea. And now, against Arsenal, I only had to wait a quarter of an hour for my chance. The ball rolled to me just outside the penalty area and I whipped it, first time, past David Seaman. The feeling wasn't what I'd been expecting at all. I jumped up to celebrate but, at the same time, it seemed like I should be going over and having a laugh about it with Dave. We've joked our way through shooting practice at so many England training sessions together. If he reads my intention, he'll just catch the ball as if to say: Is that the best you can do? If he doesn't, and I score, then he gets the stick. Half of me that night at Villa Park wanted to run over, jump on Dave's back, and give him a shake. I was really pleased with the goal but because of everything that came later in the game, it's only me that seems to remember it now.

When you score in a big game, you always hope your goal will be the winner. But Arsenal came back strong, and in the second half things seemed to be going their way. Dennis Bergkamp scuffed an equaliser and, five minutes after that, Roy Keane was sent off for a second yellow card. You could tell they thought they had us. All we could do was dig in and hope for the best. *Whatever happens, they're not going to score.*

Then, right on full-time, Arsenal got a penalty, down at the end where I'd scored my goal, which seemed so long ago now it might have been in a different game. *Oh, no. Bergkamp's taking it. He never misses.*

Lucky for us, Peter Schmeichel knew better and he dived to his left to save it. I ran up to congratulate him and put my arms around him.

'We're going to get a goal now!' he bellowed at me.

Then he pushed me away. I mean, really pushed me. I went flying. We had to defend the corner and I think everybody was too busy concentrating on marking up to notice me stumbling away.

The ninety minutes ended 1–1 and we went into extra-time. To be honest, it was a bit like a training game: attackers vs defenders, with Arsenal camped around our penalty area. But then, with about ten minutes left before penalties, Patrick Vieira – of all people, one of the best midfielders in the world – misplaced a pass on halfway. Ryan Giggs got onto the ball and just started running. Giggsy was one of the few of us who had any legs left because he'd come on as a sub after about an hour. He kept going and going, beat a couple of defenders, and when the ball bobbled off his shin it took him past Martin Keown, who was standing off him. Ryan was on an angle, to the left of the Arsenal goal. *He's got to square it across the six-yard box now.*

Instead, he just smashed the ball in at the near post, into the roof of the net. All the United side of the ground erupted. Giggsy was running along in front of them, waving his shirt in the air. Loads of the supporters were spilling onto the pitch. I got to him, too, and I can still remember the smell of the fans around us: one bloke, in particular, must have been chain-smoking the whole game and he grabbed hold of me. I couldn't get the smell of his cigarette smoke off my shirt and out of my nostrils for the rest of the game.

When the final whistle went, United supporters came pouring onto the pitch again and it got a bit scary for a while. I got lifted up onto some people's shoulders. Someone was trying to pull one of my boots off as a souvenir; someone else had hold of my shirt. I leaned over in all the din and tried to say to one of the fans who was carrying me: 'While you've got me up here on your shoulders, could we try and head over towards where the dressing rooms are?'

Like I say, it was a little frightening; and I was out on the pitch for what seemed like ages. I think I was the last person off. I was enjoying the moment, though. Times like that don't come along too often, even if you're playing for United, and I just wanted to experience it all. Finally, I managed to find my way back to the changing rooms. The atmosphere was fantastic but completely different to the madness outside. No jumping around, no shouting the odds: everybody, the gaffer included, was just sitting there, glowing. Something special had just happened. It was about as good a game of football as I'd ever played in. Right up there, as it turned out, with our next semi-final which came along the following Wednesday night.

We hadn't played well in the first leg of the Champions League semi against Juventus. They'd come to Old Trafford and got a 1–1 draw, which was almost as good as a victory because of the away goal. We had to win in Turin now. Nobody was ever supposed to win in Turin. Five minutes into the game, Juventus were 1–0 up and battering us. After ten, they were 2–0 up and still battering us. I found myself thinking back to those semi-finals against Dortmund and the chances we'd not taken. Was this going to turn out to be another year when we missed out on the final?

Sometimes in a game, when you're struggling, someone produces a moment of brilliance, like Ryan Giggs had at Villa Park, to turn everything on its head. Other times, it's the team as a whole that finds something, which was what happened at the Stadio Delle Alpi. Maybe Juventus relaxed a little, I don't know, but we put a few passes together for the first time in the game. About twenty minutes had gone and we were still 2–0 down; but it didn't feel like we were out of it. I remember us going close and me turning to Gary Neville:

'They're not that good, Gaz. We can win this, you know.'

Just a couple of minutes after that, I took a corner on the left and Roy Keane came in with a fantastic header to get it back to 2–1. You lose count of how many great games Keano has played for us. That night, though, was special even by his standards. He scored the goal and, soon afterwards, got booked: he knew, and we all knew, that meant he was going to miss the final if we got there. But his head didn't go down for an instant. All he cared about was winning that game for United. Who were we to argue? Who were Juventus to argue? As soon as we pulled one back, you could sense it turning. They started panicking all over the field. Yorkie equalised before half-time and then Andy Cole scored the winner about five minutes from the end.

It's an ambition for any player to be involved in the biggest games for your club and your country. The European Cup Final, though: that was a mission at United. Every one of us knew that winning it was what the boss wanted more than anything else in football. When we came off at the end of the game in Turin 3–2 winners, we knew we were almost there. We had good enough players; it felt like luck, perhaps, was starting to run our way when we needed it to; and there was a spirit in that team, that season more than ever, which made us all feel like we couldn't be beaten. Every game we played during the last couple of months of 1998/99 was a cup final in its way: if we'd lost any game, in the League, in the FA Cup or in Europe, it would have meant the Treble had gone. No-one knew if we'd ever be in the same kind of situation again and, so, none of us wanted to miss a single game of it, even though the gaffer kept coming up to us and saying he could rest us if we were feeling tired. We were on the kind of roll where you'd finish one game and the adrenalin kidded you into believing that you could play another one the following day, however heavy your legs were.

The Premiership title was between us and Arsenal, as close as the FA Cup semi-final had been, and they had their noses in front almost to the end. We had two games each left to play and, the night before we visited Blackburn, Arsenal were away to Leeds. For weeks we'd been waiting for them to slip up. I watched that game at Elland Road on television. The tension's terrible: you can't do anything about it, can you? Right at the end, Jimmy Floyd Hasselbaink scored and it felt like I had. We went up to Ewood Park the next night and drew 0–0, which meant as long as we beat Spurs on the last day of the season, we'd be champions again. The Treble came down to ten days in May, starting at Old Trafford: our final Premiership game.

All the press had been saying it would be easy: that Tottenham wouldn't want Arsenal winning the League. On the day, especially in the first half, it didn't seem easy at all. *How could we have come this far and be playing this badly?* I missed a really good headed chance. Dwight Yorke hit the post and, then, Tottenham ran up the other end and Les Ferdinand scored. It wasn't what was meant to be happening. Just before half-time, though, the ball got played into me and I whipped a shot into the top corner and ran off to celebrate. I watched the video of the game later and the look on my face after I scored that equaliser gave me a bit of a shock. I've seen that expression on other players' faces: at Preston after I scored from the free-kick, up at Blackburn the night I made the mistake of arguing with Roy Keane. I've seen it on the faces of United fans crammed in at Old Trafford. I don't think I'd ever seen it on mine: that desire, wanting to win so badly; it looked like fury. *Smile, mate. You've just scored.* But, at the time, all the frustration of that first half came out, along with the tension that came with knowing what was at stake. I just ran off towards the supporters, screaming.

The gaffer was a bit calmer than I was and he changed things around at half-time. We were surprised, and so was the crowd, that he took Yorkie off and brought on Andy Cole. It took all of a couple of minutes to prove his point: right at the start of the second half, Andy went round the keeper and scored what turned out to be the winner. There were a few nervous moments at the end but the job had been done. In the dressing room afterwards, nobody mentioned Newcastle at Wembley or Bayern at the Nou Camp. Nobody mentioned the Treble. Nobody had to. It seemed like it was ringing round the dressing room, inside my head and, I'd guess, everybody else's. *This is it. We're going to do this now.*

Two cup finals in a week: I was happy, of course. It meant two new suits. I think Gary Neville organised things with Prada – blue suits, white shirts, blue ties, not bad at all – for Wembley on the Saturday. I volunteered for Europe. For the Champions League I wanted us to have something really special. My only instruction came from the manager: whatever I got, it had to have a United club badge on the jacket pocket. Earlier in the year, Donatella

Versace, who was quite friendly with Victoria, had invited me out to Italy for the Spring Fashion Show. When I rang up to say we were in the European Cup Final, they said they'd design our outfits: a light grey suit, a white shirt, a charcoal tie with a little United badge on it and then a much bigger badge on the jacket. Maybe I'm biased but I thought they were the business. All my footballing life I'd had the importance of looking the part drummed into me. I couldn't let Stuart Underwood or Eric Harrison or the lads and the gaffer down when it came to the Nou Camp, could I?

The final against Newcastle was more straightforward than any of us had been expecting. We were flying and played really well. Once Teddy scored the first goal, everybody in the ground knew we were going to finish off the Double. During the week before the game, the boss had told me that he was thinking of resting me. Because of injuries and Keano's suspension we were going to be short of numbers in midfield the following Wednesday. Obviously it was his decision, in the end, that I started on the Saturday, too, but I can still remember pleading with him: it was the Cup Final, after all. I didn't want to miss a single moment of this.

One strange thing happened during the course of beating Newcastle 2–0 that Saturday afternoon. I went in for a challenge with Gary Speed and his elbow caught me on the mouth. I'd cut my lip. It really stung – killed me – for the rest of the game and, when we were climbing the steps in front of the Royal Box to pick up the FA Cup, it bled quite a lot. Gary Neville pulled his shirt down over his fist and went to wipe some of it away: I didn't know how bad it looked. What I did know, though, was that it was sore enough not to want anyone near it. Back at the hotel we were staying at that evening, I met Victoria who'd come for the dinner. We were in our room and I took a sip from a glass of mineral water and suddenly realised that it was dribbling out through my lip. I couldn't understand it at first. The cut had gone right through. I closed my mouth and blew, and water came spurting out through the hole: it was a weird party trick to celebrate winning the Cup.

Thinking back, it feels like we had a couple of weeks after that to get ready for the European Cup Final against Bayern Munich. Actually, the game at the Nou Camp was the following Wednesday. Time just seemed to move really slowly: it was a new experience for all of us and I think we were just taking in every moment of the build-up. This was something absolutely massive, after all. Having won the Premiership and the FA Cup already, it felt like we weren't under any kind of pressure. I remember everybody being really relaxed, just looking forward to it. And I'll never forget, either, what the gaffer said to us in the dressing room just before we went up the tunnel to play in the biggest game of our lives.

'Trust me: you don't want to have to walk past the European Cup at the end of the game tonight. Not being able to pick it up would be the most painful thing you'll ever feel in football. Make sure you don't end up having to just look at that trophy, not able to touch it, knowing you had the chance to win the thing but then let that chance pass you by.'

I don't know how much the boss's warning helped focus us on what we had to do. The fact that it stuck in my mind so clearly says a lot, I think. What I know for sure is that every word he said about the pain and disappointment was true. We didn't have to endure it but you just have to watch the video of the game. Look at the Bayern Munich players as they go up to get their losers' medals. Some of them glance at the trophy – sitting there, waiting for United – and you can see, in their eyes, that they're devastated. Most of them can't even bring themselves to lift their heads and look.

Brooklyn was only two months old and Victoria hadn't planned to come to Barcelona. She doesn't come to many United away games anyway: she's wary and so am I. In the end, though, this was the European Cup Final; this was, just maybe, the Treble. Tony and Jackie babysat and Victoria came out with a couple of people to look after her. She may not know all that much about football but she supports me and enjoys the sense of occasion and the excitement of the big games. I was really pleased she made the trip although, before kick-off, I got nervous. If Victoria comes to a game, I can't relax until I've spotted her in the crowd and I know she's all right. At the Nou Camp, she did have a bit of trouble getting settled. I was looking up to where I thought she should be and it wasn't until we came back out, just before kick-off, that I saw her and had my mind put at rest. I think Victoria was pleased she made it. I remember what she said to me after the game:

'That was unbelievable. I've never experienced anything like that in my whole life.'

Which just about took the words out of my mouth. Unbelievable is exactly what it was. Because of the injuries and suspensions, I played central midfield against Bayern. I know, whatever I might say or other people might think, the manager always preferred me to play wide on the right. But with Scholesy and Keano missing through suspension that night, he put faith in me playing in the centre and it meant a lot to me that, afterwards, he praised my performance in that position when he talked to the press. And I loved it in there, alongside Nicky Butt. I was right in the thick of things, involved all game long.

It was hard, though. Unbelievably hard. And, to be honest, not the best of games. Bayern scored early on. They were a strong side, very well organised, like all German teams. We knew them and they knew us: we'd drawn twice in those group games earlier in the season. It felt like they were sure they were in control of it all. And, especially in the middle of the second half, they looked more likely to score another goal than we did to equalise. Peter Schmeichel made a couple of great saves; they missed a couple of chances. That twenty-minute spell, though, instead of taking the heart out of us, lifted us. They had a shot that came back off the crossbar and into Peter's hands. *All these chances, why haven't they scored again? Keep going and you never know. This could still happen for us.*

All of a sudden – none of us knew how close we were to full-time – we got a break. I turned on the ball, beat my man and played it out to our left. Ole had come on as a sub just a few minutes before and he won a corner. I sprinted over to take it. I remember that, even though the pitch at the Nou Camp is so big, you hardly have any room down by the flags to take corners. I saw Peter come charging up into the Bayern area and tried to steady myself. *Don't mess this up. Just float it in and try to put it in a dangerous area.*

I sent it over. The ball bounced out to Giggsy. He mis-hit it and it bounced through to Teddy Sheringham, the other sub, who knocked it in. Teddy was so close to being offside. But he wasn't. And we were level, 1–1. Everybody went up. I just went mad. I swear I felt like crying. At that moment, it felt like the whole season caught up with us. I was shattered. I looked over and saw Gary, celebrating on his own. He was happy but he couldn't get his legs to carry him over to the rest of us. People came running over from our bench. Every single person on the pitch, every single person in the crowd must have been thinking the same thing. *Here we go. Extra-time.*

The thought of another thirty minutes of football barely had time to sink in. Maybe the gaffer was the only person inside the Nou

Camp that night who wasn't already looking ahead to the final whistle. I glanced over towards our bench. Steve McClaren was trying to say something to the boss, trying to reorganise the team. The boss was ignoring him, just waving him away. Was it my imagination or was he acting like he knew we were going to score again? He was screaming to us to get back to halfway and kick off as fast as we could.

Almost at once, we won another corner. It was all happening so quickly that, when I went over to take it, I could see United supporters still jumping around, shouting into their mobile phones, and celebrating Teddy's goal. I think the Bayern players were still trying to get to grips with what had just happened, too. In the blink of an eye, I'd whipped the ball over and Ole had got to it and we'd scored again. Even after the celebrations, even though the second goal was already well into injury time, Bayern did get the ball forward one more time. My legs had gone. Everybody's legs had gone. *Oh, no. Please don't score now.*

Someone just booted the ball away from our penalty area and the whistle went. I don't know where it came from: the sound of that whistle was like an electric shock and I got this last burst of energy. I ran – sprinted – with my arms stretched out beside me, almost the length of the pitch and down to our fans. Most of the lads had just fallen on the floor: collapsed with exhaustion. Which was probably the best thing to do, but I couldn't help myself. The roar that broke out from the United supporters when the game finished was deafening and I felt like I was being shot out of a gun towards them. I don't know if I'll experience moments, or see celebrations, quite like those ever again.

We were out on the pitch for what seemed like hours afterwards, having a private party in the warm Spanish evening air: the lads who'd played and those who hadn't been able to, and the thousands of United fans who'd taken over the Nou Camp for the night. These were the supporters who'd welcomed me back to Old Trafford at the start of the season; who'd stuck by me after France 98, no matter what flak I was getting from anybody else. You could see on people's faces how much what had just happened meant to them and they could see how much the United players were enjoying being out there celebrating with them. It felt even more special for me: if it hadn't been for the supporters at that first Premiership game of 1998/99 at Old Trafford, I'm not sure I'd have been there at the Nou Camp on the season's final night. I'll never forget what they did for me. I know they'll never forget what we did for them in the dying minutes of the biggest game of them all.

It was pretty mad in the dressing room, too, once we finally found our way back there. Champagne was flying everywhere. Albert, the kit man, got thrown into the Jacuzzi. Everybody seemed to be singing, screaming and laughing. We'd played a lot of football together, and now was the right time to go a bit crazy together. Eventually, people started getting dressed. We were looking forward to meeting up with our families. I remember just sitting in my place in the dressing room, watching it all go on around me, and trying to take in what we'd done. I looked over to the far corner and that huge trophy, the European Cup, was just standing there, on top of a bench, all on its own.

This is my chance. I found the United club photographer:

'Will you take some pictures of me holding this?

I walked back up the tunnel, past the little chapel and out onto the pitch again. Half the floodlights were still on. Half of them were off. There were strange shadows being cast across that huge stretch of turf, and the empty stands just sort of loomed in the darkness. You could still imagine an echo of the crowd shouting and cheering during the game. It was an amazing feeling. *Forty minutes, an hour ago, this place was full of people. We were playing out there. We were getting beaten out there.*

And then I looked down at the trophy, which I'd set on the grass in front of me. It made me shiver. For a moment, I felt like the thirteen-year-old boy who'd jogged out onto this same pitch for the first time, nervous about meeting FC Barcelona's star players and trying to imagine what it would be like to play at their ground. I picked up the European Cup and the photographer snapped away. One of the proudest moments any player could ever experience in his career and I found myself standing there, in the half light with a winners' medal hanging round my neck, feeling humble in the face of what had just taken place. I got the same sensation later that evening, when the players walked into the hotel room for dinner. Victoria was there, my mum and dad too, along with all the families and closest friends. Everyone stood up at their tables and clapped. My wife – soon to be – called it unbelievable. She got it just right.

I hung onto that trophy. I thought I could make it my job to get it safely out of the ground. I walked out into the car park to look for the coach. Everyone else seemed to have drifted away and there was this eerie quiet in the air. The one or two voices you could hear sounded like they were coming from miles away. I looked up and saw Dad walking towards me. He just appeared out of the gloom, from nowhere, walking along with Mum and some other people. It wasn't as if we'd arranged to meet straight after the game: I'd been expecting to see them back at the hotel. Ninety thousand people inside the Nou Camp that night and your mum and dad are the ones you bump into by chance. We were the only people there.

Dad didn't need to say a word. He hugged me. It felt like he was crying or, at least, trying hard not to. And my eyes were pricking too. The two of us knew what it had been like when we'd met less than a year before, in another car park, after the Argentina game in Saint-Etienne. My parents knew better than anybody what had happened to me since that night. It had happened to them, too, in a way. That's how it is with your children. Their lives become the most important part of your own. I knew what it felt like to be a father now, of course. So I put down the cup and just hugged my dad back.

I Do

8

'Beckham. Here. I want a word.'

'Victoria hates it up north . . .'

'David is joining Arsenal . . .'

'. . . or, if he isn't, he's going to buy a helicopter to fly up to Manchester three times a week.'

There was plenty of speculation when we bought our house just outside London. The truth was a lot simpler, but also a lot less controversial. The story needed to shift newspapers, I suppose, which meant that the boring and the obvious had to make way for something people could talk about. Actually, Victoria didn't have a problem with Manchester at all or with me playing there. And as for me, I had absolutely no intention of ever leaving United. I think even the gaffer read more significance into us buying a new place than there was. He was aware of the gossip and pulled me to one side:

'Why have you bought that?'

His main concern was probably that I might end up trying to commute from Essex for training. In fact, even after we talked, I think he spent a year or more believing that, secretly, that's what I was doing. He didn't realise the place was a building site. I did my best to explain:

'London is where I'm from and that's why I've bought a house there. When I finish playing, I'll move back: my family's in London and so are lots of our friends. That's all it is. We're a family now, boss: Mr and Mrs Beckham. We've got our first baby boy. And when I retire London will be the natural place for us to call home.'

Once Brooklyn arrived and we knew we were getting married, I think instinct kicked in. We knew we wanted somewhere to bring up a family, somewhere we could always call home. We had a pretty good idea where we wanted the Beckhams to be based: north and east of London, near our parents, and not too far from the motorways. We knew we wanted space for Brooklyn to run around, safely and in privacy. We knew we wanted room to have friends and family over without having to squeeze anyone in. We wanted to be able to throw a decent party. Me? I had to make sure I had enough space for a snooker table and a long enough wall for my collection of signed shirts. It was time to stretch out a little after a year and a half of living out of suitcases, stopping at Tony and Jackie's or at the apartment in Cheshire.

The place we found was in Hertfordshire, on the edge of a little village called Sawbridgeworth. The first place we looked at belonged to the boxing promoter Frank Warren. I liked it but Victoria wasn't sure: perhaps it would have been too big for us. The house in Sawbridgeworth hardly needed a second look: Victoria fell in love with it straight away. The buildings and the grounds were the right sort of scale. I know people call it Beckingham Palace but it's a family home when all's said and done. It's manageable without needing an army of helpers. There was plenty of work to be done to it, and maybe that was what got Victoria so excited about it. I'm like her in that I've got very particular tastes in things: you could say we've got a liking for 'subtle over-the-top', the pair of us. What Victoria had, though, was the imagination to see how she could turn the place into somewhere we'd love. She also had a dad who had the knowledge and found the time to organise the details. Tony was the unpaid project manager for Sawbridgeworth when he wasn't running his own building business. I bet he had no idea what he'd be taking on when we said: please, we need someone we trust. It took the best part of four years to make all the changes that Victoria had imagined the moment we first drove through the gates.

Sawbridgeworth was about putting down roots. Until I pack in playing, though, I'm the same as any other footballer. It's something you take on as part of being a professional: your life revolves around training and games. It has to. Even one of the biggest days of my life, my wedding day, had to get squeezed into its place in the middle of the United calendar. At least there wasn't a World Cup or a European Championship to rush off to over the summer of 1999. Once I'd come down from the incredible high of the Nou Camp that May, and once I'd been convinced I should take off the European Cup winners' medal I had slung round my neck for days afterwards, we were able to concentrate on the planning, and all the excitement, of the Beckhams' own cup final: David and Victoria getting married on the fourth of July.

It's fair to say the Big Day took some organising. It's also fair to say I didn't have that much to do with it. We knew what we wanted: the general idea. Life had turned into a fairy tale since the Prince met his Princess and that's how we wanted it to feel. But when it came to the details, Victoria did most of the hard work. Together, we imagined something special, not just for us but for our families and friends too. Then, the day-to-day inspiration came from the bride. We talked. I didn't have anything sprung on me at the last moment. And, in the middle of all the bustle and arrangement-making, I was allowed to have my say. But it was Victoria, and her mum and sister Louise, who took on the responsibility for getting things right.

Through the 1998/99 season, and after what had happened in

the World Cup, we'd had to get used to the idea of thinking about security in relation to almost everything we did. But we weren't going to compromise on the day for our family and friends. We didn't want to slip away and get married in secret. We wanted a wedding to remember, both for ourselves and for the people we care most about. A big day would mean big security, though, and that pushed us towards two big decisions. One was to do a photo deal with a magazine: we realised that OK!'s desire to protect their exclusive would go a long way towards protecting our privacy at the same time. The other was to find someone who could take some of the pressure off the bride. So we hired a wedding co-ordinator, Peregrine Armstrong-Jones. I can't say I'd ever met anyone named Peregrine before. He was pretty upper-upper but a really lovely bloke who did a fantastic job for us: he understood what we were hoping for and made sure that was exactly what we got.

Between them, Victoria and Peregrine found our castle in Ireland at Luttrellstown. It had everything we needed and, best of all, something we might never have thought of if it hadn't been there already. The local church was a little drive away but, in the castle grounds, there was a little folly: ancient, tumbledown and a bit magical. The kind of setting in which you could dream about saying: I do. Once the bride and her sidekick saw it, ramshackle as it was, the decision was made and Peregrine got to work. There was a stream running underneath the folly and he created this setting straight out of a picture book of times past, with branches reaching overhead, fairy lights and flowers everywhere. Just enough room for about thirty members of our families and very closest friends before the big bash for everyone up at the castle later on. It was fantastic.

I loved every minute of the build-up: tasting the food, trying the wines and choosing the music. Everything went really smoothly – amazing, really, considering how complicated the arrange-ments were – until it came to getting the bride's frock across the Irish Sea. Now, bear in mind I wasn't supposed to see Victoria's wedding dress until the day. The people at *OK!* were so nervous about things that they chartered a small private plane to take us to Ireland. Brooklyn, me, Victoria, her mum and dad, sister Louise – with her baby, Liberty – and brother Christian had all squeezed in before the crew told us that the big box with the Big Secret wouldn't fit in the hold. Which meant the dress had to come out of the box to get it in through the passenger door. So I was sent off to stand on the runway with my eyes shut for twenty minutes. I had to sit with my back to the thing all the way to Dublin and, of course, once we touched down, we had to go through the entire routine all over again. I wasn't supposed to see it and, of course, we had to make sure that any cameras couldn't either. Pity: the afternoon would have made quite a good silent movie.

We got to the castle two days before our wedding day. Mum and Dad flew out and other guests started arriving the following evening. We had a big dinner for everyone the night before. After the meal, Victoria and I went out in the castle grounds for a walk together. We headed down to the marquee where the reception was going to take place. There was a little grove that had been made out of branches, and holly and flowers, which people would have to walk underneath to get inside. I'd brought along a couple of glasses and a bottle of champagne. I was telling Victoria, again, how much I loved her and, all of a sudden, this soft rain started falling. On a warm summer's evening, it felt perfect. I couldn't have imagined anything more romantic.

Eventually, bride and groom had to go their separate ways for the night. Back at the castle, Victoria, of course, had the best room in the place: our wedding suite. I had to make do with another guest room downstairs. Before I went to bed, the United players and some of my mates got together: it wasn't very wild as stag evenings go. Everyone was pretty tired and we just went through and had a couple of drinks and a frame or two on the snooker table. Two o'clock and sober, that was me. I wanted to look half-decent the following morning and I wanted to be sure I'd remember every second of it.

I got back to my room and started fretting about my speech. I knew I wanted to thank Mum and Dad for everything, Lynne and Joanne too, to thank Jackie and Tony and Victoria's brother and sister for making me so welcome into their family: Christian had turned into something like the brother I'd always wanted to have. And then to talk about Victoria who, by this stage in the proceedings, would have become my wife. I was starting to think that finding the right words to describe what I really felt might just have to wait for a glass of champagne and the spur of the moment. I rang Peregrine:

'Sorry, Peregrine. My speech. I'm still not sure I'm saying what I want to. Or if I'm saying it the right way.'

He was still awake or, at least, pretended he was:

'No problem. I'll be right up.'

Five minutes later, I was standing at the end of my bed and Peregrine had pulled a chair up in front of me:

'Go on, then. Let me hear it and I can give you a few pointers. I'll be the audience.'

I was a bit embarrassed but he assured me I would be on the day too, so this was good practice. Almost as soon as I started, he was clearing his throat loudly and coughing. As I ploughed on, he started throwing in comments like:

Above left to right:
'Where's yesterday's
United result?'

Last call for Barcelona…

The Nou Camp wasn't
just about sightseeing.

Right: At least I knew who
Terry Venables was.

Below: Barca's star Brits,
including Steve Archibald, Mark
Hughes and Gary Lineker, with
three Bobby Charlton Soccer
Skills prize-winners.

Far left: Top class. My PE teacher at Chingford High, the late John Bullock.

Left: Home from home. With United landlady Eve Cody.

Below: The family, silver. Celebrating United's 1996 Double with Victoria, sister Joanne and Mum and Dad.

Top: Something special. United's
1992 FA Youth Cup winning team.
I'm in the front row, second left.

Above: Wedding Day for Lynne
and Colin, October 1999.

It must be love.

Right: Pride and joy.
Brooklyn and Romeo.

Above: My England debut, against Moldova in Kishinev, 1 September 1996.

Right: Celebrating with The King, Eric Cantona.

Far right: 1997 PFA Young Player of the Year, with other award winners Alan Shearer and Peter Beardsley.

Bottom: 'We'll have you, Beckham.' Upton Park 1998.

Right: 'I've made a big mistake here.' Saint Etienne, World Cup 1998.

Far right: Off. Physio Gary Lewin ushers me past manager Glenn Hoddle on the England bench.

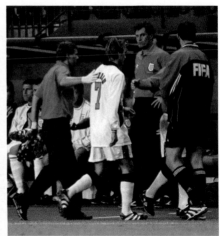

A couple of Reds.
Me and Gary Neville.

'That's not very funny.'

He started rattling his chair: anything, really, to try to throw me out of my stride. He knew the speech was going to be all right: we changed a couple of things but I didn't even use my script on the day. He was just trying to give me an idea of how standing up there, doing it in front of an audience, might feel. By the time Peregrine had finished giving me a hard time, I was ready for bed. At least I'd had some help. The Best Man, Gary Neville, had had to sweat through it all on his own.

The next morning, I was pacing about in the corridor getting myself nervous about what lay ahead. I found myself outside Gary's room and I could hear talking. He couldn't be on the phone: there wasn't one in the room. The stone walls of the castle meant he'd be lucky to get decent reception on his mobile. I couldn't help wondering what he was up to. I opened the door as quietly as I could. Gary was standing there in front of the mirror, holding a can of deodorant in front of his face like a microphone, practicing his speech. I knew how he was feeling, of course, after the time I'd had the night before. But I burst out laughing anyway. Gary did too. It was going to be a big day all round. I realised how seriously he was taking it when the manicurist arrived. And I was honoured: Gaz had waited for my wedding day to get his nails done for the first time in his life.

The guests who'd been invited for the ceremony in the folly were starting to arrive. It was the proper thing, and gave me something to think about other than how nervous I was. I got ready and went down to the main reception to say hello. Melanie, Emma and Mel B from the Spice Girls, were almost the first to get there. They've always been lovely with me, even though I get a bit shy when I'm around them. At least, with the Girls, I didn't have to force myself to make the conversation. They took care of that. They seemed as excited as I was, wanting to know everything that was going on. Mum and Dad were there, too, just to keep my feet on the ground.

Usually, the Best Man drives, doesn't he? I'd decided I wasn't having that. I'm the world's worst passenger anyway and, although it was only two minutes from the castle to the folly, I reckoned that would be enough for Gary to take us off into the mud. What's more, the groom's car was a Bentley Continental. I wasn't going to miss driving that. I was paying for it, after all. We drove down and I saw the inside of the folly for the very first time. You could hear helicopters spinning overhead, looking for pictures but, once you'd walked up these mossy, old steps and through the doorway, the sound of the stream running underneath us drowned everything else out. It was like stepping into the pages of a fairy tale: little lights twinkling above us, red roses everywhere, ivy creeping up the walls and the scent of a forest floor. Victoria had planned all this down to the last detail and it was beautiful. I gulped back the first lump in my throat of the day.

The Bishop of Cork, who was performing the ceremony, was already there, dressed in his deep purple robes. He was a lovely man. And a mad Manchester United fan, of course. He actually arranged for the folly to be blessed so that the wedding could take place inside it. There are twelve bishops in Ireland and, since our marriage, the other eleven have nicknamed the Bishop of Cork 'Purple Spice'. I stood in front of the altar that Peregrine had made out of branches and twigs, while everyone else made their way inside. A violin and a harp were playing. It was perfect and peaceful and I could feel myself shaking like a leaf. Sweating, too: it was really warm in there. I looked around: our families were all there, aunts, uncles, my Nan and Grandad, the Girls, my mate Dave Gardner, Gary Neville's mum and dad; just a couple of dozen people in all. And all of us expectant, waiting. I heard another car pull up outside the folly: Victoria.

I was wobbling, even before I saw her. There was a swell in the music. *I'm going, here.*

Tony, Victoria's dad, walked in. *That's it. I've gone.*

And Victoria stepped inside. I looked around. I had Brooklyn in my arms and I could feel my own eyes pricking. As I turned, the first person I saw was Emma Bunton. She was in floods of tears and, of course, that was all I needed to set me off. I was sniffing away; someone had to hand me a tissue. And then I saw Victoria. I married her because I love everything about her: the looks – the legs – her personality, her sense of humour. She was the person I felt I knew and understood better than anybody I'd ever met. We were always meant for each other. But, in those moments as she walked through the folly towards the altar, I saw somebody completely different. It was one of the most incredible experiences of my life and very difficult to put into words. It was like seeing this amazing person fresh, for the first time all over again. Was it the dress? The setting? The fact that we were about to become man and wife? Victoria was everything I knew – and knew I wanted – but she suddenly seemed much more than all that, too. I thought I knew how I felt about her but I wasn't prepared at all for how I was feeling right at that instant. Victoria was more beautiful than I'd ever realised or could have imagined.

No question, you could have wrung that tissue out. Victoria came up alongside me and I couldn't help myself. I leaned over and kissed her. The bride looked at me, as if to say:

'We rehearsed this last night and I don't think you were meant to do that.'

The ceremony started and everything was fine until we got to the point of actually saying: 'I do'. Then, the pair of us went. Voices started trembling, the tears started trickling again: both of us this time.

We kept our wedding outfits on for the reception when everybody else arrived. Only Elton John and partner David Furnish weren't able to make it on the day. Elton had actually said he'd sing at the reception, but he got taken ill on the morning of the wedding. We missed them but it was the kind of situation where we were more worried about Elton's health than we were about them not making the wedding, and I think Elton was more worried about letting us down than he was about how rough he was feeling. As it was, we were just happy it didn't turn out to be anything serious.

There were nearly 300 friends and relations present for the meal in the marquee. It's a wonderful feeling looking out across a room and seeing so many of the people who've meant something in your life, all together and enjoying themselves. We ate but, just before the desserts, Victoria and I went to change. I loved my suit and would probably have kept it on but Victoria didn't have much choice. Part of her gown was a corset that had been made for her by someone called Mr Pearl, this amazing little guy who wore a corset himself every day and even had a rib removed to make his waist seem slimmer. By this point, Victoria's outfit was starting to get really uncomfortable so we went up, with Brooklyn, to the wedding suite and put on clothes for the rest of the evening.

We had these thrones for ourselves – and a high chair for the boy to match – which were up at the top table. The whole thing was tongue-in-cheek, of course: we were at a castle, weren't we? And the pair of us were Lord and Lady of the Manor for the day. Our little squire had a purple suit of his own and looked fantastic in it. I think he took to it like I had taken to my pageboy outfit at another Beckham family wedding all those years ago. The moment we got ourselves settled back in at the reception, though, Brooklyn decided he'd eaten something he didn't fancy and threw up all over himself and me. You can always count on your kids to make sure nobody's in danger of taking things too seriously.

Wiping sick off myself and Brooklyn was just the right preparation for the speeches.

Thanks to my son, and to Peregrine, I think I got away with mine. The only joke afterwards was that, every few minutes, I'd seemed to find myself saying:

'Well, ladies and gentlemen, I'd like to start by saying . . .'

Tony's speech was next and was just right: really loving. It was lump in the throat time again for Victoria and for me. I think he understood just how we felt ourselves.

'David and Victoria grew up fifteen minutes away from each other. Even though they never met, so much about their backgrounds and upbringings have been the same. They've both tried to make something of themselves and worked hard at their own lives. When Victoria was going off to dancing school, David was going off to football practice. They've each worked really hard to achieve what they have. And now they're really lucky to have found each other after all this time.'

And then, to Gary: without me knowing, my best man had asked Victoria to lend him one of her sarongs. By the time we got to his speech, everybody had had enough wine to be right in the mood. I didn't have a clue what he was going to say. Or do. It was a good start, anyway, him standing up wearing this sarong. Gary was really funny, although maybe the funniest thing of all was by accident. Every time he cracked a joke, he forgot to take the microphone away from in front of his mouth. What happened to all that practice with the can of Sure? It meant you could hear

Gary giggling away to himself at his own jokes. He was as nervous as I'd been, but Gary was great. The whole day was.

Although we'd borrowed Peregrine's nanny for the night, Victoria and I took Brooklyn up to get him ready for bed. We went back downstairs and through into the tent where the party was going to carry on: there were cushions and pillows and drapes everywhere, this very oriental, kind of Indonesian, setting. The bride and groom, of course, had to have the first dance of the evening together, while people drifted through after the meal. Then, for a couple of hours, it was a chance to go round and say hello to everybody, catch up and have pictures taken before, at the stroke of midnight, everybody came outside for a big fireworks display. Which was amazing: even Victoria and I didn't know exactly what to expect. They were perfect: the spectacular treat to top off our perfect day.

I was so happy, so proud: content as I'd never been before in my life. Victoria and I were thrilled to be Mister and Missus. And when you're feeling like we were, you assume everybody else will be equally delighted. After all, in the world of football, managers are usually pleased to see their players marry and settle down. But during those first days and weeks after our wedding, it seemed I might be destined to be the exception that proved the rule.

Pre-season training was round the corner and, like any new husband, I was keen on a honeymoon. The first-team squad was split up anyway: most of the lads were off to Australia on tour, whereas the England contingent, who'd trained earlier in the summer on international duty, had a little extra time off. Maybe it was a mistake, but I asked if I could have a couple days more so that Victoria and I could spend a week abroad together. Actually, I didn't ask; my agent, Tony Stephens, did. He was seeing the United chairman, Martin Edwards, on business. They'd talked about the wedding and Tony mentioned that I'd love the couple of extra days to make going somewhere exotic worthwhile. We didn't fancy getting on a plane and then having to turn round at the other end to come straight back. Martin Edwards didn't think there'd be a problem with that but, when the gaffer got to hear about it, it sounded to him as if I'd tried to go behind his back. He wasn't best pleased and let me know about it. Never mind the blast down the phone, I had to settle for a whirlwind of a honeymoon and then report back – before the other England lads turned up and while the rest of the first team were on the other side of the world – to train with the reserves.

We might have only recently won the Treble. We might have been going into a new season believing we could do it again. But never mind all that: the gaffer was going to make sure that nobody started taking anything for granted. He was probably trying to bring me back down to earth: I'd just lived through the most amazing six months of my life, feeling like things couldn't be going any better, at Old Trafford or at home. If he'd asked me, I'd have told the boss I didn't need the knock he gave me at the start of pre-season. I suppose it's always been part of how things are done at United: any hint of anybody getting above themselves and someone – a team-mate, a member of staff or the gaffer himself – was there to knock you down again. I didn't think it was right, but I understood why the boss had reacted the way he did. As always, he was doing what he thought was best for the team. There was only one thing for me to do: knuckle down and get on with it.

Since that amazing semi-final against Arsenal, the team had felt invincible: we went into every single game sure that we'd win it. And that confidence rolled on into the new 1999/2000 season. We made a great start and, for the next nine months, hardly looked back. Even the odd defeat – I remember we got turned over 5–0 at Chelsea – didn't stop the momentum. How happy I was at home somehow made me even happier to be playing football – for United and for England, too. After France 98, even at the lowest of times, I hadn't ever wondered about continuing to play for my country. Whatever other people were saying, I was proud to be an international footballer and I'd never thought about stopping even if that might have been a way of easing the pressure on me. My only doubts were about whether, in the long run, I had an England future under Glenn Hoddle. I always had the feeling that he'd have looked for a way, sooner or later, to leave me out of his plans.

Back in the autumn of 1998, we'd made a pretty poor start to qualifying for the next European Championships. England supporters weren't happy and some of the media seemed to be campaigning for a change of manager. Even so, when that change happened, and the way it happened, came as a real shock. I don't know how much of it all was Glenn's fault and how much he was stitched up by the press. When I first heard that he'd been quoted talking about disabled people and their past lives, I knew straight away it was going to turn into something huge. Overnight, it seemed that everybody, including the Prime Minister, was having a say on it. Once they're in the headlines, stories move so quickly that no one really has a chance to think. At the start of February, just a few days after the interview had been published, Glenn was gone. There was a crazy press conference to announce it at the FA, where one England fan had to be dragged out kicking and screaming. Despite the fact I'd had real differences with him as England manager, I knew that must have been a very hard afternoon for Glenn.

Howard Wilkinson came in as caretaker manager for a couple

of friendlies. When the FA made their permanent appointment, they couldn't have picked anyone more different than the man who'd gone before. I'd always admired the way Kevin Keegan's teams played and enjoyed listening to him talking about football. I respected his passion and his honesty. I was really excited, joining up with England for the first time with him as manager, for a qualifier against Poland at Wembley. I've always thought that, in a perfect world, it would be good to be able to combine Hoddle's strengths with Keegan's. Glenn is a very good coach who, I think, struggles with relating to some players. Kevin is an absolutely fantastic man manager. Right from the start of our first sessions at Bisham Abbey ahead of that Poland game, Kevin's enthusiasm lifted everyone. He inspired you about what you could do as an England player. Come the Saturday and a beautiful Spring day at Wembley, everyone was up for it. The fans were up for it as well. Scholesy got a hat-trick and we just blew Poland away. I don't think there was anyone in the country who didn't think Kevin was the right man for the England job and all it took was that 3–1 win to convince him to take it on full-time.

There was a great atmosphere around the England camp under Kevin but it was hard work getting to Euro 2000: we ended up having to play off against Scotland. We won 2–0 at Hampden Park on the Saturday but then, at Wembley the following Wednesday, Don Hutchison scored for them before half-time and, to be honest, by the end we were hanging on. The important thing, though, was to have qualified. We had six months to forget about how we'd done it and concentrate, instead, on putting things right in time for the Championships. I thought we'd be okay and I had faith in Kevin as England manager. By the time we were squeezing past Scotland, I'd found good reason to put my absolute trust in him as a man, too.

In mid-October 1999, we had one week to play two Euro 2000 qualifiers. We played Luxembourg at Wembley and then four days later, on the Wednesday, we took on Poland in Warsaw. I was in my room at the England hotel on the Friday night before the first of what were going to be two really important games for England. My mobile rang. It was Victoria, calling from her mum and dad's. She'd have known, the night before a game, that the hotel wouldn't have been allowed to put her through to my room. It didn't help that the line wasn't great but, in amongst the hisses and crackles, I heard what I needed to. The police had been in contact about a tip-off they'd received. They believed someone was going to try and kidnap Victoria and Brooklyn the following day, while I was at Wembley, playing football for England. Suddenly, it was like feeling everything was slipping away from beneath me. *What do I do? Who do I tell?* It probably didn't help Victoria that I was so shocked, hardly able to take in what she'd told me. I didn't know what to say, other than:

'I'll call you straight back.'

The first person I spoke to was Gary Neville. Without even thinking about it, his reaction was:

'You've got to tell the manager. Go and see Kevin.'

I made my way through the hotel to his room. I knocked on the door and went in. I'm sure Kevin could see for himself something was wrong. I was shaking; I felt sick. I could hardly find the breath for it but I told him what had happened. The first thing Kevin did was let me know he understood what I felt like which, when you've lost control like I had, is the first thing you need to hear.

'David, I've been in a situation like this. When I was playing in Germany, me and my wife had death threats made against us. I know this is horrible. We need to go to where your wife and son are. We'll go together. We'll sort this out.'

It was ten o'clock at night by now. In minutes, we were outside the hotel in a car – me, Kevin and Ray Whitworth, England's team security officer – and I was calling Victoria to tell her we were on our way. We drove to Tony and Jackie's. As soon as we walked in, although he'd never met Victoria or her parents, Kevin took control of the situation. He knew me and could see for himself the state Victoria was in: we needed him to be calm and know the right thing to do.

'The best place to be is our hotel. We've got the whole place booked to ourselves. We've our own security. Nobody's getting in. Pack a bag. Get Brooklyn. David and I will go back now, sort the rooms out, and we'll meet you there as soon as you're ready.'

Tony and Jackie came, too. Kevin had been just brilliant when we needed him most. He'd done it all without even thinking twice about it, even though there was a game the following afternoon. Never mind his qualities as a manager. This was Kevin doing his best for us just because he could, not because he felt he had to. I'll never forget his attitude to that situation that night: none of us could have been in surer, safer hands than Kevin's. We had a good relationship before it happened and, obviously, we still do now. He would have done what he did, though, for any of the England players. In fact I really believe that, if Kevin had found himself in those same circumstances and able to help, he'd have done what he did for anybody at all. He's a great man.

Victoria and Brooklyn slept in my room. The next morning, all Kevin was concerned about was what I felt I should do.

'David, I understand what you went through last night. If you want to play, that's great: I want you to. If you don't feel sure about it, that's fine too. I want you to make your own mind up. You know how you feel. Do whatever you think is right.'

I played and we beat Luxembourg 6–0. That meant the game

in Poland in the week would decide our fate in the qualifiers. It was a huge game and Kevin was under all sorts of pressure to get the right result. Even so, on the Sunday night before we left, we had the same conversation again.

'If you need to be close by your family, don't worry. You don't have to come over there with us. You can stay here if you need to and look after Victoria and Brooklyn.'

I sat down with Victoria and asked what she thought would be best. My instinct was to stay but she saw the situation for what it was.

'We'll be all right. We've got people to look out for us now. This is your job. It's England. You should go.'

I did; and Victoria was right. It was what I needed to do, even though the game in Warsaw was horrible and ended up being a 0–0 draw. It meant we had to wait a couple of months for the result of a Sweden game, when they beat Poland at home, before we knew we'd made it through to that play-off against the Scots.

By Christmas 1999, things had been decided and, even though it hadn't been spectacular, England would be going to the European Championships the following summer. New Year 2000, meanwhile, and United were heading off to the other side of the world. As European Cup holders, the club were asked to participate in the first-ever FIFA World Club Championships in Brazil. No question that it was an honour, good for United and good for the reputation of English club football. The catch was that it was scheduled to take place in Brazil in January. Beforehand, the whole thing turned into a storm, especially when the news broke that, because we'd be out of the country on the weekend of the third round games, the FA had decided to let United miss the whole of the 1999/2000 season's FA Cup.

It was an argument in which everybody in football wanted to

have a say. Everyone knows that the FA Cup is a fantastic tournament, the oldest knockout competition in the world. It was said that because United, as the holders, weren't going to be in it, all its tradition and credibility were going to go out the window. It was special treatment for one club at the expense of everybody else. Sometimes it felt like the issue was just being used as an excuse to have a pop at United. I don't see we could have done anything else in the circumstances. I think everybody knew we had to go. Even if the new tournament was an inconvenience, it was a world event – a FIFA competition – and to knock it back wouldn't just have damaged us. It would have damaged English football.

To be honest, it was something we talked about in the United dressing room as much as everyone else did outside Old Trafford. We were looking forward to going to Brazil, looking forward to playing clubs from all over the world. But nobody was happy about missing out on the FA Cup. Think back to that semi-final against Arsenal the previous season and the final against Newcastle: those games, and that competition, meant so much to us. It didn't feel right not to defend the trophy. Perhaps we could have been given a bye through to the fourth round while we were away and then joined in when we came back, I don't know. That was for the FA and the club to sort out. When it came down to it, it wasn't up to us: it had been decided, we were going, and that was that. You grow up with the routine of the English football season and, just at the time you're usually getting ready for giant-killings, heavy pitches and the worst of the weather, we were headed off to sunshine, beaches and 100-degree heat.

I don't know about anybody else, but I don't regret the experience at all. Despite what happened to me personally and despite the fact that the tournament itself has been long forgotten about since, I wouldn't have missed it. For a start, it did us a lot of good as a team, being away together for that length of time and getting recharged for the rest of the season back home. We'd have won the Premiership anyway, I think, but we did come back from Brazil in pretty good nick. And with half-decent tans as well. As things turned out, it really was like a holiday for me. I got sent off in our first game, against Necaxa of Mexico, which meant I missed the next one and then played just twenty minutes of the last one, against South Melbourne, by which time we were already out of the tournament.

It was a horrible feeling, getting a red card for the first time as a United player. I went into a challenge for a high, bouncing ball just near the halfway line. I didn't go into the tackle with any intention other than winning the ball, so when the ref said I was off I was shocked more than anything else. I've seen it on video since and I must admit that, on telly, it looked a bad challenge. I didn't think it was, though, and I was relieved that the gaffer didn't either. He was really angry after the game: not with me but with the match officials. I think the way their player reacted had a lot to do with why I was sent off. I probably should have been more aware that we were in South America and that, perhaps, things weren't quite the same over there. I was absolutely crushed by it that evening, although I have to admit that, within a few days, lounging by the pool while the rest of the lads were confined to their hotel rooms before the game against Vasco da Gama, I didn't feel quite so disappointed about how things had worked out.

Being in Brazil was fantastic. I remember one evening wandering down to Copacabana Beach on my own. You hear about it but it's beyond anything you'd ever imagine without being there. The beach just stretched away for what seemed like miles. There were goalposts and little sets of floodlights planted along the whole length of it. And, as far as the eye could see, kids – thousands of them – out playing football on the sand. No wonder Brazil are world champions. All these youngsters were either playing games or doing tricks, like keepie-uppy and head tennis or showing off flicks and turns in twos and threes. The level of natural ability was unbelievable. A couple of them recognised me and asked me to take some free-kicks while their mates went in goal. If football's got a soul, that's where it lives: on that beach. I'll never forget my evening out there with those kids.

Brazil in January was hot. Great weather for a holiday or a walk by the sea at night. But for playing competitive football? I think it was a lesson for all of us. People laugh about the English going abroad, what we're like in the sun. When it came to United in Rio at the World Club Championship, the jokes weren't far wrong. The first time we arrived at the Maracana stadium, we were already sweating from the walk from the coach to the front door. We walked into the changing room and I remember some of the lads were actually in the middle of a conversation about how hot it was. Next thing, everybody's gone quiet. Standing there in the middle of the room were seven beds with oxygen masks hanging down. I don't think any of us knew what to say. *What were we in for here?*

When we went out to warm up – is that the right phrase, at one o'clock in the afternoon and in temperatures of over 100 degrees? – Albert Morgan, the United kit man, had fitted us out in our regular gear. The Mexicans were jogging around in vests. We ran out wearing black training tops, all trying to head for the tiny patches of shade by the touchlines under the stands. Albert's great, but we gave him stick about that afternoon for a long time afterwards. None of us will ever forget those thirteen days in Brazil. It was an honour to play for the club there and to meet some of the people: the kids on Copacabana Beach and other youngsters, in youth projects up in the *favelas*, the slums, that we visited while we were in Rio, representing United and enjoying the privilege of learning about other people's lives for ourselves.

We came back feeling great. As good a time as I'd had, I couldn't wait to see Victoria and Brooklyn. I couldn't wait to get back to some mud, wind and rain either, to get on with the rest of the season. We might not have had the FA Cup to look forward to but, while we'd been away, no other team had been able to catch up on our lead: the Premiership was there to be won. And we were still in the Champions League. The first game back was against Arsenal at Old Trafford and they almost caught us cold. We ended up drawing 1–1, though, and it was a game they maybe needed to win more than we did. From then on, it felt like we were just picking up where we'd left off. I was so relaxed and enjoying my football so much, why would I have stopped to think what might upset the roll we were on? There was a kind of ambush waiting for me, of course, but I'd not have been any better pre-pared for dealing with it even if I'd somehow seen it coming.

On Saturday 12 February we took a 3–0 hiding at Newcastle. That didn't help the gaffer's – or anybody else's – mood over the following week, as we built up to another big game that weekend, away to Leeds. As with players at most clubs when there's not a midweek game, we were given some time off: I was down at the house in London, planning to drive back on the Wednesday night for training on Thursday morning. During the day, Brooklyn was really unwell. With a first child, maybe there's an extra intensity to your feelings about things because you don't recognise symptoms: everything to do with being a parent is new, after all. Maybe now, with Romeo, I'd not have worried like I did back then. By around seven that Wednesday evening, though, Brooklyn was running a fever and had gone all floppy. I was holding him in my lap and just getting no reaction from him. We didn't know what was going on: any mum or dad will know how scary that is. By the time the doctor had been and told us Brooklyn had gastro-enteritis, I'd already made the decision to stay at home for the night and get driven to Manchester early the following morning.

Brooklyn was so rough and I hated seeing him like that. When we eventually got him off to sleep – who knows what time of the night it was by then? – I stayed in his room and slept for a few hours on the bed next to his cot. I woke up and got away by six the next morning: the plan was I'd be able to sleep a bit more in the back of the car on the drive north. But I couldn't get my boy out of my mind: how sick he'd been and how wrong it felt to be leaving him and Victoria behind. Victoria had said I should go, that Brooklyn would be fine, but all my instincts were telling me that my place was at home with them, at least until I knew for sure Brooklyn was going to be all right. I needed to see an improvement in him for myself. Twenty minutes up the motorway, I asked the driver to turn round. And, to be honest, even if I'd known what the consequences were going to be, I'd still have made that same decision.

I rang United to try and speak to Steve McClaren. I'd only ever missed one day of training before in nine years as a pro and was sure that, if I explained, the club would understand. I couldn't get through to Steve so I left a message:

'Brooklyn's really struggling. Is it all right if I don't come in? I think I should stay with him.'

No one called back.

In hindsight, the one thing I should have said on that message was that I was calling from London, as opposed to Manchester. The tension between me and the gaffer over my family life, though, made me guess that just mentioning London would have been enough, on its own, to infuriate him. By ten, Brooklyn had woken up and was obviously much better. Within an hour I was back in the car, on my way to Manchester. I rang Steve and got through to him. It was about midday, when the lads finished training, and I asked him if I should come into Carrington that afternoon to do some work on my own. Steve told me I didn't need to:

'But, David, I should tell you: the manager's not happy.'

I didn't think I'd done anything wrong but, of course, now on the phone to Steve wasn't the time to talk about that. I thought, anyway, that by the following morning everything would have smoothed itself out. I was wrong.

I got into training on the Friday morning and Steve McClaren told me the boss was angry and wanted me to go and see him. I got on with training, assuming I'd talk to the gaffer afterwards. Instead, while we were in the middle of a possession routine, he came storming over, said something to Steve and then shouted at me:

'Beckham. Here. I want a word.'

Suddenly, I'm in the middle of a row with the Manchester United manager in front of the entire first-team squad. I tried to stand my ground but the boss wasn't having any of it:

'Go and train with the reserves.'

In front of the other lads, that was a huge insult: a huge blow to anyone's self-esteem, especially someone who didn't think he'd done anything to provoke it. I refused and said I'd go back inside the Carrington complex. I walked back across the training pitches, went to the changing room, got dressed and walked out to my car. Something made me stop, though. *It's a big game on Saturday. Don't make things worse. Be professional about this.*

I went back inside, got changed again and went into the gym

to work on my own. After about half an hour, Roy Keane came through on his way back to the dressing room. I wasn't sure what was going on or how I should be reacting. I asked Roy what he thought I should do. He said it straight out:

'You should go and talk to the manager.'

It was what Roy would have done himself. I should have ignored his advice. I went to the gaffer's office, knocked on the door and walked into the biggest dressing down I've ever had in my career. As he saw it, I had my priorities all wrong. I apologised for feeling how I did about the situation but I didn't back down.

'It's not that I didn't want to be here at work but, as I see it, my first priority has to be my family. My son was ill and that's why I missed training.'

The boss thought differently:

'Your responsibilities are here at the club, not at home with your son.'

Don't get me wrong: I could see the gaffer's point of view, with the whole club to think about at an important time in the season, even if I didn't agree with him. What really tipped a big argument over into becoming a blazing row was a photo in that day's papers of Victoria at a charity function on the Thursday night: the evening after the morning I'd missed training. By tea-time, Brooklyn had been back to his usual self and Victoria had decided, while he slept, to honour a long-standing commitment which meant her being away from the house for a couple of hours. That wasn't how the boss saw it, though:

'You were babysitting while your wife was out gallivanting.'

That word: gallivanting. It was the sneering tone I thought came with it that made me flip:

'Don't talk about my wife like that. How would you feel if I was disrespectful like that about your wife?'

I should have waited before going to see him. I'd expected him to be angry with me. I hadn't expected that I'd lose my temper as well. He told me not to report for the Leeds game, not to meet up with the rest of the team.

I went back downstairs, got changed again and left. I couldn't believe that the boss would leave me out at Elland Road because of all this. But that's exactly what he did. I turned up later in the day as I usually would have done, hoping things would blow over. I travelled with everyone to Leeds overnight and the boss announced the team – without me in it – at the hotel the following morning. When we got to the ground he announced the substitutes: I wasn't even on the bench. By then, the whole thing had come out in the papers and there were photographs of me sitting in the stands that afternoon, watching us win 1–0. Thinking back, it seemed as if the publicity surrounding the situation was what really wound things up. I just wonder whether it was the pictures of me coming away from the training ground that Friday, and the stories that came out with them, which forced the gaffer's hand and made him follow through with the threat to drop me. Might things have been different if the whole business had been taken care of in private?

After the Leeds game, I was away on international duty. When we got back to Manchester, I sat down with the boss, Steve McClaren and Gary Neville to sort things out. That meeting, at least, was out of the public eye, which I'm sure helped us put things straight. After everybody had had their say, the gaffer summed it up:

'Let's forget this now. Let's get on with things, eh?'

I was genuinely relieved. The boss was the last person in the world I wanted to fall out with. Not just because he's scary when he loses his rag; not just because it could mean me missing games.

As far as my football career was concerned, the gaffer was the man who'd made everything possible for me: from day one of my time at Manchester United, he was the father figure in what had become a second family for me. Old Trafford had been home now for almost as long as Mum and Dad's had before it. No matter how angry or hurt I might be about how he was treating me, I understood everything the boss did was motivated by his wanting to do the best for United. And I knew how much he'd done for me personally, as a player and a person, since I'd arrived at Old Trafford as a boy. Maybe how important my relationship with the gaffer was to me was the reason feelings ran so high.

That afternoon, after training, I was shopping at the Trafford Centre. As I came away from the shops to get back in the car, my phone rang. It was the boss:

'Where the hell are you?'

'Eh?'

'Where the hell are you?'

'I'm in my car.'

'Don't lie to me. You're in Barcelona, aren't you?'

I nearly laughed out loud:

'I'm in my car. I'm just driving out of the Trafford Centre.'

The gaffer wasn't having any of it:

'My mate has seen you at Barcelona airport.'

What could I say? I described the car park at the Trafford Centre, told him which shops I'd been in. There was a long silence:

'OK. Goodbye.'

I found out later that, five minutes before he rang me, the boss had rung Gary to find out where I was and tell him what he'd heard. Because of what had been talked about at the meeting earlier that same morning, Gary had put the phone down and just thought to himself:

'Dave, after all that's gone on, please don't be in Spain.'

It was such a weird sting in the tale. I couldn't believe we'd had the conversation. The boss knows people all over Manchester, knows everything that's going on with the players. People must tell him things they say they've seen or heard all the time: someone had just told him I'd got off a plane in Barcelona. The problem with those stories is that they must really wind the boss up, whether they're true or not, which doesn't help me or whoever else the stories are about. I don't think I could have lived my life better from a professional point of view: looking after myself, being careful about things like drinking and staying out late. When I went down to London to see family and friends, I never let the travelling get in the way of my job. For a game on a Saturday, Wednesday evening would be the absolute latest I'd ever be driving back to Manchester. The rumours, though, which had led to the row I hoped we'd just seen the back of, had made the gaffer believe I was up and down the motorway every other day. He wasn't annoyed with me for the sake of it – I knew that – but because he genuinely believed the life I led away from football was interfering with what really mattered: winning games for United. And nothing I could say could convince him he was wrong. I could do something, though, to try and set things straight: play.

We were flying. The World Club Championship had been a break from the intensity of the Premiership and I think we came back feeling really strong. I won my place in the team back after the Leeds game and, between then and the end of the season, we drew two games and won the rest in the League. We finished champions, 18 points ahead of Arsenal, and the gap at the top said it all. We'd only lost three games all year and nobody else had been able to live with that. Obviously, going to Brazil had meant we couldn't defend the FA Cup. The season's biggest disappointment, as it turned out, was that we didn't defend the Champions League either. Our experience in Europe meant we'd learned how to get through the group phase even if we lost the odd game or didn't play at our best in others. Once you get to the knockout stages, though, it's different: real cup football and against some of the best teams in the world. In the quarter-finals in 2000, we were drawn against Real Madrid.

The first leg at the Santiago Bernabeu, we drew 0–0. They played some great football but we had the chances to win – you always get chances against Real – and played well. An away goal that night in Spain would have made all the difference. As it was we were really looking forward to getting them back to Old Trafford. We thought we could beat them. So did our supporters. So did the press. Real Madrid didn't. This was before the days of Zidane, Figo and Ronaldo but Real had great players – I think the boss said he thinks that Raul is the best there is anywhere in the world – and they scored great goals in Manchester and beat us before we really got going. There was no shame in losing to them. They went on to win the competition after all. But we were shattered. We had our chances but didn't take them.

It was a little like the first half of our game in Madrid in 2003: they had this spell, for fifteen minutes after half-time at Old Trafford, when everything they did seemed to come off and we couldn't get near them. I remember their left-sided midfield player, Redondo, the Argentinian, did this unbelievable dragback to take the ball past Henning Berg. He crossed and Raul just had a tap-in. It was brilliant. We'd lost one goal in the first half, then Raul got his two and, before even an hour of the game had gone – a game that we'd never felt out of – we were 3–0 down. We came back in the last half hour: I scored, Scholesy got a penalty, but they held on and we were out.

It didn't make up for being beaten but I was pleased about my goal that night. I'd skipped away from Roberto Carlos and arrowed one into the top corner. I've played against him a few times, for United against Real and for England against Brazil. Everybody talks about how great Roberto Carlos is going forward but, that night especially, he proved he could defend too. He's the best left-back in football. People say that he leaves space behind him because he bombs forward all the time, but the bloke can give people five- and ten-yard starts and still get back to get his tackle in. I always loved games against him: if it was Roberto Carlos, then it was either Real Madrid or Brazil. You knew you and your team-mates were up against just about the best in the world.

After going out of Europe, the important thing was not to sit around feeling sorry for ourselves, however desperate we'd been to prove ourselves by winning the European Cup again. I think one of our strengths, and something that always set United apart, is how we reacted to a defeat. It's a special spirit: during games, the team doesn't know when it's beaten. And when we did lose a game, however big the disappointment, you knew everybody would be back next match to make up for it. It's the same spirit that fires up United teams to go on the kind of long unbeaten runs, like in 1999/2000, that win championships. The gaffer has a lot to do with it. The coaching staff at United, as far back as Nobby Stiles and Eric Harrison, have always been able to inspire that attitude, too. Even in youth cup and 'A' team football, we always seemed to have the ability to come back from low points, in the course of individual games and after we'd suffered defeats.

You could call it stubbornness. We finished 1999/2000 as Premiership Champions. The unwillingness to settle for second best, that intensity and desire: they're in the make-up of the club. At United, a professional attitude ran through everything we did.

Whatever the secret was, I think it was particularly strong, particularly obvious, amongst the group that grew up together in the nineties: me, the Nevilles, Paul Scholes, Ryan Giggs and Nicky Butt. Roy Keane used to wind us up, laughing about the 'Class of '92', but, of all people, he's the kind of player who recognises when the other players in a team are up for the battle.

There was a sense of togetherness amongst us that I don't think you could ever buy or recreate. It grew over time because we'd all been at United together for so long. We had complete faith in each other. None of us got carried away as individuals. The last thing we'd ever do was let one another down. And one thing was always the same: we lived for playing football – playing football for Manchester United. In recent years, especially since we missed out on winning any trophies in 2002, some pundits and even some United supporters started talking about the time when it might be best to break up the 'Class of '92'. Obviously, I've now had to leave that group behind, but as for the others, I genuinely believe the club would risk losing something – a spirit, a United spirit – that's been very important to its success. It's something not many clubs have; and it's something that might be impossible for Manchester United ever to replace.

The Germans

9

'Go out and enjoy yourselves ...
We're a better team.'

It doesn't seem to matter that football is a team game. When things go wrong, someone always has to take the blame. Take England, for example: in the World Cup, it was me in 1998 and Dave Seaman in 2002. At the European Championships in 2000, Phil Neville was the player who was made scapegoat for us not matching up to the public's expectations. For the media and for some supporters, it seems there always has to be a hero or a villain. I'm not saying that people don't have every right to have their opinions about the England team. Sometimes I wonder, though, whether they realise that what they say or write about us does get through. Footballers may tell you they don't read the papers or listen to the radio but, believe me, we know when we're getting stick and, however strong we try to be, it leaves a mark on our confidence and attitude.

Of course, picking out – or picking on – an individual isn't just something that happens when it comes to international football. There was a spell in the autumn of 2002 when United weren't doing as well as we knew we should be. There were all sorts of reasons for that, to do with injuries, suspensions and the team as a whole taking a dip in confidence and concentration. I was having my own problems, which I'll come to later on. Some people seemed to decide it was all Ryan Giggs' fault. Nobody in the dressing room, players or staff, saw it that way. But a section of the Old Trafford crowd weren't happy and, naturally, the papers and the radio phone-ins picked up on that. It came as all the more of a surprise to the players, and I'm sure to Ryan himself, because United supporters have been fantastic down the years, and especially loyal and encouraging to the home-grown boys.

As soon as it became a big story, most United fans got behind Giggsy. He might have been experiencing a dip in form, but no one with any idea about football thinks he's anything but a world-class player. And, more to the point, no one with any feel for United would even begin to question an amazing career at the club just because the team as a whole wasn't firing like it should. I wouldn't, for a minute, say supporters don't have the right to speak their mind about United; after all, they pay the players' wages and those of everybody else working at Old Trafford. The players have to live up to the fans' highest expectations of them, it's their job. Having a go at one player like that, though, I don't understand. It just makes things more difficult for that player and for the rest of the team. In general, I'd say the Old Trafford crowd is more patient than most. They know the game and they know the players. Real United fans knew Giggsy would be back flying, as he proved during the last six months of that season, on our way to winning the League.

When it comes to England, ever since I've been involved at least, there's always been that same tendency to lump everything onto one bloke's shoulders when the team's seen to fall short. When you think that we're representing our country, not just our clubs, on international duty – and that millions of supporters are watching on television every time we kick a ball at a major tourna-ment – you realise that being the one to carry the can is even more painful and humiliating. I remember, when we were younger, some of us would turn up to prepare for England games and half joke about who we thought would be to blame this time if we lost. Looking back now, it wasn't even half funny. I think players being made scapegoats didn't just undermine the particular lads who were singled out for the stick. I think it held back the England team as a whole. And maybe it still does.

There's always pressure on the England players and I understand that: I'm patriotic, too. I'm an England fan and I want us to do well as a country. But in World Cups and European Championships, I think that pressure sometimes makes players scared to try things, makes them nervous about taking risks and really expressing themselves. It's a fear of failing and the memory of what happened to me in 1998, for example, or Phil Neville at Euro 2000 is in the back of some players' minds. Look at Brazil: they're relaxed whatever's happening. I remember, during the World Cup quarter-final in 2002, looking across the pitch – this was while we were 1–0 up – and Ronaldo was having a laugh and a joke with the referee.

Of course, none of the Brazilian lads are going to go back to Brazil to play their club football the following season: maybe that helps them not worry about what might happen if things go wrong. England players know what kind of stick they can get and I really believe that being nervous about it holds some of us back. Even though I've been through it myself, it still crossed my mind once I'd got home after the World Cup in 2002: what would have been said and written about me if I'd missed that penalty against Argentina? I could be wrong. It's not something I've talked about with the other lads. I just have this sense that, in the really big games, a fear of failure sometimes stops us turning in the kind of performances we're capable of and which the fans want to see.

For whatever reason, Euro 2000 didn't go the way any of us would have wanted it to. Phil Neville took some of the blame for that. Kevin Keegan came in for a lot of criticism too. But with the team spirit that Kevin had created since coming in as England manager, we all felt we were in it together. And that meant all of us taking the responsibility for England getting knocked out so early on. Although we'd had a difficult time in qualifying, we still went off to the tournament expecting to do well. Before our arrival in Belgium and Holland, our training camp in France was much more relaxed than the one organised by Glenn Hoddle before the World Cup two years before. By the time the tournament began, everybody was really excited, and looking forward to getting started.

If you look at the opening twenty minutes of our first game that summer against Portugal in Eindhoven, you'd have to say we were in exactly the right shape and the right state of mind. They were an excellent team, with world-class players like Luis Figo and Rui Costa, and they put us under pressure straight away but, every time we broke upfield we looked like we were going to score. I sent a couple of crosses in: Paul Scholes got on the end of the first one and Steve McManaman put in the second. We were 2–0 up before any of us had had time to feel how the game might be going. To be honest, we were surprised by the position we found ourselves in. We should have gone on to win the game but, almost straight away, Figo ran through and blasted one into the top corner and everything changed. Everything started to go wrong. They equalised just before half-time. Michael Owen went off injured, then Steve McManaman too. And the Portuguese got the winner in the second half.

For a neutral, it had been a great game. For us, though, and for the England supporters, it was really disappointing. To have been playing as well as we had early on, and to have scored two good goals but then let the game slip away, was unbelievably frustrating. The fact that we'd played some good football and been beaten by an excellent team didn't ease the pressure at all. Even though I thought I'd had a decent game, I felt really down at the end: losing 3–2 wasn't the start we'd been hoping for at all. For those few minutes after the final whistle I was off in a world of my own. Perhaps I should have had my head up, steeling myself, because there was trouble waiting for me as I trudged off the pitch.

Victoria had travelled over to Holland for the game. She'd obviously come to support me, but I remember feeling nervous about that before kick-off. We'd been told that our families would be seated in a secure, enclosed area but that hadn't happened. I looked across to see her in the crowd and, to be honest, I was worried about how safe Victoria was going to be. She was with her dad and they had trouble before and after the match, getting pushed around and abused by people who were calling themselves England supporters. She'll never go to a game like that, in those kinds of circumstances, ever again.

Some of those same idiots were waiting for me, too, when I came off the pitch. As I walked off towards the tunnel, after we'd been to applaud the England fans, there were five or six blokes, in seats behind the dugouts. They started having a go, first about me, then about Victoria. And then – the most horrible thing – they were shouting this stuff about Brooklyn. It still makes me feel sick to my stomach thinking about what they were saying. I was so angry; but I bit my lip. What can you do? You're powerless to stop it, aren't you? I just stuck my middle finger up towards them and headed straight down to the changing room.

Since France 98, people having a go at me, inside and outside football grounds, had become something that happened so often that I'd almost learned to live with it. It always hurt but I got better at blocking it out, I suppose. What really shocked me was the abuse since Victoria and I had got married and started a family; instead of this earning us a little privacy and respect, it seemed to have made things worse. You'd have to ask the people who abused us why they did it. Envy? Contempt? Nothing better to do? All I do know is that, on that particular afternoon in Eindhoven, after I'd spent ninety minutes running round for the England team and we hadn't got a good result to show for it, my guard was definitely down. What those blokes said hurt and disgusted me and, because I was so shocked by it, I couldn't help but react.

By the time I'd gone down the tunnel with the rest of the team, the moment had gone as far as I was concerned. I was lucky that Kevin Keegan had been only a few paces behind me as we came off the pitch. He'd heard every word that had been screamed in my direction. He didn't mention it straight away in the changing room. The more important thing was to talk about the game we'd just played and to start getting heads back up for the next one, against Germany, in Charleroi. I got changed and followed a couple of the other lads onto the coach. I phoned Victoria. She was telling me what had happened to her and Tony, getting in and getting out of the ground. I don't think I'd even had time to tell her what had been shouted at me when Paul Ince came up the aisle:

'Did you stick a finger up at the crowd?'

I just nodded.

'They got a photo of it. One of the press boys has just told me the picture will be in the papers tomorrow.'

By the time we got back to our hotel, Kevin had found out what was going to happen too. He'd been asked about it in the press conference after the game. We were sitting down to dinner when he came up to me:

'David, I heard everything. You've got nothing to worry about. Don't take any notice of anything you read in the papers. I heard exactly what was said. Don't worry. I'll back you.'

He said exactly the same to anyone else who asked. He told the press – and, perhaps, the representatives of the FA who'd have been concerned about repercussions – that he knew the full story and was completely behind me. It was Kevin who gave people an idea of just how far the abuse had gone, how personal and how spiteful it had been; the idea of anybody thinking that stuff about someone, never mind shouting it at them, was horrible. In that kind of situation, no player could have asked for better support from a manager. Kevin Keegan was ready to stand shoulder to shoulder with me. That's exactly what Alex Ferguson would have done in the same circumstances. I think both Kevin and the gaffer understand how much it means to players to know their manager, whatever happens in private, is going to stick up for them when it comes to facing the media.

In Eindhoven, it wasn't that Kevin felt he should back me because I was one of his players. I got the impression he'd been really shocked and upset by what he'd heard coming from the crowd. And, as it turned out, I don't think he was the only one. Of course there was a big fuss in the next day's papers and, of course, there were people saying some of the same things they'd said about me after what had happened in Saint-Etienne: *he's an idiot, a disgrace and he should never play for his country again.* But it was different this time. I had the England manager behind me and people had a better idea why I'd reacted the way I did. In Eindhoven, I'd been goaded not by an Argentinian midfield player but by people wearing St George's crosses and England replica shirts. Perhaps people, now, could understand why I'd reacted even if what I'd done hadn't been right. I'd been pushed – for two years now – and I'd snapped. I think there were writers and supporters alike who decided that I'd been pushed far enough and deserved the backing Kevin was giving me. Almost straight away, I could sense a change in the media and the public's attitude towards me.

I know, sometimes, your memory plays tricks. Things don't always happen as quickly or as dramatically as you remember them. But, after Eindhoven, I know for a fact that things changed almost overnight. What happened when we came out to warm up before the Germany game I'll never forget. Since being sent off against Argentina, England fans hadn't needed much prompting to turn against me. Playing my club football for United didn't help. Especially in the old days at Wembley, all the United lads had got used to the stick. Some supporters used to boo when Gary or Phil Neville's names were announced in the team. The abuse we'd get at away games for our club used to carry on when we turned out for our country. That all changed, for me at least, in Charleroi.

Five days after we'd lost to Portugal, we were playing Germany in a tiny stadium in a tiny Belgian town. I know there were crowd problems in the main square but we were kept away from all that and the important thing for us was the atmosphere inside the ground. It felt like a little league ground, with the crowd right next to the pitch and the noise was fantastic, most of it from the England fans. The place was already packed when we came out to warm up about 35 minutes before kick-off. It was an amazing moment for me. I jogged down towards our supporters and, for the first time ever, I heard them singing:

'One David Beckham. There's only one David Beckham . . .'

It sends a shiver down my spine remembering it now. At the

time, I couldn't believe I was hearing it. Like I say, I'm an England supporter as well as an England player: our fans chanting my name meant the world to me. Just like the crowd at Old Trafford had helped me put Saint-Etienne behind me, those supporters in Charleroi made me forget all about what had happened after the Portugal game the previous Monday. It made such a difference, knowing our own crowd – the people who pay good money to come out to major tournaments and follow the England team – were on my side. From that afternoon on, I believe attitudes towards me changed. I'll never know how important Kevin's backing was, but I really believe that events in Eindhoven finally helped people realise what I had been through after two years of abuse.

I felt fantastic going back down to the changing room to get ready for kick-off. When we came back out, I'd have run through a brick wall for my country. And, to be honest, that's what the Germany game felt like we were having to do: it was hard, really hard. The ninety-odd minutes were absolutely terrible as a game of football. But considering we hadn't beaten them in a competitive game since 1966, the result more than made up for that: England 1 Germany 0.

I'd set up our two goals against Portugal and was feeling pretty confident about my game. Just after half-time in Charleroi, we got a free-kick a couple of yards inside Germany's half. Gary Neville came running up to me:

'Take a quick one. Come on.'

You can't knock the bloke. Gary's always up for it, wanting to be involved, but just then I didn't want to just tap the ball to him and get back into open play.

'Gary, just go away.'

I don't think he was all that happy about me sending the free-kick long but I went ahead and did it anyway. It swung enough in the air to miss two German defenders and Alan Shearer ran on to it at the far post and stuck it in. It turned out to be the winning goal. In the middle of the celebrations, Gary came up alongside me:

'Great cross, Becks.'

Like it had been his idea all along. Gary drives you mad some-times but I can't think of anyone I'd rather train or play football with. He's got a perfect attitude to the game. Once the final whistle had gone, we were all out celebrating on the pitch while the supporters were going crazy: we'd beaten Germany and won our first game of the tournament. I remember Gary, though, coming up to me and putting things into focus:

'We should get off the pitch. We haven't done anything yet. We haven't even qualified out of this group.'

And he was right. We still had Romania to play. We just needed a draw against them to go through from the group, but everybody knows now how that game turned out. Romania were a good, technical side, even without Gheorghe Hagi who was suspended, but they weren't that good. We should never have got ourselves into a position where they could put us out. After going a goal down, we got ourselves 2–1 up and should have gone on to win the game from there. After they equalised, it felt like we didn't have the belief in ourselves to get back at them. We were hanging on for the draw. All it took then was one misjudgement, right at the end, to put Romania into the quarter-finals instead of us.

I was standing near the halfway line when Phil Neville slid in on their player and the penalty was given. It was a strange moment. Unreal: it felt like it shouldn't have been happening, like it was part of another game, not the one we'd been playing for the last ninety minutes. I felt so bad for Phil. He'd had a good game that afternoon and a good tournament. When the final whistle went, I found myself thinking about him straight away. *I know what's going to happen, what's going to be said about you now.*

I went over and put an arm round him. There's nothing I could have said or done, though, to stop him getting shouldered with the blame for us losing to Romania and going out of the competition. The stick he got wasn't as fierce as I'd had after France 98 but it was enough. More than enough. No wonder England players sometimes go into big games wondering if they're going to make the big mistake and get ripped apart for it afterwards. Like I've said, for the England team to really move on, we need to get over that way of thinking.

That afternoon in Charleroi, around the ground and back in the changing rooms afterwards, there was this sense of disbelief. After the high of beating Germany on the same ground just a few days before, to follow it with the result against Romania was devastating. The win the previous Saturday had lifted everybody's expectations – the fans', the media's and the players' themselves – and, in a split second, all that had gone. It was hard to take. You can't help but dream along with the England supporters, even if the manager and team-mates like Gary Neville try to bring you back down to earth. We felt crushed, like the fans, to be going back home so soon.

The minutes in the dressing room afterwards and then the first days in England are a blur to me now. I remember thinking back, during that time, to 1999 and how the Bayern Munich players must have felt after United won the European Cup. It's not like the opposition have taken the lead and are beating you two- or three-nil, controlling the game. One minute everything's there in front of you, the next it's snatched away. It happens so quickly and you've no time to do anything about it. It just kills you. I saw it on the faces of the Bayern players the night United won in

Barcelona. I have so much respect for them: they came back from that disappointment and won the trophy a couple of years later. To react the way they did shows the kind of strength of character the England players needed to find after Euro 2000.

It wasn't just the players who took criticism when we got back to England. The manager had to face a lot of it too, which at least took some of the pressure off Phil Neville. Given the way Kevin's teams, including England, play the game, I suppose it was bound to happen. It was the same when he was in charge at Newcastle: people love to watch his sides play but, when things don't work out, it's easy to say Kevin takes too many risks and doesn't put enough time into working on defending. I don't need to say again, though, how highly I think of him as a manager and as a man. The players knew, deep down, that what had happened in Belgium was our responsibility, however much anybody else wanted to point the finger at Kevin.

In international football, there's never time to go back to scratch and work out new ideas. As soon as one tournament finishes, you move on to try to qualify for the next one. In the autumn of 2000 we had our first games on the way to the 2002 World Cup. Of all teams, our first competitive fixture was against the Germans again, this time at Wembley. After we'd beaten them in Charleroi, many observers had said they were the worst German team ever; maybe they assumed that we'd just need to turn up to beat them a second time. So despite what had happened over the summer, expectations were right up there again. That October the day had an extra edge because it was the last game we were going to play at Wembley before the place got pulled down.

There was so much build-up, so much looking back over the stadium's history, especially to the best afternoon of them all in 1966. Wembley was packed, of course, and when we went out to warm up you had the feeling everyone had come for a party, never mind a World Cup qualifier. Actually, the game was awful, as frustrating as any I've ever played in. Germany got an early goal when a free-kick from Dietmar Hamann skidded away from Dave Seaman and then they just sat there and bottled the game up; the pitch didn't help but we never really built up any momentum. They had lots of players behind the ball and probably looked more likely to score another goal on the break than we did to get an equaliser. I picked up a knock on my knee and I had to be substituted just before the end.

I went and sat on the bench, huddled up against the rain, and listened to the atmosphere around Wembley getting more and more sour. When the whistle went and we'd lost 1–0, the last the old Wembley heard from England supporters was them booing us off. To lose the last game at Wembley – and to lose it to Germany – was one of the worst experiences I've ever had in football. I walked down the touchline towards the changing rooms just a few yards ahead of Kevin Keegan. I could hear the abuse he was getting from fans near enough to the running track to make themselves heard. It wasn't personal, what was being shouted at him. Instead, they were telling Kevin what they thought of him as England manager. Second-hand stuff, lifted from the back pages, saying he didn't have a clue – which was really harsh and insulting towards a man who'd achieved so much during thirty-odd years in football. It hadn't taken long for everybody to forget that Kevin had been first choice, by a mile, to take over when Glenn Hoddle resigned.

I was surprised at what happened when we got down into the changing rooms but, because I'd been listening to what those supporters had been saying, I had an idea why Kevin made up his mind so quickly about what he should do. I could understand him, after taking that stick, wondering if it was worth it. Even so, what actually happened in the hour after that Germany game came as a huge shock. We hadn't even started changing. Most of us were just getting something to drink. Kevin walked in and stood in the middle of the room. Then he told us he was leaving:

'I have to be honest with you. And honest with myself. I've gone as far as I can with this. I'm calling it a day. You've got good times ahead of you. You're very good players.'

I know it was an instant decision because even his assistant Arthur Cox, who knew Kevin better than any of us, didn't know what was coming. He was the first to speak up:

'No, Kevin. Don't do this.'

I remember my reaction:

'Kevin, we want you as England manager.'

It was all falling apart and now we were losing Kevin Keegan. Personally, I didn't feel let down. I wouldn't have said a bad word about one of the best managers I've ever worked with. Kevin felt he knew what he had to do and he'd made up his mind completely. He told us he was going to step down. Then he told Adam Crozier, the FA Chief Executive. And then he told the press. What a way to finish things off: all the great things that had happened at Wembley, and all the good times we'd had with Kevin, ended with the rain tipping down, people angry and upset and the England team looking for another new coach. I look back now to that miserable afternoon and think: *Why couldn't we have changed our minds and had one more game there? One more chance to give Wembley the send off it should have had?*

As it turned out, with the delays to the new National Stadium, we could have done that. Instead, you just have to hope that us losing to Germany isn't the only memory of Wembley that people are left with. Better to remember the great FA Cup Finals and

Euro 96 and winning the World Cup back in 1966. From a football point of view, of course, if we'd been told before the game in October 2000 that we were going to lose to Germany that afternoon but then go on to beat them like we did in Munich a few months later, every single one of the players would have settled for that. A lot had to happen to the England team first, though, before that particular dream could come true.

Really important international players, leaders and captains like Alan Shearer and Tony Adams, had come to the end of their England careers, or were just about to. There was a group of lads, including my generation of United players, who now had the experience of two major tournaments – and two major disappointments – behind us. Following us, there were lots of talented young players waiting for their chance. When Kevin left, everybody seemed to agree about what needed to be done to get England going again. Before Sven-Goran Eriksson was appointed, Howard Wilkinson looked after the team for a couple of games and then Peter Taylor came in as caretaker manager for a friendly away to Italy. Everybody was saying:

'Shake things up. Go with the young players.'

Maybe Peter knew he wasn't going to be in the firing line that comes with doing the England job full-time. More likely, that's just what he's like as a coach: he was the one who had the bottle to change the international team around, to recognise what needed to be done and then to go ahead and do it whatever the doubters said. All the young players who've come in since should remember that it was Peter who was the first to take the chance with a new generation of players. It wasn't that he gave out a lot of new caps. What he did was give the younger lads the opportunity to come together as a team. Sven's been a huge influence but Peter got things started. Personally, I owe him, too. And always will: Peter

Taylor gave me the England captain's armband for the very first time.

I'd only ever skippered a side once in my career. During my first year at Old Trafford, I was captain of the youth team that won the Milk Cup in Northern Ireland. Lack of experience never stopped anyone dreaming, though. Once I'd established myself as an England player, I'd started to have ambitions – which, of course, I kept to myself – to make the next step, which would be the greatest honour of all. I've always believed that you should set yourself the highest of goals. I got as far as having a meeting with Kevin Keegan after Alan Shearer announced his international retirement. I wanted the England manager to know that I believed I could take on the job as captain. Kevin didn't say yes or no. But he did say he thought I would make an England skipper one day.

By the time Kevin had left the international set-up, I think people were starting to talk about the possibility of me being up to the job. I have to say there were at least as many people against the idea at the time as were for it. And obviously it wasn't something I could make happen myself: I just had to wait and see, along with everybody else. The night before Peter Taylor announced his squad for the friendly game against Italy, Victoria was away and I was staying at Gary Neville's house. My phone rang at about eight o'clock in the morning. I'm not the best at getting up early, so my first, blurry reaction was: *Who the hell's that?*

I picked up the phone and managed to mutter:

'Hello?'

The voice at the other end was wide awake.

'Hello, David. It's Peter Taylor.'

I came to my senses very quickly indeed. I was out of bed and on my feet.

'Oh. Hello, Peter. How are you?'

The caretaker manager hadn't just rung up for a chat. I'll never forget what came next:

'Sorry to ring this early but I'm about to announce the squad. I've picked a young group and some new young players. I think the right thing is for you to captain them. I've got absolutely no doubt about you being ready for the job. I wanted you to know before I tell anybody else.'

I had to sit down again for five minutes. It crossed my mind that I might still be asleep. Had that phone call really happened? I was frozen to the spot by what I'd just heard: so excited, so proud, humbled by the thought of it. I phoned Victoria. I phoned Mum and Dad. Something like this hasn't really happened until you've shared it with your family. And then, still sat on the bed, I found myself thinking: *It's fantastic. But I don't want to be England captain just for one game. I want the job to keep.*

Once that was in my mind, I calmed down a bit. I didn't run in and jump up and down on Gary's bed. We had breakfast later and I just told him what had happened, almost matter-of-factly:

'Oh, by the way Gaz. I've been made England captain. Pass the cornflakes.'

I must admit I'd always seen Gary as a skipper, either at United or with England. As it turned out, it happened to me first. He was as pleased for me as I'd have been for him. It was some way to start a day before the drive in to train. I think the news got to Carrington before I did and I got some stick from the United lads, who insisted on calling me 'Skipper' for the rest of the morning.

I didn't really talk to anyone about how to approach the captain's job. I'd seen how other people did it. I knew my own character, and that I had to find my own way. I realised that the shouting and hollering wouldn't be for me. It was going to have to be about going out there and playing, working hard, and hoping to lead by example. Joining up with the rest of the squad for the first time as skipper was great. The whole experience was, even though I put myself under pressure: I couldn't just relax and enjoy the moment because I was aware, the whole time, that I didn't want this to be a one-off. I had to try to make sure that a new full-time manager would agree with the decision Peter Taylor had made.

I was chuffed Peter had given me the armband and, in hindsight, I'm grateful that he picked the squad he did too. I was captaining a young side: I felt I had the experience and that I could take that extra responsibility. It might not have seemed so natural a progression if senior players like Paul Ince, Tony Adams or Alan Shearer, who'd been captains themselves, had still been involved. I might not have taken things so much in my stride. Even so, some people weren't sure about me in the role. It helped that Peter made it clear he believed in me. It felt like my team-mates did too. There were enough really young lads around for me to feel like an old man in the England set-up.

Leading the team out at the Stadio Delle Alpi – never mind it was a friendly, never mind the ground wasn't full – was one of the proudest moments of my whole career. Peter Taylor might have taken a risk with me and with the team, but I don't think we let him or England down. We lost 1–0 to a very strong Italian side but deserved better. Emile Heskey terrified their defence all night long and we made plenty of chances but couldn't score. Personally, I knew I'd never felt like this playing for England. Since that night, people have said to me that they saw a change in me almost as soon as I pulled on that England armband. I know the incident they have in mind when they say that.

We were about ten minutes into the second half and it was still 0–0. We'd had a couple of half-shouts for penalties earlier in the game. This time, the ball got crossed in and ricocheted up in the air. I didn't know where the challenge came from but I remember being barged out of the way as the ball dropped towards me. It was in the area and a couple of England players appealed for the foul. I went down on the floor. As I got myself to my feet, the player who I guess had bumped me, Gattuso, was shouting and screaming at me. Maybe he thought I'd gone down too easily. Or that acting angry would keep him out of trouble with the referee. Anyway, I went to run off and he grabbed hold of my shirt. I turned back and looked at him. It was the kind of split-second which, in the past, might have seen me react in the wrong way. Here, I just wanted to get on with it: I was England captain and had to be bigger than that. I jogged away from him. And from trouble. In the event, Gattuso had got away with it. A couple of minutes later, he went down our end and scored with a screamer from thirty yards which turned out to be the winner.

Peter Taylor had done a really good job. The new England coach was in the stands in Turin that night. The argument about a foreigner, Sven-Goran Eriksson, taking over running the national team had been going on for a couple of weeks. It even came up in the England dressing room. I understood people's concerns. I know they wanted an Englishman who'd be up to taking on the responsibility of being in charge of the England team. But the situation we found ourselves in was that the country was desperate for success, desperate to see the national team play some decent football. We needed to get the best man for the job, whatever his background. And Sven was, and is, one of the most respected managers in the game. Fortunately, it didn't take long for most of the doubters to forget all their worries about the fact that Sven was a Swede: the results and, just as important, England's performances soon saw to that.

Before he took the England job, I'd never met Sven. I don't

228 \ David Beckham: My Side

think I'd even played against any of the club sides he'd managed. In football, though, you know bosses by their reputations: word gets round about the very best. That, and the trophies he'd won, told you the new man deserved our respect. As far as the players were concerned, we knew what we needed to because we knew what he'd already achieved in the game. I was first introduced to Mr Eriksson when we joined up ahead of his first game in charge, a friendly against Spain, at Villa Park. When we got to the team hotel, I got a message that he wanted to see me.

It was just a chance to say hello, and to let me know a little about how he planned to approach the job. Sven had been going round the country watching dozens of games. There'd been so much talk about him ahead of that first match in charge. Even a hoax phone call, put in to him by a radio DJ pretending to be Kevin Keegan, went out on air in Manchester. One of the questions had been about me: would he keep me as captain? And Sven had said yes. Obviously, I hadn't taken that at face value and I'd been worrying – really worrying – for the week leading up to our first get-together. Lucky for me, I heard what I was desperate to hear almost at once:

'You'll be staying as captain. I think you'll make a great England captain. You're a good enough player and a player others can look up to. Anybody who doubts that, it's your job to prove them wrong.'

What he told me, and told the rest of the team, was pretty simple. Sven wanted England to play good, attractive football. But he also wanted us to play effective football. The training was relaxed, especially because Steve McClaren, Peter Taylor and Sammy Lee were all part of the coaching staff at first. There was nothing revolutionary going on: Sven was calm, was prepared to let other people get on with what he wanted them to do and just got involved himself when he needed to make his point. And when he did that, every player listened. Never mind his reputation, Sven had a real presence that commanded respect and attention. The players knew straight away that England had got the right man in charge. The rules were clear and simple and you didn't cross them. We were treated like men, given respect and, at the same time, expected to take responsibility for ourselves. I believe it's an approach every England player has responded to.

Despite it being only a friendly, there was a definite buzz in the air at Villa Park – this was the start of something new, wasn't it? – and we beat Spain 3–0. We all knew that the first real test would be the next World Cup qualifier. After losing to Germany and then drawing in Helsinki, the game against Finland at Anfield was pretty much win or bust. If we didn't take all three points, we were going to have a real problem getting to the play-offs, never mind qualifying automatically by winning the group. This was a genuinely competitive game and we needed to come up with a result as a team. Personally, as the new England captain, I felt I needed to come up with something too.

At Villa Park, perhaps because I'd just played the first half, I'd not been satisfied with what I'd been able to do, although the team had played well. At Anfield, even before the kick-off, things felt completely different. The stakes were so much higher: it wasn't just me who was really hyped up. We were just starting to take England games to different club grounds around the country after Wembley had closed down. Everybody knew the atmosphere would be great at Anfield, although nobody was quite sure what kind of reception the United players would get at Liverpool's home ground. We shouldn't have worried. Whether they were Liverpool supporters or fans from around the country, the sound of the Kop chanting my name before kick-off made the hairs stand up on the back of my neck. It was great for me personally, but, much more important, it gave you the feeling that everybody had rallied round England and rallied round Sven.

Early on, we were flying. We made chances. There was a great energy in the team. Passes went where they were supposed to go. It felt really good. And then Finland scored. The ball bounced past Dave Seaman off Gary Neville's knee, a lucky goal, but it meant we were 1–0 down. *Oh, no. Not again.*

Then Michael Owen got an equaliser just before half-time from Gary's cross, which meant we went in for the break feeling pretty upbeat about our chances. Confident even, although I know our supporters probably weren't. We came back out for the second half and I got what turned out to be the winner. The ball came across from the left to the back of the area and my first touch took it down at an angle that made shooting the easy option. I swung at it, the shot took a nick off a defender and the ball flew into the far corner: my first goal for England from open play. I spun round and the first person I saw was Teddy Sheringham, warming up on the touchline. I launched myself, and jumped on his back celebrating. Dave Seaman made a great save towards the end. He always seemed to do that in the really big games. We had other chances as well. But my goal had won it: scored at the Kop end, too, which made it even sweeter.

We had to beat Finland just to give us a chance. Germany in Munich was five months away and we knew we had to keep ourselves in the hunt, at least, until then. We had qualifiers in Greece and Albania and friendlies, too, ahead of us. Now was the time to find out about ourselves as a team. Sven trusted the young players he'd inherited from Peter Taylor – a whole generation, really, mid-twenties and under – and gave us the time and the games to build up our confidence. Over those early months there was a bit of a United feel about how things developed. There still is. And I don't just mean because of myself and Gary, Phil, Butty and Scholesy.

It's hard to tell exactly what brings a successful group together. There's the obvious: good players, good coaching, good management. To turn individuals into a team, though, something else needs to happen, especially at international level where the players come from clubs all over the country. Being together, playing together and winning and losing games together all make a difference. An international coach has to try and make it possible for a side to develop despite injuries, dips in club form and how little time the England team has together apart from the few days before fixtures. The players have done their bit and, like I've said, maybe the age of the squad helped. But Sven deserves some of the credit, at least, for creating a better team spirit than I can remember us ever having had with England before.

There have been times in the past when we'd meet up and you knew who would be with who straight away. Cliques were in place along the lines of the senior and younger players or according to rivalries between clubs. It's a natural thing to stick with your mates. We were as bad as anybody: the United lads used to be famous for keeping to ourselves. So much of that has changed now. I'd say there's a real bond, a real mutual respect, amongst the current England squad and that makes a difference when we go out and play. We could all feel it starting to happen within months of Sven taking charge. The way the new manager dealt with his players made a big difference too.

I remember the 4-0 win against Mexico at Pride Park, in between qualifying games in the Spring of 2001. There was a moment in that game that summed up the new spirit in the England camp, that gave me a feeling we could go to Munich and get a result and take it on into the World Cup the following year. Quite early on, one of the Mexican defenders came through the back of me. It wasn't too serious: I just limped away and got on with it. But within about a minute, Stevie Gerrard had gone flying into this same player – legally, he played the ball first – and left him rolling around on the floor. Looking after your mates: it's an attitude I knew well enough from United. It's an attitude you'll see in every team that wins games and trophies.

We beat Greece in Athens and Albania in Tirana, which at least made us favourites to finish second and qualify for a play-off to reach the World Cup Finals the following summer. To win the group and go through to Japan and South Korea automatically, we knew we'd have to win in Munich. And, even though things had been going well under Sven, I don't think there were too many people who fancied our chances of doing that. Nobody beats the Germans in Germany, do they? For once, expectations weren't too high, so that took some of the pressure off us. We didn't have to worry too much about letting the supporters down. The one person who'd said all along that he thought we could win the game was the manager. Sven's never one for talking big to the press before games but, since taking over, every time he'd been asked about the Germany game, he'd said that he thought we were good enough to win. Maybe his confidence, over the months and, then, in the days leading up to the game on the first of September, found its way into the players' own minds without us even realising it.

Whatever the reason, by the time we were sitting down to dinner at the hotel in Munich on the Friday night before the game, I found myself looking around and listening to conversations and wondering if I could ever remember being with an England team that seemed in such a positive state of mind. I had my own doubts about the game the following day, but they were to do with whether or not I'd be fit to play. I went up to my room later and spoke to my mate Dave Gardner. He asked me how I thought we were going to get on. The couple of hours with the rest of the players had convinced me.

'I think we're going to win.'

The silence at the other end of the line told me there wasn't the same kind of confidence back at home. But I wouldn't have said it to Dave if I hadn't believed it. And I wanted to be part of what I thought was going to happen. I was worried that a groin injury I'd picked up playing for United against Aston Villa the week before wasn't going to heal in time. It had turned out not to be as bad a tear as I'd thought when it first happened, so I'd joined up for England training with the rest of the lads although I wasn't fit enough to train with them. I had a week on my own, getting treatment, hoping for the best and hating every minute of it. Being captain made it even worse: I wanted to be involved in everything. Instead, the first time I was able to work with everybody else was at the stadium, late in the afternoon before that Friday night dinner.

I went out half an hour early with Gary Lewin and Alan Smith from the England medical team to check my fitness: running, turning, hitting dead balls. It's a strange feeling, even more so with a place in the team for such a big game at stake. You want to stretch yourself to make sure you're strong enough to play and won't let anybody down. At the same time, you can't help but hold back a little because you don't want to break down at the last minute and miss out on your chance. Anyway, Gary and Alan were happy and gave me the all-clear to join in with the main session. It felt great: the rest of the squad were in such good nick. I found myself wishing we could have a go at the Germans there and then.

I was almost waiting for the nerves to start jangling but the lads were just as confident over breakfast as they had been over dinner the night before and, even an hour before kick-off in the changing room, everyone seemed calm and relaxed. We went out to warm up and everything seemed right. Everything, that is, apart from my injury. I still wasn't sure. I knew I wanted to play but I knew I had to do what was best for the team. Those few minutes running and stretching, though, made all the difference and I came back in convinced I could make it. When the time came, in the minute or two before the bell rang to tell us to go out for the game, Sven sat everybody down. What he had to say was pretty simple but tapped into everybody's mood:

'Go out, enjoy yourselves. Be confident: they're a good team but we're a better team. Play well. And three points.'

Sven always finishes with that: 'And three points'. I stood up and led the team out into the tunnel. The physios had talked me into putting on a pair of lycra cycling shorts just to keep me warm and to give a bit of extra support. Even standing in the tunnel, I knew I'd made a mistake agreeing to wear them. I've always been the kind of player who needs to be comfortable with what I've got on: not just my boots but the rest of my kit too. If I've got blisters, I can't wear an extra pair of socks or a plaster on a sore toe. Maybe it's all in the mind, but I know it makes a real difference to me. Waiting to go out for this huge game, I felt like I'd been strapped into these things. It wasn't really the right moment, though, to be changing my mind.

We kicked off and, in no time, we were a goal down. Carsten Jancker scored for the Germans. I'd not even had long enough to stop worrying about not feeling right. The injury wasn't bothering me but the cycling shorts were. Surely, if the groin was going to go, then it was going to go anyway. I jogged across to the touchline and peeled them off. One of the papers got a photo of me stripping off by the dugout and ran it the next day with a jokey headline about the England captain changing the game by changing his shorts. Getting rid of them did change things for me: I felt better straight away, freer and able to run more easily. I didn't give the injury another thought for the rest of the game.

Usually, going a goal behind would have been the worst possible thing that could happen. Give Germany a head start and you expect them to organise behind the ball and hit you on the break. That's exactly what had happened at Wembley, wasn't it? Here at the Olympic Stadium, it didn't bother us at all. Nobody panicked, nobody started having second thoughts. It felt like it had at the Stadio Delle Alpi with United, the night we were 2–0 down to Juventus but came back to win and reach the European Cup Final. Michael Owen was really pumped up. He had things under control but I'd seen the fire in his eyes before kick-off. Now we were behind, he was shouting at anybody in earshot:

'Come on. We can win this. We can beat them.'

And we all knew he was right. Five minutes later, Michael got the equaliser – the first of his hat-trick – and we never looked back. We were that sure of ourselves. I think the Germans picked up on it and their nerve started to go. Oliver Kahn, one of the world's best goalkeepers, had one of his worst-ever nights. It turned into one of those rare games in which everything you could possibly want to happen does. Steven Gerrard's goal, right at the end of the first half, was a great strike. It flew in from twenty-odd yards: his first goal for England. Even better, it went in at the perfect time for us. If a game's tight, nicking the lead just before half-time gives the team that scores it a real edge psychologically. He'd missed qualifying games through injury but Stevie made up for it that night in Munich. We're so much better balanced with him in the side. He's still young but he's like a Roy Keane or a

Patrick Vieira: he tackles and will run all day; he can pass and he'll score goals. He's got the complete midfield game: it's no coincidence that England rarely lose with Steven Gerrard in the eleven.

I don't know about the other lads but I was more nervous at half-time than I had been before the game. I remember going into the changing room, 2–1 up, and not being sure how we should approach the second 45 minutes. After a first half, Sven always lets everybody come in and settle for five minutes: sit down, unlace your boots, get a drink, whatever it is you need to do. There were conversations going on between players straight away, with everyone buzzing:

'Do we go out and try to defend 2–1? Do we attack and hope to get another goal that'll win it?'

I think we all knew we didn't need to change anything. That's what Sven told us too. There were more goals there for us and we could trust our defence to defend. The second half was like playing in a dream. Michael got his second goal just a few minutes after the kick-off. And then his third. And then Scholesy rolled one through for Emile Heskey to score too. I remember when Emile's shot went in, I turned round to look at the bench to see how people were reacting: it was the same as what was going on in the stands and, I'd guess, in front of the telly back at home. The subs and the coaching staff were just falling about, hugging each other. You could read people's lips:

'Five-one. Against Germany. In Germany. This is unbelievable.'

There were still twenty minutes left. Twenty minutes in football heaven. It was strange: I was involved in the build-up to the fifth goal and I had my work to do during the game; but I wasn't as much in the thick of the decisive incidents as I sometimes am playing for England. I was playing but it felt like I had the luxury of watching at the same time. I was part of it but I was admiring what these lads alongside me were doing as well. All we needed was to keep the ball. Which was what we did, getting the Germans more and more wound up. We're not a team to showboat: our players aren't the kind to rub anybody's nose in it with little flicks and tricks. But we kept passing to each other and, as long as we were doing that, they couldn't get a touch. And it wasn't just playing out time, either. We felt like we wanted to beat Germany 10–1, never mind five.

Right after he blew the final whistle, the referee, Pierluigi Collina, came up and asked for my shirt. He must have known he'd just been part of some history being made. I think he's the best referee around, so I was happy enough. There weren't many Germans in the mood for swapping shirts, after all. I think Collina was quite chuffed when I asked for his in return. All I wanted to do then was get across to the England supporters. Thousands of them had come out to Munich and the second half had sounded like we were playing at home. The noise was fantastic. I've always said that England fans are the best in the world. Put the tiny percentage of idiots to one side: our fans travel everywhere with us and give us amazing support. I'm sure every England supporter inside the Olympic Stadium could have told you stories about horrible trips to the middle of nowhere in the past and the disappointment of poor England performances. Every one of them knew how it felt to lose to rivals like Germany and Argentina. Those supporters deserved 5–1 at the Olympic Stadium as much as we did. I'm sure, as it was for the players, that night was one of the best of their lives.

Back inside I discovered I could hardly speak. My throat felt like I'd been forced to smoke twenty cigars, one after the other, over the past couple of hours. I knew I'd talked and shouted a lot during the game. Had I joined in with some of the England singing in the second half too? There was a wonderful atmosphere in that dressing room: we were so proud and so happy but we'd done all our jumping around out on the pitch. Now there was calm. Some players were getting massages, others were steaming in the showers and the rest, like me, were sitting in their places, slowly taking off kit, sucking on water bottles and just drinking the moment in.

Without Sven saying anything, I think every England player was already starting to think about the next game in four days' time against Albania. Anybody who wasn't was hearing all about it from the likes of Gary Neville. What had just happened was unbelievable but it wouldn't mean anything if we didn't win next Wednesday at St James' Park. You live a life in football, as a supporter or a player, for nights like Germany 1 England 5. From game to game, though, putting the history and the glory to one side, the opposition doesn't matter. Victory always means the same thing. As Mr Eriksson says: it's another three points.

I sat in my place, leaning back against the wall. I thought back to Wembley on a wet Saturday afternoon less than a year before. And to Kevin Keegan, in the dressing room after we'd lost 1–0, telling us he'd taken England as far as he thought he could. I remembered the press and plenty of our supporters writing off the World Cup adventure before it had even begun. In my heart of hearts, I knew I'd have been hard pushed, back then, to disagree with the doom merchants. Losing to Germany was a blow. For me personally – and for England, I thought – losing Kevin had felt like the end of the world. Now, eleven months later, we were on the brink of beating our old rivals to the post.

Who knows what might have happened if Kevin had decided to carry on? I believe in him as a manager. Just look at what he's achieved at Manchester City over the past couple of years. And I've got limitless respect for him as a man. Sometimes, though, change happens not because anybody wants it to but because it has to. I loved playing for England under Kevin. A year later, I was captaining my country under Sven-Goran Eriksson. The new manager had brought through a new generation of England players and given us the chance to develop as a team. Sven and Alex Ferguson couldn't be more different in their approach to individual players. The way they went about trying to build successful teams, though, was exactly the same. As far as the England side was concerned, the performance and the scoreline in Munich were all anyone needed to see how successful the Swedish revolution had been.

My Foot in It

10

'This isn't going to be our day, is it?'

We all knew it was going to happen, although not many of us had ever believed it would. Soon after the gaffer signed a new contract in 1999, he said it would be his last and that 2001/02 would be his final season with United. His reasons seemed obvious enough: he wanted to relax a little after twenty-odd years as a manager up in Scotland and then at Old Trafford. He wanted to travel. He wanted to see his family. He probably wanted to be able to spend more time at the racecourse. Even before Rock Of Gibraltar made him famous as an owner, we knew he loved horses with the same passion he loved football. On one of my last days out with the lads as a United player, the boss took us all over to Chester races. It was a great afternoon. Even though I felt by then, in late April 2003, that I was being pushed to the fringe of things at Old Trafford, the togetherness for those few hours was as good as it had ever been in my time at the club: it was a real United family outing. The gaffer himself was having such a good time, you couldn't help getting into the spirit of it yourself.

When he'd first told everybody about his plans for retirement, it had seemed something that was a long way in the future. But during 2001 it started being written about and talked about more and more. There were stories about the boss becoming an ambassador for the club, especially out in the Far East. There were reports about disagreements with the board, and the boss saying he was going to cut off all ties with Old Trafford. The players didn't know any more about the speculation than what was in the papers. It wasn't until what was meant to be his last season had kicked off that it began to sink in, after he sat us down and told us he would be leaving the club the following May. Once we started work, it wasn't something the players thought about every day or talked about in the dressing room. We didn't have to. I don't think any of us could really imagine life at United without Alex Ferguson in charge. Players would have arguments with him: I definitely wasn't the only one. And, in whatever walk of life, when you're in the middle of a row with your boss, you wish he wasn't your boss. Most of the time, though, if you ask any United player they'll tell you that working for the gaffer means you're working for the best in the world.

The day I arrived at Manchester United, as a teenager away from home for the first time, the boss knew my name. He knew my mum and dad, and my sisters. He knew everything about me. And he made me feel welcome. It was as if I was leaving one family and joining another. That's a great strength in any manager: to make players feel like he knows and understands and cares about them. Look how the gaffer hung on for Ruud van Nistelrooy, stayed in touch with him all through his comeback from rupturing his cruciate ligaments. He kept reassuring him that he would come to Old Trafford eventually. Players recognise that kind of loyalty. No wonder Ruud paid him back with all those goals to help United win the Premiership in 2003.

The boss has always known how to make the new boy feel at home from day one. Even more important is that, once that relationship has been established, you never feel he'd turn his back on it. Like a father, the United manager was there to protect you, advise you and give you a piece of his mind for as long as you were part of the family; as long as you were part of the club. Young hopefuls and established stars: the boss makes them all feel special, and he makes sure they realise how special the club is. There have been players, like Dwight Yorke or Jaap Stam, who've done great things for United, but who suddenly found themselves on the outside without a way back. Something they said or did had convinced the gaffer they weren't right for the club. In the end, maybe I turned out to be one of those players too even though, at the start of the 2001/02 season, I'd never have imagined that happening.

By reputation, the Manchester United manager is short-tempered and miserable. Well, the boss is both from time to time. But then, isn't everybody? What people outside the dressing room never see is how inspiring he can be when he's working with players. They don't see him, either, when he's having a laugh and a joke with the lads. When he thinks it's right, he does relax when he's around the team. If the dressing room's buzzing after a great win, he'll be wearing the biggest grin of the lot. I'd say the boss is right in keeping a professional distance from his players most of the time. He's careful not to be closer to one lad than to another, even if his relationships with one or two, like Eric Cantona or Roy Keane, were always different from the rest.

The boss understands football like very few other people. That means whatever situation the team's in, either during a season or during a game, the players have the feeling he knows exactly what to do. He's aware that he's got the power to change things and he's never afraid of doing that, even when the best thing to do is nothing, whatever anybody else might be saying. I think everyone's heard enough about 'The Hairdryer'. It's been talked about so often, you might imagine that's what life is like in the United dressing room all the time. It isn't. What people outside Old Trafford should understand is what everyone inside the club already knows: whatever the gaffer does is what he thinks is right for the team at a particular time.

I remember an amazing game, the week before England played Greece in 2001, down at White Hart Lane. I was so hyped up for the afternoon. I was captain of the United first team for the very first time. The way the gaffer let me know was typical: he just dropped the players' match tickets into my lap before dinner at the team hotel the night before. Handing those tickets round was the skipper's job. I didn't even have time to turn around and start getting emotional: the boss was already away down at the other end of the room. I was so proud, especially as I knew Grandad, who still followed Spurs, would be there with Mum and Dad.

Being skipper would have been enough on its own to make the afternoon stick in my memory. And I still remember it for that. I bet nobody else does. Too much else happened besides. At half-time, we'd had it: Tottenham were winning 3–0, hammering us. You'd expect a manager, when his team's played that badly, to try and shake up his players. You'd expect him to be doing his nut. That afternoon, the boss came into the changing room and was completely calm about the situation. There were no recriminations. There were no angry words. I was sat on the floor, thinking the game was as good as over. I looked around and I could see the other lads, heads down, feeling the same way. The boss just walked in and perched himself on the skip which all our kit had been packed in for the trip down to London. He didn't say much beyond:

'Let's keep the score down now.'

But he knew his players well enough, and trusted us enough, to let us react for ourselves, in the way he expected we would.

I'm sure I wasn't the only player who suddenly found himself thinking: *I'm not going to lose to Spurs like this.*

We went out for the second half, Andy Cole scored early on and we turned it around. We beat them 5–3. It was one of the most amazing 45 minutes of football in which I've ever been involved. And it had been really important that the boss had been so cool and reassuring at half-time, just when you'd have expected him, or any other manager, to be blowing his top. He's a very demanding man but, in all my time as a United player, the gaffer was the one person who always seemed to have even more faith in us than we had in ourselves.

As I've said, the boss made players feel special: when he told you he was pleased with something you did, in a match or in training, that counted for something. I'm not sure what the gaffer thought about me getting the England captain's job. He didn't say anything to me about it at the time, although I remember reading quotes from him in the papers. He said he didn't really see me as a skipper and wasn't sure that it was a very good idea. But during the qualifying campaign for the World Cup, after we'd beaten Germany, he actually made a point of saying to me:

'You've surprised me. This has made you a better player. Maybe a better person. I'd never thought you could be a captain.'

To hear that from the gaffer meant a lot to me, like when I was a boy and Dad had told me he was pleased about something I'd done. It was always the gaffer's way of handling players, keeping them focused: to lift them up when that was what they needed and then knock them down if he thought they were getting above themselves. When I first got into United's first team as a regular, my squad number was 24. The following season I was given the number 10 shirt. That meant a great deal to me: Denis Law and

Mark Hughes had both worn it before me. Maybe the history that went with the number was why I scored so many goals wearing it. I remember, though, the summer we signed Teddy Sheringham, the boss actually took the trouble to phone me when I was away on holiday in Malta to tell me he was taking that squad number off me. No explanation, no alternative and no argument. I remember saying to Gary Neville at the time:

'What's he done that for? Why would he phone to tell me that? Did he just want to make sure he ruined my holiday?'

I was devastated, trying to work out what I'd done wrong. Then, a month later when we turned up for pre-season training, he had a new shirt ready: the number 7. The boss handed me Eric Cantona's squad number. The surprise of that honour stopped me in my tracks.

As well as preparing teams for games, the gaffer was always very careful to prepare each individual too. In the dressing room, whether it was before a Champions League match or before a pre-season friendly, he made sure I knew what he expected from me. And he gave me the information or advice I needed to make sure I was up to that. He takes whatever time he needs with each of his players. And that tells you he values what every single player can bring to the team. By the autumn of 2001, I'd already known the gaffer for a very long time: his experience, though, meant I was still learning from him almost every day. Look at his record, at United and, before then, at Aberdeen. The idea of him not being there was going to take some getting used to. Like everybody else inside and outside Old Trafford, I couldn't help wondering who could replace him.

There are great managers around and lots of them – like Martin O'Neill and Giovanni Trapattoni and even Sven-Goran Eriksson – were talked about for the United job. At Old Trafford, though, the job would take more than the right CV. Any new manager would have to be like the gaffer is: a man with a mission. It's why so many people admire him so much. It's also why he winds so many other people up. Whatever the gaffer says or does, it's never: I want this for Alex Ferguson. It's always: I want this for the club. He is Manchester United, through and through. Anyone who cares about United, anyone who really understands football, recognises that. Even after we'd won the Treble, although he recognised what an achievement it was for us as a group of players, he was immediately thinking about the future. About the need to go on and match what we'd just done and then better it next time round.

The desire to bring success to Old Trafford was what had driven every single one of us on; for the best part of fifteen years, in the case of me and the Nevilles, Paul Scholes, Ryan Giggs and Nicky Butt. The boss, though, was always more intense than anyone: never sitting still, always concentrating on the next challenge. I'd say his drive was more important to our success than anything else. He didn't spend too much time saying it in public, but the players knew the boss valued what we'd achieved. In my case, I was sure he recognised – back then, anyway – that, whatever else was going on in the rest of my life, I would never let United down through lack of effort. Above everything, I was a Manchester United player. Since I'd arrived at Old Trafford, of course, that had meant working for the boss.

Early on in 2001/02, our form was up and down. Lots of pundits jumped to the conclusion that uncertainty about the gaffer was the explanation. There were all sorts of rumours that we got to hear about, like that the boss regretted having had to tell us he was leaving because it meant we weren't frightened of him any more. I can honestly say that wasn't true. None of us wanted him to go but, once we were into the week-in, week-out business of training and playing games, the idea of May coming and the boss packing it in didn't really affect us. We definitely couldn't use it as an excuse for losing games. My only concern was about who'd be replacing him. I was sorting out a new contract at United and I was worried that my relationship with a new manager might not be as good as the one I'd always had with the gaffer. For all that I'd been a United supporter, Alex Ferguson was one of the main reasons I'd left London and signed for the club when I was a boy. Even so, any doubts about the future didn't get in the way of playing for United in the here and now.

If the team was unsettled, it probably had more to do with having lost Steve McClaren over the summer. I've already said how highly I rate Steve as a coach. In June 2001 he left United to become manager at Middlesbrough. With the gaffer expected to leave, I don't think it was a case of Steve wanting any kind of guarantee that he'd replace him. He just wanted to know he'd be in with a chance. I think there were meetings behind the scenes and it became pretty clear that United didn't see him as the future number one. So, when Steve was offered the 'Boro job, nobody was surprised he took it. And all of us, including the gaffer, wished him well. During that season, the boss stepped in to take training from day to day: he's a decent coach as well as everything else. Never mind winding down for retirement, the boss was more involved than ever in 2001/02. Steve was a big loss, though: sessions with him were really enjoyable and, technically, right up to the minute. He knows how to communicate information to players better than anybody I've ever worked with. In his couple of years with us, he'd made his mark at Old Trafford just like he had in the England set-up.

Of course, I still had the chance to work with Steve on international duty, as he stayed on with England, while he was managing 'Boro, until after the 2002 World Cup. We'd been together again for the game against Germany in Munich. And, four days after that, we were up at St James' Park for Albania. Steve talked about lifting ourselves for it. So did Sven. The Wednesday night after the Saturday afternoon was the time to make the 5–1 result count: another three points for the taking. But being ready for it didn't make any difference. Albania at home turned out to be a much harder game. The players were tired. There was expectation in the air again, especially after what had happened in Munich. People thought that, if we could beat Germany 5–1 away, we could beat anybody. Well, we beat Albania but it was close and it wasn't a performance to remember. They were already out of the World Cup and had nothing to lose. They got plenty of players back behind the ball and had a go on the break. They looked like they were enjoying themselves. I can't say we did. The best that could be said was that we stuck at it. We won 2–0 and got our three points.

So it came down to Greece at Old Trafford. Beating Albania meant we went into our last qualifying game level on points at the top of the group with Germany but with a better goal difference. Perhaps it would have been easier – on everybody's nerves, at least – if we could have gone straight on to that game the following weekend. We'd have been tired but we were so disappointed by how we played against Albania that we'd have had something to react to and something to prove. If we'd played Greece that Saturday I think, like a club side, we'd have kicked on and beaten them. Instead we had to wait a month. A month during which everybody needed to concentrate on winning games back with their clubs. A month for doubts to set in ahead of the match that might decide England's international summer. Those weeks dragged and, once the squad got together again, so did the days building up to the game itself.

We met up on the Sunday and stayed at the Marriott Hotel in the suburbs of Manchester. It seemed like we were rattling around there together for ages, just wanting to get on with Saturday afternoon and what we had to do. Inside the hotel, just like outside it, everybody was talking about the importance of the game and about what automatic qualification for the World Cup would mean. Did we have to win? Would a draw be enough? What about goal difference? You can get suffocated with all that. What was important was that beating Greece would mean it didn't matter what the Germans did. That was what we had to keep in focus. It didn't help that the media and England supporters seemed to think the hard work was over and that we were on to a home banker. We had five days for nerves and anxiety to set in. Saturday came and there was far more tension about than there should have been.

I was on edge as much as everybody else, although I had more to help me get through it than some of the other England players. First, the game was at Old Trafford. I'd come on as a substitute the last time we'd had an international there, against South Africa, back in 1997. Now, 6 October 2001, and I was a United player leading out the England team as captain. Who wouldn't be looking forward to a moment like that? Second, we were playing in an all-white strip. During the week, the England kit man came to find out if I thought he should ask Sven if we could. United's all-white change strip, the England version or even Real Madrid's colours, come to that: I've always loved that kit. And the England manager agreed that we'd wear it against Greece. I had that and my home ground to look forward to. What I didn't know too much about in advance was that I was going to meet an angel in the tunnel at Old Trafford that afternoon.

The first time I heard about Kirsty Howard was from my Dad in midweek. He phoned to tell me about her:

'She's a lovely girl, David, but she's not well at all. She's going to come out for kick-off with you on Saturday. Make sure you take good care of her.'

Dad had been involved in the arrangements along with the FA and that's why he knew all about Kirsty and the Francis House Children's Hospice she's raised so much money for. That phone conversation was as much as I was told. When we arrived at Old Trafford on the Saturday afternoon, before I went into the dressing room to get changed, I went down to the tunnel to meet her. Kirsty was waiting for me with her mum and dad and a couple of people from the charity. She was standing patiently, a little girl with a smile almost as big as she was. I saw that smile before I even noticed the oxygen cylinder Kirsty has to wheel around behind her. I sat down on the step next to her and we talked for a few minutes; about what she had to struggle with, her being born with her heart the wrong way round and some of her other organs out of place. She explained how she was trying to raise money for other children at the hospice where she got her treatment. I asked her how she was feeling and, before she could answer, someone behind us said:

'Do you want to give him a kiss?'

For the first time, Kirsty seemed a little bit embarrassed but she gave me a peck on the cheek anyway and we had a bit of a cuddle. It was time for me to go. I stood up and said:

'I'll see you in a minute, though, won't I? When we go out on the pitch?'

Kirsty looked back up at me. She nodded and smiled and I went back in to the changing room. I was miles away. It took me a minute or two to realise that the atmosphere was weird, quiet.

Not like this England team. Nobody seemed to have much to say to each other. Sven said:

'Make sure we get the ball moving quickly.'

Which was exactly what we didn't do for the rest of that afternoon, of course. The bell rang and it was time to go out. In the tunnel, I came up alongside Kirsty and took her hand. She's got the tiniest little hands you could imagine, just big enough for her to wrap one around one of my fingers. She held onto me. I asked her if she was nervous:

'No.'

I had to smile.

'Well, there's 65,000 people out there in the stadium waiting for us, hoping we're going to get to the World Cup. If you're not nervous, you must be the only person here who isn't.'

'No, I'm not. I'm not nervous.'

She looked up at me and gave me that smile and that was enough to tell me she was fine. We walked out into the roar and the sunshine. The cameras were on Kirsty all the way to the centre spot. I hardly needed to ask if she was okay. She was just so graceful and so poised. I wish us players could have been as relaxed as she was: the coolest person inside Old Trafford. She was great.

Since that afternoon, Kirsty and I, and Victoria too, have become really good friends. We help her with fundraising whenever we can but I wouldn't want anyone to think that's all our relationship is about. Kirsty's an amazing person, so full of life and energy. When you're with her, you don't think about what's wrong with her or the fact that she's hanging on for her life against all the odds. You see past that cylinder, past what you might call her disability. You see her personality, her determination to make a difference for other people, her happiness in the face of it all.

She's the bravest person I know. I remember the summer of the 2002 Commonwealth Games in Manchester when I ran with the baton into the stadium and met up with Kirsty before the two of us met The Queen. All the way round the running track, I was convinced the flame on the baton would blow out, or my tracksuit bottoms would slip down, or I'd trip on a trainer lace. As soon as I was face to face with Kirsty, though, all the nerves disappeared. Suddenly, it was this private moment, as if it was just the two of us in the stadium together: you look into her eyes and what comes back to you is calmness and inspiration. Kirsty's smile takes you out of your own world and into hers, where she takes it all in her stride. *England captain? Her Majesty the Queen? Thousands of people watching in the stands? Pleased to meet you, I'm Kirsty Howard and this is all just fine by me.*

That's how it was as we made our way to the halfway line at Old Trafford. I'd been fretting all week. Suddenly, I wasn't thinking about the game at all. I wasn't thinking about how big the occasion was or how desperately we wanted to win. I just wanted to be sure Kirsty was all right, walking beside me. The girl touches every single person she meets. She glows. In my memory, meeting Kirsty at the start of the afternoon is up there with scoring my goal at the end of it.

Eventually, Kirsty had to find her way off the pitch and I had to remind myself we had a game of football on here that needed winning. You're never sure until you kick off but we were right to have been worried about Greece. They were really up for the match, despite having already missed out on qualification. I remember one or two of them having a go at us after challenges, although not speaking Greek, I haven't got a clue what they were actually saying. They played well and we just couldn't get started. The players were uneasy and the crowd picked up on that. The game felt flat, like we needed a goal just to get us going. The trouble was, after half an hour or so, I found myself thinking that I couldn't see us scoring one. Ten minutes later, disaster: Greece scored. It was a sloppy goal, too, and between then and half-time we didn't find anything like the rhythm we needed to get back into the game. From thinking we needed the win to be sure of our place at the World Cup, we were in a position where we had to start thinking that at least a draw would give us a chance. At half-time, Sven wasn't panicking.

'We need to lift the tempo. We're waiting for things to happen. We need to push on and be the team that's making things happen.'

The start of the second half was better, but not by much. Nobody said anything but I just got it in my head that I needed to go looking for the ball. I was angry. Angry with myself. Angry with the Greek players who were having digs at us. Angry about the situation we'd got ourselves in. It was hot, a dead pitch and we looked tired. It's not right to rely on anybody else in that kind of situation. You have to try and do something about it yourself. It wasn't a case of thinking it was my responsibility or something I had to do as a skipper. It simply felt as if it was time to take risks. If I wasn't getting the ball in my position, I decided to try and get involved somewhere else. I remember Gary Neville shouting at me:

'You'll get caught. We've got to keep our shape or they'll break off us and score again.'

In almost any other game, Gary would have been right. But that afternoon against Greece, for once, I decided to take no notice of Gaz. I tried running at players and drew a couple of fouls around the area. It was the kind of afternoon, though, when every free-kick was going high or wide however hard I tried. Nothing seemed to be going right for us, at least until about twenty minutes into the second half. The Greeks had been attacking and almost scored, which might have finished us off. Nigel Martyn, in goal, threw the ball out to me, on the left wing. I'm sure Gary was thinking: what's he doing over there? I sort of barged past one player, took another one on and, ten yards outside the corner of their box, the ref gave a foul which probably wasn't. It was too wide of goal for a shot. Teddy Sheringham was just about to come on as a substitute in place of Robbie Fowler. While I was waiting for the changeover, I noticed a piece of red card on the pitch by the ball. I grabbed it and flung it away from me. I was so frustrated I was blaming our troubles on the litter by then. As Teddy jogged past me, he said:

'Watch me. Just watch me.'

I knew what he meant: we'd played that many games together for United. I lifted the free-kick towards the space I knew Teddy would run into. All he needed was a touch: he knew exactly where the ball was going, beyond their goalkeeper and into the far corner. We were level and back on track for the finals. But for only a minute. We'd hardly finished celebrating before Greece broke away and scored again. *That's it. This isn't going to be our day, is it? We're heading for the play-offs.*

I was frozen to the spot. I could see other players' shoulders sagging at the same time, the same thoughts running through their minds. We kept going, of course. You have to. But I couldn't see us scoring again. Another couple of free-kicks; another couple wide of the post. Maybe that was why I was running round like I was. The frustration of getting chances with that many free-kicks, seven or eight of them during the game, and not getting a single one on target. It was the last minute and Nigel didn't have time for anything other than a big boot downfield. Teddy went up for it. He did well. I don't know if he really got a shove in the back or not but it was enough to get a foul, just left of the D, five yards outside the Greek penalty area.

I put the ball down. Teddy came over as if to grab it and take the free-kick himself.

'I'll have this.'

I'd missed a few that afternoon but I wasn't going to give this last one up.

'No, Ted. It's too far out for you.'

I don't know why I said that because it wasn't. But Teddy looked up, looked at their wall, and let me get on with it. I knew this was our last chance. I tried to slow my nerves down by blowing out a couple of long breaths. Teddy did what he always does. He's great at it: behind the wall, he finds where the keeper is and stands in front of him, without obstructing him. Just at the last moment he'll move away and it throws the keeper's positioning out every time. Without Teddy doing that, maybe the Greek keeper would have got across in time to make the save. I was just concentrating on making sure the shot was on target. I ran up and the moment I made contact with the ball, I knew this one was in.

Anyone who was at Old Trafford that afternoon, anyone who was watching on television, won't need reminding that I got a bit carried away after the goal. Teddy went and got the ball out of the back of the net. I was gone, celebrating with Rio and Emile and Martin Keown, not even remembering that we might need another goal and the win. It was a fantastic feeling and it wasn't just me who lost it completely for a minute or two. Martin's a great professional and a very funny man. I'd never seen him like it: it makes me laugh now, thinking back to the look on his face and his eyes popping out of his head. He was hanging off me, laughing and screaming:

'That's amazing! That's amazing! That's why you're the man!'

All of a sudden, though, it dawned on us that this might not be over. We might need to score again. Germany were playing Finland at home that same afternoon. They'd been drawing at half-time: if it stayed the same in Manchester and Munich, we'd be through. Right at that moment, I was far too excited to be working out the permutations. I ran back to halfway and saw Steve McClaren standing on the touchline. I shouted across to him:

'What's the score?'

'Nil nil.'

'Is it over?'

'Nearly.'

The Greeks kicked off and lobbed the ball forward. I remember praying we wouldn't get caught cold again. Once the ball had gone out of play, I called out to Gary Neville:

'What happens now? If they draw, do we win?'

Gary managed to make sense of what I was trying to ask him and nodded his head. We got a throw-in and Steven Gerrard rushed over to take it. He still thought we needed another goal. He threw the ball to me just as the final whistle went. I picked it up and kicked it up in the air as high as I could. All the other England players came rushing over towards me. Ashley Cole had been substituted but he came charging across from the England bench, followed by the rest of the squad. I felt so proud, my free-kick taking us through to the World Cup finals. We knew we'd done it even before the tannoy announcer came on the PA:

'And the final score from Germany is . . .'

Suddenly there was silence all round the ground. I get a little shiver when I remember it.

'. . . Germany 0 Finland 0.'

This roar – I'd never heard anything like it – erupted around Old Trafford and the sound of it followed us back into the changing room. It was strange: people were going mad, bouncing off the walls, the coaching staff and the subs. Back in the quiet underneath the stand, though, most of the players were just blown out, down even: we knew that we hadn't played well and the heat and the effort of the afternoon hit people hard. I found myself thinking about all the free-kicks I'd missed rather than the one I'd scored. We went back out on the pitch for a lap of honour and that helped lift us: we could be proud and excited that we would be going to the World Cup Finals after all. I've just one regret about those mad scenes in the sunshine at Old Trafford. Michael Owen was out with a hamstring injury and was analysing the game for television. We should have got him down to be part of those celebrations: his hat-trick in Munich had been so important, getting us all to where we wanted England to be.

There's a phone just outside the home dressing room at Old Trafford and, when we came back in, the first thing I did was ring Victoria. She was out in Italy working, desperate that she'd missed the game. She'd made sure she found out what had happened and now she wanted me to tell her what it felt like. My heart was pounding, adrenalin was still charging round inside me, my mouth was bone dry. Every time I went to speak, my voice cracked and nothing came out. Victoria knows me well enough: the little gasps and croaks were enough for her to understand exactly what was going on at my end of the phone. She may not know all that much about football but Victoria knows what it means to people. And she knew what an afternoon like the Greece game meant to me.

Mum and Dad told me afterwards about how the supporters around them had celebrated: for once it wasn't just me who had trouble holding back tears. I was so pleased that I had so many people who mattered to me there, watching at Old Trafford, that afternoon. As well as my parents, who sat outside because that's how they prefer to watch games, I'd taken a box for Tony and Jackie and Brooklyn, and also for the American R&B singer, Usher, who'd come as my guest. When Sven first took over as England manager, he wasn't happy about music being played in the dressing room before games. He'd put a stop to it, in fact. The players had worked on him, though, and I think he came to realise how positive a part of our preparation it could be. And Usher, that year, was always on the CD player before kick-off. He had a new album out in the summer of 2001, called '8701', and had come over to England to promote it. He'd got a message through that he'd like to meet me and I'd invited him along to Old Trafford. I was a big fan of Usher – I still am – and I met him in the players' lounge afterwards:

'David, David: that's the most amazing thing I've ever seen.'

I got him a signed shirt, we had photos taken, the works. He was lucky. If you were going to watch a football match for the first time, you couldn't have got a much more dramatic one than that game against Greece. Meeting Kirsty, the game itself, my goal, being with my family and Usher afterwards: all that was great. One other moment from the day will always stick with me too. To get to the players' lounge, I had to walk along the side of the pitch, past where the old tunnel at Old Trafford used to be. The press working area is just there, to the left as you climb up the stairs, and there were still a couple of dozen football writers sitting, working on their reports. As I walked past, one of them stood up and started clapping. The next thing I knew, they were all on their feet and giving me a round of applause. That's something that never happens. Thinking back to after France 98, it's certainly not something I'd have ever imagined happening to me. I hope those guys know how good they made me feel that afternoon.

Usually, the English press takes some pleasing. Not as much as Alex Ferguson, though. When we got back to Carrington, the gaffer's first words to me were:

'I hope you're going to work that bloody hard now you're back at United.'

I knew better than to be surprised by the gaffer but that comment hurt a bit anyway. I came back into training on a high, all of our England players did. And, because of that, I couldn't wait for the next game for my club. I enjoy the big moments but I really don't believe I'm someone who gets carried away with them. I didn't arrive at training expecting anyone to pat me on the back and say how well I'd played. It wasn't something for me to get big-headed about. I was just turning up to work at United in a very good mood. The boss obviously didn't see it like that. At least, he didn't see me like that. He thought what I needed was to be dumped back down to earth.

It must have been a strange season for the gaffer. Maybe he wished he hadn't had to tell anyone he was retiring. Like I've said, I don't think it affected the United players. If the boss was reading in the papers day after day that it did, though, perhaps he started to believe it himself. I don't know what made him change his mind. I just remember him telling us he had. It was early February 2002. We were in the changing room at Carrington after training one morning.

'I'm staying on.'

It was as simple as that. I remember Gary Neville clapping and one or two of the other lads joking:

'Oh no, you're not are you?'

We were all really happy: me more than anybody, although, in hindsight, it probably meant the beginning of the end for me at the club. Back then, I didn't have any idea what was going to happen between me and the boss over the next seventeen months. I can still remember that lunchtime and the mix of relief and excitement that came with hearing that the only manager I'd ever worked for had decided to stay as boss of Manchester United. Alex Ferguson had been the making of me and the club. Why wouldn't I have been happy to know he was carrying on?

The gaffer's decision definitely gave us a lift and we had a good run in the second half of 2001/02. Not good enough to win the League, though: Arsenal were absolutely flying and won their last dozen games and the title. They won the FA Cup too: Middlesbrough and Steve McClaren, of all people, knocked us out in the fourth round. Our best chance was in Europe. We played Deportivo La Coruña in the first group phase and lost to them twice but, come the Spring, we drew them in the quarter-finals and those previous results didn't mean a thing. We played them in Spain first and won 2–0. The team played so well, especially considering Roy Keane had to go off with a hamstring injury just before half-time. I scored one of my all-time favourite United goals that night. I got the ball, about thirty yards out, and whipped a shot in early. The goalie hadn't been expecting it: he was caught a little off his line and it dipped in over his head.

I actually got the first blow on my left foot at the Riazor stadium. There were about five minutes left and I had the ball over by the touchline. As I cleared it, Diego Tristan, their centre-forward, came in with his foot high and caught my standing leg. Every player knows how dangerous that kind of challenge is and the pain I got straight after it made me think he might have broken my ankle. As it was, there was just a cut and some bad bruising. Even so,

I was on crutches and couldn't put any weight on my foot on the journey home. I remember there were one or two pictures and headlines wondering if I'd be fit for the World Cup, never mind the second leg at Old Trafford. I had scans as a precaution, but everything was fine ahead of the game a week later. At least, that's what I thought.

I was really looking forward to the return game: it's always exciting against Deportivo. The first quarter of an hour, they really had a go at trying to get back in the tie. We ended up winning 3–2 and going through to the semis. By the time that had happened, though, I was in a hospital bed. Just as we were starting to get a grip on the game, twenty minutes in, I went in for what looked like a 60/40 challenge in my favour fifteen yards outside their area. I think the other bloke, Aldo Duscher, decided to even up the odds: another Argentinian midfield player leaving his mark on my life. All I was thinking about was winning the challenge: you never worry about getting a knock at the same time. I made it to the ball just before him and nicked it away but Duscher arrived, two-footed and studs up, and caught me and my left foot instead.

I remember lying there, dumped on the floor, and holding my foot which was killing me. I tried to get myself up but, as well as it hurting, the foot had gone floppy. I couldn't stand on it. They carried me over to the touchline. I was still thinking I'd run it off.

'Just spray something on it. Put some water on it. It'll be fine.'

They did that but then, when I went to stand, I almost fell over. I just couldn't put any weight on the foot at all. The pain wouldn't let my boot even touch the ground. The United doctor was bending over me. He took the boot off and felt around where I told him it was hurting. It was like something giving way inside: what should have been firm felt flimsy. I could actually feel the bone moving. I said it before the Doc did:

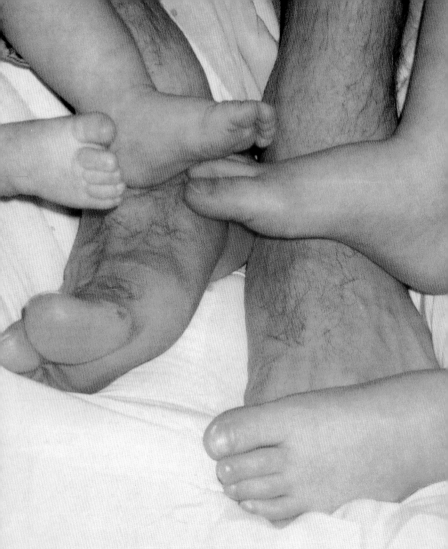

Best feet forward. The boys make their marks.

Left: Mr & Mrs. The Beckhams' big day.
Above and below: Signing then slicing. The formalities at Luttrellstown Castle.

Hair today. The changing face of.

United born and bred.

Left: Down and out against Romania at Euro 2000…

Below far left: …eight days after the disappointment against Portugal.

Below left: 'Don't worry, I'll back you.' England boss Kevin Keegan was always very supportive.

Bottom: 'I want the job to keep.' England captain for the first time, against Italy, 15 November 2000.

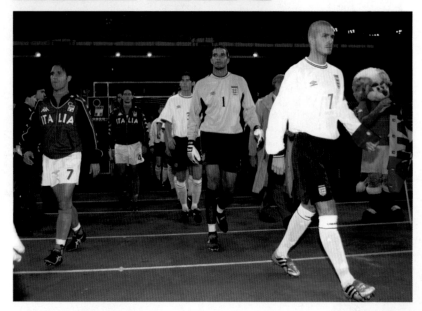

Above: Amateur dramatics at the FIFA World Club Championships, February 2000. My only sending off as a United player.

Right: Happy days. Training at Carrington, Spring 1999.

Left: Every schoolboy's dream. Lifting the FA Cup, Wembley 1999.

Far left: 'Here, David. I want a word.' Sir Alex Ferguson takes charge.

Left: Who's your money on? Roy Keane and Alan Shearer have a difference of opinion.

Below: Unbelievable. Completing the Treble at the Nou Camp, 1999.

'It's broken.'

'Yes. I think it is.'

He nodded and I thought: *What about the World Cup?* And I slumped back.

'I can't believe this is happening.'

They got me onto a stretcher and took me around the side of the pitch to the changing room: there was no other way but past the photographers. I couldn't remember the last time I'd had to come off injured during a game. Throughout my career, I'd been so lucky. Why had that luck run out now? I looked up towards where Victoria always sat when she came to Old Trafford. She was on her feet straight away and I saw her pick up Brooklyn and make her way downstairs. When I got into the treatment room, I asked one of the lads to fetch her. I knew she'd be worried. I expected her to be even more upset than I was but Victoria was really strong for me during those moments when it was all starting to sink in.

'Don't worry,' she said. 'It'll get fixed. Everything's going to be fine.'

Brooklyn was there too. He wasn't sure what was going on.

'Why aren't you playing any more, Daddy? What's happened to your leg?'

Laughing at my boy didn't do me any harm just then either. I knew we were going straight to the hospital.

'Hey, Brooklyn. We're going in an ambulance.'

His eyes widened:

'Are we?'

Doctor Noble, the United surgeon, was in the treatment room with us. I wanted to know there and then:

'What's the longest I'll be out?'

'We'll know as soon as I've seen the x-ray.'

They got me down to the ambulance and agreed that it would

be all right for Victoria and Brooklyn to come with us. Once we'd all got inside, they strapped me to a bed so that my foot wouldn't move around on the way. I got the driver to stick the blue light on for Brooklyn. At least it was turning into an exciting evening for him. The ambulance man must have put his foot down for us: we had to get across Manchester to the Royal Infirmary in Whalley Range and seemed to do the trip in about five minutes flat.

I had my x-ray almost as soon as we got to the hospital. Victoria went through to look at the results with Doctor Noble and she came out to tell me what they'd seen.

'The bad news is it's broken. The good news is that, if everything goes well, you should be fine for the World Cup.'

The first bit was no surprise. The second bit was what I'd been waiting and hoping to hear since the moment I'd been clattered by Duscher. Victoria left it to Doctor Noble to explain the injury. I'd fractured the second metatarsal, a tiny bone between the toe and the rest of the foot, which usually has enough flesh around it to keep it out of harm's way. It's very rare to damage it, apparently. But try telling Gary Neville or Danny Murphy that: they both missed the World Cup because of the same injury. The doctor confirmed that he thought I'd have just enough time to recover. I hung onto that over the next few weeks, even when I had my doubts about being ready: never mind the bone healing, I knew I needed to be match-fit for England as well.

The following morning, I couldn't believe what we woke up to. What was my foot doing on the front page of the papers? Sven was one of the first people to ring me, although it may have been less about: 'Are you all right?' and more about: 'Are you going to be fit?' It was good to hear from him. He told me that, whether I was fit to play or not, he'd want me to come out and be involved at the World Cup. Sven's support then, and later, made a real difference to me. At the hospital, they'd put my foot in a cast. Dwight Yorke picked me up in his car and took me in to training at Carrington. The United medical team took the plaster off and replaced it with a thing called an air cast, a sort of inflatable boot. When it was pumped full of air, it protected my foot in the same way the plaster cast would. But I could release a valve and take this thing off in order to work on my ankle and my leg. Even after a day or two in plaster, my calf and ankle had shrunk. The air cast was a way of trying to make sure I wouldn't suffer any more muscle wasting than was unavoidable. After I'd done my physio, I could re-inflate the blow-up boot again and hobble away on crutches. It was a couple of days later that I sat down with the doctors and talked through what I needed to do to give myself my best chance of being ready:

'Whatever you tell me to do, I'll do.'

I didn't want to be in Japan as a cheerleader. I knew that the United physios would give me all the help I needed. The work was down to me: resting my foot and keeping weight off it for a month or so but there was plenty I could still do to help cut down on the time I'd need to get myself ready for football again once the broken bone had healed. I'd be in at Carrington for as long as the physios thought was worthwhile. When I'm injured – and now was no different – I'll always be ready to push myself as hard as I can to give myself a better chance. On my days off, Terry Byrne would come over to the house and keep an eye on me while I did extra rehab. I could do running in the deep end of my pool, making sure my foot didn't touch the bottom. I could work on my overall fitness in the gym. The World Cup was all the motivation I needed, however fed up I was with the routine of working on all those machines.

Usually, a player's left with the day-to-day progress of an injury to deal with on his own. During that April and May, though, it seemed like there were a few million England supporters looking over my shoulder, having the same worries as I was. The fans' good wishes helped me along. Gary Neville was there for me too: he phoned as soon as he got away from Old Trafford after the La Coruña game. A fortnight later, I was watching the first leg of the Champions League semi-final against Bayer Leverkusen on television, the night he picked up the same injury. The moment Gary went down I knew what had happened. And I knew that, if I was touch and go for the World Cup, Gary had no chance. He just didn't have time. If I'd been him, I would have been devastated. But Gaz is so positive in his attitude: whatever he was feeling inside, he did his best to stay upbeat. He deserved better than to have to miss three months of the following season as well because the foot needed an operation to put things right.

I was worried about the summer and I was really disappointed to miss the end of United's season. Bayer Leverkusen put us out of the Champions League on away goals. I'm sure we'd have had a great chance of beating Real Madrid at Hampden Park if we could have got to the final. It was a frustrating time for me and a frustrating time for the club but I knew that, with the gaffer staying, United would push on again next time round. I couldn't imagine that I wouldn't be a part of that when it happened. I was in the middle of negotiations over a new contract. I knew what I wanted to do and I was pretty sure I knew what the club wanted to do. Modern-day football, though, is never as simple as that. The negotiations, and the newspaper speculation, had already spun on for over a year. Now was the time to set things straight.

I never thought seriously about anything other than signing a new contract with the club I loved. It was just a question of getting the details right: a new deal was going to mean a major commitment on both sides. I needed to know that United respected my value to them and I don't think United directors Peter Kenyon and David Gill, who handled things at the club's end between them, had a problem with that. They certainly did everything they could to make things go smoothly and made sure they honoured every single promise. I'm very grateful to them for that. I'm grateful that I had the right man sitting on my side of the table as well.

Tony Stephens had been my agent since 1995. He'd been a director at Wembley in the past and was working as a consultant on the project to build Huddersfield's new ground, the McAlpine Stadium, when I first got to know him. I remember one time in particular: Tony invited a group of the young United lads – me, Gary, Phil and Ben Thornley – to a Bryan Adams concert. We ended up wangling our way onto the stage for what was a pretty amazing night. That same evening, Tony actually had another quite important bit of business going on in the area at the same time: arranging a transfer for Alan Shearer, a player he was already looking after, from Blackburn Rovers to Newcastle United.

I'm not sure when or where we were actually introduced. I do remember clearly, though, something Tony said during our very first conversation. It's stuck with me ever since:

'Football's the most important thing, David. That's what you do. You must make sure nothing ever gets in the way of that.'

Later, when we talked about him representing me, Tony described his job as making sure I didn't have to worry about anything other than playing. The problem we had at United now, though, was a tricky one. He and the gaffer didn't get on; or, at least, the gaffer didn't get on with him. I should have known: when I first told the boss that I'd signed up to be represented by Tony, which happened a few months after we'd met, I got ripped into on the spot.

'What do you need an agent for? Haven't you always been looked after at the club?'

Tony made a point of telling the boss, too, as he'd never have thought to start work with me without him knowing. He went round to the gaffer's house to do it face to face. There are stories that the gaffer ended up chasing Tony down the street. That never happened but I do know Tony got an even worse grilling about it than I did.

I think back to times during my career at Old Trafford when the boss was worried or angry about me; I remember situations where we fell out. Those bust-ups always seemed to get blown up out of all proportion. They happen at every football club all the time without having to make headlines. I think we could have kept a lid on things and settled differences sooner if the boss and my agent had had the kind of relationship which meant they would have been able to pick up the phone to each other.

The frost between Tony and the gaffer wasn't what held up negotiations over my new deal at Old Trafford, though. It was a pretty complicated bit of paperwork, especially because my image rights had to be built in somewhere so that United could use my face and name as an individual in their commercial operations. I think it took something like two dozen meetings before everything was squared away. I'm happy I only had to show my face at one of them. It might have needed a year and a half to come up with the right contract but, as far as I was concerned, the talking was all about details. In the meantime, it was interesting – flattering, even – hearing that other clubs, big European clubs, might be interested in signing me if things didn't work out at Old Trafford. But all that was daydreaming. I never wanted to do anything else but sign on the dotted line for the only club I'd ever played for. I knew that. Tony knew that. And so did United.

As the 2001/02 season wore on, we got closer and closer to the right deal. I wanted to be able to sign out on the pitch before a game at Old Trafford. After all the speculation, I wanted the people that mattered – United's supporters – to see it happen for themselves, especially as I hadn't been able to play since the Deportivo game. The last home game but one was against Arsenal. That was the night I'd set my heart on and I did what I could to hurry Tony along. As it turned out, there were a couple of tiny last-minute hitches. Just as well. Arsenal came up and won 1–0 which meant they won the title; and did the Double, in fact. It was a real low point for the club, to lose it in our own backyard. Although I think the disappointment spurred us on the following year, that night wouldn't have been the ideal time to celebrate me signing a new deal. That waited until the following Saturday instead, when we were at home to Charlton. It was perfect. The sun was shining. The gaffer came out on the pitch with me and gave me a hug in front of 65,000 fans. No doubt at all, Old Trafford was where I felt I belonged. I'd known all along the new contract was going to happen, whatever anyone else had been saying, but putting pen to paper was still a really satisfying moment.

My future felt settled. The second metatarsal, the medical experts told me, had healed. Suddenly everything was clear. I just had to concentrate on getting myself ready for England and for a World Cup that was now only a couple of weeks away. We had the send-off, at home in Sawbridgeworth, the next evening. Come Monday, we'd be leaving for Dubai to start our preparations for Japan. The idea was to combine a party for the England squad with an event which could raise money for my principal charity: the NSPCC. We even managed to sell television rights for the night to ITV. All of that money went to the NSPCC as well. Some of the arrangements had to be left to the last minute. I didn't know who Sven was going to take to the World Cup, so we couldn't be sure which players to invite until the squad was announced. In the meantime, we had a great time putting together the guest list. Lots of friends from football, of course, football greats from the past, and stars from other sports along with some famous musicians and actors as well.

To help raise more money for the NSPCC, we set just a few tables aside for paying guests too. We got in touch with my sponsors, people Victoria works with, and other companies we thought might be keen. They were all taken in no time. People knew it was going to be a special evening, I think, and they also knew their money was going to a good cause. Even though I was a crock and might have had the time to help for once, Victoria took charge of everything. She's got a gift for it: how things should look, when things should happen, what's there for people to enjoy. And she pays attention to the last detail.

I only got home from Manchester the evening before and so things were a bit of a rush. There was time, though, for one present. I gave Tony a watch to say thank you for all the work he'd done in negotiating the contract I'd signed on the pitch at Old Trafford 24 hours earlier. That turned into quite an emotional scene in our kitchen in the middle of the Sunday afternoon. And at the same time, of course, we had our families, our kids and their kids, running backwards and forwards in amongst the last-minute arrangements for the party and our bags, half-packed for Dubai the following day.

Eventually we were dressed and ready. We had photos taken – more money for the charity – and then headed towards the marquee where it was all happening, up behind the house. To get there, you had to walk through our little plot of forest which has a kind of Japanese feel to it anyway. We'd taken that as the theme for the whole party. Except for the bouncy castle: lots of the players had brought their children along and so we had one blown up for them next to the grown-ups' tent. Brooklyn walked alongside me. We had matching outfits: a knee-length Japanese-style jacket over the trousers, with a red sash around the waist. I don't know about me but my boy looked very cute indeed. And we wore flip flops because my left foot still wasn't comfortable in a shoe at that point. It was all going on in my garden but, because Victoria had thought it all out, I felt like one of the 400 guests. I couldn't wait to see what she had waiting for us up through the woods.

Lanterns were lit all the way through the garden. There were gymnasts and acrobats spinning around the flower beds and between the trees. There were dancers, martial arts experts. Surprises everywhere. Mis-Teeq sang, the R&B singer Beverley Knight, too, and Russell Watson, the opera singer. The marquee where dinner was served was really two connecting marquees. The first had been decorated like an oriental garden. There were thousands of orchids that had been flown in from Japan and Indonesia, and a little bridge, with carp swimming in a pool underneath, which you had to climb across to reach the main tent just beyond it. You walked through huge curtains hung at either side. There were geisha girls welcoming people. And then the tables, all beautifully laid – Victoria had decided on everything down to the napkins and cutlery – stretched away in front of you. It was all red, black and white: one of the most beautiful settings I've ever seen in my life.

That was when I started getting nervous, looking around at the people we'd invited, some of whom I'd never even said hello to before. I'd asked Ray Winstone to come just because he's such a great actor and I wanted the chance to meet him. I knew I was down to make my first speech since our wedding day. I was England captain and all these people were round at my gaff. I couldn't get out of it, could I? I knew where I wanted to lead up to: giving Victoria a present to thank her for making the evening happen. But before that? Well, there were other thank yous and then something about the NSPCC and UNICEF, the United Nations childrens' charity with which Manchester United were involved. I knew I should say something about the abused children we were raising money for. I was so worried about leaving something or somebody out, I had it all written down on little pieces of card. Eventually I got onto something more personal and I was able to put the cards down. Not long before, I'd visited a kids' shelter down in South London. I sat in a room in front of a couple of dozen of these youngsters who all had terrible stories to tell. You could feel something like hostility in the air: not towards me, particularly, but towards the whole world. They were kids with chips on their shoulders and I wondered, at first, whether this had been a good thing to agree to do. The questions were absolutely direct:

'How's Posh, then?'

'What cars have you got?'

'How much money do you earn?'

They weren't worried about how the hostel staff or me or anyone else might react. I knew I couldn't say I didn't want to answer their questions. They'd all lived through things that I'm lucky I'd never had to face: rape, prostitution, drugs, time in jail. A few answers from me were the least they deserved. The grown-ups were looking at me to see what I wanted to do.

'It's fine. I don't need to check the questions first. Let them ask what they want.'

That afternoon turned into one of the most rewarding things

I've ever done away from football. Obviously there weren't any press there: this was just me and the kids talking. I relaxed. They did too. After a while, I think we decided we liked each other and ended up laughing and joking: about football, about my life, about nothing in particular. My defences came down and, during that time, so did theirs. I couldn't change anything that had happened to them but it made a difference to me that at least we were able to connect with each other. By the way they acted towards me, it seemed that made a difference to them too. Maybe telling the story of my afternoon at the kids' hostel was strange in the surroundings we were in that evening, but it was what I needed to do to explain why I'd wanted the party to take place. And why I wanted everyone to be generous when it came to the charity auction. Which they were: Ant and Dec were the auctioneers and our guests stumped up over £250,000.

We had a fantastic evening. Victoria and I had to call it quits about midnight. Some of the players, and other people who had brought their families along, had already left but there were plenty still enjoying themselves when we went back to the house to get ready for bed and Dubai. It might have been late but there was still time for my Ray Winstone moment. I heard somebody at the front door. I went down to open it and Ray was standing there. It wasn't until he stepped forward that I realised how much he'd enjoyed himself. Maybe he hadn't realised either. He'd come to say thank you but, instead, he tripped on our step and landed face down in the hall. Actors know how to make a big entrance. Like I say, it was a really good night: good memories for us all to take away to Japan.

I know the United medical staff weren't all that happy about me going off to Dubai with the rest of the England squad to start our preparations for the World Cup. I think the gaffer assumed the week would just be a jolly and that I'd stand a better chance of being fit if I stayed in Manchester and worked with the physios at Carrington. I knew that, even when I went off to play for my country, I was still a United player. If the club had really put their foot down I'd have done what they said without thinking twice. Sven wanted me to be with the rest of the players for the two weeks leading up to our first game and Gary Lewin, the England physio, and Doc Crane, the England doctor, were two of the best in the business. At one stage, the FA offered to take a United medical team along with us. To be honest, it was an argument I wanted other people to have. I didn't think it was right for me to be involved in any row. I was ready to go along with whatever decision was made behind the scenes. And that decision, eventually, was that I went.

Early on Monday morning, 13 May 2002: lying in bed next to Victoria at home in Sawbridgeworth. Everything in the house was quiet. Somewhere in the distance outside, I could hear the last few people making their way home from the party and climbing into waiting cars. I reached down and touched my left foot: a little sore since Victoria and I had started the dancing in the marquee after dinner. In a few hours we'd be off to the airport. I had eighteen days ahead of me, eighteen days to make sure I'd be right to line up against Sweden on the other side of the world on 31 May. I got a little chill feeling deep down at the base of my spine. Excitement? Or dread? Four years ago, I'd been getting ready to head off to the last World Cup. How much had happened since then? 1998 already seemed so long ago: Argentina, a red card and the rest. But, at the same time, it seemed as if the next challenge had stolen up on us in the blink of an eye. Just having the chance to be involved in a World Cup is a dream and a privilege. And every player knows that during the month of that tournament your career, and your life, can change forever. Mine had in France, in the harsh glare of a floodlit evening in Saint-Etienne. I shut my eyes and sank back into the dark. What was waiting for me, and waiting for England, this time out in Japan?

Beckham (pen)

11

'What's going on here? I can't breathe.'

I wonder now: *Did that week in Dubai help finish me off as a United player in the eyes of the boss?*

I was out in the sunshine with England instead of being back at Carrington, clocking up the miles on the treadmill alone. I know the gaffer wasn't best pleased about that. I had the feeling he wasn't too happy, generally, about the extra responsibility – and the extra attention – that came with me captaining England. And he probably wasn't keen, either, on the fact that Victoria and Brooklyn were in Dubai with me. It didn't matter that I thought that marriage and fatherhood had settled me and had a positive effect on me as a player. The gaffer had always thought my family was a distraction from the serious business of football. He'd said as much to me often enough since I'd met Victoria. He thought my life at home got in the way: for me and for him.

I'd long since decided that it wasn't an argument worth having. Was an argument ever worth having with the gaffer? I wasn't going to convince him that being fulfilled as a person could only ever be good for me as a player. And, obviously, nothing he said was going to change how much I loved and cherished my family. It was great having Victoria and Brooklyn with me out in Dubai.

Sven thought it would be good if the players had their families around them. We were hoping to be away in Japan for the duration of the World Cup, after all. I remember talking to him about it before we left England, while he was planning our schedule. He believes in players having time with their partners and with their children. Most other countries see it that way. I remember at France 98, the Danish team were staying at a hotel just down the road from us and had their families with them in the same complex. At first, Sven wasn't sure how the English players felt about having family with them, so he asked me, as captain, to sound them out. In Dubai we had activities organised for the kids in the mornings around the pool and barbecues for everyone in the evenings. The families enjoyed each other's company and it helped draw the lads closer together at the same time.

Having Victoria and Brooklyn there left me with a clear head to concentrate on the one thing that mattered, the World Cup, and me being fit for it. I worked with one of the England physios, Alan Smith, every morning on my own. I was just starting to run, just starting to test the metatarsal injury. I had to try and build up to something near match fitness too. I wasn't able to join in with the regular squad training which was going on every day at the same time. The balance was just right in Dubai: hard work and then the beach and some sunshine, with our families there to enjoy it with us.

I still had doubts whether I would be ready to play in our first match against Sweden. Some days I'd wake up feeling ready there and then, others when it just felt I was starting to run out of time. I was desperate to play in a World Cup as England captain. To give myself and the team the best chance, I thought that meant playing from the very first game. Even before I left England, I'd done everything I could to hurry along the mending process. Now, in Dubai, I was able to put weight on the injured foot. As well as starting to run, there was other work to do before I'd be ready just for a training session, never mind for a game. People might have seen pictures of me on a trampoline. I definitely wasn't ready for jumping up and down. Those exercises were about teaching my leg how to balance again. As well as the muscles losing strength, the tendons and ligaments forget how to do their jobs. I'd have to stand on one leg and balance when a ball was thrown to me, then change legs. The next stage after that was to volley the ball back instead of just catching it. At the end of every day, the physios would sit down with the England doctors and talk through what we'd done. The medical team would do that with every injured player. Then, Doctor Crane would meet up with Sven in the evening to make sure the manager knew exactly how I was doing from day to day.

I was glad to be around the other players who weren't bothered about anything but starting the tournament. Picking up on everybody else's excitement made me feel more positive about what I had to do. I don't know if it was being captain that made me feel older; or being conscious of the experience I had now, four years on from France 98. I liked watching the younger England players: they were excited about the build-up, the new suits, the kit, the attention and everything. But as far as the football was concerned, the World Cup for them just meant more big games to look forward to. They weren't scared of anything and that kept them very relaxed. It was the likes of me and Michael Owen, Gareth Southgate, Martin Keown and Dave Seaman who'd been there before and understood just how big a World Cup was and how much was at stake for us all.

The week in Dubai gave the players some time to rest after a season at home that had only just finished. It didn't seem long before I was saying goodbye to Victoria and Brooklyn and travelling east with the squad. There was going to be so much travelling during the World Cup itself that we decided it would be too much for our families. We were going to be based in Japan for the tournament but we stopped off in South Korea for the first of two warm-up friendlies. We checked into our hotel and you could see the change of mood on the players' faces. We were here now. This was where the World Cup was going to take place. That first match was a good jolt for us, as we only drew 1–1 with the Koreans in Seogwipo. We experimented with a few things and nobody was at it full pelt, but it was obvious South Korea could play; and they were incredibly fit. Which was more than could be said for me. I wasn't even close, eleven days before our first proper game.

Sven had taken on this Dutchman, Richard Smith, as one of four masseurs who travelled with the squad to Japan. Somebody stuck up a card on Richard's door that read 'HOUSE OF PAIN'. They weren't far wrong. Richard would work deep, deep into where your injury was. I can't describe what it felt like. It just made your guts turn over it hurt so much. But it worked. Thanks to Richard I got there in the end and, later, Michael Owen made the Brazil game because of him working on his groin injury the day before.

Our other friendly was in Japan against Cameroon the following Sunday. Although I couldn't play, the medical team thought I needed the boost of being involved with the rest of the lads so I led the team out for the warm-up. It was a decent game to watch despite the players holding back in challenges, for obvious reasons, and the final score was 2–2. That afternoon, I found myself thinking back to my lowest point in the whole rehabilitation process. Quite soon after the injury happened, England had a friendly against Paraguay at Anfield. The squad met up at a hotel in Cheshire and Sven invited me along. He wanted me to be part of our build-up because he believed all along I was going to play in Japan. I got there for dinner and it was good to see all the other lads but, at that stage, I was still on crutches most of the time. The next morning, when the squad went off to train, I found myself sitting on my own at the hotel, watching daytime television. For those couple of hours, I was really down. If I couldn't even get along to watch training, never mind be part of it, what chance did I have? Now, here I was, within touching distance. But I still wasn't sure. Was I days away from all that rehab work paying off? Or days away from a disappointment that I just couldn't imagine myself having to face?

The opening game against Sweden in Saitama was still a week away. Sven didn't push me. He wanted to give me as long as possible. But he couldn't afford for that to interfere with preparing the rest of the team. With a longer-term injury, the doctors will always set you weekly targets. That's partly so they can make sure you push yourself on to the next stage, whether that's running on hard ground or twisting and turning or hitting a ball with full force. But it's also to make sure a player doesn't get depressed by focusing too far ahead. Psychologically, the secret is to concentrate on what you're doing from day to day. Now, though, I'd reached the point of no return. Would I be able to take part in a competitive game by the end of the week? Sven knew – and I knew – that the time had come when a decision had to be made. If I couldn't join in full training in the days before the game then, obviously, playing was out of the question. I know the medical team were confident about my foot but not so sure about my overall fitness: I'd been out a long time. The decision was the manager's to make. Wednesday arrived, the very last day he could afford for me not to be working with everybody else. I'd known all along that Sven would want to take a chance on me as long as the odds were in mine, and England's, favour. He knew that I hadn't come this far or worked this hard to duck out at the end of it. Even if I didn't feel one hundred percent, I was sure I could make it. After breakfast, Sven asked me the question:

'Well, are you fit?'

He knew the answer and I didn't pick up any trace of doubt or tension in his voice. He wanted to hear it from me and to know I was confident. It crossed my mind that, if I'd broken my foot in a Premiership game the following weekend rather than against Deportivo in midweek, me and the England manager wouldn't have been having this conversation. It was that close. I gulped a little air and tried to keep it as short and nerveless as Sven had done.

'I'm fit.'

'Good. Let's go.'

The first session with the rest of the boys was difficult. I'd been working really hard, running and kicking a ball. This was the first time I'd had to risk physical contact. I should have seen it coming: as soon as we were into a game, the first crunching challenge came in from Martin Keown – who else? He didn't actually make contact with the injury: it was a clump across the back of the legs. I couldn't help the instinctive reaction. I tumbled over, expecting the worst: angry at Martin, angry at Aldo Duscher, angry at everything. It took a second to realise that, for the first time in a couple of months, somewhere else was actually hurting worse than my foot. Pain's never given me so much pleasure. Like I say, I should have been waiting for him. Martin will always be the one to test you: he'll whack you, challenge you to be up to it, find out if you've got the nerve. He knew and I knew that, come Sunday, there'd be someone ready to do the same thing he had just done. The difference would be that if a Swedish player did it, it would be in the hope that I wouldn't get up again. Here, I scraped myself off the floor and carried on. If I could survive Martin, I could probably survive anybody. The foot was really sore even before we'd finished the session, but I was just pleased to have got through it. Working with the other lads lifted me for the rest of the week.

It was a great squad to be part of, especially once we arrived in Japan and the players started looking forward to getting on with the tournament. The atmosphere amongst the group we had out in Japan was special. What was going on outside the camp, though? I don't think any of us had ever seen anything like it. It started the moment we got off the plane in Tokyo: walking out through the terminal was unbelievable. There were thousands of Japanese waiting to meet us: mums, dads, children and teenagers, who'd made England their team for the tournament. They were wearing our shirts. It was almost like a pop concert, with fans waving, shouting, pushing forward, and the police struggling to hold them back. As we climbed onto the coach, I caught one old lady out of the corner of my eye: well into her seventies, I'd say, with snow-white hair and a bright red stripe dyed through it. Parents were holding their children up above the bobbing heads. These kids were too young to have a clue who I was, but lots of them had copied my haircut: the blonde streak and the mohican. And had the number 7 on their shirts. It was chaotic, but in a polite way that's maybe characteristic of the Japanese. They were excited to see us, so positive about the team and about the English. I think their attitude had a lot to do with why there weren't any crowd problems during the World Cup, even though people had been worrying about trouble happening for months leading up to the tournament. Instead, it turned out the people there had a real passion for football and loved being with the English: we're passionate about the game in the same way. And it wasn't just the players who were welcome. Our supporters were too and, credit to them, England fans made the effort in return. That spirit is what World Cups should be about.

For a player, of course, the World Cup is all about playing. Leading England out at the stadium in Saitama, for our first game of the 2002 tournament against Sweden, will always be one of the proudest moments of my whole career. The setting, the occasion and the privilege of being at the head of the line as captain of your country at a World Cup: my heart was beating out of my chest. It's a schoolboy's dream but it's the kind of dream you don't dare have. And here it was, happening. The atmosphere was terrific. One corner with a few thousand Sweden fans; the rest of the stadium red and white, our own supporters and the Japanese who'd decided to make England their team. Fractured metatarsal? So what? I could never have allowed myself to miss this.

Pity the game wasn't as intense as the build-up. We played some good football, especially early on, but somehow the game didn't feel like it could decide where it was going. There weren't many chances. Where were the big tackles and the confrontations? You couldn't honestly say you saw it coming but, 25 minutes in, we got the first goal. I took a corner on the left and Sol Campbell arrived and got a perfect header in. Sol went running off towards the other corner flag to celebrate. I was just going mad on my own, as if it was me who'd scored. I turned round and put my arms up in the direction of the Swedish supporters, who'd been giving me plenty of stick. They were still laughing. Maybe they knew that their time would come.

Scoring's one thing. Setting a goal up for someone else is a fantastic feeling as well and, that night, I was so pleased it was Sol who got it. We go back fifteen years together, to training with Tottenham as schoolboys, and he doesn't score many. Against

Argentina at France 98, in extra-time when we were down to ten men, he'd had one disallowed which, if it had stood, would probably have won us the game. Now, he'd kicked us off in 2002. The trouble was, we didn't push on from that. We were ahead but we were cautious, tense, sitting back on the lead. And then in the second half, we lost our shape. We didn't keep the ball. Our passing was all over the place. And Sweden kept on coming at us. Unlike our goal in the first half, you could see theirs was due. We just lost concentration, as a team, at the wrong moment and gifted them their equaliser. When a rushed clearance from Danny Mills was blasted into the net by Niclas Alexandersson, it would have been easy for people to blame the Leeds defender for the goal. I didn't think it was his fault. There were two or three other mistakes in the build-up as well. I made a point of getting near him.

'Come on, Danny. Let's keep going.'

A couple of minutes later, Sven took me off. It was my first game since Deportivo at Old Trafford and, to be honest, I was feeling it. The foot was sore but it was more about match fitness. Early in the second half, I'd been thinking: what's happened to my legs? I'm sure Sven could see me puffing a bit and knew we had other games ahead of us and that was why he brought on Kieron Dyer. Even so, I wasn't happy about being substituted. It was the first time I'd ever felt angry about one of Mr Eriksson's decisions. Watching from the bench, I got more and more frustrated as the game drifted away to a draw.

The 1–1 scoreline wasn't a disaster for the first match of a major tournament, but we were really disappointed with our performance. I think that was why we didn't go over and thank the England fans inside the stadium after the final whistle. We were criticised for that in the papers the next day and accused of snubbing our fans, but that wasn't true. We'd had fantastic support and I think the players disappeared into the changing room because we felt we hadn't lived up to it. What we did all realise afterwards was that, whatever the reason, not applauding our own fans was a mistake. As captain, maybe it was down to me to give the lead, even though I'd been on the bench. All the players talked about it together the following day and we promised ourselves and the supporters that, in future, we'd make sure we recognised them being there and behind us.

Back in the changing room, it felt like we'd lost. I couldn't remember having seen this England team so flat. Even the England masseurs, Terry Byrne, Steve Slattery and Rod Thornley, couldn't lift the players that afternoon. It was the first time I'd seen Sven really try to shake players out of a mood.

'We've got two big games ahead of us. Don't even think about letting yourselves get depressed about today. It's not a problem. We've drawn 1–1. We didn't lose, did we? Come on. What's wrong with you, lads?'

I'd not been in the best of moods myself, partly because I was still annoyed about the manager having taken me off. I hadn't expected that at all. I listened to Sven in the changing room, though, and realised that, as captain, I should be doing what I could to be positive. It was still a pretty miserable evening. We'd all been building up to the World Cup Finals and the players were really down about having let our first game slip away.

The next day we had no choice but to forget about Sweden. We had four days to get ourselves ready for what was always going to be the biggest game in the group. Now, it was a game we really needed to win. One of the best things about Sven-Goran Eriksson as a manager is his ability to judge what players need at any particular time. He says the right things to have each individual in the right frame of mind for a game. Just as important is that he always seems to know exactly what we need physically as well. Between games, in a situation like a World Cup, he works hard when the team will benefit from that but he'll ease up in training sessions if our bodies aren't up to it. He wasn't going to 'punish' us with a schedule because we hadn't played well against Sweden. He and Steve McClaren just built us up slowly towards Friday night's game against Argentina in Sapporo.

That week, we even got a little break from the kind of strict diet that's part of being in a training camp these days. I have to own up: it was the best idea I had all summer. We'd been away from England – and away from fast food – for three weeks already. And I was starting to miss the occasional burger and fries. I assumed there'd be a few of the other lads feeling the same way. I talked to Sven, who thought it wouldn't do any harm, and then had a word with the England chefs. On the Wednesday night we all trooped down to dinner. The doors of the dining room were shut and there were two giant golden arches stuck up on them. We all went inside and there was a McDonald's takeaway mountain waiting for us: more burgers, cheeseburgers and chips than you've ever seen piled up in one room in your life. It was a complete surprise to all the players. We just devoured everything: it was like watching kids going mad in a sweetshop. And it worked. We did it again before we played Denmark. Maybe fast food was what was missing from our preparations for facing Brazil.

With England, we always do a lot of work on the other team. It's the job of Dave Sexton, a United manager back in the seventies, to talk us through our next opponents. He'll discuss each player in a twenty-odd man squad. Then he'll show us a video, the equivalent of Playercam when you watch games on Sky Sports, which picks out that player: this is what he does when they're attacking;

this is what he does when they're defending. Dave will then explain exactly what he thinks we should be doing to counter what that player can do. It's almost like planning a military operation. Carlos Queiroz brought a lot of the same ideas into our preparation at United during my last season at Old Trafford. That kind of work with players is being done more and more in football. Everybody seems to have the latest technology now. Instinctively, I'm a bit old school. I'd just like to go out and play. But I understand the importance of knowing your opponents' strengths and weaknesses inside out. A tiny advantage is often all you need to win a football match at the top level.

It goes without saying: we couldn't wait for Argentina. The prospect of the next match was what shook us out of the depression after the draw with Sweden. I really admired how the lads prepared themselves for a game against the World Cup favourites. Self-belief is such an important element in football. Argentina were one of the best teams in the tournament. Every England player went into the match convinced we were going to beat them. There was that strength of mind in every individual, and through the team as a whole. In hindsight, the draw against Sweden had made it simpler for us: we went out on the Friday night knowing we had to get a result.

England vs Argentina is one of world football's great fixtures. It had been a huge game back at France 98. Because of what happened in Saint-Etienne, the build up to Sapporo in 2002 was even more intense. All the hype beforehand was about England – and the England captain, in particular – getting the chance to settle a score: the papers had been talking about 'revenge' and 'destiny' and 'Beckham' ever since the draw had been made. Half the players on both teams had been involved in the game four years before. On the Argentina side, that included Seba Veron who'd become a team-mate at United in the meantime. Whenever I see the pictures of my sending off in France 98, I can see Seba urging the ref to show me the red card. We never had a serious conversation about that incident: it had nothing to do with us playing together for United, after all. But we did joke about the rivalry between our countries: team days out always seemed to include me and the other England players singing 'Ar-gen-tina' and him singing 'In-ger-land' back. I saw Seba before the game in Sapporo and it was still relaxed and friendly between us. He started trying to wind me up:

'You must be very tired, David. I bet your foot's been really hurting you.'

'No, I got a rest at the end of the season, didn't I? I've never felt so fit in my life.'

I'd been fighting the nerves a little; natural enough when memories of four years ago kept flooding back into my mind. I couldn't help it. Every question I was asked, every conversation I had, with the press and with England supporters, seemed to be about Simeone, about a red card and, now, about having the chance to put things right. I was still worried about the metatarsal, too. It felt fine but I didn't like the look of the pitch and how it might play in the humidity of a stadium with a roof. I'd fretted about what boots to wear. Long studs would have stuck in the turf, which might have hurt my foot over the course of ninety minutes even though I'd have better traction. In the end, I settled on a moulded sole.

I spoke to Victoria on the phone before we went to the stadium. She'd stayed at home: Romeo, our second son, was on the way. But even on the other side of the world, if anyone knew how to make me feel relaxed about the situation, it was Victoria. I told her how I was feeling; she wished me luck of course:

'Just enjoy it. Do your best. Back here in England, everybody's going mad. We can't wait.'

I was trying to think positive thoughts. We even talked about what it might be like if I could score the winner; rather that thought in my mind than the opposite: *If something were to go wrong tonight, Victoria, I don't know if I'd be able to go through all the stuff that happened last time again.*

Then, just as we were getting ready to say goodbye, she gave a little chuckle:

'Now don't do anything stupid, will you?'

I laughed and the tension lifted.

'I don't know. I'll see how it goes. Maybe I should just go out and kick one of them for old times' sake.'

I'll never forget the passion, the sense of purpose, in our changing room before we went out to face Argentina. The beat from the Usher album, '8701', was booming through everybody's heads. I looked at Michael Owen: he had this aura about him, pure undiluted concentration on the job in hand. I looked at Rio Ferdinand, at Sol Campbell: their faces had those same calm, fixed expressions; the same intensity burning away behind their eyes. *This is it. How can we not win this tonight? Come on, England.*

I'd never heard us like this before. The noise was echoing in the tunnel while we lined up with Argentina; English voices – the players' voices – shouting, growling, urging one another on, as if we were going into battle. And, from the off, a battle is what it was. Batistuta's tackle on Ashley Cole about a minute into the game was horrible. Later in the game and he'd have been sent off. It was a chance for a big player to put down his mark. We'd talked beforehand amongst ourselves about not showing Argentina anything in the way of respect. We could be sure they wouldn't be showing us any. That lunge from the number 9 said it all, from their point of view. But it broke a spell: it shocked everyone in the stadium, players and fans. Never mind Sweden. Never mind four years ago. Never mind Beckham's foot. This was the challenge: were we strong enough to face it? The atmosphere inside the Dome was electric. Every England supporter could sense it, I'm sure: every one of our players seemed to rise to the occasion at that instant. *Face it? We'll do better than that.*

It took me longer to settle into the game than my team-mates. By the time my foot had warmed up enough to stop giving me twinges of pain, we were already playing really well, a different team to the one that had struggled less than a week ago. We were first to the 50–50s, Nicky Butt was all over the pitch, getting his foot in, nudging us forward. Even at 0–0, it already felt like our night. Owen Hargreaves got injured early on and Trevor Sinclair came on in his place. On another evening, that might have disrupted our rhythm. Another player than Trevor might have needed time to find the pace of a World Cup game. Instead, he just grabbed his moment. He started running at Argentina, terrorising experienced defenders like Placente and Sorin. He was ready for this. It was his night to make sure all those miles in a 747, when he'd been in and out of the squad and finally in again, had been worth the flying.

Argentina had one or two chances. We had better ones. Michael turned in the area and shot across their goalkeeper, Cavallero. I was already in the air, sure it was in, but the ball came back off the far post. Then I found myself with the ball at my feet about six or seven yards outside the Argentina penalty area. Shoot or pass? I wanted to keep the ball moving: Michael was already making a run in behind one of their defenders. Suddenly, I'm over. Someone had come in from behind and clipped the back of my heels. I had no idea which Argentine player had done it. I was sure it was a free-kick, though. Good range and position for me as well. I shouted out towards Pierluigi Collina, the referee. He'd spotted the foul but he'd also already seen something I hadn't and was playing advantage. I looked across. Twenty yards away from me, the ball had broken forward and suddenly Michael Owen had it and was twisting past Pochettino, just inside the box. The defender stuck a leg out as Michael edged beyond him.

'Penalty!'

I'm sure I shouted it out. I know every England supporter did. As I saw Michael tumble, I knew Collina would see it and would be brave enough to give it. He'd been strong enough to play on when I'd screamed at him for my foul. There was a split second of *déjà vu*: I'd known I was going to score, hadn't I? I'd talked to Victoria about a winning goal and finally squaring away Simeone and Saint-Etienne. Had I dreamt this scene the night before? Or had I seen what was about to happen just before it did? As quickly as those thoughts were in my mind, they were gone. I had to get to the ball. I had to be the one to score. A hungry feeling, in the pit of my stomach: dread. And it wasn't a voice in my head exactly, but the realisation, right then: *Everything else I've done in my life, everything that's ever happened to me: it's all been heading towards this.*

I knew Michael would be ready to take the penalty himself.

'Do you want me to have it?'

'No. I'm having it.'

And I was there, the ball in my hand, putting it down on the spot. *What have I said? What have I done?*

I was glad Collina was in charge. He wasn't going to let anybody mess about here in Sapporo. South American players are very good at putting pressure on you, at trying to intimidate and unsettle opponents. I had good reason to know that better than most, so it didn't surprise me. The ref, the keeper and Diego Simeone, of all people, were standing in front of me, between me and the goal. I took two or three steps back. Simeone walked straight past the ball towards me. He stopped and offered his hand as if he expected me to shake it. *Should I? No chance.*

I looked beyond him – through him – towards the goal, trying to blank him out. Then, as I turned, Butty and Scholesy came from behind me and pulled Simeone away. *My mates. I like that.*

I looked down at the ball before running up. It all went quiet. Everything was swirling around me, every nerve standing on edge. *What's going on here? I can't breathe . . .*

I remember forcing in two big gulps of air to try and steady myself and take control. For the last two penalties I'd taken for United, I'd hit the ball straight down the middle of the goal and the keepers, diving to one side, had been nowhere near them. *Same again now, David.* I was far too nervous to try to be clever. Not nervous for myself any longer. This was all about the team I was captain of. I've never felt such pressure before. I ran forward. And I kicked the ball goalwards as hard as I could.

In.

The roar.

IN!

Not the best spot kick you've ever seen. But, for me, for all of us that night, just absolutely perfect. I'd run up, hit it and – knowing, instinctively, it was a goal – kept on running towards the corner flag. The nerves, the pressure and four years of memories just fell away. In those few seconds after the ball settled in the back of Argentina's net, I could see flashbulbs fire off around the ground. As each little explosion died against the blur and colour of the stands, it took something that had happened, something that had been said or written since my red card in Saint-Etienne, away into the night sky with it. The look on my parents' faces at Heathrow when I got back to England, that picture of an effigy of me hanging outside a pub, the snarls from the crowd at Upton Park, and all the rest of it: gone. The film that had been running in my head for so long just stopped dead. Burnt away. Out of my mind for the first time in four years.

Arms outstretched, I sprinted across the grass towards our supporters with a team of England players in red shirts doing their best to get to me before I could disappear into the crowd. I couldn't have wished the burden away. I had to live through it. What had happened in 1998 had done a lot to make me the person I'd become, captaining my country at another World Cup in 2002. But with one kick, it was all off my shoulders for good. Right at that moment I was sure that if I leapt up I'd be able to fly. Suddenly, the other lads were in the air and down on my back. Sol first, then Trevor Sinclair. Rio was there, holding me so tight I could barely catch my breath. This wasn't just my moment. It was a moment for all of us. And then, just as suddenly, came the reminder that we weren't in a Golden Goal situation here. Argentina were going to kick off. A minute later we were going to hear the whistle, but only for half-time, not for the end of the game.

In the changing room, there was no shouting, no screaming. It was quiet, charged; as if the room wasn't big enough to cram in the energy of the players inside it. *Wouldn't it be great if my goal was the winner?* We went out and, in the second half, picked up where we'd left off in the first. No standing back this time, like we had against Sweden. No giving away possession; not early on anyway. We went looking for another goal. The England back four were a brick wall. Further forward, we were picking off Argentina's passes and then playing around them. Teddy Sheringham came on for Emile Heskey and almost scored. If their keeper Cavallero hadn't punched away Teddy's volley from the edge of the box, after we'd passed it from one end of the pitch to the other, it would have been one of the greatest-ever England goals.

Nicky Butt was the best player on the park. It was fantastic to see him prove himself on this stage. He wasn't even guaranteed a start in midfield at United, never mind for England, but he got his chance here because Steven Gerrard missed the tournament through injury. Nicky's a quiet lad, with a really dry sense of humour. He'd never be a character to say: look at me, look at what I can do. But here he was, against what many were saying was the best team in the world, running the game. Other people saw for the first time in Japan what we'd known at United all along.

In the last twenty minutes, Argentina got hold of the ball and started to play. It wasn't that they looked that good: they were just keeping possession by force of will more than anything. We couldn't seem to stop them piling forward. *Please don't score.* I was starting to feel really tired; this was only my second game since I'd broken my foot. I remember Sven calling across to me with about ten minutes to go:

'David, are you all right?'

I didn't shout back. The expression on my face said it all. *Don't even think about taking me off. I've got to be on when we win this.*

Seba Veron had been replaced at half-time by Pablo Aimar. He was the one player who looked like he could unlock something for them. The longer the half went on, the further forward he got, which meant our midfield players were dragged deeper trying to stop him. We ended up with the rest of the team stepping on the toes of our back four. Argentina were firing in shots and crosses. And they had some good chances. For supporters watching on television at home, that final quarter of an hour must have been unbearable. Dave Seaman made a couple of great saves. Sol and Rio kept diving in the way of Argentinian attempts on goal. It was fantastic but I wanted it over. I was out there trying to defend with the rest of the lads but half-wishing I could be hiding behind the sofa with my eyes shut, like the England supporters back home.

When the final whistle blew, Rio and Trevor came running towards me. Such a great, great feeling. For us and for the fans. I rang Victoria out in the tunnel about half an hour after the game. I was well past putting things into words by then and couldn't hear a word she was saying either. She was at her mum and dad's. They had a houseful of family and friends, all of them shouting and singing away in the background. Later on, I called Dave Gardner and he told me things had gone mad back in England. He was in the middle of Deansgate, the main shopping street in Manchester. He said no traffic had been able to get through since the end of the game. There were parties going on in the middle of the road. He'd never seen anything like it. I spoke to Simon, one of the guys at my agents, SFX, and he was in London and had found his way down to Trafalgar Square. The same thing was going on there. Like I did after every game in 2002, I phoned Gary Neville too. He was so upbeat, even though he'd missed his chance with his injury. That night was the one time I heard him say:

'I wish I was there.'

Gary's a team player. The perfect team player. He knew exactly what it meant to win a big game like Argentina. He'd have loved to be part of it. I needed him to tell me what was going on back at home. He wanted every bit of detail about the party that was going on in Japan.

If there was one impossible thing I could make happen, it would be to get back to England, minutes after a great win at a World

Cup or European Championships, to see the celebrations and join in with the madness at home. I'd love to get my share of all that excitement when we score: bodies flying around through the air and people hugging and kissing each other, in London, in Manchester, in Birmingham, in Newcastle, everywhere. I love it.

Out in Sapporo, I didn't want to have to come off the pitch. If there was one England player, one England supporter still in the ground, I wanted to be out there celebrating with them. Eventually I went over to the tunnel to do a television interview and then headed back to the dressing room. I was the last one in. Terry Byrne and Steve Slattery came over and hugged me. They knew exactly what the evening had meant for me. Sven-Goran Eriksson shook my hand. He knew what it meant for the team. The Usher album was blaring out again. Rio was leading the dancing in the middle of the floor, kicking discarded kit and shin pads out of the way. I wish we could have played Brazil the following day. That same night, even. We felt so strong; everyone was still so hyped up. I'm sure we'd have won. The atmosphere in the changing room after we'd beaten Argentina made it feel like this England team was invincible.

Back at the hotel, Mum and Dad were waiting for me. They came out to every game in Japan. Mum was in tears – just what I needed to start me off – and I think Dad was having to hold them back as well:

'I'm so proud of you, son.'

Tony Stephens made his way there after the game. He's a football fan as well as an agent working in the game, and he'd had a great night along with all the other England supporters inside the Dome. He came up and gave me a hug:

'That was unbelievable, David. Who is it writing your life?'

The room they'd set aside for us was very Japanese: a big, pale grey room with nothing on the walls; large rectangular tables set with white cloths; food and drink laid out for people to help themselves. It wasn't exactly the way you'd set things up for a big party. Tiredness was starting to set in by then anyway, once we'd all shared a bottle or two. Some of the lads headed off to bed early, especially the ones who didn't have family waiting to see them. The rest of us wound down slowly together, toasting England 1 Argentina 0 with a couple of glasses of wine.

Everywhere we went that summer we had most of Japan for company. They were doing everything they could to make us feel at home, if that was possible in a country that was so different from ours. I was getting sack loads of cards and letters at the hotel from Japanese supporters.

'Good luck Beckham. Good luck England. We're very happy that you're here in our country.'

We felt we should be giving something back, finding a way to say thank you. We talked with Paul Barber from the FA and I suggested that meeting some schoolchildren would be a good idea. It was arranged for Rio and I to go down to a place not far from where we were staying, one afternoon after training. We thought it might be a nice gesture to chat with the children, a lot of whom spoke English, and leave them with some England kit and other souvenirs. We walked into the hall together and there were hundreds of them sitting in neat rows, waiting patiently. The place erupted when they spotted us. It was great, and I think Rio and I got just as big a buzz out of those couple of hours as the children did.

It would have been ideal to take the high of beating Argentina on into a knockout game against another major team. Instead, we had to wait nearly a week to play Nigeria in our last group game. A game that, now, we didn't have to win in order to go through.

Those five days were long enough for us to lose some of the inspiration from the previous Friday night. Having beaten the tournament favourites, all of a sudden we were expected to take care of anybody else in our way without breaking sweat. As it turned out, sweat was the one thing we did do in Osaka come the Wednesday afternoon.

We went into the Nigeria match wanting to win it. Finishing top of the group meant we probably wouldn't have to face Brazil until the final. And we wouldn't play them in the kind of conditions we had to prepare for in Osaka. The extreme heat had been talked about in the build-up to the tournament: games that kicked off in the middle of the afternoon would be difficult, especially against non-European sides who were used to playing in temperatures of 95 degrees plus. None of us realised how tough it would be, though, until we went out on the day to warm up. We jogged up and down the pitch once and players were looking around at each other. *How are we supposed to play in this?*

The heat stood up in front of you like a wall. Not a breath of wind. Sweat rolling off you just standing still, looking round at the stands. When it's that hot, you feel claustrophobic. The air's heavy: it wraps itself around you, stealing your breath. We knew Nigeria could play, but I didn't have any doubts about us beating them. I was just worried we might not be able to beat the conditions.

It was a game we never felt we'd lose. The longer it went on, the more it felt like we'd never win it either. Ninety minutes of hard labour. We got a 0–0 and we were through to play Denmark in the next round. There wasn't any more to be said about it: the players sat in the changing room, gulping water, throats almost too dry to drink the stuff. The match itself is like a blur in my memory now. What's sharp is how we felt for hours afterwards: absolutely wrung out, drained, physically and mentally. We all dipped over the next couple of days. We didn't doubt ourselves but we were aware that, back home, some people were wondering if the Argentina game had been a one-off. We'd finished second in Group F behind Sweden. Were England good enough now to go forward?

Talking to Victoria and Brooklyn helped keep me going. I missed my family. I had a videophone set up in my hotel room and I could talk to Victoria face to face: when your wife's seven months pregnant you want to know about every last kick and twinge. We'd plenty to say without even mentioning the games I was playing out in Japan. Time on the phone to home was a break from football and a break from the tension. I even got to see and talk to Brooklyn on the videophone: he would sit there chatting to me or showing off his new bike as he rode it round and round the bedroom.

I had a bad feeling about the Denmark game beforehand. It might have been due to exhaustion after the heat in Osaka, but I thought there was more to it than that. We knew we'd probably face Brazil if we got through; and people were already looking ahead to that even though we had this game to win first. Denmark were well organised and a physically strong team; almost all their players played in England or, at least, had done so during their careers. I thought it might turn out like our first group game against Sweden, where the opposition's familiarity with the England players had done them a favour but not helped us at all. I believed in this England team. Believed, in fact, that we had a chance in 2002 of doing something that hadn't been done since 1966. But I wasn't sure we'd be in the right frame of mind to turn that into a result on the Saturday afternoon.

Before the game, I took one look around the dressing room and knew I was wrong. We were as ready for Denmark as we had been for Argentina. The players' faces and their body language were just right: no fear, no distractions, no tension. Everyone was focused, waiting for kick-off, more relaxed than I'd ever seen an England team. Niigata was another new stadium for us, but the lads looked like it had only taken the previous evening's training session to make it feel like home. An atmosphere like that amongst players takes on a life of it's own, You look at your mate; he looks like he's up for it. So does your team-mate next to him. And you're radiating confidence yourself by the time the look falls on you. It's an energy that runs through a dressing room in the minutes before kick-off. That afternoon, I knew we were set.

As we came up the tunnel and out on the pitch, I found myself looking at Denmark's players instead of my team-mates. The way they walked, eyes darting backwards and forwards: you could sense how nervous they were. It maybe wasn't fear exactly, but it was something like it: no self-belief. We had a psychological advantage. The tough guys like Thomas Gravesen and Stig Tofting were doing their best, marching round and growling, as if to say they were up for the scrap. That just made it more obvious that a lot of the other Danish players looked like they didn't fancy it at all. It wasn't only me who noticed. While we were warming up, Rio called across to me.

'What do you reckon? They look scared.'

I think we had Denmark beaten before we'd even kicked off. Which was just as well: it was the one time all summer that the injury really gave me grief during a game. My foot had been feeling better and better, almost by the day. Against Denmark, though, I wore boots with an ordinary long stud. It was pouring with rain in Niigata, so I didn't have any choice. Until then, most of the discomfort had been on top of the metatarsal, but that night the pain was all underneath my foot. It felt like the studs were pushing up into the injury every time I pushed down to run or strike the ball, twisting the fracture every time I tried to turn.

The pain in my foot didn't stop me enjoying the game, though. The first twenty minutes, especially, were fantastic. We played like we didn't have a care in the world, even in a winner-takes-all game at a major tournament. Five minutes in, I put over a corner. Rio got his head to it but nobody was sure until afterwards that he got the goal because the ball hit a post, then their keeper, and finally Emile Heskey jabbed it in again when it bounced back out. I even thought about claiming it myself at the time. But I'm really glad the video replays gave it to Rio. He's such a good guy to have in the dressing room and, out on the pitch, he had a fantastic World Cup. Getting on the score sheet was the least he deserved from the summer.

Fifteen minutes later, Michael scored the second and that seemed like game over. Denmark got themselves into some good positions but we went up the other end just before half-time and Emile got his goal. The heat had worn us down against Nigeria in Osaka. The rain was just what we'd needed in Niigata. It quickened the pitch up, which is something that suits the way Sven wants England to play. 3–0 was just fine, all anyone could have asked for. And against a team who'd qualified for the second phase at France's expense. I'd have been jumping up and down afterwards, celebrating getting through to the last eight, except my foot was killing me. By the end of the game, I'd been getting cramp in it because I was running with my boot angled to one side to try and take the pressure off the sole. The rest of me was in much better nick, though. I felt fresher against Denmark than I had at any time since coming back from the fracture. And, afterwards, I had the satisfaction of knowing I'd been much more involved: I'd been part of the build-up to all three England goals.

So it was Brazil in the quarter-finals: win that game and we'll win the World Cup. I know, back at home, people were starting to take it very seriously. England were contenders. In the past, high expectations have put pressure on the national team. In Japan in 2002, though, our supporters weren't thinking anything that me and the other players weren't already thinking ourselves. Argentina? Out. The holders, France? Out. Italy? Out. Portugal? Out. The Dutch? Not even there. Who was left in? Of the teams with a World Cup history, it came down to two: Germany, who we'd beaten 5–1 in Munich to get to the finals, and Brazil. We couldn't wait for Friday afternoon and Shizuoka.

Our only worry was Michael Owen. It made a change for the fuss to be about his groin instead of my foot, although I don't remember many people, even inside the England camp, being aware of how close he was to missing the Brazil game. He was struggling with a groin strain, the kind of injury that feels worse and worse each time you play through it. Liverpool would have rested him for a couple of weeks during a Premiership season but Michael was so vital to England: a world-class player who always came up with his best on the biggest occasions. Any team in the tournament would have done everything they could to have him fit enough to start.

We certainly weren't scared of Brazil. The game was an afternoon kick-off, which meant they would probably have an advantage if the conditions were anything like they had been for our game against Nigeria. We trained at the stadium the evening before and it absolutely bucketed down. We all knew that the same again the following day would give us a really great chance. In the hotel later on, I felt like I should build a little shrine to the local weather gods and pray, before going to bed, for more rain. No such luck: I jumped out of bed on the Friday morning and pulled open the curtains. The sun was already high in the sky, beating down on a beautiful day. My heart sank: we were going to have to do this the hard way after all.

I'd never think of using the weather as an excuse. You take what you're given and then go and play your best anyway. Even so, enough people had been saying that, if it was hot, England might struggle. I've wondered since if it got into our heads. A tiny doubt is sometimes all it takes to undermine players' confidence. Before the game, we went out onto the pitch for ten minutes or so but then came inside to do our main warm-up. The Japanese found a big enough office for us to stretch in. It wasn't ideal. And Michael was getting massage right up to us going out onto the pitch. It was a close call, but he played. People know all about what Michael does but he's also tougher than anybody outside the dressing room will ever know. I'd had my time with Richard Smith, the masseur, so I understood exactly what Michael went through to make sure he could start. He wasn't going to miss Brazil for the world.

We started the game really well in Niigata. If the heat was bothering us, it didn't seem to show. We didn't wait for their players to get into any kind of rhythm. Do that and a team like Brazil can have the game won before you've even started to play. We knew we had to defend as a team when they were in possession. We couldn't let them get two-on-one against our players anywhere. When we did have the ball, the job was simple enough: don't give it away and get it into their half quickly. Everyone knows the Brazilians like to let their defenders get forward in open play. We knew we had the players to hit them back on the break. Our concentration seemed excellent and, although they had a couple of half chances – Dave Seaman had to save one Roberto Carlos free-kick – there wasn't anything going on to worry us.

Don't make mistakes. Wait for the other lot to make theirs.
There were just over twenty minutes gone when Brazil lost possession in our third of the pitch. Emile Heskey got the ball on
halfway and, ahead of him, he saw Michael starting to make a run
across his defender. Emile hit his pass thirty-odd yards towards
the corner of the Brazilian penalty area. It looked as if the central
defender, Lucio, would bring the ball down and clear. I don't
know if he caught sight of Michael and was half-worried about a
challenge, but Lucio definitely took his eye off the ball. Instead of
controlling it, he let it bounce down and away from him into
Michael's path. Great strikers don't stand still. They're already
moving, expecting to get their chance before anyone else sees
there's anything on. Michael nicked the ball away and ran into the
box. You knew, groin injury or not, Michael was never going to
be caught once he was through. And because he'd been surprised
by what happened, the keeper, Marcos, didn't come off his line
until it was too late. Michael just had to steady himself and dink
his shot beyond the keeper and into the far corner. One-nil. I was
forty yards away. It was like watching it on television. *Michael
Owen's scoring for England against Brazil. I don't believe this is
happening. I hope the video's recording.*

If it had remained 1–0 at half-time, I genuinely believe England
might have won the World Cup. But Brazil are some team. Never
mind the ability: they're completely fearless with it. Being a goal
down didn't throw them out of their stride at all. Nothing was
going to change their approach to the game. With any team other
than Brazil, if you get a lead, you expect it to force your opponents
to push forwards and start taking risks. Not them, though: they're
the best in the world and they know it; and that's the way they
play every game anyway.

About five minutes before the end of the half, Roberto Carlos had a shot which took a deflection. Dave Seaman jumped to catch the ball and hurt his neck, falling backwards. It didn't look good. There was a chance he'd have to go off. I looked away from Dave and the physio, Gary Lewin, for a moment. Ronaldo was standing with the referee, Ramos Rizo, talking about something. And then he started laughing and put his arm round Rizo's shoulder. He looked like this was him and a few mates enjoying a Wednesday night kickabout down at the local park, without a care in the world. *How can you be doing that, 1–0 down at the World Cup? This isn't over. This isn't anywhere near being over.*

Dave Seaman got up and carried on. The treatment had taken a while. If we'd played straight through, we'd have been in the dressing room by the time Brazil equalised. As it was, we were just waiting for the whistle. I remember the ball coming towards me on the touchline, just inside their half. It was from a Brazilian player who'd been looking to pass to Roberto Carlos but shinned it a bit. I was sure it was going out for an England throw which, seconds from half-time, would have been better for us than having the ball in open play. By the time Danny Mills had come forward to take it, the 45 would have been up. Roberto Carlos slid in with a tackle. I jumped in the air to let his momentum take the ball over the touchline, for our throw. Somehow, Carlos got a foot round it to keep it in play. And I was out of the game. They broke from halfway, played round Scholesy's challenge and got it to Ronaldhino twenty yards outside our penalty area. He had a trick to throw Ashley Cole off balance. He ran at Rio and then played a pass to his right to Rivaldo. In his stride, with no backlift, Rivaldo took the shot so early that Dave Seaman and the covering defenders didn't have a chance to get in the way. It couldn't have been a worse time for us to let in a goal.

Instead of going back into the cool of the changing room on a high, with a lead to defend or to build on, the momentum had been snatched away from us. The looks on the England players' faces said it all. *We're knackered. We've got nothing left.*

It was the story of our World Cup. We played our best football in the first half of games and then ran out of steam after half-time. I'm not sure how much was physical and how much was mental. I do know Rivaldo's goal killed us in Shizuoka. And I don't think there's anything that could have been said or done in the break to change that. Sven went round talking to players whose shoulders were sagging, whose heads were down. When he spoke to the whole team, he went straight to the point:

'We've played well. We should be winning 1–0. We've got to tidy things up, make sure we don't give away silly goals, and then we'll get our chance.'

Sven's never been a shouter, a manager to jump up and down. He may not be passionate in the way of an Alex Ferguson or a Martin O'Neill, but he's just as single-minded about winning football matches as they are. Sven's passion and intensity come through in a different way. He's not about frightening players or shaking them up. He's about inspiring them, giving them confidence, making them desperate to play. His approach has worked for him throughout a career in club football and you only have to look at his record in competitive matches to see that it's working with England as well. Steve McClaren worked hard in those twenty minutes too. I know Sven thought a lot of him and that meant Steve was as free to get his points across as the manager. In any dressing room, a coach or a manager can't give players what they haven't got: the job is to make them find what they need inside themselves. In Shizuoka, you could have looked for a spark but you wouldn't have found one. There just wasn't anything there.

We came out for the second half with our belief and our energy drained away. It was like Sweden all over again: we sat back, couldn't keep possession and couldn't get forward. When your legs go, your head goes too. But that works the other way round as well. It was well over 100 degrees down on the pitch that afternoon and trying to keep your concentration fixed was like trying not to screw your eyes up in the sun: we hadn't a chance. The knock we'd taken in conceding the goal had given Brazil all the lift they needed. They came out for the rest of the game playing as if winning was just a matter of time. We'd no excuses and I don't believe there was anything we could have done differently, by way of preparation, which would have made that second half turn out any differently. Brazil just got stronger and stronger the hotter it got: we'd had the life squeezed out of us by the end of the game.

Even so, it took something very weird to beat us. There wasn't an England player who gave up, although when things happen like they did in the fiftieth minute that afternoon you do start thinking: this isn't going to be our day. Brazil won a free-kick, almost forty yards out and to the left of our penalty area. We organised to defend against a cross. From that position, you wouldn't even think of the player having a shot. I was standing fifteen yards away from Ronaldhino, looking straight at him. The moment he struck the ball I could see he'd shanked it: it was a cross that had gone wrong and was heading too near to the goal. It happened so slowly, as if the ball was having to force its way through the heat to get to where it was going. As I watched it arc over my head towards the far post, there was time for all the possibilities to run through my mind: *It's going behind. It's into Dave's arms. It's wide.* Finally: *This could go in here. It's not going to, surely* . . . .

There was an eerie silence as the ball spun beyond Dave Seaman and dropped over his head but under the bar. At the time, I was certain it was a fluke. Watching it again since, I'm not so sure. Definitely there wasn't another player on the pitch, on either side, who'd had the faintest idea it might happen. Even before the disappointment of conceding the goal sank in, the thought crossed my mind. *Dave Seaman's going to get hammered for this. If we lose, it will have been me in 1998, Phil in 2000, and Dave in 2002, the same stuff all over again.*

When I'd first joined up with England six years ago, Dave Seaman had been one of the players who actually put himself out to try to make me feel welcome. Ever since, shooting practice against Dave, and the banter that went with it, has been my favourite part of England training sessions. The last person in the world who deserved stick for us failing against Brazil was Dave Seaman. Right then, in Shizuoka, I wanted to go up and put my arms around him, tell him everything would be all right. It wasn't the time, though. We were 2–1 down to Brazil. There were forty minutes to go.

I don't think many people watching could see us getting back into it. Out there playing, I never really felt like there was an equaliser in us. When Ronaldhino got sent off for launching himself at Danny Mills, you could sense the crowd in the stadium – the England supporters, anyway – were thinking this was our chance: eleven against ten. The extra man actually worked against us. Brazil, with a full team, would never change how they play. Once they were ahead, they kept pushing on, looking for a third goal. While that was happening, at least we knew there was the possibility of another mistake, like Lucio's in the first half, if we could get the ball forward on the break. Once Ronaldhino went, though, they decided to defend and protect the lead. We didn't have enough energy left to force the pace of the game, which was what they were letting us do for the last half an hour. There was no way now we were going to catch them short of numbers at the back: when they needed to, Brazil proved they could get behind the ball with the best of them. Our one half chance, when Teddy, on as a sub, got fouled on the edge of their box, came and went when the ref didn't give the free-kick. A dead ball had seemed like the only way we'd be likely to score since half-time.

Even after I'd watched them go on to turn over Germany in the final, the thought that we'd been knocked out by the world champions, the best team in the tournament by far, wasn't much by way of consolation. I thought we missed out that afternoon on a real chance of winning the World Cup. And so did all the other England players. With all due respect to Brazil, it wasn't like we'd lost the game so much as handed it over; and that was a horrible feeling. We were all down. Devastated. Dave Seaman was standing in the centre circle looking like the loneliest man in the world, never mind that he was surrounded by other England players. I went over and put an arm over his shoulder, spoke into his ear, his head bent in towards me.

'Don't worry about this, Dave. You've had an unbelievable tournament. You've kept us in games to get us this far. You had no chance: the goal was a freak. Forget about it. Don't let people see you like this now.'

Dave didn't say anything. I remembered what I'd needed in the dressing room in Saint-Etienne. I remembered Tony Adams being the one who'd been there for me. Here, now, I couldn't be inside Dave's head in those moments but I felt like I knew what he needed from a team-mate:

'Come on, Dave, let's go for a walk round. Let's go down and see the England fans.'

Those supporters were great. We knew they were as disappointed as we were but they stood in their seats, waiting for
us and applauding us when we came in front of them. No bitter-
ness, no threat towards us or anybody else; behind us to the end.
They'd been like that throughout the tournament: the best fans in
Japan. Maybe the Brazilians picked up on that spirit: their supporters were clapping us as well as their own team. They were
celebrating Brazil going through but they gave the English players
respect, too, and I admired that a lot.

When we got back and sat down in the dressing room, it was
very quiet, players thinking their own thoughts. It wasn't only the
game we'd just played. You could see ten months of top-level
football catching up with the lads in the minutes after we lost to
Brazil. It was as if the life had been drained away out of us. Sven
was the only one to break the silence.

'I'm very proud of you all. Not just what you've done in the past
three weeks but what you had to do to get us to the World Cup
in the first place. Today we're very disappointed. We thought we
could go further in this tournament. I believed we could. But this
is football. This is how the game goes. When your time comes,
it'll happen. You're good enough. You should know that.'

I was off in a world of my own. Every player in the dressing
room was. There was nothing more to say than Sven had just
said. It seemed to take forever – it was a real effort – just to get
up off the bench and get to the shower and then change. We
took a long time dragging ourselves out of the stadium. When we
finally made it to our coach, we pulled away immediately behind
the Brazilians. Ronaldhino was in the back, playing a set of samba
drums; he was so happy. I'm not surprised. His goal had got his
team to the semis. At that moment, my head ached with what-ifs.
I spoke to Victoria on the mobile:

'David, it's terrible how it's happened but we love you. I know how down you are. But we're here. We'll be happy when you're home, Brooklyn and me.'

Victoria was right. She knew how much I'd wanted to make the final. That's all she wanted for England too. But now it wasn't going to happen, we had to see things as they were. My wife was seven months pregnant. She was missing me. My son was missing me. And I was missing them both. I'd rather have been staying in Japan but the thought of going back to England and my family was the one thing that lifted me on the way back to the hotel. We said goodbye. I said I'd see them the next day.

Back at the England team hotel, the Japanese were still out in force to welcome us back: they'd stuck with us just like our own fans. Inside, there were family and friends standing at the top of this long staircase that swept up on two sides. As the players made their way up the steps, there was applause. Mum and Dad were there. *Don't start crying here.*

I hugged my parents, and nodded to one or two other people. I couldn't speak to anyone. What was there to say? I just walked straight on through reception and up to my room. Quiet, lifeless, save for the low hum of the air-conditioning. I closed the door on the afternoon. And then just crumpled up on the bed like an old man; frustrated, hurting and weary. I'd expected so much of myself and of England. We'd prepared right. Everything had felt right. And we'd missed maybe the best chance any of us would ever have. It wasn't as if I needed to sit there and start trying to work out why. Why didn't matter right now. All that mattered was the plain truth. Even then, a couple of hours after the game, I still couldn't quite take it in as a fact. The air pressure in that hotel room bore down on my ear drums. For me, for all of us, it was just empty now. There'd be the semis and a final after we got home. We'd be watching on television along with the rest of the planet. But the real thing had slipped away. For us, the World Cup was over. England were out.

Bubble Beckham 12

*'To meet a great man such as you
is an amazing honour.'*

I'd only been waiting 27 years. 1 September 2002, just after 9.30
in the morning, and our second son, Romeo, was born; a baby
brother for Brooklyn. Their dad could still remember how he'd
dreamt of having a baby brother when he was growing up with
two sisters. You'd have to ask someone who knows more about
these things than me why I'd always wanted another boy in the
house for company: it's bound to be more complicated than just
needing a little 'un to go in goal in the back garden. It's not as if
I didn't love Lynne and Joanne, after all. All I know for sure is that
when we found out Romeo was a boy, I was delighted for Brooklyn
and pleased, as well, for the little boy I used to be. I was a bit surprised by how strong those feelings were, to be honest. After Brooklyn was born and we'd started talking about more children, Victoria
and I had expected a daughter would be next. And when Victoria
got pregnant again, that was what Brooklyn had expected too.

Victoria's sister Louise, who we're really close to and see all
the time, has a little girl named Liberty. Brooklyn's been playing
with her since they were both tiny: he and Liberty are just a few
months apart in age. Maybe that's why, from the moment we
found out another baby was on the way, Brooklyn always assumed
it was going to be a baby sister for him. Victoria and I are long-term

planners when it comes to naming babies: we'd already had the names Paris and Romeo ready for a while:

'Do you want to say hello to baby Paris?'

Brooklyn would press his head up against Victoria's tummy. He was as excited as we were. We thought the explanations could wait until the baby actually arrived. One of the stranger things about our lives together, though, is the way the private things – or a garbled version of them – become public. Things can sometimes get a bit confusing for everybody because of that. Brooklyn was out shopping with Victoria one afternoon. They were in a chemist's and the lady behind the counter asked him:

'How's your mummy's new baby?'

Brooklyn must have taken to this woman because he happily told her he was getting a little sister named Paris. It took about 24 hours for that to turn up in the newspapers as fact: Brooklyn, aged three, had made the Beckham family's official announcement. It wasn't that we were trying to fool anybody: at that stage we didn't know whether the new baby was going to be a boy or girl ourselves. Anyway, just because the gossip columns and the bookmakers had got it wrong wasn't a reason for us to put their story right.

Husbands have it easy, don't they? The father-to-be just does what he can to help and looks forward to the new arrival. Before the day arrived, though, Victoria had to carry the new baby for nine months in her tummy. I love how Victoria looks when she's pregnant; I love knowing she's looking after something precious for us both; I love sharing all the ups and downs, the hopes and fears. But, for Mum, it must be hard in ways men can never really understand. I've seen for myself – twice now – how Victoria's emotions, her body, her hormones, everything, get turned upside down during pregnancy.

Romeo was born, like his brother, at the Portland Hospital in London. Some things were simpler because of the fact we'd been there before. I knew how to sneak into the Portland without being seen: we parked just round the corner from the hospital and I jumped into the boot of the car for the last few hundred yards' drive to the back door. But every baby's different and I can't imagine the whole thing would ever be routine. For Romeo, we had a last-minute panic when the doctor told Victoria he needed to do the caesarean the following morning, which meant me driving down from Manchester overnight to make sure I was there. And the day itself, of course, stands out clearly on its own: one I'll never forget.

You imagine beforehand that, once you've seen one baby come into the world, you'll be ready for the emotions when it happens again. But that's not how it was for me at all. When Romeo was first lifted up into the light in the operating theatre, the feelings of excitement and happiness, of pride and awe, just flooded through me with all the same intensity they had three years before, when Brooklyn was born. It was like it was happening for the first time all over again. It took my breath away how much I loved Victoria right there and then, how much I loved our brand new baby son. I could feel my heart grow to make room for the new life in our lives.

The best moment of all was still waiting to happen. My mum looked after Brooklyn while we were in the operating theatre. His first glimpse of his baby brother was about half an hour after Romeo was born. It was my first glimpse, as well, of the two of them together. The most wonderful feeling: Brooklyn looked down at this tiny little creature, wrapped up in fresh linen, and he just melted. He was so gentle with Romeo, so loving. He reached out and stroked his brother's forehead, the lightest of touches. I was standing there watching. No need to tell Brooklyn to be careful. He was only three years old himself, but already wise enough to know how precious Romeo was. They connected. It's been like that between the two of them ever since. I'd always wanted a baby brother. I was looking at my eldest son now and the way he was with Romeo was the way I'm sure I would have been. Those two boys together for those couple of minutes, the two of them touching, a little world of their own: their dad had never felt so happy, never felt so proud.

I like the feeling that those two boys are with me, even when I'm away from home. And not just in my heart. I had their names tattooed on my back after each one was born. There's a guardian angel there, too, looking after them both. My dad had three tattoos of his own and so the idea has been with me since I was a kid. In Dad's case, I think it was a bit of a teenage rebellion thing. I know he got a clip round the ear when Grandad found out about them. My equivalent of that was getting my ear pierced when I was fifteen, at a jeweller's in Chingford Mount. Dad went mad:

'What have you done that for? What are people going to say when you turn up for football with an earring?'

He was about as pleased with my little silver hoop as his dad had been when he pulled off the plaster hiding Dad's first tattoo. When I was a boy I sometimes talked about getting one. Mum would wince but Dad, obviously, would have been happy enough. I never seemed to get round to it then; I suppose I was waiting for the right time. It never occurred to me to have one because I liked a particular design; I didn't think about them as a fashion thing. The idea came much later, a little while after Brooklyn was born. I was talking to Mel B and her then-husband, Jimmy Gulzar, and the subject of tattoos came up. I ended up going to this Dutch guy who'd done all of Jimmy's. I'd finally realised what I wanted a tattoo to represent. Mine are all about the people in my life, my wife and sons, who I want to have with me always. When you see me, you see the tattoos. You see an expression of how I feel about Victoria and the boys. They're part of me.

Our family and the life that spins around us: sometimes we laugh and call it 'Bubble Beckham'. Victoria and I and Brooklyn and Romeo, at home, at the shops, on holiday: we're just a family that loves being together, doing what families do. Mum and Dad both have the kind of very public careers that mean our ordinary working days aren't very ordinary at all: me playing Champions League football in a packed stadium somewhere, with millions of people watching on television all over the world; Victoria cutting new tracks in a recording studio in New York; both of us jumping on a plane to go off and shoot a Japanese commercial on a beach in Thailand. And outside all of that, helping to keep the bubble bouncing along, is the fame thing: the attention, the gossip, the paparazzi and the stuff that's just made up – we know it is – but still comes with our names at the top of the page. Inside the bubble, we have family, friends and professionals who help us find a way through it all and we're grateful for that. I'm grateful we've got each other too. We've experienced some pretty weird things, along with what's been wonderful, since we've been together. It makes you strong knowing there's someone's hand you can hold. I know Victoria feels the same.

When I first met Mrs Beckham – Posh Spice – I'd never experienced the kind of hype, or the lifestyle, that came with being a massively successful pop star. Victoria was handling the situation long before I even knew what the situation was. Maybe my manager at Manchester United would have preferred me to have found a nice, quiet girl who'd stay indoors, clean the house, change nappies and have my dinner ready in the evening. Well, you can't

choose who you fall in love with. When I met the girl of my dreams
– the woman I always knew I was going to marry and settle down
with – I was swept away by her. And, as I've said, part of the
attraction was how good she was at what she did and how famous
she was because of it. Because of where Victoria was in her life
when I met her, and because of what's happened to me in my
career in the last seven years, the fame thing has been on a steady
upward curve ever since. Us being together, of course, has made
it all even more intense.

The bubble seems to expand, almost day by day, we thought.
Maybe the move to Madrid would change that: we'd try to keep
our heads down and get on with starting a new adventure, settling
in a new country, as well as at a new club. There's always a story,
though, isn't there? And even if there's not, someone's ready to
dream one up. Sometimes we wonder what would happen if it all
just vanished overnight. We'd miss some of it but we'd still have
the things that matter: each other and our children. What if the
bubble just keeps getting bigger? Do we have picture spreads
about the boys' first schools, first girlfriends, first everything else
to look forward to? We've talked about that, and laughed about
it together as well. But it's a serious question: how will it be for
Brooklyn and Romeo if they're going to find themselves having
to grow up in the public eye whether they like it or not? I think
it's really important that, in the whirl of our lives together, we give
our children the same solid base our parents gave Victoria and
me. I know that, above everything, I owe my boys the same love
and support and guidance I had at home, from my parents, my
grandparents and the rest of our family.

In some ways, that's the easy bit: loving Brooklyn and Romeo,
giving them the time and attention they need. It's a parent's
instinct, after all. The more difficult thing is helping them through

the extraordinary stuff that comes with life in Bubble Beckham; more difficult because Victoria and I are only finding out about that stuff as we go along ourselves. For a start, neither of us grew up with personal security being as much a part of everyday life as breakfast and dinner, which it is now. I don't mean the guys in blazers who hold back the crowds at airports. I'm really grateful they're there but, once we're through a terminal or wherever, those lads are gone: like us, they're on to the next job. I'm talking about the people who we trust to look after us and the boys, everywhere but inside our own four walls, 24/7.

It's been a strange road to where we are now with the whole issue of security. Soon after Victoria and I started going out together, I received a letter at my house in Worsley that contained two bullets in it and a scrawled note saying there'd be one for each of us. I can still remember standing by my pool table and the sound of the cartridges dropping out of the envelope and onto the table in front of me. That wasn't the only death threat we've had down the years, but it's the one that still makes my stomach turn over. When I came back to England after France 98, I felt threatened – really threatened – in ways I'd no real idea how to deal with. It would never have occurred to me, back then, to employ a bodyguard. I relied, like anyone else would, on the police and my mates. There were a couple of incidents at home – crashing bins, strangers outside – when I got very scared indeed. I phoned 999 and then Giggsy. The police were always great and so was my neighbour: Ryan would be round in a flash, standing there just about awake in his tracksuit bottoms, baseball bat in hand, and ready to look after a mate.

The incidents that really changed how I thought about all this, though, were the kidnap threats. My children didn't choose their mum and dad so what's always upset me more than anything is when they get involved in things they don't deserve to be involved in. Sometimes that might just be something spiteful in a newspaper column. I can deal with that myself: phone the bloke up and tell him he's out of order. That's what I've done in the past. But a threat to my boys' safety? Their lives, even? How am I supposed to know what to do about that? It's only when those things happen you realise that you have to do something, have to talk to people who think about the unthinkable for a living. You never know what may happen: when the case against alleged kidnappers got thrown out of court the year before last after all the publicity in the *News of the World*, it left us not knowing where we stood. All I can tell you is those threats felt very real – and very frightening – at the time. And if Victoria and the boys are the potential targets, I can't take any risks about how serious or not the threats might be.

If it's your family's safety you want to protect, it's very hard to judge who the right person, or people, might be to turn to for advice. Like with everything else in your life, you start with the people closest to you. I'm lucky that my father-in-law actually knows a bit about the hardware and technology side of it all: it's in his line of work. The police have always tried to see us right and we've always tried to check staff out as carefully as we could. But who hasn't misjudged a person at some time in their life? Of course, we've made our mistakes.

It's not a subject where you can ever say: this is sorted. I can't even say I'm sure I'd know what 'sorted' might be: there's not a 'How To' book you can check to make sure you're doing the right things. It's about balancing the need for a normal life with taking what precautions you can. You can't live every day making sure the world can't get near you. But you shouldn't have to live with fear either, on edge all the time, imagining that something bad could be about to happen. Right now, I feel pretty comfortable with the people we have looking after us. I trust them enough for us not to be spending all our time watching our backs.

The time after France 98 was pretty uncomfortable, to say the least. But before then, and since, it's not as if I've felt under any kind of constant threat: you're guarding against the hundred-to-one chance. But feeling secure leaves us freer to get on with doing what we do, publicly and privately. We like to take Brooklyn and Romeo out to dinner sometimes. We want to stop at the motorway services to stock up on snacks. We want to go shopping at the local supermarket, shlepping up and down the aisles and choosing what we fancy, instead of going on the internet or ordering by phone. I still feel, deep down, like the person I've always been. If I want it to stay that way, I've got to make sure I can still do the things I've always done. I've never had a problem with people wanting to chat or to ask for an autograph. How could I? I asked enough United players to sign stuff for me when I was a boy. I don't like the idea of things turning up on memorabilia websites, people trying to get rich on the back of someone else's popularity but again, it's a balance. I'd rather risk making that mistake than risk disappointing a kid who's been standing, waiting, outside the ground for an hour after a match. I know what it's like to look up to people, to admire the achievements of someone who's good at what they do. I know what it's like because I always have done myself. And still do.

I'm a fan. I always will be. I remember one night a few years ago, Dave Gardner and his girlfriend were down in London and Victoria and I took them to the Ivy restaurant for dinner. Dave got there first and he slaughtered me later about how the *maître d'* had changed his tone completely when Dave told him who he was supposed to be meeting. It went from: 'Who's this Manc?' to 'This way, Sir.' All in a split second. When we got there, the snappers were doing their stuff outside. Dave was starting to take the mickey out of me for being a face at this expensive London restaurant when we looked across the room and saw Our Man at the same time.

'It's not him, is it?'

'I think it is, you know.'

'No, no, it can't be.'

It was, though: Michael Jordan, sitting in the corner, puffing on the biggest cigar I'd ever seen in my life.

'Look. Look who he's with.'

One of my all-time heroes was there at his table, chatting with Madonna, the singer Ricky Martin and Tom Ford, who was head of Gucci at the time. I don't think Dave or I touched any of our food. We were sitting staring across at him.

'Should I go and get his autograph on a napkin?'

'No, you're not allowed to do that in the Ivy.'

Next thing we knew, a bottle of champagne arrived at our table. It was a little while after Brooklyn had been born and this was congratulations from Michael Jordan and Madonna.

Then they both came over for a chat; Victoria knew Madonna and I'd met her at Madison Square Garden the night I arrived in New York after France 98. But Michael Jordan? I was like a little kid, couldn't think of what to say to the bloke. It was some night. And by the Monday, it was all round Old Trafford. Dave had started telling people as soon as he got home. All day at training it was about Saturday night with Becks and Michael Jordan:

'What was he like? What was he like?'

I get a genuine thrill from meeting people like that: superstars as far as I'm concerned, whether they're sportsmen or rappers or actors. Dave Gardner's the one who ends up hearing about them all. Every time I go to a party there seems to be someone there I'll get excited about saying hello to: an Elle McPherson or a Michael Jackson or a Michael Caine. Most people would just think I was name-dropping. But Dave's known me long enough to see it for what it is. I still get nervous – thrilled – in the company of the people I admire. If I meet one of them I can't keep it to myself. I always have to ring up the next day to tell Dave.

An amazing part of my life – of life with Victoria – is that, sometimes, those people I'm nervous before meeting and tongue-tied when I do turn out to become friends. I met Elton John at a Versace fashion show in Italy. He was sitting next to me and did all the hard work of the 'hellos' and 'how are yous'. He'd actually met Victoria a couple of times before and just went ahead and introduced himself. After what he's done in his life, I should think Elton's long since got past being shy in situations like that. We got on really well: there just felt like an instant connection. We started spending time together and we've continued to ever since. Elton and David Furnish are Brooklyn's godparents and probably the closest friends Victoria and I have ever made as a couple. Maybe that's because, as a couple, they're like us in so many ways: very much in love and not afraid to show it. They're incredibly generous: almost the first thing Elton did the afternoon I met him in Italy was to offer Victoria and me their place in the South of France as somewhere to go if we ever needed to get away from it all. But it's not just that they're generous in the sense of sharing what they have. We've grown close to Elton and David because they're just as generous when it comes to sharing who they are.

Meeting new people, even for a shy one like me, is a pleasure. There are some people, though, who meeting is more like a privilege: The Queen; the Prime Minister; the greatest sportsman of all time, Muhammad Ali. In May 2003, straight after the end of the football season, we had an England trip to South Africa. I was on the wrong end of a pretty clumsy tackle in our game against their national team. It was the fall after it that did the damage: another weird injury. I broke the scaphoid bone between the wrist and thumb on my right hand and spent the next couple of months with a removable cast on the lower part of that arm. The injury I picked up in Durban, though, I'd forgotten about even before I was told it had healed. It's meeting Nelson Mandela on that South Africa trip that I'll always remember.

I'm a father to two boys: it's the biggest responsibility in my life. Here's a man who's been a father to a nation. Meeting Mandela was an opportunity I feel humble to have had. We were based in Durban, where the game against South Africa was going to take place three days later. We got a flight at dawn to take us to Johannesburg and were taken to the offices of Mr Mandela's charity foundation. We were all in our England blazers, there were press and other officials and staff gathered round and the morning was already getting warm. The top man, though, seemed so relaxed, leaning back in his armchair, the sunshine streaming through the window behind him.

Victoria will tell you: I've become used to a bit of public speaking since I got the England armband. A little preparation, along with the self-confidence she's given me, and I'm usually ready to go. In fact, Victoria reckons the difficult bit is getting me to stop making speeches these days. My time came to speak to Mr Mandela. I sat down and leaned in towards him. I had a job to do as England captain but, at first, I was just dumbstruck in his presence, overwhelmed with my respect and admiration for him. Did he pick up on how I was feeling? I don't know, but he put me at ease with a little pat on the back. I remembered some of what I'd wanted to say:

'To meet a great man such as you is an amazing honour. It's great to be here today. It's an amazing honour for all of us.'

Mr Mandela asked me and the other England players to support South Africa's bid to host the 2010 World Cup. I'd love to see them get it: football's the people's sport in South Africa. I'd come with United in the past and again, this time with England, you could see the passion for the game all around you: in the stadiums, in the townships, and on every street corner. I gave Mr Mandela an England shirt with his name and 03 on the back. I know he likes team colours: I still remember him wearing the South African rugby shirt after they won the final of the Rugby World Cup. He leaned forward and reached a hand out: some of his grandchildren came up to meet me and the rest of the England lads. He said quietly to them:

'This is David Beckham.'

I had my hair in tight braids and one of the press guys asked Mr Mandela what he thought about it. He just smiled:

'Oh, I'm too old to have an opinion about that.'

I'd have been happy listening to his opinion on that and anything else for the rest of the day. We all know his story but, looking into his eyes, catching his smile, following the lines across this incredibly handsome face, you couldn't help wanting to hear it from him. I don't think Mr Mandela would have been too sorry to spend a little while longer with us either. Time was pushing on, though, and we had work to do back in Durban. By the time we stumbled off the coach back at the hotel, having been up before dawn, our lack of sleep was starting to catch up with me. The afternoon drifted past in a dream. Meeting Nelson Mandela today: did that actually happen to me? I needed to call Victoria and tell her all about it before I could really believe it was true.

Whatever's happening we have to touch base. Because both

Victoria and I have had careers that take us away from home a lot, telephones have been a pretty big deal in our relationship down the years. When we were first getting to know one another, she was travelling all over the world with the Spice Girls. They even took a year away from England for tax reasons on the advice of their manager. That put pressure on the times we could actually be with each other. Sometimes I think we got to know each other down the phone line. I'd be in Manchester after training; Victoria would be in a hotel somewhere in the States, getting ready to go on stage at a 30,000-seat auditorium that night. I can remember days when we spent five hours on the phone at a time. You find out so much about the person you love and eventually marry in the first weeks and months after you meet her. There's all that history, all those details, you have to fill in. Me and Victoria learnt about each other long distance.

That's carried on ever since, of course. We married, we've had children, but we still have to be away sometimes for weeks at a time. We'll still talk all the time but it's different now. For a start, we don't mind a bit of technology: the videophones while I was out in Japan at the World Cup were just the job. And these days, of course, it's not two single people: a boy and a girl falling in love. Whoever's at home has got their hands full with Brooklyn and Romeo. We've always had fantastic support from our parents looking after the boys. But whichever one of us is at home will still be busy with mealtimes, bathtimes, bedtimes and school runs. We end up talking on the phone more often now, but not for such a long time. There'll always be something the boys need that means:

'I'll have to call you back in a minute.'

I think we're lucky. Victoria and I are as comfortable talking on the phone as we are face to face. I know I hate being away from her and the boys but it's that much easier because, if we're on the line, it's intimate and easy enough between us that I feel like we're connected, even if our words are having to be bumped across continents. We feel close enough, anyway, to keep me going until I get home. Life gets so intense and so strange sometimes that, if I couldn't ring the one person who understands it all, I'm not sure I'd always make it home with my head in one piece. Five minutes on the phone with Victoria can make sense of what's going on at my end for me, sort out the strangest problem and calm the biggest crisis. The trust and love that make it work like that are the same in any marriage. Most people's conversations, though, can happen across the dinner table when they get in from work. If I need to talk to Victoria, I'll often have to find out an international dialling code first.

Of course, with the life we live, the important thing is that Victoria and I are in it together. We both know what it's like to be successful in what we do in our careers. Partly because we're a couple, we know what comes with a certain level of fame and an unbelievable amount of attention. We're lucky we have great people around us: family and professional advisers who relieve some of the strain, help us find our way through living the public side of our lives and careers. When it comes down to it, though, it's me and the missus. Every now and again, we'll have to sit down and pinch ourselves, look at what's happening together:

'What's going on right now? What might be just around the corner?'

Whether those conversations happen over the phone or face to face, the important thing is that they happen. Life gets crazy sometimes. We'll see things, be asked to do things, be presented with challenges that we could never have foreseen turning up even a couple of years ago. Truth be told, we both enjoy the unpredictability of it all; Victoria even more than me. There's always something new going on. It's important to try to keep things under control, for our own and the boys' sakes, but every now and again – whether it's studio time in the States or a transfer, out of the blue, to a new club in a different country – things feel like they take on a life of their own. And leave us just hanging on to the slipstream. We have our tricky moments, like anybody else would. But having each other, I think, stops me or Victoria getting overwhelmed by it all.

We can talk to each other. And we can go home to Brooklyn and Romeo. It doesn't matter what's been going on around me the rest of a day. I walk into the house and, as soon as I'm with the boys, nothing else matters but them. They're more thrilling to me – every single day – than anything else in my life. People must look at the lifestyle that comes with being Mr and Mrs Beckham and imagine it's all mad, all completely unreal. Some of it seems that way to us as well. But the foundations for me are the same as those for anybody else with a family. Inside Bubble Beckham, there's another bubble: it keeps the four of us safe – and sane – inside it. My real world, where I find what I need for the rest of the adventure, is with Victoria, Brooklyn and Romeo. There's nothing unusual about that, is there? I'm myself, both feet on the ground, like any other husband and father, when I'm at home with my wife and my sons. It's like Victoria said when we were talking about the move to Madrid:

'This is a huge thing, a huge change in our lives: a different country, a different way of life. But this is just a time to get our heads down and get on with it, concentrating on the things that really matter. You play your football – and you'd better play well – and I'll do my music. And for the rest of it, we'll be where we need to be: you, me and the boys. The family.'

They matter that much to me, Victoria, Brooklyn and Romeo, that I'll travel backwards and forwards from wherever just to spend an hour or two at home. Over the years, it was never a problem for me to drive from Manchester to London to stay overnight and leave early the next morning, as long as we weren't too close to a United game. I know some people would sweat over the mileage but I've never found being behind the wheel tiring. It's always been like that with Victoria: our first date, after all, was a 400-mile round trip for me but I'm pretty glad I didn't decide to stay in that night and watch television instead. I suppose when we were boyfriend and girlfriend, especially when Victoria was out of the country for long stretches, it did get a little extreme even for me. I remember one day, during the summer holidays towards the end of the Spice Girls' world tour, when I flew to Texas and back just to spend an hour in a VIP lounge with Victoria at Dallas airport. More than once, I flew out to where she was so that we could get back on the plane and fly home together. Now? With the children to think about, I might not do those things any more. But that doesn't mean that I wouldn't still want to.

I suppose if I'm not used to airplanes by now I never will be. The passport's picked up some interesting stamps: a photoshoot in Japan, a TV commercial in Spain, a sponsors' event in Vietnam, an awards ceremony in Los Angeles. It could be anything. It could be anywhere. I'm glad someone else has to make the arrangements. It's all good business and, thanks mainly to the right advice, it's working with people I feel good about being associated with, who understand that, when it comes to my time, football always comes first. As well as paying the bills, the other stuff I get involved in is usually enjoyable too. I don't know about the cliché about a change being as good as a rest, but I do get a kick out of concentrating on something which is completely different to my usual routine. Sometimes it even means Victoria and I getting the chance to work together. That's great from the point of view of having time with each other. Our approaches to things like a filming day or a personal appearance are completely different, though. I'm pretty relaxed about it all:

'You get on with it and give me a shout when you need me.'

I like watching other people doing what they're good at, so a set or a studio can be a pretty interesting place to be.

Victoria, of course, has done far more of it over the years. The world of commercials and promotion and publicity were part of her working life even before I met her. That's probably why she's a lot sharper about it, wants to keep things moving, wants to make sure they're just right. She'll sometimes get a bit impatient with it all and those times, as it happens, she's usually right: she probably could do it better herself. I think we both do a decent job, even if we get round to it in different ways. It's just sometimes we'll wind each other up a little along the way. Mind you, that's part of the deal: life with Victoria. Her winding me up. Her making me think: have you seen this? Have you heard this? Have you done that? Her making me laugh, day in and day out. Being with her has made me look at everything, myself included, in a completely different way. I love how she is: awake from the moment she gets going in the morning. I've never known anyone be so alive: being married to Victoria is like being plugged into this no-batteries-needed energy source. And I'm buzzing thanks to her. Sometimes there's the odd short circuit but I've learnt to give as good as I get. Victoria's the best company I've ever known.

I love us travelling together. We had a fantastic time in the summer of 2003 on the promotional tour we did through the Far East. I'd been to Japan before, of course, with England for the World Cup. The two of us heading out there to do work with a sponsor called TBC was a completely different experience. There's a whole thing about blonde Western women in Japan but Victoria's something else for them: she's a role model and a star but she's accessible too. Japanese women adore Victoria – the looks, the glamour, the attitude, the whole package. The same women seem to like me too. I think that's a bit strange: you can't really imagine a movie actor or famous musician from Japan making an impact here in terms of their looks. I remember us talking to an American woman in Tokyo, who lives there and works for Def Jam records. She said that the way I look is only a small part of what's going on. In Japan, according to her at least, everyone's looking for the perfect husband, the perfect father for children. Maybe we'd think of it as old-fashioned, but I think it's a good thing, how important family life is in that society. When they look at me, they see a good-looking bloke who'd make a good partner; he likes being at home, he loves his wife and he's good with the kids. That's why, when it comes to commercials and sponsorships, in the Far East, they like Victoria and I being together. There's an interest in my football and in Victoria's pop career, but those things on their own don't explain why we get the reaction we do in Japan. It's only being there and talking to people you get an idea of how we're seen out there; and we've realised it's very different to the way people see us back home. People in England know I'm a husband and a father but I think what I do for a living is more what drives it all here.

I enjoy the Far East, even though it can get a bit overwhelming at times. As far as holidays go, if I have the choice and a couple of days available, it's a quick jaunt to the South of France. We'll often stay at Elton and David's house. And soon, once it's in shape, they'll be able to stay at ours: we bought a villa down there in 2002. With the family, though, I'll always be ready for a trip to the

States. America is such a big country – and so hooked into other sports like Basketball and American Football – that I don't have the same kind of profile there as in other parts of the world. The press like to make out that I've got this dream about 'breaking' the US market. The real reason I like going to America is actually that I do sometimes daydream about what it would be like to live there. And that's not just because the Big Macs are so much better than they are here. With not being so widely recognised in America, when I go out, I'm not in the position where I'm thinking about people looking at me. I can spend some time looking at them instead. And what I see is a passion for their own country that I really admire. The Stars and Stripes are everywhere. The way we get excited about England when it comes to big football tournaments is how Americans seem to feel about their country all year round. I get the impression that everybody there, whatever background they come from, feels like America is their country and they're proud of it. I think that makes a big difference to the way of life: people in the States seem to have a very positive attitude about themselves because of it.

We had a great time in America in the summer of 2003, even though we ended up staying in the middle of the desert just to get a bit of private family time to ourselves. Because of all the talk about a move to Real Madrid, I understood why there were so many journalists and photographers following us around in New York and Los Angeles. There were a couple of public appearances in the diary too: the MTV awards and a day training with the American women's national football team. I appreciate that you can't turn the attention on and off like a tap. That's why, when it comes to myself, I wouldn't ever complain about the media putting me in the spotlight. There have been times in my life when it's helped me, no question, especially when I was starting out as a young pro at United. And, in recent years, definitely once France 98 was behind me, I think I've had a pretty good deal from the press: they've been positive and generous towards me more often than not. The football writers really helped me settle into the job of England captain. Mostly, though, it's men who run the papers and perhaps that explains some of the snide stuff that gets written and said about Victoria. It winds me up. It winds her up, too. But then my wife's a grown up and can look after herself. The one area where I really do think the media should have a long look at what they do is getting in the faces of children who happen to have famous mums and dads. Brooklyn and Romeo haven't asked for Posh and Becks as parents. It makes me angry – more than that, it makes me sad – that I can't take the boys to a park or to the beach without the cameras coming out. It spoils it for me but that's not the point. I remember Southend with Mum and Dad, evenings after school in Chase Lane Park. Even though my sons aren't aware of it – not yet, anyway – they're being cheated out of some of the best bits of their childhoods because the press can't leave them alone.

I appreciate the role the media's had to play in bringing me the rewards I enjoy. They're part of any career played out in the public eye and, the red card in Saint-Etienne apart, I've been dealt with pretty fairly I think. Right now, I'm really pleased that most people seem to like me and respect what I do, as a football player, a husband and a father. In the back of my mind though, because of what happened after the World Cup in 1998, I'm aware that everything could change. It might be something of my own doing; it might be nothing to do with me, just people's moods changing. When you're talking about fame and what comes your way with that, you know you can't be in control all the time. If the tide turns, I can't expect to be able to stop that. All I can do is be ready for it – if it ever happens – and be comfortable enough with myself to deal with it in my life. That's another reason why it's so important to me that I look after what I feel surest about: my family. I want my wife and my children to be there for me. I want Victoria and Brooklyn and Romeo to know that I'm going to be there for them. If I have the love of my family wrapped up inside me, I'm absolutely sure that I'll be able to face whatever comes.

I grew up in the love of a family. Without Mum and Dad, none of my story would be here for the telling. Like any son, I wouldn't have grown up into the person I am if they hadn't passed on their values to me. Marriage and parenthood, I think, are the two most important things any of us ever take on in our lives. They bring the greatest pleasure and the greatest responsibility. I learned so much about both from my parents and from going through childhood in the home they made for me, Lynne and Joanne. That explains why my parents' splitting up has been probably the most difficult episode I've ever had to face up to in my whole life. To be honest, I'm still trying to face up to it now.

It's not for me to tell the story of how Mum and Dad's marriage ended in divorce. I can't tell my story, though, without talking about how my parents' splitting up has made me feel and still makes me feel. I've been through some difficult stuff in the course of my career and I think I've always been able to handle it. My life is my responsibility now and I've always reacted to challenges by taking them on. There's always a sense of needing to be in control and of trying to take charge of situations in a positive way. My parents' divorce, though, I haven't been able to deal with in that way at all. I was involved but what was happening was something completely outside my control. And that scared me, the first and only time I'd felt that way about what was going on around me. Over the couple of years when things were falling apart, I couldn't bring myself to talk about it. And talking to Mum and Dad was the thing I found hardest of all.

It may be that anyone who's been through the experience of parents' separating will recognise my emotions as the same ones they've had to struggle with. In a family like ours, your mum and dad and them being together is like the sun coming up in the morning. It's something for always. You can't ever imagine them apart, not even when you leave home and start life on your own. Probably the hardest thing to deal with has been thinking – or being made to think – that the split was somehow my fault. I remember the time and the energy they both put into me as a son and as a promising footballer. Should they have given some of the attention they gave to me to each other instead? Then, I'd never have thought about it. Did they? Now, when I think back, it's already too late to do anything about it.

However old you are when it happens, children in a divorce always find themselves feeling guilty. Or find themselves being made to feel guilty. I believe that what happens between husband and wife, deep down, is between husband and wife and nobody else; not even their sons and daughters can change the outcome. My dad's actually said to me that having my own family and not spending as much time with my parents was part of the problem for them. I did find myself wondering: would me going out with Dad, us talking, have changed anything? Should I have been there, trying to be the glue keeping them together? I couldn't help but question myself. It would have been pretty impossible to be with them more often: I was in Manchester most of the week and the odd day or two spare I needed to be with Victoria and the boys. Even if there had been more time, would me being around have made the difference? Looking back, I don't think so.

Even after it's happened, now Mum and Dad are divorced, it's still hard for me. Hard for Lynne and Joanne, too. It's not necessarily said in as many words but there's always, in these situations, a question: whose side are you on? For me and my sisters, that isn't even something we think about: they're our mum and dad and 'sides' doesn't come into it. But I can see that, for parents, there'd be insecurity. They're having a painful time, feeling guilty themselves and they don't want to lose a family at the same time as they lose a husband or wife. I see Mum a lot because she helps us with looking after the boys. I can see that Dad might feel that there's more to it than that. The only way we'll ever get round 'whose side are you on', I think, is if Mum and Dad can find a way to talk to one another again, find a new kind of relationship where there's a bit of trust between them. I really hope that will happen.

When it did become clear that things had broken down between them, even though I found it hard talking to Mum and Dad about the situation, I still wanted to help. I really don't believe I could have stopped them splitting up but I did want to do what I could to make it easier for each of them after it happened. I helped buy our family home – the house I grew up in – so Dad could make his new start there. I needed to be sure my mum felt settled and I know my Nan and Grandad were worried about her too. I bought Mum a new place out in Loughton, nearer to the house in Sawbridgeworth, where she could live with Joanne. I'd always imagined that, somewhere down the line, I'd have bought them a big house somewhere to live in together. My parents were married nearly thirty years; I still can't come to terms with the idea that they're set up now for living apart. For us – me, Lynne and Joanne – and for them, I hope that, somewhere down the line they'll become friendly enough, at least, for us all to sit down together to remember some of the great times we had.

How could it all not have made me think about my own family? The story of my parents' marriage makes me feel sad, empty inside. What was home isn't any more. Who can tell what lies down the road for you in your own life? At home with Victoria and the boys is where I feel I'm fulfilled. My marriage and my family are precious to me. So precious I don't know what life would be about without them. I want to see our children grow up. I want me and Victoria to grow old in each other's company, the two of us together always. I've got married just this once and I want it to mean what it does now, forever. Mum and Dad separating has made me even more aware of that. Growing up, I learned from my parents how to live, how to make decisions and how to treat other people. They also taught me that, if you really want something, you have to work hard for it. I think they had my football career in mind. But I've realised for myself now: that's true for a marriage as well.

About Loyalty

13

'Have you got a problem with me?'

I've never felt a disappointment like it. I really believed we were going to win the 2002 World Cup in Japan. I don't know what had made me so sure. Being captain? My foot healing in time? The little coincidences, like being allocated seat number 7 on flights, just by chance? It had definitely felt like they were the right omens pointing towards this being England's time. What I do know is that going out when we did – and how we did – left me with a real hangover into the new season back home. Victoria and I went away for a week soon after the England squad got back to the UK, but even that did nothing to shift my mood. In fact, by the end of the week, Victoria had had about enough:

'I don't know how much more of that I could have taken', she said, 'being with someone who didn't smile or show any emotion from one day to the next, who could hardly bring himself to say two words to me or to anyone else'.

She didn't need to tell me it was unfair on her. In the past I'd always tried to make sure that I didn't take work home with me, didn't get moody with my family when things weren't going well for me, for whatever reason, at United. But this was different. And when it came time to start pre-season training, I was still feeling the same, like I hadn't had a break at all: tired, heavy legs, no spark. It was all wrong. My job isn't a job at all. It's not nine to five, is it? It's not going down a mine or driving a lorry all day long. Playing football, training, is what I love doing and I knew I shouldn't have been feeling like I did: as if I didn't really want to be there, back at United already and with a new season about to get underway.

You can't just wish that kind of depression away. You get your head down and get on with what you know you've got to do. United players are lucky that the gaffer understands his players well enough to recognise how they're feeling and that they're not putting something on. Maybe because of that, pre-season wasn't as hard as it's sometimes been in the past. Even so, when we kicked off 2002/03 I still felt a long way off ready for a new season which, after the previous May had come and gone without a trophy at Old Trafford, had plenty riding on it. When you don't feel right, sometimes you need to work that bit harder, to train and play your way through it, and I was ready for that. What I didn't realise was that some of the worst of what lay ahead had nothing to do with football at all.

Victoria and I do what we can to keep our lives organised; not just to keep our own heads straight but because our schedules mean life's already complicated enough for Brooklyn and Romeo. Sometimes, though, things come out of nowhere, things you could never lay plans for. And, even if you could, you wouldn't want to because just thinking about them would have you wanting to lock your front door and never come out.

The first game in November at Old Trafford was against Southampton. Not a game that, usually, would have stuck in my mind. We weren't at our best and it was one of those afternoons when you're glad to have done enough to nick all three points. For all that every home game is a big occasion, especially when you're wearing the captain's armband like I was with Roy Keane out injured, I came off at the end of our 2–1 win with a bit of a 'that's

Made to measure.
Dressing up, dressing down.

Left: 'Wrapped up in love.' From the Beckham family album.

This page: It's an honour. Meeting Muhammad Ali, Nelson Mandela, and Her Majesty the Queen; and BBC Sports Personality of the Year 2001.

Above: Celebrating with the England fans after that goal against Greece.

Left: A pain in the metatarsal. An end to my World Cup chances?

Right: My World Cup, Japan 2002, including a draw against Sweden, a win versus Argentina and elimination at the hands of Brazil.

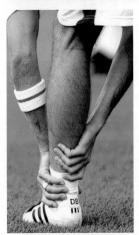

United 4 Charlton 1:
Champions again.

another Saturday afternoon' feeling. I was looking forward to seeing Victoria and heading off home for a night in with the boys.
Which meant that what was waiting for me came as all the more
of a shock.

As soon as I got to the dressing room, the gaffer said we needed
to talk in his office. Not after I'd changed. Not as soon as I could.
Now. So I clattered through, still in my boots and my kit. We went
inside. I don't know what I was expecting but it wasn't that Victoria
would be there waiting for us. She looked pale and nervous. *I'm
handling this but only just.* I looked at her, as if I expected her to
tell me what was going on: it's such a strange feeling, knowing
something's terribly wrong, just from the tension in the room, but
not having any idea what it was. I looked at the gaffer, too. He
looked drawn. It was only then, really, that I took in the other
people who were present: four of them. One I half-recognised as
a Manchester-based police officer and he introduced me to the
other three. They were from SO7, the Serious and Organised
Crime Command unit, and had driven up from Scotland Yard.

So four men standing there in their suits, with me still dripping
sweat in my United kit: it felt like we were all waiting to find out
what was going to happen next. The manager said I should sit
down and listen. What I heard I had trouble believing. I was trying
to make some sense of what was being said. *This can't be happening. This shouldn't be happening.*

I looked across at Victoria and I could see in her eyes she
already had the same question in her mind as I did. *What are we
going to do?*

After a tip-off from the *News of the World*, four men and a
woman had been arrested in London. They were part of a gang
of art thieves – four more people were picked up that night
and the following morning – believed to be planning to kidnap

Victoria, Brooklyn and Romeo and hold them to a £5 million ransom.

Victoria had already heard all this and she was doing her best to be strong about it. She'd jokingly said if they were going to kidnap her, they'd have to kidnap her hairdresser as well. Now, she was listening to the detail again, and watching me take it all in. And I was really upset. I felt my stomach turn over: it's anybody's worst kind of nightmare, although not many people will have to listen to policemen talking them through a threat that's very real indeed. Right at the start, the guys from Scotland Yard were telling us that they took this thing seriously. They'd already made those arrests and, as of right now, they were putting officers outside the houses at Alderley Edge and Sawbridgeworth.

Sure enough, by the time we got home, there was a police car at the end of the lane and a couple of policemen were on duty at the gate. We went in and there was another car in the drive, right outside our front door. I think Victoria and I were trying hard not to panic and, I've got to say, it helped that the police seemed so in control of things so quickly. That evening and the next morning, as we read the papers and watched the television coverage of it all, the truth of what might have happened started to hit home. We might have been used to seeing and hearing stories about ourselves, often to do with things we've had no idea about beforehand, but this was different. There were the pictures of the gang at the gates of the house down south and details of the threats they'd made about what might happen to Victoria if I didn't pay up: that kind of wickedness and on my own doorstep made my blood run cold. I think it was overnight that the shock really sank in for both of us.

We were upset and scared, but you can't just hide and hope it will all go away. My family's safety is the most important thing in the world; it's the same for any dad. So in the days after, it was a case of trying to work out what we could do. I lost count of the number of experts that we took advice from. Some of the time, it felt like we were just getting more and more confused: everybody had different ideas and I even had the feeling that a certain amount of politics was behind some of it, people staking claims for their own reputations at the same time as offering to help. It came down to not being sure exactly who we could trust.

In the end, the person we turned to was Tony, Victoria's dad. He'd always taken an interest in security equipment in connection with his own work and, when we bought the house in Sawbridge-worth, he'd put in alarm systems without us, until now, ever having to know the details. These security measures were sophisticated enough to impress the officers from Scotland Yard when they began looking at what improvements they thought we could make to our arrangements.

We've now got levels of security in our lives, from day to day, which we'd not even considered before the kidnap plot was uncovered. It's not easy: never mind going to work or out to social engagements, we've always wanted to be able to go down to Marks & Spencer or McDonald's like any other family. Now we have to be careful like never before. At the same time as making sure the boys are safe, we've tried not to make life too strange for them. In the day or two just after the plot was uncovered, I told Brooklyn that the policeman parked outside had come down especially to show him his car. You can imagine what a three-year-old made of that: he was out there every ten minutes wanting to sit behind the wheel and turn the patrol car's lights on and off.

If you'd asked me then, I'd have said that I'd rather not play against Leicester in the Worthington Cup on the Tuesday night after that Saturday afternoon. The manager had said he was going to rest those players who he thought needed a break. And I felt like I was one of those players. Over the years, we've some-times not played our strongest side in that competition. It's been an opportunity for younger players to come in and make their mark, like I did, down at Brighton, nearly ten years ago. But my name was on the teamsheet against Leicester; and, if I was picked to play for United, the boss knew he'd get no argument from me.

There's always a very good reason behind every decision the manager makes. You may not like it at the time – like when he'd left me out against Leeds – but, when you stop and think, you remember that all he's focused on is what's right for the team. And often that turns out to be the right thing for the player as well. It drives you mad sometimes: you feel almost like he knows you better than you know yourself. He knows that playing football is what I'm all about and decided, I think, that me captaining the team that night would help the other lads and, at the same time, give me a break from the chaos of the previous few days away from Old Trafford. Once I'm out on the park, nothing's ever got in the way of me doing my job. The manager knew it wouldn't that night either, and I got the first goal, from the penalty spot, in a 2–0 win.

I got a break in that game, too, but not the kind I needed. A few minutes before the end, I went in for a challenge with their centre-forward, Trevor Benjamin, who's a big lad, and he fell on top of me. I was left sitting there knowing something serious had happened: I could hardly breathe. Afterwards and over the next few days, the United medical staff said I'd just bruised my ribs. I trained. I even played at the weekend. They thought that, if there'd been a fracture, I'd not have been able to do either. I was con-vinced the pain meant there was more to this than bruising though and, when we followed it up, the scan showed I had actually broken a rib.

I've never had trouble with injury beyond little niggles but this was my second in less than a year: This particular knock was maybe a blessing in disguise. I never want to miss games, but even before the season started I'd been feeling tired, mentally and physically, after coming back from Japan and, now, I didn't have any choice but to rest. I joined up with England for a get-together during the international week. The whole squad was invited to Buckingham Palace, which was something I couldn't miss out on. I felt unbelievably proud, being introduced to Her Majesty the Queen again as the England captain. She asked about my injury – last season's foot, I think she meant, not this season's rib – and about our arrangements since the kidnap plot. She obviously took an interest in that, personal security being something she knows all about herself.

For what seemed like the first time in ages, we took the boys on holiday, just us for a week in Barbados. Arranging it was a bit stressful: where to go, who to tell about it and the rest. We decided at the very last minute and just told the family but, by the time we got to the hotel, the papers had tracked us down. Who knows how it happens? Someone on the plane, or at the airport, sees you and passes the word along? It meant we spent almost the whole time by the pool, which was fenced off and private. The very last day I took Brooklyn to the beach, which was only a few yards away from our villa, and the cameras were already out there, waiting. I know I'm lucky to be able to fly off to a beautiful place in the sun and enjoy the luxury; not so lucky, maybe, that I can't spend a few hours playing in the sea with my family while I'm there. Anyway, it was great to have some time to relax and just be with each other while, I imagined, life rolled on back at home.

I came back fresh and couldn't wait to be playing again, although I was still a couple of weeks short of being ready for a game. Something had changed, though, while I'd been away. Almost as soon as I started work on building up my fitness at Carrington, I began to feel a chill in the atmosphere: not around the club, but between me and Alex Ferguson. It's often like that when you're injured. You're not involved and so it's as if you don't really exist. Obviously, the gaffer has to get on with winning football matches with the players he's got.

This felt like something different, though. Perhaps if I'd known what was going to happen over the next few weeks, I'd have been able to do something about it before events spun out of control. After the ten happiest years of my life at Old Trafford, how could I ever have imagined that things were going to unravel, and so quickly, to a point where I'd find myself wondering whether my future didn't lie away from United, or even away from football altogether?

The boss hardly said a word to me at training or anywhere else. After a month of getting the cold shoulder, I decided I needed to find out what was going on. In the past, any kind of meeting with the boss would have been intimidating just to think about. I'd be standing in front of him and, before I'd said a word, my bottom lip would be starting to go. I've always been stubborn but I'm older now and more mature as a person. Most important of all, I'm surer of myself. I've got my wife believing in me to thank for that. I asked the gaffer if I could see him and said it straight out:

'Is there a problem? Have you got a problem with me?'

He did. A big problem. To be specific, it was that, instead of going straight off on holiday, I'd gone to Buckingham Palace with the rest of the England players. He reckoned I'd have been fit sooner if I hadn't waited those extra couple of days before going away. I tried to argue my case. As I understood it from the doctors, there's nothing you can do that will hurry a recovery from a broken rib: it's four weeks' rest and that's that. As for going to Buckingham Palace, I tried to explain:

'I'm England captain. Never mind that I was proud to be asked to go and meet The Queen, I'd have been ripped apart in the papers if I hadn't been there. The whole World Cup squad was there. I felt it was my duty to be there too. Ashley Cole got stick because he turned up wearing trainers. What would it have been like if I hadn't turned up at all?'

What the gaffer said next, I'll never forget:

'When I saw you turn up there, I questioned your loyalty to Manchester United.'

That stung. I couldn't believe I was hearing it, to be honest. I'd been at the club for thirteen years.

'I love United. I want to be here. But if you don't want me to be, you should tell me.'

The boss didn't answer. I walked out. And, in the days after-wards, it was like the conversation hadn't happened at all. In training, it felt like I was on the end of the worst criticism, whatever I did, for no real reason at all. The gaffer's never been afraid to change things at United. I got my chance in the first team, after all, because he sold Andrei Kanchelskis. Now it was beginning to feel like I was the one being set up for the chop. We were all used to getting stick from the gaffer: for years it had been one way of him getting the best out of his players. This wasn't like that, though. It was personal and it was humiliating. Try as I might to carry on as normal, the situation got to me. Ask Victoria: she had her own worries with Romeo being so young. And she hated the fact that I was so down and depressed the whole time. It wasn't her fault was it? But she was the one who got it in the ear day after day from an unhappy husband.

That meeting with the gaffer hadn't resolved anything. Even after I'd got back to full fitness and was playing again in the team, it seemed I couldn't do anything right in his eyes. I got more than my fair share of stick on the training ground and, away from football, it felt like the slightest thing was enough to get me into more trouble. Before Christmas, the players would go to local hospitals, taking in presents for the kids. The previous couple of years, we'd spread things around a bit by me and Victoria going to a different hospital, the Christie Cancer Hospital in Manchester, and I made the mistake of asking whether we should do the same thing again. The boss saw that as me snubbing the rest of the team, wanting to be different and wanting to be treated differently – none of which was anything like the truth – and pulled me to one side to give me a piece of his mind about it.

The day of our game against Chelsea at Old Trafford in the Worthington Cup, Brooklyn had his first nativity play at nursery school. We trained in the morning and were due to meet up at one o'clock to prepare for the game. I asked the gaffer if I could report a few minutes late: the play started at midday and lasted about an hour. Maybe I should have known not to even ask. If I'd been another kind of character, I'd have gone off anyway and then blamed traffic for me being fifteen minutes late getting to work. I'm not the only dad in the world who'd be desperate to be at his son's nursery school for something like that and I hoped the boss would understand. At worst, I thought, he might just say no; that we had a big game and he didn't want me to go. But he was furious:

'Hell, David, what are you after? What more do you want?'

Before I could say anything he just turned on his heel and

walked away. I had to take that as my answer. I was sorry to miss Brooklyn's play but I understood a manager not wanting his player to be there on the day of a game. What I didn't understand was why it was such a big deal that I'd asked. Winding the gaffer up was the last thing I'd wanted to do.

I didn't have to. This standoff just seemed to drag on. They were the worst three months I'd ever had at Old Trafford. The boss, when he wasn't having a go at me, seemed to be ignoring me. I got more and more depressed. At training, at home, I felt like just withdrawing into my shell. I'd be really quiet. Things people said to me would go in one ear and out the other. He was ignoring me and I found myself ignoring him and pretty well everything else, too. Obviously I talked to Gary, to Victoria, and to Tony Stephens about what was going on. But I really missed there being someone at the club to act as an intermediary between me and the gaffer: a Brian Kidd, a Steve McClaren or an Eric Harrison who could see things from the gaffer's perspective as well as the players', who really understood what the situation was and could advise you accordingly. The new number two, Carlos Queiroz, was a great coach, no question, but maybe because of a language barrier or because of his own background as a top-flight manager himself, he wasn't someone I'd have felt comfortable having that kind of conversation with. I don't think Carlos would have recognised it as part of his job, either. The boss himself, obviously, didn't want to talk to me. For the first time in my United career, I felt like I didn't have anybody on the staff I could turn to for help.

I've already mentioned how difficult I've found it to cope with my parents' splitting up. It goes without saying, though, that with the situation between them coming to a head and, then, the divorce going through, my own relationship with Mum and Dad couldn't help but be affected too. Any son, or daughter, who's lived through a family breaking up, will know how disorientating and confusing it is. With Dad, especially, things changed over that time. In the past, he'd have been the first person I'd have talked to about what was happening at Old Trafford. Now, he had his own problems and pressures to deal with and it didn't feel right to be looking to him for advice. Because she and Jackie – Victoria's mum – are the world's best babysitters, I was still seeing a lot of my mum around the time things started to go wrong for me at United. I've always known that she and Dad were there for me but, as far as football was concerned, Mum had given me support while Dad, I suppose, had been the one to give me guidance. Now, though, she could see for herself how this standoff with the boss was torturing her son; and how me being upset was hurting her daughter-in-law and her grandchildren too. Without me knowing, Mum decided to take it on herself to do something about what was happening.

We played West Ham in the FA Cup and Mum was at Old Trafford to watch. For the first time, I felt the depression affecting my game. I played, and we won 6–0, but there wasn't much pleasure to be got from it, especially as the boss had had a go at me about something at half-time. I remember getting changed and leaving the ground as quick as I could. By the time I was in the car with Victoria, it felt like something had to give. I felt completely powerless and just sat there, staring out into the rain, and choking back the tears. Mum came away from Old Trafford a bit later – she and Joanne were driving back to London separately – and phoned from their car:

'I've been to see him.'

My first reaction was: 'Been to see who?'

Without Mum saying, I knew she meant the boss. And then I was angry. The idea of my mum going to see my boss seemed totally wrong, somehow. She explained that it hadn't been planned, that she'd run into the gaffer by chance in the corridor and felt she had to tell him what she thought. At 27, it seemed to me that I should be able to sort out my own problems at work. It was a real surprise to me that she'd done what she had. I'd guess it was for the gaffer, too. She told me a bit about what had been said and one thing stuck in my mind:

'Do you know Sandra, the trouble with David is that everybody sucks up to him now.'

Nothing the gaffer could have said about me could have hit harder than that. I've always believed, whatever anyone else says or thinks about you, that you have to be true to yourself. When I was a kid – playing for Ridgeway, training with Spurs, starting out at United – whenever Dad had been angry with me about something, had decided my attitude wasn't right, he'd known just what to say to really get to me:

'You've changed.'

Those words, coming from him, always stung me like nothing else: they suggested I was cheating with my football and with my life by pretending to be someone or something I wasn't. Dad knew how to get to me and so did Alex Ferguson. What he told my mum after that West Ham game was his way of saying the same thing Dad had said years ago. I knew how alike they were: stubborn, for a start. Maybe what neither of them really knew was how much I'd inherited that stubbornness as part of my own character. I couldn't let myself buckle under, anyway. I was angry, at first, that Mum had been to see the boss but it made me realise that if I was this upset and this frustrated, I needed to face up to the situation instead of just letting it grind me down.

A few days later, the boss asked to see me. He wanted to talk about the arrangements for the England friendly against Australia:

the understanding with Sven was that the senior players would only be involved for 45 minutes. Of course, as England captain, I needed to know what was going on. All that was fine. Now it was my turn. I'd thought long and hard since the West Ham game about what I wanted to say to the gaffer and what I wanted to hear from him. We'd had a couple of days off and that had given me time to get a few things straight in my own mind. I needed to know if he wanted me to leave United. And, if he didn't but was going to carry on treating me the way he had been, I wanted him to know that I had one other option. I couldn't imagine myself actually doing it but it was possible: I had enough in the bank to make sure that my decisions didn't have to be about money. Rather than have my life broken apart by the game I loved, I had a choice: I could retire from football altogether. I got as far as discussing it with Victoria. I didn't want to believe, though, that things might come to that:

'Can we sort out our problem now, boss?'

'What problem? Do we have a problem?'

'Yes, we do. I'm not in the state I'm in for no reason. I'm in bits at the moment because of what you're doing to me.'

'I've not been doing anything to you,' he said.

Then he went on: 'You've been treating me the same way: ignoring me, not even looking at me in team talks.'

Which was true, but only because it had been all I could do, sometimes, to stop myself letting slip how down I was feeling. If you can't deal with something, you try and block it out.

'Boss, this has been going on for months, the way you've been treating me. At least as far back as me breaking my rib and the business about the visit to Buckingham Palace. I'm not enjoying training. I'm not enjoying football. I just can't go on like this.'

When I asked him if he really believed that people sucked up to me, and that I'd changed because of that, I think it caught him off guard. It was a strange moment – a moment of uncertainty – not like anything that had ever gone on between us before. Perhaps he was surprised that Mum and I had talked to each other about his conversation with her or surprised that I didn't mind him knowing we had. At first he denied saying it and then tried to explain what he'd meant. As far as I could see, the gaffer was missing the point.

'I don't agree with you but put that to one side. Even if you don't approve of how other people might behave towards me, is it right to blame me for it? To take it out on me the way you have been doing?'

I think the gaffer agreed with that. The principle of it, anyway. This was too important to me to just leave it there, though.

'I'm 27 years old now. I think I've grown up a bit. And I think, now, I respond better to encouragement than I do to being picked on. The way it's been the past few months: perhaps, in the past, it might have worked on me. It doesn't any more. If I'm playing well now, it's down to me and the support I get at home. It's in spite of how you're being towards me, not because of it.'

He assured me that he wasn't trying to pick on me on purpose. That he wasn't treating me any differently than he was the other players. I knew it didn't feel like that but I didn't have any choice but to take the gaffer at his word. I'd said most of what I had to say and it felt strange that the gaffer hadn't jumped back at me. It never blew up into anger. Maybe that's why the meeting didn't get to where I'd thought it might: either a genuine reconciliation or me telling the boss that I was planning to retire. Instead he said he wanted us to move on:

'You communicate with me. I'll communicate with you. We'll be professional and we'll go on from there.'

I stood up and went to walk out of the office. The gaffer said to me in that half-joking, slightly sarcastic way he has:

'Come here and shake my hand before you start crying.'

I didn't feel like crying. I'm not sure it felt like the time to shake hands either, but I did. I left feeling that nothing had been resolved; that nothing had really changed. The next morning at training, though, it felt like something had. The gaffer was completely differ-ent, or seemed to be: positive, encouraging, friendly even. For a while, it was great. It seemed as if the meeting had, after all, done the trick. It was all I needed to lift me out of the gloom I'd sensed myself slipping into. Not getting it in the neck every other day meant I could enjoy training and playing again like I hadn't for weeks. It felt like me and the boss had found our way past some-thing: the tension that had been between us since the broken rib and my visit to Buckingham Palace.

I was wrong. In fact, it was the calm before the storm.

The Sunday before I went off to join up with England, we played Manchester City at home. Earlier in the season, we'd lost the derby 3–1 at Maine Road. I hadn't played, so that couldn't have been my fault. Just as well. The next day, Gary Neville told me that, in the dressing room, the gaffer had been as angry as he'd ever seen him after a game. The result at Old Trafford wasn't much better. We conceded a late goal and drew 1–1. The gaffer picked me out for criticism in the dressing room afterwards, saying I'd given the ball away too often. I could only think of a couple of passes that had gone astray. I didn't rise to it, I just sat and let him have his say, but then, during the week, regretted that I hadn't. If I'd stuck up for myself that afternoon rather than waiting until after our next home game, perhaps things wouldn't have blown up in our faces the way they did.

People say a change is as good as a rest. The week England

lost 3–1 to Australia at Upton Park, it certainly wasn't. The senior side played the first half and we never really got going: it was a strange atmosphere, knowing that after 45 minutes the young players were going to come on instead, a completely different team. The Australians, most of whom play their club football in England, were really up for it and they were worth their two-goal lead at the break. I was really angry about what was happening. As soon as we got back to the dressing room, I asked Sven if I could play for at least part of the second half as well. I thought we owed it to the England supporters and to ourselves to try and put the situation right. He said no, that the arrangements had been made and so it wasn't a good idea. This was a friendly and a chance for him to have a look at players like Wayne Rooney. If you think about the Euro 2004 qualifier against Turkey at the Stadium of Light later in the season and the difference a certain seventeen-year-old made in that game, I suppose nobody can say Sven's decision wasn't the right one against Australia.

Our next competitive games were weeks away, so nobody was looking that far ahead. After losing to Australia that night in February, the England manager and the players took a hammering in the press. There had been criticism of Sven ever since the World Cup. Our first European Championship qualifier for 2004 had been a really hard game, on a terrible pitch, away to Slovakia. We won but that didn't seem to matter: we were criticised in the press for playing without any style and without any passion. Me, I thought it was a great three points. Then, at home to Macedonia, despite playing some good football during the game, we only drew against a team we were supposed to beat easily. The flak got worse and, all of a sudden, it was as if the people who'd disapproved of Sven being appointed England coach had spotted their chance to try and hound him out of the job.

A lot of the criticism was focused on the fact that we'd fielded two completely different teams and on the club versus country debate. Ridiculous things were being said, like Sven not being strong enough to face up to the Premiership managers. For me, it wasn't a choice of playing for United or playing for England. United had been my life, as far as football was concerned, but that didn't mean I wasn't proud every time I played for my country too, especially as captain. Reading and listening to the fuss, I found myself wondering what the gaffer would be making of it all. Wondering if my career as an international footballer – as well as the way I lived my life as a husband and father – might be part of the 'David Beckham Problem', as the Manchester United manager saw it. Of course I could think about all that, but there wasn't anything I could do about any of it right now. The important thing was getting back to Carrington to prepare for Arsenal at home in the FA Cup fifth round.

I remember the boss getting us all together beforehand. It wasn't just the England lads who'd been away from Old Trafford on international duty:

'You're back at the club now. It's a big game on Saturday. Make sure you get your heads right for it.'

There was a chill in the air between the two of us again. Something had annoyed the gaffer. I didn't know what. All I knew was I could feel the tension and I was convinced things were going to snap. I remember talking to a mate on the Friday evening before the Arsenal game:

'Things aren't right. Something's got to him. Something's going to happen tomorrow.'

The game didn't go well. Arsenal scored from a lucky deflection off a free-kick. At half-time, the gaffer said he wasn't happy with how I was playing. That it wasn't my job to be a right-back. I should be pushing up, further forward, on Ashley Cole, he said. I couldn't understand what he meant. I looked across at Gary who, of course, was playing behind me, and I could see he didn't agree with him either. There wasn't any point in me saying anything. We were only 1–0 down, we'd had as much of the ball as they had, and we had 45 minutes, now, to put things right.

It got worse, though. Early in the second half, Edu put a little ball through for Wiltord and Arsenal were two up. I didn't play well. Nobody else did, either. We trooped back into the dressing room afterwards. I took my boots and shin pads off straight away because I'd got a kick on my leg and been substituted. The boss came in, shut the door, took his jacket off and hung it up on a hook. His first words were:

'David. What about the second goal? What were you doing?'

Was he blaming me? I was taken completely by surprise.

'It wasn't my fault. Their bloke's made a run off someone in central midfield.'

The boss kept going: 'We told you about it before the game. The problem with you is you don't let anyone talk to you. You don't listen.'

I couldn't believe it. I'd been listening – and wanting to listen – my whole career. I'd listened to the gaffer since the first day we'd met and I was listening now.

'David. When you're wrong, you've got to own up.'

'Boss, I'm sorry. I'm not wrong here. This wasn't my fault and I'm not taking the blame for it.'

'No. Take the blame is what you're going to do.'

Everybody in the dressing room could hear what was going on. Surely, everybody else knew I was right: you could have pointed your finger at half a dozen of the team in the build-up to Arsenal's second goal. But it was all down to me, according to the boss. I felt like I was being bullied, in public, and being backed into a corner, for no reason other than spite. I was trapped. And I swore at him. Something no player, certainly no United player, should ever do to the manager. What happened then still doesn't seem real now, thinking back to that afternoon.

The boss took a step or two towards me from the other side of the room. There was a boot on the floor. He swung his leg and kicked it. At me? At the wall? It could have gone anywhere, he was that angry now. I felt a sting just over my left eye, where the boot had hit me. I put one hand up to it and found myself wiping blood away off my eyebrow. I went for the gaffer. I don't know if I've ever lost control like that in my life before. A couple of the lads stood up. I was grabbed by Giggsy first, then by Gary and Ruud van Nistelrooy. Suddenly it was like some mad scene out of a gangster movie, with them holding me back as I tried to get to the gaffer. He stepped back, I think quite shocked at what had happened. Probably a minute, at most, was how long the real rage lasted. I calmed down a bit and went through into the treatment room.

One of the medical staff stopped the eye bleeding. I was in there for about five minutes. As much as anything, the doctor and the physio were trying to make sure I didn't go back and start at it again. Eventually, I told them I was all right and went through into the changing room. I got dressed and started to leave. As I got to the door, the gaffer was there:

'I'm sorry, David. I didn't mean to do that.'

I couldn't even bring myself to look at him, I was still that angry about what had happened and didn't want to react. I didn't say anything, just walked straight past and through into the players' lounge. Victoria was there. I wanted to get out of Old Trafford and home.

'What's wrong? What have you done to your eye?'

I told Victoria I'd tell her later but she wanted to know right away. I explained what had happened and, all of a sudden, Victoria was as angry as I'd been. She'd had to live with how low I'd been for most of the season. And now she thought she could do something about it:

'He can't treat you like that. I'm going to see him right now.'

I don't know what Victoria might have said or done if she had. I wouldn't want to get into a scrap with my wife. I knew it wasn't right to stay and insisted we left there and then. Later that evening, the eye started bleeding again and I had to call out the doctor. He came round and sealed the wound with a couple of steristrips.

I should have known what to expect. It's hard to keep secrets these days and, even before the Arsenal and United players had left Old Trafford that afternoon, the story of what had happened – or, at least, bits of it – had got out to the press. I walked out of the house in Alderley Edge the following morning, with my hair pulled back to stop it falling against the cut over my eye and, within a couple of minutes, someone had taken the photo that was all over Monday's papers. Along with all the other emotions I was trying to get to grips with, I felt like Exhibit A.

It's bad enough having a row with your boss. It makes setting things straight all the harder when it seems like millions of people are looking over your shoulder, waiting to see what's going to happen, speculating about what might before it does. For a couple of days, at least, when I didn't feel like I was wandering around in a daze – how and why had things between me and the boss come to this – I was still seething about what he'd done in that dressing room, accident or not. Even though he'd said sorry straight afterwards, now this thing was in the public eye, I really believed the gaffer's apology should be made public too. I certainly didn't think it was up to me to make the first move.

Outside Old Trafford, the whole thing became this huge issue. In a way, everybody else saying what they had to say, whether they really knew or understood what had happened or not, made me concentrate harder on seeing the row for what it was. We'd had a big argument, me and the gaffer. I'd said things I shouldn't have. He'd reacted. Badly. And now I had a little cut over one eye. The tension of the past few months seemed to explode in those few moments. Only the boss could tell you what he'd been feeling but I knew – and he'd said so straight away – that he hadn't meant that boot to hit me, however angry he was. That much of it was a fluke. I thought things through. United had a huge game midweek against Juventus in the Champions League and I didn't want a personal problem between me and the boss to get in the way of our preparations.

I realised that, whatever the gaffer said or did, I could draw some of the sting from the situation ahead of the game on the Wednesday night at Old Trafford. It felt like the right thing to do: for me, for my team-mates and the club. I released a statement saying that what had happened had been an accident; that it was behind us now and that all that mattered was focusing on beating Juventus. Which we went on to do, 2–1. The gaffer made a point, after the game, of saying publicly that I'd played particularly well. I appreciated that. And the next time we sat down to talk, it was about football. There wasn't a big meeting or anything. We watched the video of the Arsenal defeat. The boss pointed out where he thought I'd been caught out of position for the second goal but he also admitted that half the team had actually been in the wrong place at the same time. It was as close as I was going to get to an admission that singling me out for criticism in the dressing room that afternoon hadn't been fair.

At any other point in my career as a United player, we'd have called it quits there and then. A month later, it would have seemed as if nothing had ever happened. I didn't realise, though, in the days after that Arsenal game, what I know now: the boss and I had already reached a point where there was going to be no turning back. Had Alex Ferguson already made up his mind about David Beckham back then? Decided he didn't want me at the club any longer? Even if he had, I bet that it didn't have him any better prepared than I was for how things would turn out over the coming six months.

United Born and Bred

14

'For the first time, it was my relationship with the club that was slipping away.'

Turkey were fantastic at the 2002 World Cup. Their passing, their movement, their edge. They play the right way and it makes them a great team to watch. For pure football, their two matches against Brazil, in the group and, then, in the semi-final, were the best of the summer. They came back from Japan and South Korea supposedly the third best team in the world. And, of course, we'd pulled them out of the hat for the Euro 2004 qualifiers. From the moment the draw was made, the England–Turkey games were always going to be the ones to decide who'd qualify from Group 7. And here we were, 2 April 2003, after dropping points at home to Macedonia earlier in the season, knowing we had to get a result against Turkey at the Stadium of Light to give ourselves a decent chance of finishing top – especially with our last qualifier being the away game in Istanbul at the end of October.

Although I think we need to have a national stadium for England games and FA Cup Finals, I've really enjoyed playing international football at different club grounds around the country. It's given people who otherwise would never have made the trip down to Wembley the chance to see England close up and I'd say the relationship between the fans and the players is better because of it. It feels like club loyalties get pushed to one side on these days and supporters get behind the team as a whole. It seems a long time ago now that England supporters would boo United players when their names were announced in the line up. For pressure games, it's helped us to have a passionate crowd close up to the pitch, cheering us on. We were all looking forward to playing Turkey at the Stadium of Light: the atmosphere there is as intense as at any ground in England.

I don't blame Sunderland Football Club for what happened off the pitch that night. The crowd trouble before and during the game was a real blow, like going back to the bad old days: the idiots, too many of them to ignore, letting the rest of the England fans – and the England team – down. Afterwards, I found myself thinking that having to play our next game behind closed doors might not be such a bad thing. That was the threat from UEFA when they had their inquiry into the racist chanting and the pitch invasions at the Stadium of Light. I felt so strongly that I said it in public. If it took England having to play in an empty stadium to make people realise the damage done to our game by the racists and the troublemakers, then so be it. I don't know how happy the FA were at the time about me speaking my mind but, before we played Slovakia at home in our next qualifier, we recorded an appeal to the supporters to get behind the team in the right way. I wasn't at the Riverside Stadium that night. My booking against Turkey meant I was out for the game. Everybody's told me, though, that the supporters in Middlesbrough did England proud. We changed the way people around the world thought about our fans during the 2002 World Cup. I hope that continues. It would be awful to qualify for the European Championships and then find ourselves banned from Portugal because we've let things slide.

The crowd trouble took some of the shine off the night at the Stadium of Light. There were as many headlines about the hooligans as there were about the team. That was a shame because it was another England performance of which we could all be proud. We beat one of Europe's strongest teams 2–0 and went top of our group. The previous Saturday, we'd been away to Liechtenstein and won by the same score. The pundits, as well as some of our supporters, had given us a roasting: how could England expect to be at the finals if they struggled to beat a bunch of part-timers? But football's about results. We'd had a bad result, even though we'd played some decent football, down at Southampton against Macedonia. Other than that, despite playing in some difficult conditions, we'd won all our games in Group 7. Sven always says it: get three points. You win the games you're expected to win and it doesn't matter too much how you do it. When the big games come round, that's when you expect to find your big performance to match.

Turkey retain possession as well as any team in the world. It's what they base their game around and, if you let them, they'll take a defence to pieces. Sven and his assistant Brian Kidd, Steve McClaren's replacement, said how important it was for us to break up their rhythm and to impose our own game on them instead. As captain, I thought it was up to me to try and lead by example. In the first half I did fly into a tackle or two and it cost me a booking but that's not something I regret. I know it sounds a bit old-fashioned but getting stuck into Turkey was what we needed to do. They had their fair share of the ball but never got time to settle into any kind of pattern. I felt, all night, we were the team that would score. Turkey hadn't ever seen many like Wayne Rooney: none of us have. Even though he didn't score, the lad lifted us – and scared them to death – every time he got the ball.

Michael Owen was making great runs off him and I was sure he'd get the goal. As it turned out, though, Michael picked up an injury after an hour and Darius Vassell came on and hit in a rebound from Rio Ferdinand's header. David James made one fantastic save and then Kieron Dyer won a penalty. Well into injury time and the game already won: it wasn't exactly Argentina at the World Cup. It felt fantastic whacking it in all the same.

So much of the season had been about doubt and frustration and anger. I took off towards the corner flag at the Stadium of Light and those emotions might just as well have been worries from another lifetime. I couldn't have wanted better: here we were, never mind the doubters, turning in a performance up there with the games in Munich and Sapporo. Sven was buzzing afterwards, handing all the credit to us. When we don't play well, he always seems to be there, ready to take the stick. When we win, he'll just nod and say to people:

'The players were fantastic tonight. I'm very pleased for them.'

Heading back to Manchester, early Thursday morning, I couldn't help but take all the positive energy of the night before down the motorway with me. Could I put the problems between me and Alex Ferguson to one side? Gary Neville always used to say the boss got after every player at least once a season: that was his way. You couldn't argue with the results. He'd always got more out of us, hadn't he, year after year? Maybe things could be different for me between now and the end of the season. We'd made a mess of things in Cardiff and lost 2–0 to Liverpool in the Worthington Cup Final. We were out of the FA Cup too: I wasn't ever going to forget that. But we were still right up there in the Premiership. It was going to come down to us or Arsenal again, I was sure. And in the Champions League, we'd drawn Real Madrid in the quarters. One way or another, nobody ever got bored playing for, or watching, United. I was as desperate as I'd ever been to be involved. The European Cup Final, to be played at Old Trafford, was less than two months away. More history was there to be made.

We were out on the training ground when we found out United would play Madrid. As far as I can see, it's the best game in Europe. Not just because it's between two huge clubs but because of the way the two teams play football. We knew from past experience how good the games would be to play in. We knew what the atmosphere would be like as well. Who doesn't get excited, stepping out to play at Old Trafford or the Bernabeu? All of us at United were convinced that, if we could beat Real, we could go on and win the competition. You could feel the buzz everywhere you went around Manchester ahead of those games against Madrid.

I seem to remember that it was right around the time the draw was made – two weeks before the first leg – that stories started appearing in the papers about me being transferred to Real. I knew those rumours were nothing to do with me and didn't imagine they could be anything to do with the club either. I thought the gaffer was right when he put them down to mischief-making:

'What a coincidence that the story comes up just when we're getting ready to play them.'

He was right to be annoyed. We wanted to be ready for Madrid and we had a big game in the League the weekend before: Liverpool at home. My hamstring had felt a little sore after the Turkey game. Nothing serious: I didn't think it would keep me out of the next United game. I was in the players' lounge on the Saturday morning. We had an early kick-off against Liverpool. I got the call from one of the coaches, Mike Phelan, that the boss wanted to see me, so I went through to his office.

'I don't want to risk you, David. I want to save you for the game in the week. You've got this sore hamstring. I want to hold you back for Tuesday night.'

I never made it easy for the gaffer to give me a break. I never want a rest. I never want to miss a game. I can't help it: I just always want to play. Not that there was any point – now or ever – in me trying to get him to change his mind.

'I know what you're saying but I'm not going to play you. And that's it.'

I went out, muttering:

'Okay. Fine. If that's what you want.'

I was on the bench but at least I understood why, however annoyed I was about it. I'm not quite as mad for Liverpool games as Gaz is. He's always got himself into trouble, over the years, winding their supporters up. But, if I could, I'd always want to play against them too. Especially after the stick we'd taken, losing the Worthington Cup Final at the Millennium Stadium. Especially on an afternoon when Liverpool were a goal behind and down to ten men after five minutes. Sami Hyppia got sent off after conceding a penalty and Ruud scored. It was 2–0 by the time I got on for the last half hour. We ended up winning 4–0. I was involved in the last two goals and felt great: we'd done what we needed to in the Premiership and made up points on Arsenal who only drew. I'd come off the bench and got straight into the game and the hamstring the boss had been worried about hadn't bothered me at all. Now, Monday, we'd be off to Madrid.

Real have so many world-class players. Their stars, the *galacticos*, are as well known here as they are in Spain. We're able to watch La Liga on television every week these days and we knew most of them from previous games anyway. I'd also run into one or two of the Real lads in the past. I'd gone out to Spain with some of the other United players in early 2003 to shoot a spaghetti Western-style Pepsi advert for television. All of us were dressed up like Clint Eastwood – stubble, leathers, the lot – on a set that had been built to look like Nowheresville in the Wild West. With a bit of help from a horse, I had a shootout and won against the Madrid keeper, Iker Casillas. Then Roberto Carlos, at the end, stepped out on the boardwalk with his hair cut into a Mohican – who could they have been thinking of? – and gave me a look as if to say:

'If you want to talk about free-kicks, you'd better talk to me.'

When you're up against the likes of Raul and Zidane, Luis Figo and Ronaldo, there's always the danger of going out and playing against the reputation instead of against the player. Even at the very top level, you sometimes have to pinch yourself: you're not here to get these blokes' autographs, after all. We prepared well for the game in Madrid and trained at the Bernabeu late afternoon the day before the game. Even when it's empty, it's an amazing stadium. In the course of a training session you get what you never have time for in a game: the chance to look around and take the place in. I'd played there before but, that Monday, it got to me. The scale of the place, the sense of tradition: it's got an aura, like Old Trafford does. The history of half a century of great games, great players, success and silverware just seemed to hang in the early evening air. Almost as soon as we came off the pitch, I was on the mobile to home:

'I've never had a feeling like that. The place is giving me the shivers. I can't wait for tomorrow night.'

After dinner that evening, we watched a video that Carlos Queiroz had put together. I think the idea was to make us think less about what a good team Real were and more about why we had a great chance of beating them: it showed highlights of the best things each United player had done in games during the season so far. It was the right kind of inspiration and made us fancy our chances for Tuesday night even more.

I've talked to Mum about the game at the Bernabeu since. She was up in one corner, on the first tier, with all the United fans. She says she had the strangest feeling when we ran out before kick-off, which she never mentioned to anyone else: a cold tingle ran up her spine. She was convinced then that I would end up playing at this stadium for Real Madrid. For all the paper talk, I'd no intention of ever making the move at that time and Mum knew that. What's more, she would never have wanted me to leave England: it had been bad enough me moving to Manchester, hadn't it? She couldn't help her intuition, though: she just made sure she kept it to herself. While Mum was having her moment, I was down there and grinning from ear to ear during the warm-up. You come out of the tunnel into the glare of floodlights and the din of a 75,000 crowd who demand the absolute best. If you're a player and that setting doesn't turn you on, you might as well forget it: the alternative is to get intimidated by it, in which case you'll have lost the game before you kick off.

Mum was right to sense that something significant was about to happen for her boy that early April evening. I could pick out any number of incidents that took me down the path to what happened that summer. I've already written about some of them. My big moment at the Bernabeu wasn't anything spectacular but I think it played its part in taking me back there as a Real player. About five minutes into the game, we got a free-kick just inside the Madrid half. I took it and, just as I struck the ball forward, I felt my hamstring tighten. It didn't tear. If that had happened, I wouldn't have had any choice about what to do; I'd have come off and been laid up for the next three weeks. I'd have missed the second leg at Old Trafford, no question. In hindsight, I guess I should have given the bench a wave and made my excuses. But that's not me. It's not most players. We'd just kicked off in what felt like one of the biggest games of our lives. I was desperate to play; desperate to impress in this stadium and against these players. It was uncomfortable but I convinced myself I'd run it off. And so I carried on.

Over the next forty minutes, Real played football like I'd never seen it played in my life. It wasn't that we were bad: we made chances all the way through the first half and if we'd taken one early on, it might have made for a different game. I doubt it, though. When they had the ball, they were making runs off us all over the place. It might have looked like we were standing back, watching them play. I think the truth was that they were getting so many players involved every time they came forward that we found ourselves defending one man against two or three all over the pitch. It meant there were holes for us to play in when we had the ball but the Real players were too busy running past us to worry about what was going on behind them. That's why they're so good to watch when they have that kind of night.

As if the team play wasn't good enough, Luis Figo scored an impossible goal early on to give Real the lead. He was about 25 yards out, on the left wing, maybe fifteen yards short of the byeline. I remember looking over and thinking:

'That's a good position for a cross.'

But a cross wasn't what Figo had in mind. He took a little pass from Zidane, checked back and then hit it right-footed, all power and swerve, over Fabien Barthez and in under the bar at the far post. You're happy if you've got one or two players who'll do something like that for you: Real have got half a dozen. I know the gaffer rates Raul as the best centre-forward in the world: Ruud van Nistelrooy would probably get sixty goals in a season playing alongside him. At the Bernabeu, Raul scored either side of half-time. We looked shot to pieces.

But United don't lie down for anybody. That's the gaffer; that's Keano and that's anybody who wants to play for the club. I talked to people afterwards who were watching on television. They said that, at 3–0, it looked like it was going to be 7 or 8 the way Madrid were playing. But we kept getting our tackles in when we could; kept trying to pass the ball when we had it and, eventually, we got our goal. Ruud deserved it: when we'd been under the cosh, he'd been playing their back four on his own. At 3–1, with an away goal, we had half a chance. Right at the end, I missed one that would have made it 3–2. That really would have given us something to chase at Old Trafford. When the game ended, I was looking down at the pitch, catching my breath and putting a hand to the back of my leg, which was starting to tighten up. Out of the corner of my eye, I saw Roberto Carlos coming towards me. He was smiling. I straightened up and looked at him. Now, he was laughing. I didn't have a clue what about. There was something a little crazy about the moment. I didn't know what to say or do. I smiled back as we shook hands. I could hear the camera shutters clicking and I remember thinking: *That won't make a very good picture back in Manchester.*

The gaffer didn't say much afterwards. We'd all had enough nights in Europe together to have a pretty good idea what had gone wrong. There was no need for him to lay into us. What mattered was that we got ourselves up for the second leg.

Paul Scholes and Gary Neville were pretty low. They'd both got bookings and were going to be suspended for the game in Manchester. I felt bad for Scholesy. He'd missed out on the European Cup Final at the Nou Camp in 1999 because he'd been suspended for that as well. He's intense about his football, passionate about playing for United. Real at Old Trafford was another huge game. I've been playing football with Scholesy half my life, for United and for England. Think about the two of us, as people, and you'd probably say we've not got much in common. Paul's quiet. He's so private that the other lads are always giving him grief about it. The rumour is that he turns off his mobile straight after training and doesn't turn it on again until he's five minutes from Carrington the next morning. And as for his home number, he's given it out to so few people down the years he's probably forgotten what it is himself.

Scholesy's always just kept his head down and got on with football. I don't know a Premiership player, apart from him, who hasn't got an agent. Actually there's quite a few things that set Scholesy apart. He's an amazing one-touch player, who scores all the goals from midfield any manager could ask for. Plus he's got a temper as scary as Keano's or the gaffer's once he gets going. Like I say, we played through some history together at United and I hope we'll play through some more with England over the next three or four years. I've always got on well with Paul but you're never going to have a dressing room full of people who want to go out to dinner with each other every night. For a team to be successful, what you have to have is players who respect and trust each other. And it goes almost without saying – just look where we've been together – that I respect and trust Paul as much as any player I've ever known.

After the final whistle at the Bernabeu, we went down to say thanks to the United fans. The club competes in the Champions League season after season. I wonder sometimes how people find the time or the money. They do, though. There are Reds away in Europe in their thousands wherever and whenever United play. I was hobbling a bit by then and when I got back to the dressing room, I was on the treatment table for a long while. The hamstring was really sore now the game had finished. It kept me out of the team for the Premiership match against Newcastle the following Saturday. I was frustrated about it but there was nothing I could do. It meant I missed the game that put the stamp on our season. I think winning 6–2 at St James' Park was the result that pushed us on to winning the League. Ole Gunnar Solskjaer came in and did really well in place of me.

I was back training with everybody else first thing on the Monday morning. We were away to Arsenal on the Wednesday night: as far as the Premiership goes, the biggest fixture of the season. We'd got ourselves into a position where, as long as we didn't lose at Highbury, it would be very difficult for them to catch us over the last four or five games. The way we were feeling, we thought we'd win every game until the end of the season anyway. I was pretty confident I'd play. I knew I was fit enough to. No manager likes to change a winning team and 6–2 away was definitely a winning team. Even so, the gaffer had usually brought me back into the United side after a game's rest or games missed because of injury. I felt I was part of his best eleven. I didn't find out otherwise until the day of the game. We were having our pre-match meal. The gaffer came and sat next to me:

'I'm starting with Ole. I can't change the team.'

I couldn't help but be disappointed, but I didn't feel like an argument over it. I wasn't happy but the gaffer was doing what he thought was best. My job was to sit on the substitute's bench and be ready.

Because of the speculation about my future, people pointed to the boss leaving me out against Arsenal as proof things weren't right between us. As far as I was concerned, though, I was a

United player, and me not playing at Highbury wasn't going to change that. It was a strange night: not much of a game when you compared it to the stuff that had been played in Madrid, by both sides, the previous week. But it had all the tension and drama anybody could have asked for. Ruud scored. Thierry Henry scored twice and then Giggsy equalised. Sol Campbell got sent off. Patrick Vieira had to go off injured and didn't play again for the rest of the season. At the end, the gaffer went running onto the pitch, punching the air. He's always loved beating them and I think he knew the 2–2 was just what we needed. I remember being in the tunnel afterwards, talking to Sol about the sending off. Gossip gets round players as well and the rumours hadn't really stopped since the last time we'd played Arsenal, back in February up at Old Trafford. I remember Thierry Henry coming past us. He looked at me and raised an eyebrow:

'What's the matter? Why weren't you playing?'

Then he laughed:

'You can come and play for us if you like.'

I laughed too.

The gaffer was really pleased with what had happened. I actually remember him saying, particularly, how well he thought Ole Gunnar Solskjaer had played. Even so, come the Saturday and home to Blackburn, Ole was on the bench and I started a game for the first time since we'd been beaten in Madrid. Blackburn were on a really good run and played well but we won 3–1. I was happy to be back in the team and happy with how I played. But something still didn't feel right. The obvious picture was that I was fit again and the gaffer had wanted to give me a run out before the second leg against Real the following Wednesday. Everybody assumed I'd be playing in United's biggest game of the season. Except me. Over the weekend I became more and more convinced the gaffer was going to leave me out for the second leg. I talked to some mates about it. They all said the same thing:

'No chance. You'll play. It doesn't matter what's gone on, you'll play.'

In the couple of days leading up to the Madrid game, I did my best to concentrate on our preparations like everyone else, but the thought that I was going to be dropped just nagged away at me like a sore tooth. Gary and I always used to joke that we'd learnt how to tell – from how the boss was behaving towards us – if he was getting a shock ready for us.

'He was nice to me yesterday. So he's going to leave me out of the team tomorrow.'

That instinct, after so many years working with him, told me that the gaffer's manner leading up to the Wednesday night was all wrong as far as my chances were concerned. No harsh words, no wind-ups, no little digs: it was as if I wasn't even there. Out at Carrington on the morning of the game, we were playing head tennis before the training session started. The gaffer pulled me to one side. He just said what he had to say, and what I knew he was going to say:

'David, you're not going to start tonight. You'll be on the bench.'

I flinched. Although I'd been expecting it, to hear the gaffer say that was like being hit between the shoulder blades. It suddenly felt as if the whole of the season had been about him building up to doing this to me. I was on the outside looking in. *Real Madrid: an important game, son. Too important for you to play in.* I could taste the anger and the disappointment in the back of my throat. Sometimes, your feelings are so confused and so complicated you're frozen to the spot. I looked at the gaffer, tried to look into his eyes: nothing there for me. I shook my head, turned round, and began walking back to the changing room.

'David. Come back here. Don't walk away from me.'

The boss didn't shout. He didn't lose his rag. It was as if he was asking me, not telling me, *David, please come back. I want to finish what I was saying.*

As if there was anything that needed to be said. I just kept walking. Thinking back to that scene now, I'd say that if the gaffer had still cared about me as a person or as a player, we'd have had a row there and then. He wouldn't have let me walk away from him like that. It was different for me. I had to keep going, to make sure I didn't say or do anything that I'd regret later. I was a professional footballer, with responsibilities to myself and to the club. I needed to behave like one, not make things worse.

When I found out the starting eleven, frustration made way for disbelief. Ole Gunnar Solskjaer had done really well playing in my place off and on during the season. If I stepped back from my own disappointment for a moment, I could understand the gaffer picking him ahead of me. Which of us would be the best choice to start wide right against Madrid came down to a matter of opinion and it would be a manager's job to make the judgement. I could see, after how he'd been playing, it would be hard to leave Ole out. He's been so patient in his time at United, game after game as a sub. No-one could say Ole hadn't earned his chance. What I couldn't believe – and what made me sure that the gaffer was leaving me out for personal rather than football reasons – was seeing Seba Veron's name on the teamsheet. Don't get me wrong. Seba and I get on really well and I think he's a marvellous player. I'd never resent him getting a game ahead of me. But what was the gaffer thinking? Seba had been out injured for seven weeks. He'd trained for just a couple of days: hadn't even been fit enough to be a sub against Blackburn four days before. But, for the biggest game of the season, he was in ahead of me. Nine months of what felt like hard knocks and, now, the hardest of the lot. I was shatterd by it: my football world snatched from under my feet.

I went in and got changed without saying anything to anybody. Most of the other lads were already heading off to have lunch. I went out to the car. I had to let Tony Stephens know what had happened: it felt to me as if this was something that would make staying at United more difficult. For the first time in my life, I wondered if playing football somewhere else might be better than playing it here. I needed to let someone know how upset and angry I was. Tony couldn't believe what I had to tell him. He said that trying to behave as if everything was fine was the right thing to do: sit on the bench and be ready when I got the chance he thought I would. He was sure this could all still be an opportunity for me. I can't say I was as confident as Tony sounded but talking to him calmed me down a bit at least. I rang Victoria. She needed to know what was going on too.

You look to your wife for support and what do you get? From Victoria, I always seem to get just what I need. It was another of those times when the pressure was becoming that intense I wasn't sure I knew how to handle it. Like during the build-up to the game against Argentina in Sapporo. Since that boot had hit me, my situation and my future had been talked and written about to the point where I was getting suffocated by it all. You know you're in trouble when you start to think: well, maybe they're right. Even when you're the person it's happening to and you actually know that they're wrong. Victoria understood how much playing against Madrid meant to me. She knew why I thought, after the injury at the Bernabeu, I had to play – and play well – at Old Trafford. So Victoria let me talk and then said her bit:

'So you're on the bench. Well, don't forget to take your Preparation H out there with you. You spend more time sitting on that bench than you do playing. Piles will be next.'

'Eh?'

'And make sure you keep a smile on your face so, if the camera's on you, nobody will know there's anything wrong.'

We laughed, both of us. She meant what she said. She was telling me just to get on with it, which I knew was what I had to do. But she's the only person in the world who could have said it to me the way she did. Victoria brought me back to the real world. It didn't matter, the day of a game, how I was feeling. What mattered was that the team went out and beat Real Madrid. By the time I got back to Old Trafford, I'd got a lid on the morning's emotions. I got changed, went out for the warm-up with the rest of the lads. Walked round the dressing room, shaking hands and wishing my mates good luck. And then got a sweatshirt on, made my way along the touchline from the tunnel and climbed the flight of stairs to squeeze in alongside the other subs. The seven of us sat tight and watched United start the job of trying to pull two goals back against the best team in Europe. We sat and watched. And I waited.

I tried to keep that smile on my face too. Or, at least, keep a frown off it. I knew the cameras would be cutting away to the bench. I knew how much fuss had been made in the media about me being left out. The evening was supposed to be about the game, though. Not about a player falling out with his boss. I didn't want to take the focus away from the players out there. If there was anything to be said, I could say it if I got on. Meantime, it was all about not letting on how sick I was feeling. I wonder if any other game, against any other team, could have made me forget, even for a minute, where I was and what had happened that day. Real Madrid were 3–1 up, in a position they didn't need to take any risks to protect. But they just came at us the same way they had at the Bernabeu, pinging passes about, making runs off our players, looking like they were going to score every time they attacked. I was swept away in it along with 67,000 others.

Ronaldo destroyed us. Raul was out with appendicitis, so the big man was on his own up front and Madrid played an extra midfielder, Steve McManaman. Steve and Zidane, Figo and Guti along with Roberto Carlos were free to get up and support Ronaldo whenever they wanted. As if any of them needed an invitation. As if Ronaldo needed any help. He scored a fantastic hat-trick in the hour he played. I got the call from the coach Mike Phelan to go on a couple of minutes after Ronaldo's third goal. I was desperate to be out there. Not to make my point now, just to be involved in an amazing game of football: we were 3–2 down on the night, 6–3 down on aggregate, half an hour still to play. United were definitely in the game, even if the tie seemed long gone. The atmosphere when Seba came off and I went on was a bit eerie. He'd played well and deserved the applause. What was weird was that, when I stepped up the slope to the touchline to replace him, it sounded as if the cheer I'd usually get stuck in some people's throats. I could understand the United fans not knowing where they stood with me right at that moment.

'Whose side are you on? Whose side are we on?'

It was uncomfortable. But the uncertainty in the crowd just made me all the more determined to make a mark in the time we had left. A minute or two after I got on, Ronaldo was subbed. He'd had a great game. He'd won the tie for Real. Everybody inside Old Trafford knew it. The whole crowd got to their feet and gave the bloke the kind of ovation a United player would have got. Never mind we looked like we were going out of the Champions League. The Manchester crowd knows its football and they knew they'd been privileged to be there, watching Ronaldo play. I've got my own reasons for having great memories about United's supporters: they always stood by me when I needed them. But I felt really proud of them in a different way that night, watching their reaction as Ronaldo walked off, hands above his head, clapping back.

If I enjoyed Ronaldo's moment, I enjoyed my own even more. We got a free-kick on the edge of the Real penalty area, just to the right of the 'D'. If I'd been picking and choosing, I might have wanted to be a yard or two further out. The closer you are to goal, the quicker you need to get the ball up and then down again to beat both the wall and the keeper. This one looked like a tricky 50 pence worth to me: from this range and against this opposition. I'd practised it tens of thousands of times on my own, on a training pitch – Wadham Lodge, the Cliff, La Baule, Bisham Abbey, Carrington – after everyone else had gone home. Teaching my foot, my leg, the rest of my body how it felt when I got it right. And learning how to make it right more and more often. So that now, head swirling, gasping for breath, the future bearing down on me like a dead weight, I could switch distraction off like a light. It's the ball in front of you. The glimpse of white goalpost you can see beyond the wall of defenders. It's the spot on your boot and the angle at which that meets the ball. Step up. Strike. All the practice leaves you knowing, instinctively, when one's on its way, barring a save. I was up in the air before the ball had even settled in the net behind Casillas. It's flown in. Nothing to do with the circumstances. I was celebrating what I'll remember as my best free-kick ever in a Manchester United shirt.

At 3–3 in the game, I was buzzing. I felt like I'd been plugged into something. Still two-down on aggregate but there was more in this, I was sure. But then, all of a sudden, Madrid players were coming up to me and having a chat, while the football – this incredible match – was crackling on around us. First, Guti ran alongside me and asked me if we could swap shirts at full-time. Then, Roberto Carlos was grinning at me again:

'Are you coming to play for us?'

Ten minutes left and it was Zidane's turn.

'David? Your shirt?'

I was chasing around, still trying to make things happen. Those players weren't trying to distract me or wind me up. They were just stone cold sure they could beat us all night long. Why not sort out the formalities now? Maybe they were right to be so relaxed. Maybe they did always have enough that, however close we got to them, they'd just find another gear. Five minutes from time, though, Ruud made a great run into the box. His shot came back off the keeper and I stretched out at the far post and toed it over the line as me and Ivan Helguera fell down in a heap together. I could glimpse supporters' faces in the crowd behind the goal in the Stretford End. Not just celebrating, but their eyes widening:

'What's going on here?'

Because of their away goals – Ronaldo's goals – we still needed another two to go through. But there was enough time to get them. The Real coach, Vicente del Bosque, brought on an extra defender: for the first time in three hours, Real were going to try and hold on to what they had. I got one cross in that Ole, who'd played really well, couldn't get proper contact on. It was the kind of chance that, five minutes into a game, he'd have scored from. And then we got another free-kick, on the edge of their box. It was almost dead centre and, this time, my shot went over the bar. There went my match ball.

We'd won the game, but lost the tie. I couldn't help it. Of course

I was disappointed we were out of the Champions League. As we shook hands with the Real players, there was a moment or two of: if only. And then, elation washed over me. I felt more fulfilled by the 30 minutes of football I'd just played than I had by any game all season. The crowd, when I'd come on as a sub, had seemed a little subdued. The reception I got after the final whistle was better than any I could remember at Old Trafford. I'm always the last player off anyway and after the Real game I wanted to hang around and soak it up. I certainly wasn't saying goodbye to Old Trafford that night. The opposite: I thought I'd done all I could to put doubts about my commitment and worth to the club behind me. During the ninety minutes, it had been all about the team. Now, though, I let my feelings show and went to the four corners of the ground to return the applause.

By the time I got back to the dressing room, I had Guti and Zidane's shirts under my arm. And a warm glow inside. I remember the gaffer saying to me quietly:

'You played well, David.'

I wondered if he thought then that he'd made a mistake about me and about the team that night. It wasn't the time, or the place, to ask.

'Yeah. Thanks, boss.'

I've never been changed and out of Old Trafford so quickly. Half an hour after the game, I was at the Malmaison Hotel in Manchester to meet Tony and Ellen Healy, Pepsi's Marketing Director, for dinner. They must have thought I was on something: I was that high. I hadn't felt so clear about things, happy in myself, for what seemed like months. I wanted to talk about the game. About my goals. About the crowd. About Ronaldo and the rest of them. I had a grin on my face all evening. I kept ringing Victoria who was away working in the States. I told her everything that had happened the first time I called. But I kept ringing back to say it again. I missed her being there. I went on from the Malmaison to the Lowry to have a drink with Dave Gardner. The two of us went over the whole night again. We had to. The weirdest thing, though, happened just as I was getting ready to leave. I half thought I was being set up. This Spanish guy, a Real supporter, came over. He didn't speak much English. There was quite a lot of thumbs up and 'good game' going on. He motioned to me: an autograph. On his shirt. He turned round for me to sign. He was wearing the No. 7, Raul's shirt.

When I got back to the house in Alderley Edge, everything was quiet. Mum had got the boys off to bed for me. I poked my head round the door but decided not to wake them up and tell them about Daddy's great night. I was still hyped up: sleeping would have been out of the question. I made myself a bowl of noodles and ran myself a pint glass of iced water. I put the television on: Manchester United versus Real Madrid. I hadn't taped it. When I'd left home eight hours earlier I'd had other things on my mind. This was a second broadcast of the whole game. I slurped my noodles and settled into it. The hat-trick. The free-kick and scrambling my second goal. The free-kick I'd missed: I was annoyed with myself, watching it. But then the camera cut away to the gaffer's reaction and my blood ran cold. He was craning his neck, watching. He turned away as the ball went over the bar. Then, when he looked back, his face just told me everything I needed to know. His rage, his frustration: and it was all Beckham's fault. He reacted as if I'd just lost us the game. As if, in that moment, I'd just got us knocked out of the Champions League. Maybe anybody watching the pictures would have seen the same. Maybe you needed to have lived through the past six months to really understand what was obvious to me:

'It's over. He wants me out.'

Something sank in as I sat there with the last few minutes of the game flickering past on the television. The gaffer had had enough. I'd grown up as a person and he didn't seem to like what I'd become. I already knew that, deep down. Now it looked like he'd seen enough of me as a player, as well. As a player wearing a United shirt, anyway. His face in the seconds after I'd missed that second free-kick made me feel like a door had just been slammed in mine. I'd been flying all evening. I genuinely believed what I'd done during the game would force a way back in for me. No chance. If it was anything to do with the gaffer – and, of course, it would be – I was sure I was finished.

There were three League games before the end of the season: three games to win to make sure United took back the title. I played every minute of those three games: away to Spurs, at home to Charlton and away to Everton. The rumours that had me going to the Bernabeu kept circulating. The gaffer had said he'd thought they'd disappear once the quarter-final was out of the way. They didn't. It seems with some stories, once they get a head of steam on, they have a life of their own. We won 2–0 at Tottenham and, between then and the next match, there were quotes from Spanish newspapers saying Real weren't going to buy me.

'Never. Never. Never.'

The next day, everybody was saying that 'No' obviously meant 'Yes'. Hadn't Real said they weren't going to buy Ronaldo a year ago, too? I won't pretend that the attention that I was supposed to be getting from Real, and from other clubs, didn't make me feel better about myself. Reading that they might want me was reassuring at a time when it seemed like United didn't. But the speculation was getting in the way. I wanted to get on with playing. I'm sure the gaffer wasn't happy about the distraction, either.

Maybe that's why it felt as if I was involved, but out in my own private Arctic. The mood – for me, at least – before the Charlton game was intense in all the wrong ways.

I scored the first goal in a game we had to win to keep Arsenal behind us. The shot took a deflection, going in at a strange angle. My reaction wasn't the obvious one, either. Rattling around in my head had been the question: was this my last game at Old Trafford for United? A lot of other people had been asking the same that week. As I wheeled away towards the supporters at the Warwick Road End, the instinctive joy that comes with a goal collided with the thought that I might never be doing this again. The celebration juddered. I was happy to score but choking back tears at the same time. We beat Charlton 4–1. It turned out to be enough to win us the League, although we didn't know that until the following day when Arsenal lost to Leeds.

Meanwhile, we celebrated another win with the United supporters: if this was going to be a farewell to Old Trafford, I was happy there'd been a goal for them to remember me by. I found myself standing next to Gary and feeling very sad as I looked around the place I'd got used to calling home. He leant over. He asked me what was wrong. I told him:

'They're having talks with other clubs.'

Gary just didn't want to think it was true. I know we're best mates. I also know how much he loves Manchester United. He wouldn't ever have wanted me and the club not to be together. After I'd changed and had something to drink in the lounge, I took Brooklyn out on the pitch for a kickabout. Old Trafford was empty, sunshine still creeping over the roof of the stand. If I was going to go to pieces, that would have been the moment: the place looked beautiful, still echoing with the voices of the 60,000 Reds who'd been jammed in there an hour earlier. Brooklyn just wanted to play, though. He didn't want his dad getting emotional on him with an open goal waiting. It was a bittersweet afternoon. I'm glad I finished it in the company of my boy. I was starting to feel resigned to my fate.

And then, one last time, it all changed again. Was it just the relief of winning the title? Did we all relax, including the gaffer? For a week, never mind the gossip in the papers, all seemed well in the world. During training, I felt like I was welcome, like I belonged, for the first time in months, the boss laughing and joking with me in the way he had for most of the last ten years. The game at Goodison was a trip down the East Lancs Road to pick up the silverware. We were already champions before we kicked off on the last day of the season. The atmosphere in our dressing room during those few weeks had been as strong as I could remember at any time during my United career. I loved it now, feeling back in the thick of things with the lads. For a few days, anyway, those moments in front of the television watching the gaffer seemed not to matter. I couldn't really believe I'd ever have to walk away from this group of players, this marvellous football club. I enjoyed the celebrations after beating Everton 2–1 as much as anybody. I'd even scored the first goal. Because we'd had to come from so far behind to beat Arsenal, this Premiership trophy was one we'd really had to work hard together to earn. We hadn't lost a League game since the turn of the year. On the pitch at the final whistle, as we paraded the trophy, and in the changing room afterwards, I felt part of it all again. If you'd asked me that afternoon if I was leaving United, I'd have told you:

'Not in a million years.'

I won't ever forget the feeling: winning in a United shirt. The million years, though? I was gone in less than five weeks.

Two things happened in the middle of May after the season

ended. The first was that United's chief executive, Peter Kenyon, said that if someone came in for me offering enough money, the club would have to think about selling me. I know how things get taken out of context, but to me that sounded all wrong. I didn't want to leave. Peter had asked me himself, face to face, a year before and I hadn't changed. I thought I knew what the gaffer's feelings were but I believed things between us could be straightened out as long as the club still wanted me. Now, it didn't sound to me like they did. On 14 May, I had a new United contract put in front of me. I know some supporters probably thought: well, if you want to stay at Old Trafford, why don't you just sign it? Maybe that was what the boss would have been thinking as well.

My previous deal, agreed less than a year before, had taken a year and a half to sort out. The club had been very fair and open in their dealings with me over it. Now, all of a sudden, they stuck a new one in front of me as if to say: sign this or forget it. Despite what some people said or wrote at the time, my future at United was never going to be about money. In fact, the new contract included a pay rise. I remember talking to Dad about how I felt:

'The only reason I'd ever leave United is if I could see they wanted me to. Well, at the moment it feels like they're not really bothered either way.'

There wasn't time to sit at home and wait to see how things might turn out. This wasn't a situation I was in control of anyway. I was off to South Africa for a friendly with England. That trip ended in another ride in the back of an ambulance after I broke a bone in my hand early on in the game. Then it was home and a rush to pack bags and get off on our summer holiday in the States. The travelling backwards and forwards was just about right: just how I felt. I didn't know what was going to happen: one day I'd be feeling my time was up at United, the next that things could still be worked out for me to stay. Tony kept me up to date with what was going on back in England. He's always had a good relationship with the United people – the gaffer apart – and they were honest with each other about what was going on. The club were talking to some of Spain's and Italy's biggest clubs. So was my agent.

As far as I was concerned, signing a new United deal was still possible. Most days, despite everything, it was still what I wanted to do. That made what happened next even more of a bolt from the blue. While in the States, we were staying out at a resort in the desert, relaxing away from it all. I'd just woken up one morning. There was a message on my mobile from Dave Gardner.

'Have you heard what's on the news? Are you all right about it?'

All the time we were away, I knew there'd been stories claiming I was rushing around trying to look busy, making a name for myself in America. I assumed Dave was talking about that stuff. I texted him back:

'Yeah, fine. Don't worry about it.'

Minutes later, Tony was on the phone to put me straight. The story had come as a complete surprise to him as well. We knew – everyone knew – that Barcelona were one of the clubs who were interested in signing me and that one of the candidates in the presidential election at the Nou Camp had promised to bring me to Spain if he won. It was a huge jump, though, to the press release issued by Manchester United that Tony read out to me over the phone:

'Manchester United confirms that club officials have met Joan Laporta, the leading candidate for the Presidency of Barcelona. These meetings have resulted in an offer being made for the transfer of David Beckham to Barcelona. This offer is subject to a number of conditions and critically to both Mr Laporta being elected President on Sunday 15 June and Barcelona subsequently reaching agreement with David Beckham on his personal contract. Manchester United confirms that in the event that all of the conditions are fulfilled then the offer would be acceptable.'

Was I in earthquake country? I couldn't believe what I was hearing. No word from the gaffer, no word from anybody at the club, after a dozen years at United. Just the plain, bare announcement dated 10 June: we're selling him. Mr Laporta, with all due respect, wasn't even President yet but a deal had been done. It was like they couldn't wait to get shot of me. Maybe they thought I was worth more before the Presidential election than I would have been after it. I just sat down on the floor where I was. I was angry all right. I didn't like the news, and how I'd found out about it, some time after the rest of the world, was humiliating. Tony and I talked about what to say and what to do. Later that day, SFX released a statement for me:

'David is very disappointed and surprised to learn of this statement and feels that he has been used as a political pawn in the Barcelona Presidential elections. David's advisors have no plans to meet Mr Laporta or his representatives.'

I know now that Manchester United regretted it coming out the way it had. They'd been under pressure, not just from the media but also from the club's stockbrokers: if something was happening they had to let the City know about it. But that wasn't the point, as far as I was concerned. I'd just heard the truth, hadn't I? I wasn't just up for sale. I'd been carted as far as the checkout. Something shifted inside me. I'd been uncertain about my relationship with the Manchester United manager all season long. Now, for the first time, it was my relationship with the club that was slipping away. And that broke my heart. I had to start thinking seriously now about starting a career away from Old Trafford, after a lifetime of knowing that playing for United was all I'd ever wanted to do.

Barcelona are a great club: history, tradition, players, everything. I was honoured they wanted me. Just as I felt honoured when I heard about the two big Italian clubs who were interested in me as well. Deep down, though, as soon as I realised I might be leaving Old Trafford, there was only one club I wanted to join. A club as big as United and, over the years, even more successful. A team that included some of the best players on earth. From a football point of view, there was only one choice. Even more so once the President, Florentino Perez, had let us know that he was interested in me. It had to be Real Madrid.

This wasn't just a football decision, though. There were so many things to think about. This was something so huge in our lives – for me, Victoria and the boys – that, at first, I think we had trouble even knowing where to start thinking about it. For Victoria, with a career of her own, it was the first time a decision this big had felt like it was out of her hands. For the boys it meant a complete change from everything that had grown familiar. For all of us it meant a new language, a new culture, a new life. We talked to each other, Victoria and I. We talked to our families and to friends. But you can go on talking and never get things any clearer, can't you? The one thing I was absolutely sure of was that if I didn't go with my family, I wasn't going anywhere at all. We were on our way back to England and then, within a couple of days, we'd be off again to the Far East on a promotional tour arranged months ago. I was determined we couldn't run off to the other side of the world before we'd made up our minds.

Sunday 15 June at the house in Sawbridgeworth. Sunshine and a perfect day for a family barbecue. And everyone here to help us with the hardest choice we'd ever had to make. Stay in Manchester and sign that new contract? Or leave England? And for where? As it happened, it was also the day of the Barcelona presidential election. The first thing I needed to do was talk to United. I knew the gaffer was away on holiday so I rang Peter Kenyon. I needed to know exactly where I stood. I asked him what the club felt about the situation and what the gaffer thought.

'Well, David, if I'm honest with you, it seems to us that the relationship between you and the manager might never be the same again.'

When I asked what his position was, Peter didn't seem to want to commit himself. But then I asked him what he'd do if he was in my shoes.

'Well, looking at it, I'd say you've had great years here but if something else is there, that might be a great challenge for you.'

I'd heard what I'd expected to hear. Even if it hadn't been what I'd been wanting to hear: that United wanted me to stay. I said:

'Knowing how the manager feels, hearing what you're saying to me now, maybe this is the right time for me to think about looking elsewhere.'

I hadn't actually said: I'm leaving. But Mr Kenyon thanked me for what I'd done at Manchester United anyway. I felt the club's mind was made up. Now it was up to me.

I got on with helping get stuff ready for the barbecue and then, about an hour later, I telephoned the Real President, Florentino Perez. Although Tony had met Senor Perez before, it was the first time I'd ever spoken to him. It was the eve of their last game but one of the season. I knew Senor Perez's son wasn't very well and wanted to wish him a speedy recovery. I wanted to wish Real good luck for the game, away to local rivals Atlético Madrid of all people. It would go down to the wire in La Liga. Real had to win to be in with a chance of beating Real Sociedad to the title. Atlético was a huge game: I felt a bit embarrassed that all the transfer speculation might be distracting from it. Before I made any kind of decision, though, I felt like I needed to talk to Senor Perez. He wanted to know where we were with everything.

'At the moment, I'm still a Manchester United player and until I settle things at this end, it's not right for me to talk about moving to Real.'

Real had made their contact. And United were prepared to talk. He's a remarkable man, Senor Perez. He's powerful but there's nothing loud about him. He's inspiring to listen to. He was that day, too, even through a translator:

'I understand. All I want to say to you now, David, is that if you come to Madrid you won't ever regret it. We don't want you here for the publicity or to sell shirts. I think you are one of the best players in the world and we believe you can make our team a better team.'

By the time I hung up, I knew what David Beckham the footballer needed to do next. There was still a massive family decision to be made, though, and after the barbecue we talked about it for hours. Tony was there for a while. He talked to Mum and then, later, spoke to Dad on the phone. He explained the situation to Victoria's mum and dad as well. Then he said to us:

'You know the options. Staying at United, moving to Madrid, moving to one of the other clubs that are interested in you. You don't need to think about the details, contracts, money, anything else. You and Victoria need to just decide what would be best for you as a family. Once you do, we'll try and make it happen.'

Over the course of the evening, things that had seemed scary when we'd first thought about them – leaving England, settling in a new country, learning a new language – started to seem more like an opportunity for all of us. I was so excited about the idea of Madrid, the football club, that it was easier for me to get excited about Madrid, the city, and Madrid, the way of life, as well. Victoria didn't have that to push her towards the move but she was brave enough, and we were honest enough with each other, to recognise that it was the right thing to do. And that it was something that, if we were together, could be something great for all of us. She'd lived through the last year with me and knew how unhappy I'd been as things went wrong in Manchester. She understood the situation perfectly.

'United don't seem to want you. Real have said they do. And now you want to play for them. Me and the boys want to be with you. Let's go.'

It was two in the morning when I rang Tony:

'Real Madrid.'

It was as simple as that.

Well, simple for me anyway. Victoria and I were leaving the country for Japan on the Tuesday evening. Real wanted to have things squared away so that everybody could focus on La Liga. They'd beaten Atlético 4–0 on the Sunday evening and Real Sociedad had lost 3–2 at Celta Vigo. A win at the Bernabeu the following Sunday and they'd be Spanish champions for the 29th time. Tony wanted a deal agreed – a rough outline, at least – before we flew out. It was time for all the speculation to come to an end. Easier said than done. I know how hard my lawyer, Andrew, my accountant, Charles, and Tony, Sam and the rest of the team at SFX worked over those 48 hours. The people at the Madrid end, too, who also had to come to an agreement with the United board. It helped that signing for Real is pretty simple: every player puts pen to almost the same pieces of paper; you agree the salary and to split new image rights' deals 50/50. It also helped that they trusted us enough to conduct the negotiations without employing an agent. There's detail, though, like there always is and it's not any easier to reach agreement when there are two different languages involved. Eventually, early on the evening of Tuesday 17 June, the transfer fee and my contract had been agreed in principle. Victoria and I were already at the airport, making our way from the lounge to the departure gate, when Tony called:

'Everything's fine. I bet there are cameras pointed at you right now, aren't there?'

There were, as we hurried along the corridor.

'Well, just be sure you and Victoria realise they're taking pictures – the first pictures – of you both walking into a new adventure, a new world, together. It's all agreed. Enjoy yourselves.'

I whispered to Victoria:

'It's done.'

And suddenly the frowns of two people hurrying off to catch a plane were wiped away by smiles from ear to ear. We had tickets for Tokyo but we knew, right then, we were headed off towards the rest of our lives.

The tour was exciting enough anyway: shooting a couple of television commercials; photographic sessions; meeting sponsors and public appearances in Japan, Thailand, Malaysia and Vietnam. People were buzzing about us being there and, by the time the plane touched down, buzzing about the news of me joining Real Madrid. In England we still don't realise what a passion there is for football in the Far East. It was so busy. Every minute of every day seemed to be accounted for. But the reception we walked into everywhere, and the fact that me and Victoria were enjoying it together, made it more than a flying visit for work. Victoria had seemed tense while things remained undecided and she'd been feeling unsure. Now these were settled, she let herself get excited – almost as excited as I was – about what lay ahead.

Everything had happened so quickly. I felt like I'd been running alongside myself for the best part of a month, just trying to keep up with what had been happening to us. It's the story of my life: you're on to the next adventure so quickly, there never seems time to take in the one you have just had. Suddenly, though, one day in Thailand, what had been a blur seemed to slow down long enough for me to glimpse things in focus. It's always the same questions, when you find the time for yourself to ask them:

'Who are you? Where have you been? Where are you going?'

We spent one lovely day down by the beach near Hua Hin, filming and shooting stills for a Japanese sponsor, TBC. The setting was beautiful: pale milky sunshine, little resort villas clustered up amongst the palms away from the promenade, the sand stretching away to water so clear you couldn't tell where the beach ended and the sea began. There were hammocks to laze in between takes while you watched the crew racing around, trying to convince each other, and anybody else who might be watching, that they were working really hard. Always with filming, as the time passes there's more pressure to squeeze everything in before you have to finish. People start to get a little tetchy, hurried and tired. Almost the last shot of the day, we actually went down onto the beach. Eight Thai lads, about nine or ten years old, appeared: they'd been hidden away somewhere waiting for the highlight of their day. The highlight of my day, too, as it turned out. We were shooting a sequence where I was playing football with them: no goals, just us chasing each other across the sand. There was a tatty old ball chucked across for us to use. The director told us:

'You just play. The cameraman will keep up with you best he can.'

Me and the lads were just in shorts. We'd nothing on our feet to spoil the feel of the sand and the ball and we scuttled, backwards and forwards, nicking the ball away from each other. You'd try a little trick, all one- and two-touch, and slip a pass to the person nearest you who, for that moment, looked like he might be on your side. There, in the warm breeze of late afternoon, I suddenly felt lifted away. I could have been the father of any one of those boys. Any of them could have been me, a youngster, sweat running down my temples, in the middle of a five-a-side over at Chase Lane Park. They could play a bit, these lads. I realised it was the first time I'd had a game since I got injured against South Africa in Durban. We weren't doing the bloke with the hand-held camera any favours: we'd forgotten all about him. Lost in the game. Like boys – this boy included – have always been and always will be.

Back at the hotel that night, we ate and went to bed. I guess it was the travelling catching up with me. How long had I slept? Two hours? Three? My eyes opened wide in the darkness. Victoria was fast asleep beside me. I hadn't been woken by a dream or anything else: I lay still for a moment or two, half expecting I'd just drift off again until morning. It wasn't as if I was fretting about anything. My body clock had just decided this was time for being awake. No point arguing. I started being able to pick out the room around me. I slipped out from under the mosquito net and went through to the bathroom. I found a bottle of water and padded back, the cool wood floor under my bare feet.

Victoria, I thought, probably didn't want me to shake her awake for a chat. The television was far enough away from the bed that I thought: *if the sound's turned down, it won't disturb her.* I let my hand run across a low sideboard until it settled on the remote. I carefully pulled a chair across the room, up close, a yard or so from the screen. I switched on and sat back.

That little crack of electricity and then the picture comes swimming up to the surface. As things come into focus on the bright screen in that dark room on the other side of the world, my mouth drops open. I'm watching this team in an all-white kit. The others are in red and white stripes. I squint to try and pick out individual players. That's Luis Figo. This is Real Madrid. And there's Zidane, stabbing a ten-yard pass into the penalty area, away from the defender, into the path of Ronaldo's arcing run. The big man's not even had to break his stride. He doesn't have to give his first touch a second thought. Because his first touch is a shot from fifteen yards, across the keeper, into the far corner. Roberto Carlos is there, jumping all over him. On the screen the caption comes up: Real Madrid 3 Athletic Bilbao 1. Just as well: I've got the sound turned down.

And it's only then that I realise. I'm watching Real keep the ball for minutes at a time, passing amongst themselves, twisting and turning away from challenges, playing out the twenty minutes that remain. Thousands of miles away, Real are winning La Liga, right now. Because of the time difference, I'm watching it live in the middle of my night. The final whistle goes and the celebrations begin. Streamers and confetti come cascading down from the stands. Fireworks explode over Madrid. The floodlights snap out, everything goes black – for a moment I think there's something wrong with my television – and then spotlights pick out the Real players, all in t-shirts, white as their kit, saying: 'Campeones 29'. They carry the trophy – their trophy – along the touchline, dancing around it, holding it up to the four corners of the Bernabeu.

I'm breathless watching. Gasping at the spectacle. Gasping at the sight of my future. I glance across and can just make out the outline of Victoria under the bedcovers: my wife's still sleeping tight. No need to wake her, even for this. We'll be there soon enough.

I'm sitting alone, knees tucked up under my chin now; perched on my chair in front of the television as the air cools before morning. I shiver and then I'm aware I've got this huge smile on my face: a boy from Chingford. United born and bred. And going to play for Real Madrid.

15

For Real: Hala Madrid!

'David esta como nuevo. Fisicamente esta perfecto.'

My Manchester United contract expired on the last day of June 2003 and I arrived in Spain to sign my name at the Bernabeu for the first time the following morning. The Real adventure was about to begin.

Whatever doubts and worries I had seemed to be blown away within a minute or two of climbing into the car that Real Madrid sent to collect us – me, Victoria, Brooklyn and Mum – from the airport. We soon realised we were all in for a pretty dramatic 48 hours.

Six motorcycle policemen surrounded us. Fine: a few blue lights and sirens always make Brooklyn's day. And then we nosed out onto the motorway. It was like something out of *The French Connection*. We barrelled down the outside lane, then across into the inside lane, then back outside again. Other traffic was left to fend for itself. The paparazzi kept up, in their cars and on their motorbikes, as best they could. And as dangerously as they could. The schedule had my first stop as the hospital where I was going to have my medical. If the crash that seemed about to happen every thirty seconds did happen, at least I was headed towards the right place. It wasn't until much later in the day that I realised it wasn't just the police and the press: everybody in Madrid drives like they're chasing pole position for the Spanish Grand Prix.

When I'd first spoken to Real, I'd thought it was only fair to let them know that I was a bit uncertain about the idea of moving to another country with my wife and my children. Would I feel settled enough to be single-minded about my football? I knew I'd have to be if I was going to make a success of a career with the club. I could hardly believe how understanding they were. None of my concerns came as a surprise to them. Perhaps it's to do with how things are in Spain, where family life is really important to everyone:

'Your family must be as happy here with us as you are, David.'

They took it for granted that they'd try to help us feel at home. While I was dropped off at the hospital, Victoria and Brooklyn and Mum were whisked away to look at some houses that Real's people thought we might be interested in. I wished I could have gone with them but I knew there'd be time for me to join in with the househunting later. While they headed off to the suburbs, I kept my appointment with Doctor Corral.

We galloped round that medical: cardiovascular, biomechanics, blood, urine, electro cardiogram, x-rays and scans. Then Senor Corral, Real's club doctor, got his hands on me. We were done and dusted in just over two hours. A camera from Real Madrid's TV station followed us up and down the corridors of the Zarzuela Hospital before getting the door shut in its face each time I went into a clinic for a particular test. There wasn't anybody the whole time I was there who didn't seem to be grinning from ear to ear: the specialists, the staff, other patients, the cameraman with the black eye. They checked my left metatarsal and the scaphoid bone in my right hand. Could we have a photo taken? Could we have an autograph? It all seemed very relaxed. The doctors had been given my complete medical records from 15 years at Old Trafford and I'm sure they had done their homework. Dr Corral himself gave the impression of knowing exactly what he was looking for. And was happy enough when he found it. Someone told me afterwards what he'd told the waiting press:

'David esta como nuevo. Fisicamente esta perfecto.'

He reckoned I was in half-decent nick, then. And that my pen hand was up to signing on Real's dotted line. I went to the hotel to meet up with Victoria, Brooklyn and Mum. I think the fans who'd started to gather outside the Fenix were as excited about Victoria as they were about the new footballer in town. She seemed tense, though: driving round the new city, looking for somewhere to call home. What we were about to take on had started to sink in. Me and Brooklyn had time for a little kickabout on the terrace. I wonder how much of all this he'll remember once he's grown.

The cars came back at five to take us to the Bernabeu. The stadium was just a drive up the main road through the early evening traffic: Real have built their home ground on Madrid's equivalent of Regent Street. I'd been there before, of course, as a Manchester United player but, as we swung in through the gates, I didn't recognise much. The place was a building site: cranes arching in from the road, diggers and dumpers bumping along between the piles of supplies. José Angel Sanchez, Real's Marketing Director, told me they were having to remodel the stand on the side of the ground where the players come out:

'When Santiago Bernabeu built this stadium in the forties, he put the presidential suites in the stand opposite the one with the players' facilities. It was supposed to say: our boardroom won't ever be in competition with our dressing room. Now, though, UEFA's Champions League regulations say we have to have both together.'

We went upstairs to the club offices. Nothing to do with the climb, but I felt a little breathless. And held Victoria's hand a little tighter. I think we must have come up the back way because we suddenly turned a corner and there we were: a corridor, heads poking out of doorways, half a dozen blokes in suits shifting from foot to foot. It looked like any suite of offices in any modern block anywhere in Europe. All very simple. Nothing grand, nothing flash. I liked that: Real saved their grand and their flash for out on the pitch. And there was an electricity in the air. I was excited to be there. I could tell, as people came up to shake hands and be introduced, that they didn't mind me knowing they were excited about it too.

José introduced me to the Director of Football, Jorge Valdano. Probably the man most responsible, along with the President, for bringing me to Madrid: great presence and a great smile. I don't know how old Senor Valdano must be but he's still got the build and the energy of the international player he was. I'd fancy my chances in a running race: I wouldn't be so keen on a tackle. He was one of the few people at the club who didn't speak any English, which was fine by me. The two of us were on an equal footing, weren't we? Senor Valdano showed me into the office he'd been standing outside. Carlos Quieroz stood up from behind the head coach's desk. It was a surprise to see him. I knew all about Madrid having released Vicente Del Bosque. I knew Carlos had left Old Trafford to replace him. And I knew, first hand, how good Carlos was at his job. I just hadn't known – hadn't even wondered – if he'd be at the Bernabeu already. It was an odd moment, a reassuring moment: who's following who around here? We had a hug. We'd see each other – two new boys – for preseason at the end of July.

Right now, they were ready to show me around my office. We

all trooped back downstairs, with José leading the way and doing his best official Real tour guide impression:

'And this is where the tours never go,' he said, swinging open the door to the Home dressing room. On every locker door: the image, bench to ceiling, of the Real player it belonged to. For a moment, it made me feel like an opponent again, seeing them all, almost life-sized around the walls: Raul, Figo, Ronaldo, Zidane, Roberto Carlos and their team-mates. What was it going to be like, playing alongside them instead of against them? We moved through and out into the tunnel. I could remember standing here back in April, itching to get started. It felt the same now.

'José? Is there a ball anywhere? I can't wait.'

One appeared. I gave it to Brooklyn to carry and I walked out into a narrow strip of sunlight by the touchline, Victoria beside me. It was getting late: shade stretched away from us across the low camber of the pitch. It was just our little party in the place. The Bernabeu to ourselves: the stands around us banked like mountainsides, the building work behind us finished for the day. I glanced at Mum. Three months ago, she'd been sitting over there in the far corner, watching me play for United, all her instincts telling her I'd be back to play for Madrid. I headed off towards the penalty area.

'Come on, Brooklyn. Let's score a goal.'

We kicked it between us for a minute or two. He seemed a little tired, a little distracted. This wasn't Old Trafford. I looked back at Victoria. She was watching Brooklyn. Then she let her glance stray away and around the ground. I thought I knew what she was thinking. This was a time to be brave and I'd found the right girl for that. I caught her eye: a little smile. And then José was saying:

'Shall we go back inside?'

There was a stir back up in the offices. It was time for what we'd come here to do. Senor Perez had arrived. We'd spoken on the phone but this was the first time I'd met the President of Real Madrid. In Spain, the top man at a football club is elected by the club's supporters. Senor Perez has a huge building company, one of the biggest in Europe. He's President of one of world football's great powers. But he didn't seem to need any of that hanging round his neck like a badge of office. The really big men have humility about them. You can tell how important Real's President is – and how highly he's thought of – from the respect he's given by the people around him. He'd never tell you about those things himself. He welcomed me to the Bernabeu and made a point of welcoming Victoria and Brooklyn and Mum to Madrid.

We went through to the boardroom. Everybody from the club was gathered along one side of a long, slightly curving table. They shuffled for a view while Mr and Mrs Beckham and Senor Perez sat down on the other side, the three of us bunched up towards one end. I had the President on my left, Victoria on my right. The paperwork was waiting, laid out in front of us: two neat sets on the pale oak table top. Victoria had given me a beautiful new pen to sign with before we'd left England; she'd also chosen one for the President. Maybe before we sat down would have been the time to give Senor Perez the present we'd bought him. But before we could do anything, he'd reached across the table and picked up a biro that had been left over from a previous meeting. Ink's ink, after all, I suppose. He signed. I signed. Brooklyn scooted along behind our chairs, my mum not sure whether she ought to try and catch him. No chance of this all getting too serious, then.

Now we were standing again, a deal – and the writing – done. He unwrapped the gift we'd brought from England. He gave a little grin:

'I'll keep this safe until we sign your next contract. Thank you.'

I grinned. I'd heard almost the same choice of words once before, Alex Ferguson talking to a 14-year-old United hopeful. Here I was now, 28 and England captain, excited and expectant and nervous all over again:

'You're welcome, Mr President. Thank you. Thanks to everyone. It's great to be here. I'm really happy.'

Happy wasn't the half of it. You can never know how the big moments are going to feel until you're in them. And it was only now I really understood just how big this particular moment was.

Back at the Tryp Fenix, we were expected for dinner. It's the hotel where Real's players meet up before home games. They'd set up a private dining room downstairs. I'd joined Real Madrid: this evening was to celebrate that with the people who'd made the transfer happen. My team from SFX and a handful of people at the heart of Real as an organisation: our mate, José; Jorge Valdano; Pedro Lopez Jiminez, the President's right hand man, and his son, Fabio; José Luis Del Valle, the President's legal advisor. And Victoria. Mrs Beckham looked unbelievably beautiful. Charmed the room, too. Made the blokes she was sitting with think she cared as much about football as they did. Who knows? Maybe, for just that one evening, she did.

It was a lovely couple of hours. The Madrid people had been great to deal with while we'd hurried through the deal; the guys from our side are always great to deal with: Real hadn't even bothered employing an agent. I know how tense everybody in that room had been over the past month. This was the time for them to nick the top off a cold beer. No awkwardness, no politics, no pretensions: people who'd come to like and trust each other sitting down to a meal together. Even the formalities weren't very formal. My agent, Tony, got up to say a few words. A simple toast to great partnerships: me and Victoria and, now, me and Real Madrid. I thanked everybody for all the work they'd done:

'I've not dreamed about playing for many football clubs. There's not a player anywhere, though, who hasn't dreamt of playing for Real Madrid. Thank you all for making it come true for me.'

And then, as soon as I sat down, I remembered. *Why didn't I thank the most important person of all? Why didn't I thank Victoria?*

I'd missed the moment: Jorge Valdano was standing facing us. He started speaking, in Spanish of course. At first, José was translating but, as people started getting swept up in the speech, they started throwing in their own suggestions for what particular words meant in English. It got a little confusing, but the General Manager knew where he was going and ploughed on regardless:

'Three years ago, Florentino Perez ran for the Presidency of Real Madrid. People thought of him as a cold, rational businessman and wondered if he was the right man for the job. He won the election eventually because he did the most passionate, hot-headed, impossible thing that any supporter could imagine: he bought Luis Figo from Barcelona. Senor Perez came to the Presidency with the ambition to make the football club recognised by FIFA as the most renowned of the 20th century the greatest in the 21st. To do this we needed the right players: the best players but also the players who represented football – and Real Madrid – in the best way. Raul was already here. A year after Figo, the President brought Zidane to the Bernabeu. A year after him, Ronaldo. Still, there was an element missing. We believe that you David are the player Real Madrid need to be complete. Because of your ability but also because you can bring with you a football spirit which is epitomised by the captain of England.'

You could tell from Senor Valdano's tone and his body language, even without understanding the Spanish, that he was just building up to a big finish. He took a deep breath. And José's mobile went off: one of those phones which diverts all your calls except the one you really have to answer.

'El Presidente.'

There was a lot of laughing and joking between José and Senor Perez.

'David, the President wants to tell you he's very sorry he can't be here with us tonight but he's never done it with any of the other big signings. So he doesn't think it would be the right thing to do this time either.'

A pause.

'He says: not that you aren't his favourite, of course.'

Everybody in the room was laughing now. And shouting into José's mobile that the President should just come round for a coffee.

'He says: he's at a birthday party for one of the club's directors. You could all come round there. It's not far.'

Senor Valdano was still standing through most of this, waiting to finish. Just as he got round to sitting back down, the President got round to saying goodbye. He hoped we'd enjoy the evening. Everyone at the table turned back towards Senor Valdano, ready for his punchline. I didn't need to hear any more: I'd already taken in what he'd said so far and felt honoured enough. He stood up again. You could see him deciding where to pick up his thread. And then deciding that he didn't need to bother. He laughed. His moment had slipped away too. He risked a little English:

'David and Victoria: Welcome to Madrid.'

I really felt we were.

Like I say, though: when do they sleep? There was still time in the evening for me and Victoria to be rushed off to look at two more houses they thought we should see. And there was still time for me to have my early morning moment up on the seventh floor. Tuesday had been all about taking care of business, the private side of me joining Real Madrid. Wednesday's promise was to present a new signing to the world. Brooklyn made his mind up early: other kids, a swimming pool and a back garden thanks. He and Mum headed off to the house of the parents of someone we'd met the day before. I had two interviews to do: MUTV were in Madrid to give me the chance to say goodbye and thanks to the United supporters who stuck with me, lifted me and celebrated with me during nine years in the first team at Old Trafford; then Real's TV channel wanted to get my first impressions and, also, my reaction to Roberto Carlos' statement of delight that, at long last, there'd be two good-looking players at the Bernabeu. Those two interviews, one after the other, were a bittersweet way to spend the morning. It was all very well me finding my answers. Really, I wanted to be asking the questions. I couldn't help but wonder what fans in Madrid and Manchester thought of how things had turned out.

Real decided on the basketball arena as the venue for my intro- duction to the media long before I'd decided on squad number 23. The Pabellon Raimundo Saporta is an enormous, gloomy hangar of a place with a 5000 capacity, part of a training complex they call the Ciudad Deportiva. Our cars squealed in off the main road and swept up a curving drive to the front door. There were dozens of journalist waiting outside and over to my left I glimpsed the pitch where I'd get the chance to kick a ball, a Real player now, in front of Real supporters for the first time. We hurried inside. I know the Spanish are supposed to have a pretty laid back attitude to their timekeeping but this felt like a schedule everyone was dead set on sticking to. I followed the corridor round until I was standing behind some heavy, dark drapes at one end of the gym. It was a bit like waiting for your entrance in the school play: In my mind, I ran through what I wanted to say when I got out on stage.

Just a couple of minutes before we started, José came up to explain that they'd have somebody doing simultaneous translation when I spoke.

'David, can you make little pauses to give him time to do the Spanish?'

'Well, I'd rather not José. What if I stop and then can't get myself started again?'

Making speeches isn't what I do for a living but I needed to make one here and I needed it to come out sounding right.

'Couldn't your man just try and keep up with me?'

There wasn't time to argue. In the gloom, I shook hands with Senor Perez and was introduced to Alfredo Di Stefano. I'd asked about him at dinner the previous evening.

'Is di Stefano the greatest-ever Real Madrid player?'

'No. He's simply the greatest-ever player.'

I've seen clips in ghostly black and white of di Stefano in action for the Real team that won the European Cup season after season half a century ago. Senor Perez was the Real President: the man standing in front of me was even more important when it came to the spirit of the club. In his seventies now, Senor di Stefano is still strong and commands your respect. You can sense he's proud of where he's been and of what he achieved at Real. He seemed to be proud to be here now as well, though: part of the present as much as he's part of the past. Alfredo di Stefano represents for Real Madrid what Bobby Charlton always has for United.

A hand reached forward and drew back the curtain. I hadn't even realised there were speakers near us but now music – an operatic aria – was all me or anyone else could hear, the singers' voices echoing around the arena. Some entrance. We took a couple of steps up, then walked onto the stage. The floor of the arena in front of us was crowded with photographers, flash guns firing off as we emerged. I could just glimpse people sat in the seats along the two sides of the hall, too. At first, I was doing my best to keep a smile on my face, frozen as it was. I took a deep breath and glanced down to my left where Victoria was sitting with the senior Real Madrid staff in a little cordoned off area. She was looking back up at me, as if to say:

'Go on then. This is it, you know. We're all watching you.'

I really was smiling now. Behind me was a cinema screen, huge enough to make me feel about a foot tall down here on the stage. Just for an instant, it felt like Saturday morning at the Pictures, except the film had me in it. Against a burnt yellow background: my head, the club badge, the words Real Madrid. Senor Perez stepped forward. They were going to translate me into Spanish. But there was no one translating him into English for me. They'd never have kept up anyway. It was only later that I got the President's drift.

'David is a great player, a player who's been educated in the tradition of sacrificing himself to the team. He comes to the best and most competitive league in the world. We are sure he is technically good enough and a strong enough character to succeed.'

Now, Alfredo di Stefano stepped forward with a Madrid team shirt in his hands. We shook hands, photographers calling out:

'Over here, David! Aqui, aqui – por favor – Senors!'

We held the shirt out in front of us:

'Turn it round, turn it round!'

On the back: 23 with 'Beckham' over the numerals. Nobody knew, outside the club, what my squad number was going to be.

I'd thought long and hard about which number to choose from the ones that weren't already being worn by the other players. Even Real themselves hadn't found out until late the previous night, when I'd finally made up my mind.

There was a sudden burst of shutters clicking on a couple of hundred cameras. I could hear voices out in the hall:

'Veinte y tres.'

Twenty three. Then, a moment later:

'Michael Jordan. Michael Jordan.'

He's not just a hero for me, then. It was my turn now. I stepped forward to the mike. I'd gone over the few words I wanted to say again and again. I didn't want to be holding a piece of paper. I didn't want to be wondering what to say next. More first impressions were at stake here. I cleared my throat.

'Gracias. Senor Perez, Senor di Stefano, ladies and gentlemen . . .'

I left a split second for the translator to do his stuff. At first his microphone didn't seem to be working properly. I waited. And while I waited my mind went blank. Suddenly I was aware of the forest of cameras out in front of me, people around the hall craning heads in my direction. I'm glad I've learnt to trust myself. I opened my mouth and the rest of it came.

'I have always loved football. Of course I love my family. . . .'

I looked down towards Victoria again: too right I love them:

'And I have a wonderful life. But football is everything to me. To play for Real is a dream come true. Thank you to everyone for being here to share my arrival. Gracias.'

I held the shirt – my new shirt – up in front of me.

'Hala Madrid!'

The other directors of the club came over for the team photos and then Senor Perez led us offstage and back through the corridors to a room at the far end of the building. There was a table laid out with tapas and little biscuits and soft drinks. There's a room a bit like it at every football club: a sloping ceiling and bench seats around the walls. They'd tidied this one up a bit, though. Then, I was taken through a door at the far end that led off into the changing rooms: not quite as imposing as the ones at the Bernabeu yesterday. Lines of lockers which you needed your own little padlock for. Benches in rows so close together you'd have struggled to sit opposite a team-mate after a game. The showers and toilets off to one side. Anybody who's ever played football has been in those changing rooms. They were in better nick, but otherwise they might as well have been the changing rooms at Wadham Lodge where me and Dad spent so many evenings practicing free kicks when I was a boy.

I had a new pair of boots that Adidas had delivered for the occasion. A full Real strip hung on the back of a door waiting for me. I was alone, voices down at the end of the row of benches, people waiting behind lockers for me, but nobody in my line of view. I took my time getting changed, folded my clothes on top of the bench next to me, and stood up. At the end of the row of lockers, just by the doorway out to the training pitch, was a full-length mirror. I stood in front of it and pulled my shoulders back, tucked my shirt into my shorts again and folded down the tops of my socks. That all-white of Real makes you look big. Makes you feel big. I remember actually muttering, even though there was no-one to hear me:

'Now this is a proper football kit, isn't it?'

I looked the bloke in the mirror up and down. Alone for the first time since we'd arrived in Spain, it felt for that minute or two like I was looking into my future. I got a rush of satisfaction. Then, anticipation; nerves stood on end:

'Shall we go, then?'

A couple of security guards and Simon and Andy, from SFX, came through the changing room and we walked across to Numero 2: a training pitch with low stands on one side and at one end, both crammed with supporters. It took a moment for my eyes to focus, stepping outside into bright sunshine again. I ran through the gap in the fence and a couple of footballs were chucked out towards me. I know I play for a living. Controlling a ball, keeping it up in the air, the odd trick: it's all second nature. Out on a patch of grass, though, in front of a couple of thousand supporters who are thinking: show us? It felt a bit lonely out there, to be honest, even though the reception I got from the *madridistas* was all I could have hoped for: families everywhere, cheering and waving. I waved back. The photographers got their shots of David Beckham in a Real kit for the very first time.

How long was I going to be out here? What else did we need to do? I kicked a ball up into the crowd behind the goal. I peered up into the stand in front of me, trying to see who'd caught it. Trying to get a clue as to how these same fans would take to me when I ran out at the Bernabeu, alongside the *galacticos*, for a game. I knew I'd be back in Madrid to start work on 24 July. The whirl of the last 24 hours suddenly rushed to a full stop. The significance of what had happened today and yesterday swept over me, filled my chest like a blast of pure oxygen. It felt fantastic.

Suddenly, out of the corner of my eye, while the security guards followed my line of sight up into the crowd, I saw a figure away to my left. Darting out from behind the metal frame of a floodlight pylon. A lad – eleven, twelve – tanned, black hair stood on end, a bare chest and wearing a pair of jean shorts and some battered trainers. And he was haring towards me. I think I saw him before anybody else did. There were shouts of surprise from the crowd.

The security people swivelled and looked towards me. Too late: the boy – named Alfonso, I found out later – was stood a couple of feet away from me. It was a shock but there wasn't anything about him to make me step back. His eyes were wide open, pleading, like he wanted something from me without knowing what. My instinct was to just hold my arms out towards him. He didn't need a second invitation: he just jumped at me, laughing. I caught him and held on, almost as tightly as he did. I waved away the security guys: this was just a boy who'd taken his chance. I managed to prize him off me long enough to motion over to Simon and Andy, who were in front of the other stand:

'A shirt. I need another shirt.'

We walked across and met them halfway. I tried to give the shirt to him but Alfonso just stood in front of me, tears in his eyes now. He raised his arms at either side. I dropped the shirt over his head. This was like some weird kind of ceremony going on here. I was just half-aware that people around the ground were cheering and whistling. He pushed his arms through and the shirt settled on him, almost down to his knees. He looked up at me. His eyes were like a mirror: happiness, fear, awe, the wonder of the impossible having happened. I put my hand to his face: *Oh, I know how you feel.*

Alfonso had just made a bit of a name for himself at Real. Soon, it'd be time for me to do exactly the same.

Futbol, La Vida

16

'You score two goals, we'll score four.'

I took a knock or two during my first year in Madrid. If I'd known what lay ahead, I might have chosen somewhere else to be sitting than on the physio's bed – in the dressing rooms at the old Ciudad Deportiva – while I waited to meet my Real Madrid team-mates for the very first time. It's the same at any training ground: the medical room often doubles as a bit of a social club. As well as players getting treatment, you'll often find a group of lads gathered there, chatting while they're waiting for something to happen. Now, in mid-July 2003, we were checking in for a long flight east. No sooner had I landed back in Madrid, it was time to head off for pre-season training on the other side of the world. New boy at the big school, I'd made sure that I wasn't going to be late. Being first one there didn't do much for my nerves, though.

With the standards set by the club and the demands made by the manager, you could never say you were in a comfort zone at Manchester United. But for fifteen years Old Trafford had been home for me, as a footballer at least. I knew how things worked, knew everybody I'd be likely to run into from day to day and understood exactly what was expected of me. Now, almost without my feet touching the ground, I'd been whisked off to a new club in a new country and didn't really have a clue what was coming next. I was bracing myself for the challenge: unfamiliar surroundings, a different language and another way of life. Football's football wherever you're playing it, of course, but I was pretty sure that training at Real and the demands of La Liga would be very different to what I'd grown used to back home. How much of what I'd learnt so far, as a player and as a person, was going to be of any use to me here?

It didn't help matters that I'd had some of the Spanish paper talk translated for me. Although I got the feeling that, in England, people genuinely wanted me to do well, some of the pundits here were saying that Florentino Perez had just signed me to help the club shift replica shirts. I'm confident in my own ability but, that summer morning at the training ground, there was a little twist in the pit of my stomach: it felt as though, whether I liked it or not, I'd arrived in Madrid with something to prove. For a start, I had the prospect of lining up alongside the *galacticos* to contend with.

'Hola, David. How are you?'

Luis Figo was the first other player to arrive. Handy it was him: his English is spot on. Better than mine sometimes. He sat down next to me, asked if everything was alright and then scribbled his number on a bit of paper for me.

'Any problems with anything, just give me a call.'

Of course, while we were chatting, I couldn't help thinking of times I'd seen Luis play; and of the times I'd played against him. His goal from out on the touchline at the Bernebeu in the Champions League the previous season already seemed like something from a lifetime ago, so much had changed in my life since. One of the world's great players, he was just sitting talking to me, an ordinary bloke trying to make a newcomer feel welcome. Strange: it wasn't that I was in awe of him or anything, but I felt nervous at first. Maybe I was talking to Figo's reputation instead of talking to him.

Luis had been the first *galactico* the President signed for Madrid and I already knew a bit about how controversial that transfer had been. At the time, nobody had been able to believe Senor Perez – or Luis – having the nerve to go through with it. Leaving Barcelona for Real was like leaving United to join Liverpool, only even more trouble: Luis had had to deal with all that and some of it had been pretty bitter. And then he'd had the ability and the strength of mind to live up to a £30-odd million price tag once he got to the Bernebeu.

We sat chatting but, just as I was beginning to let myself relax a little, in walked Zinedine Zidane. Then Raul. Then Ronaldo and Roberto Carlos, laughing and joking, of course. And as each of them said hello, my breath got a little shorter. *Blimey, there can't be many more of them, can there?* Before long, the whole squad was in the changing room. And, by then, there wasn't really room left for my doubts. After all, come what may, I was one of them now at Real.

And, just like at any club, the mickey-taking started from day one. That first morning, before we set off for the Far East, I'd spent an hour trying to work out what I'd need to take with me. Eventually I had three big bags packed and stuffed in the boot of the car, imagining I'd have every eventuality covered. But then I saw all the other players arriving at the training ground with not much more than toilet bags or little wheelie bags. First chance I got, I ducked back outside and started emptying my suitcases: I didn't want to look like I was going on holiday for a month. I got it down to one small bag, a toilet bag inside another bag and thought I'd saved myself some embarrassment.

In fact, I'd done the opposite. Obviously, I was the one player who wasn't familiar with the routine. We all got on the plane in our suits and, almost straight away, the other lads started changing into tracksuits and sandals for a very long flight: *Where'd all that stuff come from?* It turned out that they'd all travelled with at least as much gear as I'd packed and then unpacked in such a rush before we left. But they'd left their cases by the bus to be loaded on at the training ground and checked onto the plane for them. Now, here I was, left with not much more than the clothes I was standing up in. I shouldn't have been surprised that, instead of sympathy, there were plenty of cracks at my expense while I wandered up and down the aisle trying to borrow a pair of shorts and a t-shirt for the journey. These guys might be big stars but they act like any other footballers I've ever known: always ready to give somebody stick.

Thinking back, I think settling in as a player at a new club was made a lot easier for me by us all going away together to China for pre-season training and a couple of exhibition games. Being out there meant I wasn't coming into work every day and then going home on my own with the rest of my life – and our life as a family – to try and sort out. Getting organised in a place of our own and finding our way around Madrid and into a new life in Spain just had to be put on hold for a couple of weeks. To start with, I was in the company of my new team-mates, on something like neutral territory, twenty-four hours a day.

Instead of being shut away in our own hotel rooms, Real had booked us into a resort made up of little villas. There were five of us together: me, Steve McManaman, Santiago Solari, Esteban Cambiasso and the reserve keeper, Cesar. Stevie left to go back to England with Manchester City soon afterwards and Cambiasso moved on this last summer, but it says a lot about how well I got on with the other lads that they're the players I'm probably still closest to at Real even now.

As comfortable as I felt around the rest of the squad, I was still pretty nervous when the balls came out and we got down to training. Was it because of what other people might have been saying or was it me feeling a bit unsure of myself? Having been a first-choice player at United and with England didn't earn me the automatic right to the players' respect or a place in the team at Real.

I had the chance, away from training, to let people see that I wasn't what they'd perhaps imagined I was going to be. It was important that the players and staff I worked with saw past the media image of me, found out for themselves that I wasn't about parties and fashion and shopping. That I was someone who, deep down, just cared about his family, his friends and his football. Once the lads saw me for who I was – I don't know what their preconceptions might have been – we got along fine pretty much from day one.

I couldn't say I'd ever felt frustrated by playing most of my career on the right side of midfield for United and England. Even so, I'd had a taste of what playing in the middle could be like – especially in the Champions League Final back in '99 – and had been hoping for a while that I might get the chance to have a go at a regular place in there. It was in the back of my mind that the move to Real might make that ambition more likely to happen. Carlos Queiroz had mentioned the possibility in interviews after I signed, too. Those first days' training out in China, though, all I was bothered about was whether I'd get a place in the team at all. I'd been asked in interviews whether I thought moving to Madrid would make me a bigger star. Were they joking?

'No. I'm going there for the chance to play alongside the stars that are already there. You don't line up alongside people like Zidane and Ronaldo and Raul and imagine you're suddenly going to be the centre of attention, do you?'

The truth was that, as far as football went, I was the same as

I'd always been. I just wanted to play. And improve by playing – and training – alongside the best in the world. But it took me a few sessions before I started to relax and trust myself in the company of the *galacticos*. In fact, it needed Carlos Queiroz, in the end, to come up and say to me:

'Come on, you've settled in now. You don't need to take the easy option. Play your own game. Play your longer passes.'

He was right. I'd been feeling inhibited, trying to make sure that I didn't make any silly mistakes. Eric Harrison wasn't there but he might as well have been: I was definitely holding back on what he used to call the 'Hollywood' stuff. I shouldn't have worried: it wasn't as if the other players were putting extra pressure on me. The Brazilian lads – Ronaldo and Roberto Carlos – are two of the most laid-back people I've ever met. Zinedine Zidane, as a man, is quiet and polite, a normal guy. It's only once he's playing that he's transformed into the most talented, most perfectly balanced, player I've ever worked alongside. If anything, I think the rest of the squad were giving me the time I needed to feel comfortable. They weren't testing me. Just the opposite: they were trying to help me do well.

Carlos Queiroz, of course, speaks very good English. So do some of the players, like Figo and Solari. Even Roberto Carlos has a go, even though I don't understand a word of it most of the time. I can't pretend it was easy at first, everything flying round my head in Spanish. I'm still not speaking it as well as I'd like to be. I understand most of what I need to these days, especially in training and in games, but I've still got the same problem as I had at the beginning. Every time I picked up on a word and got the drift of what was being said, the person I was trying to talk to would imagine I'd cracked it and fly off into Spanish at a hundred miles an hour. I'd just be left with a smile on my face, nodding:

'Si, si. Porque non?'

It didn't seem as if language was going to be a problem, though, when it came to playing football. I found myself enjoying it as soon as I lined up in the white shirt for the first time. We had a couple of games out in the Far East. I got 70 minutes against a Chinese team called Red Dragons in a game that, for me, was all about work rate and doing what I could supporting the rest of the team. Then we played in Japan against FC Tokyo in the pouring rain. I got booked ten minutes in, trying too hard to make an impression. But, after that, it turned into a good night. I scored from a free-kick and we ended up winning 3–0.

Pre-season went as well as I could have hoped. It definitely helped that I already knew Carlos Queiroz and a bit about the way he tried to prepare a team after our time together at Old Trafford. He made it clear what he wanted from me as a player and I was happy that, right from the off, he handed me the responsibility of playing in central midfield. I had one date fixed in my mind the whole time we were out in the Far East: 27 August would be my first game for Real at the Bernebeu. The rest of the squad had welcomed me in and I was grateful for that. But what would the *madridistas* make of a new boy named Beckham?

We had a friendly against Valencia at the Mestella that didn't go well for me or the team. Then, in the first leg of the Super Cup – a Spanish version of the Community Shield – we were away to Real Mallorca and just never found a shape or a pattern. Worse for me, Carlos took me off ten minutes into the second half. The next day, I didn't need to understand the articles to get the drift of the headlines. Basically, people were saying: *Is that it? If it is, what's he doing in Spain?*

Maybe it was just as well I had so much on my plate now we were back in Madrid: looking for a house for us all, finding my way around, and getting my first taste of life in a new city. I spent a bit of time in the car those days before the season started. At least it didn't take me long to get the hang of the Madrid A to Z. In the midst of it all, I didn't have too much time to dwell on what I knew was being said about me, not that I would have let any of it get in the way of my own determination to do well anyway. I knew by now that my team-mates and the club believed in me, after all.

For the return leg against Mallorca at the Bernebeu a fortnight later, I was aware of what was already at stake. Perhaps they'd only ever seen me play on TV. Now I needed to let Real's supporters know that I could bring something to their club. That there was more to me than selling shirts. More, even, than getting crosses in and striking decent free-kicks. In my heart, as well, I wanted to make a success of it – in that game and the ones after it – because I wanted people at home in England to be proud of me: not just my friends and family but also fans who I knew would get a kick out of the England captain doing well in La Liga.

Ever since I was a boy, playing until it was too dark to see in Chase Lane Park, I've always felt most comfortable – most myself – when I was playing football. Whatever else I had on my mind, wherever I was and whoever I was with, I could just lose myself in a game. Now at Real Madrid, just like at United, I'm aware of how important it is to concentrate on what you're doing, whether it's in training or during a game. And I'm lucky, maybe, that I've always been able to do that. Dad made sure it was second nature to me. It meant that during the first few months at the Bernebeu, however uncertain things were away from the club, I could clear my mind and throw myself into my football. Maybe I needed to do that more than ever last season. What's sure is that things couldn't possibly have gone any better once I got the white shirt on in a home game for the first time.

Everything that had gone wrong in Mallorca seemed to come right at the Bernebeu. Almost from kick-off, you could tell it was going to be our night. Raul and Ronaldo both scored and then, about quarter of an hour from the end, Ronaldo got away down the left wing. I was on my way forward but I was thinking: *He'll not cross it here. He's bound to cut in and go for goal.* He swung it over, though, and I could tell it was going to miss out Guti at the near post. As I jumped, I could see the goalkeeper coming to challenge and just concentrated on keeping my eyes open. It was a fantastic cross. I was in the right place for the ball to hit me on the head and go in, without me having to direct it at all. I could hardly believe it was happening. *My first game at the Bernebeu and I've just scored my first goal for Real Madrid.*

The other players all rushed over towards me. Roberto Carlos hugged me and lifted me up off the ground. I think the rest of the team understood what the moment meant to me every bit as much as I did. The Real crowd had been great with me all night, never mind what doubts I'd had beforehand. My first touch of the game, I chested the ball off to someone in midfield – a simple touch to a team-mate – and the fans were all up on their feet clapping and cheering. It felt like they wanted things to go well for me and the goal towards the end of the game capped it off, for me and for those supporters.

I'd been so unhappy during my last few months at Old Trafford: in and out of the team, in the wars with the gaffer, unsure of what was going to happen to me next. Now, in those few seconds as I celebrated on the pitch with a new set of team-mates who'd already done everything they could to make me feel at home in the Real dressing room, I knew for sure that, by moving to Madrid, I'd done the right thing. *This setting, these players and this team: it's all just what I need.*

I thought about that goal after the game: *Ronaldo crossing for me to score? That wasn't in the brochure, was it?* Surely I'd come to the Bernebeu to make chances for *him*. The league season started the following Saturday with us at home to Real Betis. And, two minutes into the game, Ronaldo did it again. This time, he got to the bye line and cut it back. I just had to get there to make sure of a tap in. That was a couple of goals I owed him and the season hadn't even really started. We went on to win 2–1 and I had a hand in the winner, too. I passed long for Zidane. He crossed. Ronaldo sidefooted the goal.

I couldn't have dreamt of a better few days, a better start to a career at Real Madrid. I was on a high, the team was on a high. It felt as if, almost overnight, my game had been lifted a level by being with the players around me. I don't know about the lads, who had all been very positive from the beginning, but the Real crowd and the Spanish media seemed to decide overnight I wasn't such a bad idea for Senor Perez and the club to have had after all.

If I had to describe myself as a player, I'd put my work rate pretty high on the list of things I will always try to bring to a team. But it was that part of my game that seemed to take people in Madrid by surprise. I've always understood that chasing back and getting tackles in – fighting for the team – are important parts of the game and that supporters want to see players doing it. I'd been brought up with that attitude at United. It wasn't going to be any different at Real. It made a big difference to me, though, to know it helped get the crowd on my side here in Spain.

It wasn't just Spanish fans either. I got a real thrill from seeing English people in the stadium for home games as well. The Bernebeu is a dream destination for any football supporter anyway, but I ran into some of those day-trippers and lots of them said they'd come out specially to see me play in the white shirt. It felt almost as if playing in Spain was an extension of me being England captain. I'm very patriotic so anyone who knows me would realise how those fans being in Madrid made me feel. And there was even better to come. At the end of November I was at Buckingham Palace to receive an OBE from the Queen. To be recognised in that way for doing the thing I love best, made the day one of the best of my life. All my family around me, too: I couldn't have been more proud.

Back in Spain, we were flying: the first month of the new season, Real went unbeaten until we lost to Valencia at the Mestella. It was the best start the club had made in ten years. But maybe there were signs even then, thinking back, which were a glimpse of what was going to happen to us later in the season: losing out to Valencia in La Liga was where it all ended, obviously. I also picked up my first injury, the first of many, in a draw at home to Villareal. The club sold Claude Makelele – a very good defensive midfield player – to Chelsea and we never really replaced him. And, even when we were playing well, we were shipping goals, like we did when we beat Marseille 4–2 in our first home game in the Champions League. That was a scoreline that came back to haunt us in the quarter-finals, wasn't it?

Naturally, I wasn't thinking then about what might go wrong later on. I was happier playing than I'd been for a more than a year and some of what the team was doing going forward during games was amazing. I remember one weekend we beat Valladolid 7–2 at the Bernebeu, playing football that made me half wish I could have been up in the stands watching as well as out on the pitch doing my bit. For one of the goals, I sent a 50 yard diagonal ball across to Zizou and he volleyed it in past their keeper. I remember running across to celebrate with him in the Valladolid penalty area and laughing out loud all the way over: *That's unbelievable. This is all unbelievable!* Then, on 1 November, we beat Bilbao 3–0 and went top of the league.

For me personally, those first four or five months of the season were as enjoyable and as satisfying as any I can remember in my career. The crowd was behind me. It seemed I was part of the team already. I felt I belonged. I even stuck away a couple of decent free-kicks against Malaga in La Liga and Marseille in the Champions League. It was all rushing by, almost too quick and too exciting to take in. We were scoring goals, winning games and I heard people starting to talk about Real doing what United had done in '99: winning the Treble. I've learnt never to look that far ahead – we hadn't even reached Christmas – but, in early December, a trip to the Nou Camp did bring back memories of that Champions League Final against Bayern.

The emotions around football don't come much sweeter than the night we beat Barcelona away for the first time in twenty years. I've always loved playing in games that are special for supporters and special for the team. For Spain's two biggest clubs, that means *El Derbi*. I remember there being a lot of talk before the match about the treatment I might get from Barça's crowd after their President had done the deal with United to take me to the Nou Camp before I joined Real. I did get a couple of eggs chucked at me when we arrived at the ground but I didn't really get too much stick during the game. I think the home crowd was still saving all that for Luis Figo. It didn't stop him having a blinder, though, and we won 2–1. Roberto Carlos and Ronaldo scored and the celebrations at the end felt as if we'd just won a cup final: beating Barça means that much to the club.

In the run-up to the winter break, I really did feel as though I'd found my feet; and found a rhythm to life at my new club. The match day routine around Real's home games is simple enough and usually I'd be wishing the hours away before a Saturday or Sunday night. We'd train the day before and then have lunch together. I'd head back to the hotel – or to the house once we'd rented it – and that would be time I'd really miss being with my family. I'd be knocking around the place on my own until Victoria bought me a Sharpei – we called him Carlos, as in Roberto – to keep me company. He's a lovely dog and great with Brooklyn and Romeo but, evenings in before a game, I'd be sat trying to relax by watching a video with Carlos alongside me on the settee. I'd look at him – the wrinkles drooping down, those big brown eyes – and I'd have to smile. *You look just how I feel, mate.* If I was lucky I might nod off for a bit before dinner and, after I'd eaten, I'd be getting to bed around ten.

On the day of the game, all the players make their way to the Bernebeu for around twelve. It's quite a change from the club suits at United or even our Ridgeway Rovers blazers. At Real, everybody can turn up in jeans and t-shirts – whatever we feel comfortable in – because, as soon as we get to the ground, we change into club tracksuits. We'll usually have an hour or so out on the pitch: loosening up, stretching, perhaps going over something that the coach wants to concentrate on in that evening's game. We all pile onto a team bus together to go back into town to the hotel the club uses before home fixtures to have lunch around two. Then, after a couple of hours to ourselves in our rooms, we'll have a pre-match meal together before travelling up to the stadium for the game.

I love the glamour and the excitement that comes with home games at the Santiago Bernebeu. Even at the weekend, the games kick-off late in the evening at 9 or 9.30. There's that extra buzz in the air you get when playing under floodlights. As if the place doesn't have enough atmosphere anyway: I think it's the best stadium in the world. The crowd's very different to an English crowd. Spanish people dress up for football in the way that we might dress up to go to the theatre or to a party. The supporters turn the evening at the game into a very big night out. They want to see Real win but they almost take that for granted. And they're pretty quick at getting the white hankies out if we don't. What the *socios* – the members – really want is style: to be entertained by Raul and Figo and Roberto Carlos and the rest of us. When a game kicks off and the place is full, flags waving and a wall of noise, the Bernebeu's spectacular. You can't help but rise to the occasion: we have to live up to the sense of expectation.

I suppose there's always been a tradition of doing things in style at Real Madrid and the modern-day version of that is the *galacticos*. Since he became President, Florentino Perez has always brought at least one big-name signing to the club each summer. Raul, of course, grew up at the Bernebeu and was already here when Senor Perez came into office. Figo, Zidane and Ronaldo followed. Although everybody else – supporters and the media – talks about the *galacticos* as the stars of the show, in the dressing room it's not like that at all. Players are players and we all just get on with it. And we all seem to get on.

The one thing that being described as a *galactico* does bring with it is heavy legs now and again. The President's big signings are expected to play just about every game, unless they're injured or suspended. I can understand that: it's logical that the Board feels they and the fans should get their money's worth. Maybe, though, that policy had something to do with why the team faded so badly during the second half of last season. If we'd had a slightly bigger squad – we never really replaced players who left, like Steve McManaman and Claude Makelele, or who went out on loan, like Fernando Morientes – the knocks and the bans we picked up after Christmas might not have cost us so dear. That said, given the choice, I'd always want to play. That's how I've always been and I think if you asked the other lads they'd tell you the same.

Lining up with those players and pulling on that white shirt: it was every bit as exciting as I could have imagined it would be. Days in the office were pretty special as well. There wasn't a morning all season I wasn't looking forward to getting into training. I've always enjoyed the preparation for games but, here at Real, there was so much learning to do. It'd be a dream for any player, wouldn't it? I might have won league titles and a European Cup, I might have played for my country at World Cups. But working alongside people like Zidane, Ronaldo and the rest every day has been an education. I'd drive up to the Ciudad Deportiva each day with a smile on my face, knowing for certain that, over the next couple of hours, I'd be seeing other players do things that would amaze me.

Tricks, control, attempts at goal from impossible angles: and they do it all in games too, of course. The very first week I was at Real, I saw Ronaldo get the ball off the floor and under control *nine* different ways in training: nine different tricks I'd never seen anybody do before. It wasn't only that these players had the technique to pull the things off. I was just as impressed by them having the imagination and the daring to try them in the first place. And, of course, if your team-mates are having a go, you soon find that they're inspiring you to push your own limits as well.

The attitude of the players was very different to what I'd grown used to at United. It wasn't complicated. *If you score two goals, we'll score four.* And, until the tail end of the season, that's what tended to happen more often than not. Obviously, at United, we were confident about our ability as a team and went into every game believing we'd win it. It was something different again at Real, though. I remember the Brazilian players laughing and joking when we were beating them in the World Cup quarter-final in 2002 and it felt like that same self-belief – *We'll always be able to out-attack the opposition* – existed in the Bernebeu dressing room too.

It's a very different approach to the game and you see it every-where in Spain: in training, on street corners, on the beach. The Brazilians are the masters at it but I think that most foreign players seem to have been brought up in the same way, more or less. In training, we'd do our running, our weights and the rest but, really, sessions were all about stretching and fine-tuning your technique. As often as not, between routines or during a small-sided game, someone will come up with a trick, a way of doing something with the ball, that's completely new. For the new boy, training at Real was about a lot more than simply getting ready for the weekend's game.

And I see it everywhere in Spain. Whatever age you're talking about, it seems that young players here have an edge, in terms of technique, over their English counterparts. That's not to say that it's a case of: *They've got it right and we've got it wrong.* You see kids out here who'll get a tap on the ankle in a game and that'll be it: they're off. In England, in the same situation, I know I'd have had someone like my dad or Eric Harrison, shouting: 'Come on, get up! Don't let the other team see you're injured.' It's just a different mentality and I don't think I'd say one's better than the other necessarily. But I do know I'm very happy to be experiencing what I am here in Spain.

The technical quality in La Liga is incredibly high. I can pick out individual players at other Spanish clubs who've impressed me, of course. José Antonio Reyes, when he was still at Sevilla, abso-lutely tore us apart when they beat us 4–1. Roberto Ayala, the

Valencia centre-half, is a fantastic defender: I'm probably as tall as him but I remember going up for a high ball with him in the centre circle at the Bernebeu. As we jumped, I felt his knee in the back of my shoulder. *With that kind of spring, no wonder he wins all his headers.* And I think Joaquin, the winger at Real Betis, is a very good player. But what's really impressed me is how good the standard is right through the league. Every player at every club has good touch and is comfortable with the ball. Nobody's easy to play against because, if you lose possession, it's always such hard work getting hold of it again.

With so much else being new to me, the fact that I already knew the coach at Real probably helped me settle in. Talking to the other players, I got the impression that Carlos Queiroz had a very different approach to the man he followed into the Real job, Vicente del Bosque. I know all the lads who'd been here with him thought the world of del Bosque and I'd have liked the chance to work with him too. He won Champions Leagues and La Liga titles with Real, so he must have been doing something right, mustn't he? Now, though, I'm already enjoying working for the man who replaced Carlos in his turn, José Antonio Camacho, who's a legend at the Bernebeu because of what he achieved here as a player.

I know that most supporters are as happy about the new boss as we are. Senor Camacho is a Real man, through and through. He's got a great record at club and international level as a coach as well. His reputation at the Bernebeu and his standing with the home crowd were both built up over years. I think he played over 400 games for the club. I know I've got a long way to go before I can have that same kind of relationship with the *madridistas*. Even in my first few months, though, I was lucky enough to have my moments. One in particular I don't think I'll ever forget.

We were at home to Deportivo La Coruna, the week after we'd

won at the Nou Camp. The game finished 2–1 but it seemed to me it was a lot more comfortable than the scoreline suggested. Of course Depor have an old mate of mine in their line-up: Aldo Duscher, who broke my metatarsal at Old Trafford before the World Cup in 2002. That afternoon at the Bernebeu – and I'm still not really sure why – I had a falling out with another Argentinian, Lionel Scaloni. We went to ground together in a tackle on the halfway line and I tried to jump over him to get to the ball. Next thing I know, he's come straight through the back of me. It looked like it was going to go off for a second or two but the ref came over to calm things down and asked us to shake hands. I held mine out but Scaloni wasn't having any of it.

At the end of the game, I was more worried about Duscher than my new mate. Twenty minutes from time, he'd asked me to swap shirts afterwards and I'd said I couldn't: I'd already promised mine to a little boy I'd met beforehand. Duscher took it as a snub and wasn't happy at all but, as the players left the pitch, it was Scaloni who came over and started having a go at me. The bloke definitely wanted a fight. And maybe when I was younger I'd have given him one. Now, though, I wasn't going to back down but I wasn't going to bite either. I put my hands behind my back, just stood my ground and smiled at him: I couldn't do much else because I didn't have a clue what he was saying.

The seconds ticked by, very slowly indeed. It was a strange moment: he was screaming his head off at me but I slowly realised the huge crowd had gone all quiet while the two of us were standing nose to nose halfway to the touchline. Almost as soon as I was aware of the silence behind the racket Scaloni was making, I broke away from him. I jogged into the centre circle and clapped the Real fans. The reaction I got was unbelievable: they were cheering and chanting my name. It wasn't just about the game; it was about what had been going on between me and Scaloni too. That was done now, without anything silly having happened, and all the rest of the players seemed to have made it down the tunnel. The Santiago Bernebeu had been left to me and the *madridistas.* The hairs went up on the back of my neck. *'Beckham! Beckham!'* It felt like they were telling me: *You're one of us now.*

'Vengt y tres'. Welcomed by the great and the good at Real, including Senors Di Stefano (yellow tie) and Perez (far right).

'You're one of us now.'

Taking chances, taking knocks
and taking guard during my
first season at the Bernebeu.

Left: David Beckham, proud husband.
Above: David Beckham OBE, proud subject.
Below: And tonight Matthew, I'm going to be…
Right: Smiles all round: Romeo, Brooklyn and Dad.

What might have been: the corner from which Sol 'scored' for England against Portugal.

Still no happy ending: out on penalties in the quarter-finals of Euro 2004.

Ready for 2004/2005.

It's Christmas

17

'You make your own luck in football: we weren't making any.'

It should have been enough. I think most players are the same: if your football's going well, then everything else seems to fall into place in your life. That's certainly how it had always been for me in the past. But now, even though we were top of La Liga and progressing in the Champions League, and even though I was playing what felt to me like the best football of my career – doing things in games I'd never done before – I was homesick for the first time I could remember since I'd headed off north as a teenager to start my professional career at Old Trafford.

Obviously, spending time away from Victoria and the boys, living on my own in a hotel, I didn't find easy. I'm a home-loving lad and always have been. When I went off to Barcelona as the prize-winner at the Bobby Charlton Soccer School, even though I loved every minute of what I was doing, I was desperate to get back to Mum and Dad and Chingford after the first week of the fortnight. Now, in Madrid, even when we had days or the odd week together as a family, I still found myself missing England. You don't realise how important day-to-day surroundings – the places and people you know and even the sense of humour – are to you, I suppose, until you're away from them all. I was enjoying so much of my life in Madrid and felt so fulfilled playing football for Real but, at the same time, it began to creep up on me just how much I missed the familiarity of life back home in England.

Probably the most difficult thing was getting used to – no, not getting used to, having to put up with – the intensity of the media intrusion that's been part of everyday life for me in Spain, and for Victoria, Brooklyn and Romeo too. I know back in England our own press have got a reputation for being dogged when it comes to chasing around after stories about the private lives of people who are in the public eye. And I know, first-hand, how ruthless they can be about it. Here, it was different and, if anything, even more difficult to deal with. Nothing I'd experienced before had prepared me for what was waiting for me in Madrid.

I don't think the club had foreseen it all either: they'd been sincere, I know, when they told me how happy they thought we'd be in the city, how much they thought we'd enjoy the Spanish way of life. But the attention of the chasing pack just never let up. There were only a handful of days during my first year at Real when I wasn't followed around by three or four cars, full of cameramen and photographers, from the moment I left home for training in the morning until I shut the front door and turned out the lights at night. Even on what should have been my own territory, I was aware they were parked up in the street outside the house or the hotel, waiting at the gates of the Ciudad Deportiva or tucked just out of sight down the road from any restaurant or shop where I'd stopped.

I'm used to the attention that has come mine and Victoria's way over the past few years but, in Madrid, the constant presence of what they call *La Prensa Rosa* – the Pink Press – wore me down as each week passed. It threatened, for a while, to wear us down as a family as well. Here in Spain, it seems there's a fascination for the details, however boring they might be, of your everyday life and I found that hard to cope with when it was staring down a lens at me, and at us, day after day.

I don't really know if it was just me – or just me and my family – who had to deal with the kind of pressure we felt we were under. From talking to the club and to other players, I got the impression that most of the lads had had a taste of it but that what was happening to us was on a different scale altogether. I think the club itself was taken a bit by surprise. Real are a very professional organisation and, of course, they've got their methods for keeping things under control. It was obvious from the off, though, that whatever they did wasn't working when it came to the Beckhams. I certainly wouldn't blame the club for not being able to help me better in handling the situation. It all came as a surprise to me too.

It wasn't only the cars full of paparazzi. They were just the most obvious sign of what was going on. There are papers, magazines, shows, whole TV channels that are given over to this stuff, pretty well twenty-four hours a day. With so-called famous people as the only subject, they've got to have something to talk about and, if there isn't a story, they'll go ahead and make one up anyway. Some of it's so ridiculous you just have to laugh. I remember going out for dinner one evening with my personal manager, Terry, and his wife, Jennie. I've known both of them for fifteen years now, long enough for me not to give us being seen together a second thought. The next day, one of the TV stations was running footage of the three of us and claiming that Jen was *a mystery blonde, the secret woman in David Beckham's life.*

I think I'm a pretty patient person, but I found myself losing my rag over some of the gossip and rumours that turned up last autumn. As a family, we were trying to find our feet in Madrid and these stories just seemed to be making that more and more difficult. It felt like we were trapped: everything we did was gossiped up into a big issue. When Victoria and the boys weren't here, it'd be reported that they didn't like Madrid and that I was out partying every night. When they were in Spain, we couldn't just be having that time together as a family. Instead, it had to be that there was a crisis and Victoria was only out here while we dealt with our problems; problems that didn't exist other than in some people's imaginations. They were always looking for an angle and, of course, some of the more hurtful stories, even though they were rubbish, found their way back to England and to our families and our friends.

We'd planned to all come to Madrid and settle straight away: find a house, find schools for the children and get started with learning Spanish together. Over the course of the first few months I was at Real, though, we found ourselves having to think again. I love the city we live in now and I love the Spanish people but there were certain things Victoria and I weren't comfortable with at all. I lived in a hotel for the best part of four months while we looked for somewhere to live. We'd decided to rent first before buying. It's what most players do when they move to a new club in a new city and gives you a chance to find an area and a house that you're going to be happy with in the longer term.

Eventually, I was going stir crazy – nice as the hotel was – and we rushed into a rental which we got charged well over the odds for because it was the Beckhams moving in. And then, when people found out we'd just taken a year's lease – how do they find that out in the first place, by the way? – everyone started saying: *Oh, you see. They don't like Madrid. They're leaving after a year.* At the same time, we had looked around for a school for Brooklyn to go to and that had turned out to be even more difficult.

We met head teachers, read prospectuses, found out everything we could in advance. But when it actually came to going to look around the place we had in mind with Brooklyn before making a decision, the situation got completely crazy. We walked up to the school and there must have been fifty or more people – photographers, film crews, journalists – waiting for us. There were others – dinner ladies, cleaners, who knows? – hanging out of the windows shouting down at Brooklyn for his autograph. I couldn't believe it: *Leave him alone! He's a five-year old boy!*

Back in England, Brooklyn had settled in at school the year before and was just starting to feel confident in that environment. At his age, so much of it is learning about making friends and getting on with other people. No fuss: he and the other children and the teachers just got on with it. We sat down together that evening after we'd been to the school we'd chosen in Madrid and Victoria and I made the decision together: until things settled down, we couldn't put our children through this. We'd wanted to give life in Madrid together a go, right from the start, but now it seemed obvious that we had to find another way to make it work, for the time being anyway.

I remember talking to one of the other Real players who told me that, when his little boy had started school, there'd been camera crews outside, filming his son and his friends in the playground, for the first three months. We weren't ready for that and we didn't think Brooklyn was either. At that stage, we couldn't see what else to do: we both agreed that if we were going to have to live apart for a while and just be together at the weekends then that was what we'd do. We made a family decision. We knew what was right for us – and, most importantly, right for the boys – at the time.

I think Romeo's young enough that any strain we were feeling has mostly passed him by. He's happy as long as he's around

Mum, Dad, his big brother and Carlos. But I hope none of it will have upset Brooklyn over the past few months. Obviously, we did what we could to make light of it all for him. When he was in Madrid at weekends, if he and I wanted to go somewhere together – to play for half an hour in the park, perhaps – we'd lie down on the back seat of the car and pull a blanket up over us.

'I'll tell you what, Brooklyn: let's play a hide and seek game.'

He doesn't seem to take photographers and the fuss too seriously, anyway. The boys went skiing in France at Courchevel and, because Real gave me a couple of days off at around the same time, I decided to fly over and see them. Obviously, I knew I wouldn't ski but just being together made it worth going. When we came out of our chalet and the flashbulbs started going, Brooklyn turned round to me and asked what was going on. I told him the men wanted to take photos of him because they knew what a good skier he is. I could see him having a think to himself about that. And then he gave a little smile.

'No, Daddy. I think they want to take my picture because I'm so handsome.'

I just laughed. I wasn't going to argue with that.

We decided to have last year apart but we always knew we'd want to think it through all over again before the summer. There's nothing Victoria and I want more than a routine like any other family: for me to be able to drop Brooklyn off at school on the way to training and pick him up again in the afternoon; for us all to be able to sit down together in our own home for dinner in the evening. I love my boys and they like it when I'm around: that first season in Madrid was hard on me and hard on them, too. Victoria and I could say to ourselves: *It's difficult but it's just for this little while.* It's not like that for children, though, is it? They can't see ahead and make plans; they don't necessarily understand why decisions get made. Come the spring, with us a bit wiser about how life in Madrid was going to be for us, we started making our plans for being a family together again here in time for the new season. We can't be sure if things will be any easier this year but it's what Victoria and I both want and it's what our family needs. At least, we won't be taken by surprise by it all next time around.

I'm grateful I've got help right here when it comes to making the big decisions; particularly the most important ones, the ones that involve football. I've known Terry Byrne for a very long time now. Terry's been the England masseur, so we've spent a lot of time in each others' company. He'd probably tell you that's meant a lot of me talking and him listening. What's certain is that Terry became a really close friend, someone I knew I could trust and whose opinion I respected. At the start of 2003/04, he was still working for Watford. Gianluca Vialli had worked with Terry at Chelsea and had taken him to Vicarage Road as General Manager. After Luca left, Terry had become Watford's Director of Football, responsible for transfers, scouting and the youth system at the club.

During my first couple of months in Madrid, as I began to get an idea about what a four-year contract might mean in terms of the day to day, my instinct told me I needed to have someone out in Spain with me who I could rely on. Tony Stephens had done a lot for me during our time together but SFX, the company he works for, are a big organisation with clients all over Europe. Everything seemed different in Spain: my responsibilities and what I needed to make sure I met them. I now felt that SFX and I were moving in different directions. I talked to Victoria and she agreed it was time to bring things back to basics. Above all, I decided I needed the daily one-on-one with someone who I could trust to be as focussed as I was. When it came to thinking about who the ideal person might be, Terry was the first and only name on my list.

There have been some difficult days and weeks since I moved to Spain. If Terry hadn't agreed to leave Watford – and leave England – with Jennie to come and work with me here, things might have got out of hand once or twice. Within a couple of weeks of saying yes to a job as a personal manager, Terry had flown out, got himself somewhere to live, and found us an office that was somewhere we could meet people, take care of business and – from time to time – escape from it all, right in the heart of the city. It's funny to think people wondered about how committed I was to a new life in Madrid. That office was bricks and mortar proof of me putting down roots here. Terry understands me and he understands football. I get the right stuff from him, not what he thinks I'd like to hear. The success of my time at Real has had – and will continue to have – a lot to do with Terry and Jennie having come out to Spain to be part of the adventure.

As much as I was enjoying my football, I was really looking forward to the first Christmas break of my career. More than anything, it meant time with my family over a couple of weeks when, back in the Premiership, I'd have been grabbing an hour or two with Victoria and the boys in between games and training. My body felt like it could do with a break too. Real Madrid are like Manchester United: for the opposition, the game's always a cup final, which means the intensity in La Liga never drops. In central midfield, I was getting more whacks too. I'd picked up my fair share of little knocks: the groin strain against Villareal, a kick on the foot against Valencia, a hamstring pull against Partizan in the Champions League and a thigh injury against Leganes in the Copa Del Rey.

It was the first time in ten years that I'd have the whole of Christmas Day at home. I knew that would mean a lot to Brooklyn: I'm the worst putter-together of toys in the world and for the last few years he's been in tears by the time I've had to head off to join up with United. Part of it was Brooklyn not wanting me to go, but he also wanted to know who was going to finish building his new things and then put the batteries in them the right way round. That was Dad's job, after all. There are sacrifices at home every player – and his family – have to get used to when playing football in England. No wonder, really, I couldn't wait to try out how they did things in Spain.

A proper Christmas? I couldn't help myself. I took Victoria and the boys off to Lapland for a day to meet Santa Claus which, when we got there, didn't seem at first like the best idea I'd ever had. It was the coldest I've ever been – minus 30-something – and as soon as we got off the plane the air you breathed in made it feel like your nose was going to freeze and drop off. Brooklyn and Romeo were wrapped up in so many jumpers and coats that I don't know how much of it they got to see. Once we got used to the shock of it, though, we had a fantastic time. The boys met Father Christmas and saw his reindeer. We took a ride across the snow on a sledge, had a huge dinner together and then stayed overnight. I don't know about the rest of them but I wouldn't have missed it for the world, even if we won't be rushing back to the Arctic again for a while.

It was a wonderful couple of days. We got back from Lapland on Christmas Eve. Come bedtime at home in Hertfordshire, Brooklyn and I got a glass of milk for Santa and put it out by the fire with a mince pie and a tangerine. We'd actually met him now, of course, and wanted to look after him properly. After we'd got the boys off to sleep, Victoria and I had a glass of red wine together while we wrapped all the presents and put them out round the tree. Just before we went up, I drank the milk, took a bite out of the mince pie and then got some snow powder, sprinkled it on the soles of a pair of Timberland boots and marked out some footprints between the chimney and the tree. I sprinkled some glitter around, too, and scribbled a note from Father Christmas for Brooklyn and Romeo to find in the morning.

When I was a boy, on Christmas morning Dad would always get Lynne, Joanne and me to wait at the top of the stairs so he could go and see if Santa had been. He'd turn round shaking his head: *No, not yet.* And then laugh as we all charged down to see for ourselves. I do the same thing with Brooklyn now. I love those few moments before he realises I'm joking. Both boys were so excited: almost as excited as me maybe. Then, early afternoon, we were able to sit down together to a real family dinner: parents, grandparents, brothers and sisters, uncles and aunts, everybody. It was great. And, for once, I wasn't having to look at my watch. I was still there for the turkey sandwiches and *Only Fools And Horses* on Christmas night. I enjoyed every single minute of it.

We were back in Madrid for New Year. Usually, we have a quiet night in, just the four of us but this time we decided we'd go for it. My mum and Victoria's parents came over and we went to a do at the Ritz Hotel together. It meant us all dressing up to the nines. Victoria looked absolutely amazing. The boys had identical Spanish suits on: it's a Spanish tradition that brothers wear exactly the same outfits when they go out. At about a quarter to twelve, party bags came round with fancy dress hats: my luck, I ended up looking like Biggles for midnight. On each stroke of the clock in Spain, you're supposed to eat a grape. I was struggling with that because the ones I was left with still had the seeds in and I coughed and spluttered my way into 2004. I know Mum has had some bad memories of New Years but she said that night was the best she'd ever had. That, on its own, made it a night to remember for me.

The break was only a couple of weeks but I have to admit that plunging straight back into games came as a bit of a shock to the system. The other lads at Real were probably used to the routine. For me, it meant a completely different rhythm to the season. In England, Christmas is one of the most intense times of the year for professional players. It wasn't that I let myself go or anything: I'm not a drinker and I like my sleep, after all. But, in hindsight, I think I should have done more fitness work while we were away from the club. When we came back we weren't doing any extra running or conditioning to get us back up to speed. It was straight back into it, as if we'd only been away for a couple of days. Something like forty-eight hours after reporting back, we had our first game of the new year and I'd have to admit I wasn't quite as ready for it, physically, as I'd have liked to have been.

Not that me being slightly off the pace was the problem against Murcia. No, the problem was yet another Argentine defender. What is it about me and them? The game itself was pretty hard going, not just for me but for everybody, and we were happy to get a 1–0 win against a team that struggled against relegation all season. Early in the second half, I got a gash on my ankle after a challenge from their centre-half, José Luis Acciari. I think the crowd at the Bernebeu could see straight away that it was pretty serious and gave me a big cheer for carrying on. I responded to that but, to be honest, I didn't feel too much pain at first. Adrenalin blocks so much of that out during a game.

Ten minutes later, I went down again and I rolled down my sock. I lifted it away from my leg and the whole bottom half was soaked in blood. When the boot came off, I could actually see the stuff spurting out of the cut. It was pretty obvious it needed stitching and they got me off to the dressing room. Twenty-four hours later, the ankle was hurting like I might have expected it to when Acciari actually caught me. I showed it to the Real medical people and they put me on a course of antibiotics. The gash had somehow become infected in behind the stitches. I missed the Copa Del Rey game against Eibar that midweek and then had to sit out the defeat at Real Sociedad at the weekend too, only the fourth La Liga game I'd missed since the start of the season.

If I had to pick out a turning point in the season for me personally, I think that injury against Murcia would be it. If I'd played the next couple of games, I'd have been back to the physical level I'd been at before Christmas, I'm sure. As for the injury itself, over the next few months it began to seem like my ankle had become some kind of kick magnet. Every time I got a knock, it would be right on the spot where the stitches had been put in at the start of January at the Bernebeu.

As a team, we picked up after the break where we'd left off. Ronaldo seemed to be scoring every game and, after losing to Real Sociedad, we went on another unbeaten run. Before the home game against Valencia in the middle of February, I think we were eight points clear at the top of the table. Looking back, though, that match at the Bernebeu was where the tide started turning against us. Valencia are an excellent team. They stayed strong and deserved to win La Liga last season. We'd lost at the Mestella in the autumn but we'd beaten them 3–0 in the Copa Del Rey at home at the end of January, although the edge had been taken off that night for me by getting sent off: I wasn't happy with the decision at all but I wasn't happy with having got myself into the situation where I could get a second yellow either. The referee definitely played his part in that game. Three weeks later, so did the man in charge of the La Liga fixture.

It was a Sunday night game at the Bernebeu and Valencia got a goal and were winning 1–0 until the last minute when Raul got a nudge in the back inside the area and went down. Luis Figo put the penalty away and we were happy we'd saved a point. Real being Real, though, as far as opposing supporters and some of the papers are concerned, that was only the start of the fuss. I thought we'd done enough to earn the draw but, according to the headlines, Valencia had been robbed. They must have showed Raul getting nudged on TV a million times. At the time, I thought it was a penalty and I still do even if I'd have been unhappy if it had been given against us. But it was just one incident in one game, wasn't it? No. Within twenty-four hours, we were in the middle of a national crisis. And we were the bad guys. Everybody had an opinion and most people, except for our own supporters, thought that there was some kind of conspiracy going on to make winning the title easy for us. It was crazy and I think it backfired on Real in the end.

Maybe all the publicity got to us as players. Maybe it got to referees too. For weeks afterwards, it felt like we were having decisions go against us all the time, as if nobody wanted to be accused of favouring us like the guy in charge against Valencia was supposed to have. Players getting sent off or suspended, though, was just part of it. It felt like our luck had taken a turn for the worse and we weren't playing well enough – or with a settled enough team – to get ourselves out of the rut we were slipping into. Every team has a sticky patch during a season, even when they go on to win things. Last season, though, our sticky patch cost us dear. Without the confidence and the rhythm we'd had before Christmas, we weren't able to nick the results we needed in the important games. And now, suddenly, the teams behind us in La Liga were beginning to make up the ground.

Looking back, I think we did very well, at around the same time, to beat Bayern Munich over two legs to get through to the

Champions League quarter-finals. They had most of the ball in the first game at the Olympic Stadium but, right near the end, Roberto Carlos hit a free-kick that Oliver Kahn couldn't hold onto and we got away with a draw and the away goal. It was the kind of good fortune we weren't getting in La Liga. The return game was a fantastic experience. Champions League nights are special at the Bernebeu, playing in the kind of atmosphere that had got me so excited about the place while I was still a United player. There's an extra edge in the stands. And in the dressing room too. Real Madrid, after all, have always lived and breathed for European football: nobody can touch the history and tradition that's built up at the club over forty-odd years in the European Cup.

Recently, Bayern have had a pretty good record against us but, that Wednesday night in Madrid, it just felt all along we were going to do what we needed to. Even though Ronaldo was out injured and Roberto Carlos was suspended, I thought we controlled the game from start to finish and could have won by more than just the one goal Zizou scored in the first half to take us through. And, even though we weren't playing as well as we'd done in the first half of the season, by the middle of March we were still top of La Liga, through to the Champions League quarters and into the final of the Copa Del Rey. Spain was starting to talk seriously about a Real Madrid treble.

Back in 1999, the game I've always believed made the impossible possible for United was that amazing FA Cup semi-final replay against Arsenal at Villa Park. Now, in the spring of 2004 at Real, we'd got ourselves into a similar position in all three major competitions. And it was a Cup tie that made the difference again; except what followed this time round was the whole season starting to unravel. Even though they'd got a draw against us in La Liga a few days before, we were definitely favourites to beat Real Zaragoza at the Bernebeu in the final of the Copa Del Rey and we started really well. I scored from a free-kick early on and hit the post with another. Instead of folding, though, Zaragoza came back strong. I wonder if they've ever played quite as well as they did that night. By half-time, they were leading 2–1 and deserved to be.

A couple of minutes into the second half, Roberto Carlos whacked in a free-kick for 2–2 and then Zaragoza had a man sent off. I'm sure everybody in the ground was convinced we'd go on and win the game. But, just like United had against Arsenal that night at Villa Park, Zaragoza dug in. They worked and worked at stopping us scoring. Once we got into extra-time, I'm sure they'd have settled for penalties but we had Guti sent off to make it even numbers and, about ten minutes from time, Galetti scored what turned out to be their winner from the edge of the box. That kind of blow, after 110 minutes of football, would knock any team. We piled forward looking for another equaliser but it didn't come. Every cup competition loves an underdog and you couldn't say Zaragoza weren't worth the win. That didn't make it any easier for us to swallow. The Copa Del Rey might not have been a competition that counted in the same way as La Liga and Europe, but we were shattered by losing that night.

At any big club, through the last third of a season, games are coming thick and fast. It seems as if there's never time to rest properly. Sometimes there's not the time to prepare properly either. If you're playing well and getting results, adrenalin and confidence will carry you through. But, if not, it feels as if the team never gets the chance to put things right: you're straight on to the next fixture, whether you're feeling ready for it or not. After losing to Zaragoza, we went up to Bilbao and lost 4–2 in the league at the weekend. Seven days earlier it had been Real for the Treble. Now everybody was shaking their heads saying: *Look, the wheels have come off.*

If there was ever an occasion to bring out the best in a Real Madrid team, it would be the home leg of a Champions League tie. On 24 March we were at the Bernebeu to play Monaco in the quarter-final. All season, we'd been taking too long to get started in games. I'd scored against Betis two minutes into the start of a new season. Since then it had always seemed like we were vulnerable early on. Sure enough, Monaco scored first that night and, for a while, it felt as if the belief had gone out of us as a team. But after half-time, we played some of the best football I've ever had a part in and got ourselves into a situation where the tie should have been won. Ivan Helguera equalised and Zidane, Figo and Ronaldo took us to 4–1. I picked up a booking which meant I would miss the second leg. At the time, to be honest, I didn't give it a second thought. *Surely we're through to the semis now, aren't we?*

Then, just before full-time, Fernando Morientes headed in Monaco's second. Morientes is strong. He's clever too and very good at holding the ball up, and was always a popular player at the Bernebeu. It's good having him back at the club now. That night, though: there he was, out on loan but able to play against us, and scoring in front of Real's fans. Even so, his goal shouldn't have made any difference. We were confident, after the game, that we'd done enough. Some of the stuff we'd played in that half hour when we'd scored four was as good as any we'd played all season. Maybe, we thought, the stutter was out of our system. On the Sunday we absolutely hammered Sevilla in La Liga: Ronaldo got another couple and we won 5–1.

As it turned out, we were just being set up for our fall. You wouldn't have found many people fancying a Monaco–Chelsea semi-final, would you, after we'd beaten them and Chelsea had drawn at home to Arsenal two weeks before? I saw the second leg of our quarter-final against Monaco on TV in Courchevel. I'd wanted to travel with the team but Real told me to have a two-day break instead. Watching the pictures and getting driven mad by the French commentary, I was sure that Raul's goal in the first half had killed the tie. The game was always open, though, just like the first leg had been at the Bernebeu. We didn't try and sit on the lead. Remember Ronaldo's hat-trick at Old Trafford? Killing games off has never really been the way Real Madrid play.

We could have had two or three goals ourselves in the second half but it was Monaco who got them. They went on to prove again against Chelsea in the semi-final that they could play and that they were up for a battle. Against us, their midfield player, Ludovic Giuly had a fantastic game: no wonder Barcelona went out and bought him this summer. He scored twice and Morientes – who else? – got the other. Watching the match, I honestly never thought we were going to lose until the final whistle went: right at the end, Raul missed putting a Zidane cross away by a couple of inches. That's all it took for us to go out on away goals. There's an expectation about Real in the Champions League. It's a pressure that the club takes on itself because of its history: last season we missed out on winning the thing for a tenth time. Even so, I couldn't have imagined what a blow getting knocked out would be to us until it actually happened.

Osasuna had only won once at the Bernebeu in twenty-five years but, the weekend after we lost to Monaco, they came to Madrid and beat us 3–0. It was a terrible night. We conceded horrible goals and couldn't score ourselves, however many chances we made. Ronaldo got a knock, too, that left him struggling for the rest of the season. By the end, the white handkerchiefs were waving around the Bernebeu and the fans, who'd welcomed me so warmly back in August and had expected so much from the team, were whistling and jeering as we trooped off after the game. Who knows what goes first? Is it your legs? Is it in your mind? *We've let the season slip away* was how it was already starting to feel.

We had a couple of days at a training camp in La Manga the following week: to recharge and, maybe, just to get away from the headlines and the fans giving us stick at the Ciudad Deportiva. In the Madrid derby the following Saturday, we knew we had a point to prove. All of Spain would be watching and waiting. Even though we finished the game with ten men, we held on and beat Atletico 2–1. The win put us back on top of La Liga but it was for the last time that season. Once Valencia had beaten Real Zaragoza on the Sunday, the title was out of our hands. From being eight points clear two months before, we were now two points behind and had to go into a run of games against other teams at the top who were just hitting best form. By the time we'd lost away to Depor and at home to Barça, we were pretty much finished.

Even at the end of the season, we were making enough chances to win games. The difference was we weren't scoring. Defensively, mistakes that we'd been getting away with in the first six months of the season were now getting punished every time. They say you make your own luck in football: well, we weren't making any. We lost at home to Mallorca and then away to Murcia. In that second game, the ref gave a really soft penalty against us in the first half and I got myself sent off for complaining about it. I couldn't believe it. Obviously I shouldn't have let my frustration about a busy linesman – and what had happened to our season – get the better of me but, after all the jokes about me struggling to learn the language, I got a red card because of something I said in perfect Spanish. Maybe that was why the ref decided to make a name for himself. Lots of the other lads had been shouting the same. He must just have been surprised to hear it coming from me.

That red card left me sitting in the stands, watching our last game of the season against Real Sociedad at the Bernebeu. The title had gone. Valencia had won it, which pleased their fans and just about everybody else in Spain it seemed. There's a bit of the 'Anyone But United' mentality as regards Real Madrid. We still had plenty to play for, though, because the club was desperate for automatic qualification for the following season's Champions League. I've never enjoyed watching football: I'd always rather be playing. That was especially true the evening we lost against Sociedad. They beat us 4–1. In the first half, especially, they looked like they were going to score every time they attacked. Watching from the stands, there was nothing I could do. Not that me playing would have been enough to make the difference, I suppose, but I could at least have been giving it a go.

It was a strange atmosphere at the Bernebeu on that last day of the season and I got caught up in it. The place was half empty and I don't think it was simply anger that people were feeling. There were jeers and some of the hardcore fans turned their backs on the game – literally – early on, but I think most supporters couldn't really believe what was happening in front of them. Real supporters know their football. We looked a completely different team now to the one that had been threatening to win everything for three quarters of the season. Our shape and our self-belief had just disappeared in the space of a couple of months.

As the Sociedad goals went in, I felt like covering my eyes. I'd come to this magnificent stadium, given the chance to play with the world's best players for the world's most famous team. It had seemed for six months that this amazing adventure was going to come complete with an instant happy ending. The people in Madrid, the fans here at our home, had been so warm towards me, welcoming from the start. Despite any problems along the way, I'd not regretted any of it for a moment. I didn't even regret that awful last game of the season. I just felt as if the supporters deserved better. One trophy, never mind three, would have been the right way to say *gracias*, but we failed to give them anything after promising so much. It sank in: a reminder that nobody can write their own script when it comes to football, however hard they try. At least I think Real's supporters understand that, if nothing else, since arriving in Madrid I've tried very hard indeed.

I've been very lucky in my career to play for clubs where only the best is good enough. It's the same at Real as it was at United. A season that finishes without a trophy is a season where the standard's not been met. In Madrid, winning silverware has become second nature and it wasn't really a surprise that Carlos Queiroz lost his job and the club – and particularly the President, Senor Perez – spent the summer putting things right. We've signed good players and it'll be a treat playing club football alongside Michael Owen this season. We've got a great manager in Senor Camacho. And we're all going to make sure that what happened last time doesn't happen again. After all, looking back, I don't think we were that far off last season being a very special one at the Bernebeu.

The Beckhams' first year in Madrid wasn't easy. I love it here: the sunshine, the late lunches, the siestas, the clean streets, the friendliness of the people. Spaniards are proud of who they are and they're right to be. I love the family life I see going on around me too. One of my favourite restaurants in Madrid – and I've found a few – is the *Asador Donostiarra*. The boss – *el dueno* –

is named Pedro and his hospitality sums up everything about how people in Madrid have been towards me since I arrived.

Just before I left Spain to join up with England for Euro 2004, I found myself sitting on my own at the *Asador*. I'd got into the habit of stopping in for lunch after training. Sitting on the next table was a family all dressed up for their meal out together: mum, dad, and their son and daughter. The little girl must have been about six or seven, a year or two older than Brooklyn. I looked up from my tapas and we exchanged a little smile between us. Next thing, she'd started poking her tongue out at me and chuckling every time she could catch my eye. Dad kept telling her to stop. We were all laughing. Family counts for a lot here. And, of course, it counts for a lot with me too. This coming season, I hope I'll not be sitting on my own next to a family of *madridistas* too often. I'll be with the boys and with Victoria, and who knows? We might all be talking in Spanish over dinner as well. It's slow, but I'm getting there. *Es Verdad.*

As far as football goes, I can't say my first season at Real was a success because it's about the team and we ended up without anything to show for the football we'd played up until March. What I can say is that I couldn't have asked for my settling in at a new club to have gone any better. My team-mates and the supporters made me welcome almost from the moment I got off the plane at Barajas. It's been a privilege training and playing alongside the squad at Real and I genuinely believe I've taken a step forward as a player because of the experience. I'm sure Carlos Queiroz will be a real asset to the gaffer back at Old Trafford. In the meantime, I've him to thank for giving me a first season in central midfield.

There's a museum at the Bernebeu that's stuffed full of trophies dating back through the years and where you can sit and watch clips from Real's European Cup wins from the past. What I like best of all, though, in amongst all the grainy footage and the shiny silverware is a wall of photos. They're like passport pictures blown up to about eight or ten inches square. Every single player who's ever played for the club in European competition is on that wall. The greatest names like di Stefano and Puskas, Zidane and Ronaldo, take their place alongside the others without any fuss. I'm very proud that my photo's going to have a place on that wall in its own time: an England captain who came and played his part in the story of the world's most celebrated club. And, as far as I'm concerned, the adventure's only just begun.

I know I'm going to be proud of having been a part of the life of this city too. For all that being chased around by paparazzi has been a strain and for all that I've missed England and my life and friends and family there, I've already started to feel at home in Spain. If I didn't know it already, being here and experiencing one of the darkest days in Madrid's history, 11 March 2004, made me realise how much I'd grown into the place. I found out about what had happened at Atocha when Terry phoned me early that morning at the house we were renting last season. The train station where nearly 200 innocent people lost their lives is about ten minutes away from our office in the middle of town.

I've had a handful of experiences in my life that I wouldn't want to live through again, but the Madrid bombings were horror on a scale that somehow took you outside all your own personal concerns, even at the same time as your instincts told you to pull the people you love most closer to you. Victoria and the boys were out in Spain that morning as well. Terry and Jennie Byrne came over later and stayed the next couple of nights with us.

Thinking back, I wondered why we'd never even thought, at the time, about getting away, escaping what seemed like a threat to everyone in the city. In the days and weeks after the atrocity, I think I was feeling the same kinds of emotions – anger and sorrow and disbelief – that I saw on the faces of everyone around us in Madrid. I'd been here long enough – and made enough friends – that, like everyone else it seemed, I knew people who'd lost someone they loved in the explosions. It was an awful way to realise it and it still chills me that the bombings happened at all. But the experience made me understand that what had been someone else's city when I'd arrived had become a place I thought of as *my* city now too. I've only been here twelve months, but Madrid itself – as well as its football club – has already found its way into my bones.

Let's Face It

18

'David, we may have a slight problem.'

I can think of better ways to prepare for win-or-bust games than the week we had leading up to our final Euro 2004 qualifier against Turkey. The first inkling I had about the storm that was going to break around Rio Ferdinand's head was the night before the team got together to start our build-up to the match in Istanbul. There's an idea that I'm involved in big decisions with England. People misunderstand my relationship with Sven-Goran Eriksson, I think, and imagine that our respect for one another somehow means I'm consulted about everything from travel arrangements to team selection. In fact, when it comes down to it, although I'm England captain and enjoy the extra responsibility that comes with the job, I'm just another of Sven's players. I was surprised when he called me that evening back in early October 2003:

'David, I just wanted to let you know that we may have a slight problem for Turkey.'

Mr Eriksson didn't go into any great detail about the situation. He explained that he thought it was best I had an idea of what was going on just to make sure I didn't get ambushed by it over the coming twenty-four hours. I appreciated that. He was calm about it and he certainly wasn't asking me for advice. He just thought that, as captain, I needed to know.

'The important thing, David, is that we handle what happens in the right way. It's an important game.'

A day later, the world knew as much as I did and more. I'm not sure it's for me to try and find a way through the rights and wrongs of Rio Ferdinand missing a drugs test. Eventually, Rio's case was dealt with by the FA – pretty harshly, I think – and he's had to live with his punishment. Knowing Rio as well as I do – he's an England team-mate and a former United team-mate, too – the one thing I would say is that I don't have the slightest doubt in my mind that he made an honest mistake. Anyone who knows how Rio's sometimes able to let things go in one ear and straight out the other would agree with me that his ban was all about setting some kind of example. It was far tougher a punishment than anything that might have fitted the 'crime'.

My own feelings about a mate aside, I understand that disciplinary matters – particularly anything relating to something as serious as the drug-testing of players – is for the FA to deal with in the way they think they need to for the good of football. If Rio's case had already been sorted out back then, we'd have gone into the Turkey game sorry to be missing a really good player but without there being an argument about it from anyone. As it was, though, no decision had been made. Rio hadn't been charged with anything and nobody even knew when – or if – he might be. It seemed to his team-mates as if Rio, who's as popular with the England boys as he is at Old Trafford, was being hung out to dry.

In a way, one of the reasons why the players reacted to the situation the way we did was probably down to how strong the sense of togetherness has been in the England camp since Sven took over as manager. When the story broke about Rio, United backed him. All of us knew that, in the same circumstances, we could have relied on the clubs we play for to do the same. They'd say: *Until he's charged and found guilty, we'll stick behind our player and support him.* The England dressing room, these days, feels like a club dressing room, which made the way our bosses at the FA handled the situation all the more difficult to understand. After the fuss died down, the then chief executive Mark Palios was honest enough to admit that there was a hole where the organisation's policy should have been and I hope they'll sort that problem out. At the time, it was us – Sven and the team as well as Rio – who were left up in the air ahead of one of the most important games any of us had ever been involved in.

There was never any question of us not being in Istanbul to play Turkey. As soon as we met up together, though, all of us agreed that we needed to try and get our point across. If there was a problem for one of us, it was a problem for all of us and we felt we needed to face up to the situation as a team. We had meeting after meeting together about it. I remember, at the start of the week, standing up in front of the rest of the lads and explaining the situation as I saw it. I thought we needed to decide where we stood as a group.

'Are we with Rio or are we with the FA over this?'

Everybody wrote down how they felt on a piece of paper. Every single player said he thought we should be supporting our team-mate. I wasn't happy about the situation – if nothing else, I hated those meetings – but, as a captain, I was secretly pleased that the team seemed so single-minded about how to react. All any of us wanted was to get out to Turkey and play but there was a point of principle that it wouldn't have been right for us to duck away from.

The argument went on into the middle of the week. Our last meeting about it as a team was on the Wednesday night, just three days ahead of the game. The suggestion that we might not play was only ever put to the FA in private, in the heat of the moment: we had to make it clear to the men in charge how strongly we felt. We knew – and I'm sure they knew – we'd never have let the country down by not going to Turkey. Why someone at the FA chose to make a private matter public I don't know. It didn't help them or us in circumstances where it shouldn't have been about *them* and *us* anyway. Didn't we all want the same thing? To make sure England qualified for Euro 2004?

Of course we didn't get what we wanted. In fact, the FA didn't even allow us the compromise we suggested eventually which was that Rio would travel to Turkey as part of the squad even though he wasn't going to take any part in the game. What we did achieve, though, was to get our point across to our bosses – and to England supporters – in the belief that it would be enough to make sure the same thing never happened again. In actual fact, something similar did come up a couple of months later when Alan Smith was called into a squad and then sent home again because he was waiting to hear if he was going to be charged over an incident at Elland Road during a Premiership game. Over the long term, though, I'm convinced the FA will get things straight and I'm sure that the points we made in the week before the Turkey game will have made a difference.

While we were talking – and the headlines about it all were getting bigger and bigger – I can't pretend that our preparations didn't suffer. I remember Gary Neville saying, after one training session:

'This is terrible, isn't it? We're supposed to be playing this game in a couple of days' time.'

Once we decided to put the row behind us, it felt straight away as if the whole business had actually helped us as a team. If we weren't determined enough already, we now knew something else would be at stake on the Saturday night too. It was about beating Turkey, of course, but it was also about showing we could take our sense of togetherness out into the game and use it to make sure England got to Portugal. And that's exactly what we did.

When you think about everything else that had been going on, the level of concentration in the dressing room in Istanbul before kick-off was fantastic. Everybody had cleared their minds and I knew then that we were going to do what we needed to do. We needed a draw but we were there to win. And we should have. We deserved to. We had lots of chances in the first half and then, just after the half hour, we were awarded a penalty.

Wayne Rooney played the ball through for Steven Gerrard who powered into the area, running at the defenders. It was Tugay who tripped him and the referee, Pierluigi Collina, pointed straight to the spot. I put the ball down, absolutely certain I was going to score, just like I had in the game against Turkey at the Stadium of Light. I wasn't nervous. I trust myself. I know I strike the ball well enough that, from the penalty spot, I should score every time. That night, though, just as my right foot swung back to make contact with the ball, I felt my other foot slide away from underneath me.

I've talked about it with other players and with the coaching staff since and there's one point about my technique that may help to explain what happened twelve yards from goal at the Sukru Saracoglu Stadium that night. And would happen again at the Estadio Da Luz nine months later. When I strike the ball, I plant my standing foot down on the ground – a split second before – a lot harder than most other players. Almost always, that helps both my power and accuracy when it comes to passing and shooting. But it also means that, if there's something not right – if the turf's unstable or the pitch is uneven – I've got less margin for error. So, when my left foot gave way against Turkey, I didn't just miss. I missed by miles.

I didn't have any time at all to feel angry with myself or disappointed for the team. The next moment, their centre-half, Alpay, who played for Aston Villa at the time, was in my face, screaming at me. I didn't really know what he was on about. It might have been more understandable if it had been him who'd given the penalty away, I suppose. As it was, I just tried to ignore him and get on with the game. When the ref blew for half-time, though, Alpay was back for more. As I walked off, he ran up behind me, said something insulting about my mum and then poked me in the face with his finger. I wasn't happy and jogged down the tunnel to find out what his problem was. That was just the start of it.

While I was arguing with Alpay, some of the other players – ours and Turkey's – gathered round. We all moved up through the tunnel and into the area that led off to the dressing rooms. There was a lot of shouting and shoving going on and, at one point, one of the Turkish coaching staff spat at one of our lads, Emile Heskey, I think. That was what kicked it off. None of the England players who'd seen it was going to let it go and, for a few moments, something like a fight broke out. Supporters back home, I found out later, had been able to see it happening on TV for themselves.

Once things had broken up, Signor Collina asked me to go into his dressing room with the Turkish captain. He listened while I explained what I thought had gone on and then said:

'Look, I don't care what's happened. I'm telling you now that things need to be calmed down or we're going to have a big problem in the second half.'

I'd got the lid back on things by then anyway. I just made sure he knew I understood. I've got enormous respect for Collina as a person and as a referee. It's a shame he's had to retire. By the time the whistle blew for the restart, we'd got our attention back and focussed on the game: despite me missing the penalty, we were 45 minutes away from qualifying for Euro 2004. During the second half, we came under quite a bit more pressure. The whole defence played very well but I thought Sol Campbell and John Terry, who'd come in – amid all the fuss – to replace Rio, were absolutely outstanding.

There were one or two near misses but I didn't ever believe we were going to concede a goal and it was us who had one disallowed. I think it was Ashley Cole who sent the cross over from the left. I ran in from deep and headed it in past Rustu, their keeper. I was convinced it was a goal but I heard the whistle go to disallow it almost immediately. Everybody else was sure we'd scored too. I looked over towards the bench and Gary was hugging anybody he could lay his hands on. It was bizarre, a bit like when Sol Campbell had had his header disallowed against Argentina at France 98. Some England players were still celebrating while, in the meantime, Turkey had already taken the free-kick and were heading towards our penalty area.

We survived that and everything else Turkey could manage and we held on for the 0–0 draw that we needed. Without anything having been planned beforehand, all the players – including the lads who'd been on the bench – got together in the middle of the pitch to celebrate, bouncing up and down in a huddle. It was a wonderful moment: I've got a picture of it framed on my wall at home. The team spirit, the togetherness in the dressing room and out on the pitch, I already knew we had: if anything, the problems leading up to that game in Istanbul had brought us all even closer as a group. And, together, we were off to Euro 2004.

By the time club seasons had ended in May – mine in disappointment with Real Madrid – and England met up to prepare for the tournament, the night in Istanbul and what had preceded it already seemed like a very long time ago. That had been a week during which we'd been put under plenty of pressure, none of it really of our own making, and come through with our sense of unity not just intact but stronger than ever. In the six months since, though, I'd been through more of the same. But a lot worse. I'd had to face up to the same kind of challenge to my sense of myself in my own life and I'd had to deal with it without those team-mates around me. Football's just a game. What Victoria and I had been through since Christmas definitely wasn't.

It goes against the grain with me to even have to mention it: what goes on at the heart of our life as a family is ours and no-one else's business, after all. Why a whole sorry procession of spiteful stories about me turned up in the press and on TV during my first season in Madrid I can only guess at. Maybe they were all about the individuals involved making a bit of money at mine and my family's expense. Maybe, though, there was more to them than that: sometimes it felt as if people were trying to break up my marriage. If that was what they were hoping to achieve, I hope they realise by now that they misjudged my relationship with Victoria completely. If anything, we've come through it stronger than ever. The storm around us has just made us hold each other – and Brooklyn and Romeo – closer. Maybe you don't ever know how much you love someone – or how completely you trust them – until your bond is put to the test. I don't think it's ever right, though, for a marriage to take the hammering mine did on prime time television and on the front pages of newspapers.

Victoria and I know each other – and believe in what we have together – in a way that no-one else ever will. You could say the same about any successful marriage, I suppose. We know it'll never be possible for anybody else to force us apart. Even so, what went on wasn't the kind of experience you can just shrug off or laugh about. It hurt us as individuals and as a family. The anger and frustration boil up inside you but you know, deep down, that retaliation is exactly what the people behind the stories are after. It's a fight both you and they know you can't win. In our working lives, neither Victoria nor I have ever shirked a scrap. This was different, though, because if you respond, any words, any actions – even straight denials – are then played out as the next set of headlines. It's like trying to put out fires by splashing them with petrol.

I understand how the business works: both Victoria and I have taken on careers in the public eye and we know what that means in terms of attention sometimes being focussed on us whether we like it or not. But those few months earlier this year put a strain on us as individuals and hurt us as a couple in ways nothing could have prepared us for. The stories themselves and – even worse – some people's ignorant opinions about us as a family pitched up at every turn in our daily lives. I had plenty on my plate as a player at a new club, trying to find my feet in a new life. Maybe the pressure I was feeling anyway was enough to shake me off balance. For the first time in my career, what was going on away from the pitch started to have an effect on what was happening on it. For a spell, I was doing what I'd never done before: let problems and hurt elsewhere in my life follow me out into games.

I don't know about that phrase 'going to hell in a handcart', but when we reached Sardinia in the last week in May to begin our preparations for the Finals, almost the first thing I had to do as England captain was to go and meet the gentlemen of the press on a golf buggy. It's a ridiculous enough feeling anyway, bouncing along in one of those things. Particularly if you're not out on a golf course at the time. But that wasn't why I was feeling as uncomfortable as I was while we wound our way through the hotel complex towards the room that had been set aside for media briefings.

After everything that had been said and written about me and Victoria, I'd spent a few sleepless nights fretting about how I was going to face a confrontation I knew I couldn't back down from. I'd been suspended when England played in Sweden at the end of March, which meant I hadn't been forced to deal with the situation – and my emotions – at that point. Instead, Sardinia was the first time I knew I'd have to actually be in the same room as some of the same people who'd caused so much heartache for me and my family.

I'm bursting proud to be captain of England and I've always understood that talking to our supporters – through the press – is an important part of the job. Important enough that I couldn't do the job at all without standing up in front of the media. Hurt as I'd been, I understood I couldn't turn round and say:

'I don't like what you've been doing to my family and I'm not going to talk to you.'

What's more, I'm the first person to recognise how fair most of the football writers have been with me over the years – at least since the fall-out from France 98. Their support early on had definitely helped me settle in as skipper of the England team and I knew that I shouldn't blame them as individuals for what went on elsewhere in the papers they worked for. But I didn't see how I could just ignore all that had happened over the previous few months, especially as I knew there'd be questions about it slung at me even though we were all there, supposedly, to talk about Euro 2004. I've got to thank Mr Eriksson, Terry Byrne and Gary Neville for talking to me, listening and helping me find a way through my own thoughts.

It had all been painful, but there had been a handful – three – pieces that had hurt more than most. Of all the broadcasters and newspapers who I knew were waiting to meet me that hot, sunny afternoon in Sardinia, there were three in particular who I felt had gone out of their way to damage my family and my reputation. They'd been even more spiteful and had behaved, in my mind, more unforgivably than the rest. I wanted to exclude those organisations from the press conference as a way of making it clear to them – and to their audiences – how difficult they'd made life for me.

When the media heard about what I wanted to do, they went to the FA saying that they wouldn't agree to it. Basically, their position was that if I refused to talk to three of them then the rest of them would boycott the media conferences as well. It would look as if the England captain had stopped England supporters finding out how the team's preparations were going. It may sound strange, but – unhappy as I was – I understood their attitude and even respected the position they decided on. I guess the media thought of themselves as a team. And they were sticking together like one now.

There was nothing I could do but take a deep breath and get on with it. I said my piece, wanting to make sure that nobody reading or listening would be in any doubt as to how I'd been made to feel by what had gone on, and then did my best to put those feelings to one side. We had a major tournament to prepare for, after all. And where we were – and the company we were in – was a very good place to start. Sardinia was like Dubai had been before the World Cup in 2002, only better. We worked hard in short bursts to get up towards the right levels of fitness. In between, we could relax together with our families around us. Victoria had a great time, too. I remember her saying, one evening before bed:

'This is different, you know. It doesn't feel for a minute like we're all away here together because we have to be. It's like being away with really good friends. The rest of the players and their wives are all people you'd actually choose to be here with.'

The rest of that week in Sardinia, the training afterwards and the pre-tournament friendlies against Japan and Iceland were all designed to get us ready for the tournament in Portugal. The games at Old Trafford were especially important. Sven had experimented with playing a diamond formation in midfield – and we played it against the Japanese – because he thought we needed to have a Plan B. After the first game in Manchester, I think he made up his mind that a straight 4–4–2 was what we'd be most comfortable with going into Euro 2004. When he asked me and the other players who'd be involved in midfield what we thought, we agreed: it's the system most of are used to playing in our club football. As a build-up to the tournament, though, that game and everything else only seemed to narrow the focus even more. Everybody – players and fans – had been excited about our opening fixture since the draw had been made. Getting ready for Euro 2004? It felt more like we were just getting ready for the game against France.

Usually, in the days leading up to a big game, players can't help but talk about the opposition amongst themselves, about the team and about individuals. In the run up to that Sunday night, 13 June, though, apart from during work we did on the training ground with Sven and Steve McClaren, I don't remember anybody mentioning the French. I think it said everything about how confident we felt, never mind that we were playing the reigning champions and tournament favourites. Before we left the dressing room at the Estadio Da Luz, I could see it on the face of every England player: *Nobody expects us to, but this is a game we're going to win.*

The support for us in the stadium that night was like it was right through the tournament: thousands of England fans made it feel like a home game. Nobody in the world has got a crowd to touch ours. We were confident before the game and I think, once the game started, that spread round the ground. We started really well, closed the French down whenever they had the ball and looked more likely than they did to make chances to score. About five minutes before half-time, we did. I knocked in a free-kick from out on the right and Frank Lampard nicked in at the near post and headed it past Fabien Barthez. We'd played well enough to deserve that goal. We played well enough all night to deserve more than we got.

France came out and had more of the ball in the early part of the second half but without ever looking like they were going to get an equaliser. Then Wayne Rooney picked up the ball just inside our half and went charging off, a bit like Ryan Giggs had at Villa Park in the FA Cup semi-final replay the year United did the Treble. He got himself past three defenders and into the area: it was a goal all the way. Just as he was getting ready to shoot, though, Mikael Silvestre slid into Wayne and knocked him over from behind. It was as clear a penalty as you'll ever see and I didn't think for a moment I'd do anything but score.

Maybe I was half conscious of what had happened in Istanbul and, in fact, my standing foot did slide away from me a little that night in Lisbon too. But I made really good contact and, as I hit it, I was sure it was on its way in. Fabien Barthez got a lot of stick from the English media and opposing supporters while he was playing for United. People forget he's won a World Cup and a European Championship: he's a great keeper and very strong mentally, which means he loves the kind of one-on-one situation we found ourselves facing in Portugal. I hit the penalty pretty well but his guess which way to go was better.

Looking back, I can't avoid thinking that Fabien's save cost us getting something out of the game. At the time, though, despite us being under pressure, I never imagined – until the dying moments – that we weren't going to win. France had almost all of the possession as it got nearer and nearer to full-time but they weren't really unsettling us. *We've got nothing to be afraid of here.* Almost without being aware of it, though – it certainly hadn't been the plan – we were getting pushed back deeper and deeper towards our own goal. Ninety minutes came and went. We gave away a free-kick just outside the area. *Get this away and we're there.*

I've played alongside him at Real for a season now and there's no question: Zinedine Zidane is the most talented player I've ever worked with. Now, he was standing over the ball, maybe twenty yards out. David James was organising the wall. I was on the end and shouted:

'Do you want Ashley on the post?'

At first, he said yes and Ashley started retreating. Then David decided he didn't need him there after all. Ashley came back towards the 18 yard line just as Zizou stepped up towards the ball. Did we, for whatever reason, let our concentration drop for a split second? If we did, it cost us. I'd say, though, that that equaliser was all about the quality of the bloke who took it. Never mind anything we were doing or not doing. It was a perfect free-kick.

There must just have been seconds to go. I remember trying to catch my breath:

'Well, at least we're going to come away with a draw.'

But then, in the blink of an eye, Thierry Henry was through for the first time all night. Down he went and France had a penalty. I looked around the team and couldn't see anyone who looked like they understood what had happened. Then I walked towards the edge of our area. Looking across, I saw Zidane bend over and bow his head before he stepped back to take the spot-kick: *What's that coming out of his mouth? Where did he get water from?*

Zizou was actually being sick. Was he nervous? He didn't look it when he glanced down at the ball before putting the penalty away as calmly as he had his free-kick moments earlier. From winning the game 1–0 at full-time, time added on had been long enough for the game to be snatched away from us. The French players celebrated but surely even they knew, deep down, that we'd deserved something from the game. The one player who wasn't clapping and dancing in front of their fans was the bloke who'd won the game for them. Zidane just turned and headed straight down the tunnel. I saw him afterwards in the dressing rooms.

'Don't worry about the penalty, David. Good luck in the other games. See you soon.'

I'm not sure if he meant 'soon' in the tournament – the group draw meant an England–France final was a possibility – or 'soon' back in Madrid. We swapped shirts and shook hands and he left me to get on with it.

At the final whistle, I'd gone round trying to lift some of the other players. We'd played well and those last couple of minutes had been tough on us. And, of course, nothing had been decided by the result. We still had every chance of qualifying for the quarter-finals. Even so, on my own in the dressing room, I did dwell on what had turned out to be a moment that had maybe decided the game. When Fabien had saved my penalty, I'd been convinced it would make no difference to the result. We seemed that strong in the game to me. And, who knows? Even if we'd gone 2–0 up,

France might still have had time to turn things upside down. Maybe that night in Lisbon I'd had a little taste of how Bayern must have felt after the Champions League Final at the Nou Camp back in 1999.

After losing to us in Barcelona, Bayern came back strong and won the Champions League soon afterwards. I was pretty sure England would react in the right way now, too. We had to travel north for our next game against Switzerland, to Coimbra, and knew we'd have to play it in the heat of the afternoon instead of the evening as well. And it was hot. Not quite like Shizuoka in the World Cup quarter-final two summers before, but not far off it. We weren't looking forward to the conditions but there wasn't time to be worrying about the temperature. After the Sunday night in Lisbon, Thursday had turned into a game we knew we had to win.

The first twenty minutes were pretty uncomfortable. We were a little unsure of ourselves: still shocked by what had happened four days before, perhaps, and aware now of what a mistake might mean. The Swiss, who we'd been expecting to defend, came at us and tried to force us to play our football too quickly. They made a couple of decent chances too. We'd just started to get ourselves into the game when Stevie Gerrard won the ball in their half and pushed the ball wide to me. Michael Owen's been playing international football for a long time now and that experience shows. He saw Wayne Rooney heading for the six yard box and dropped off at the far post so I could lift the ball over the last defender to him. Michael had a chance to score himself but, instead, he just floated a cross back in and Wayne nodded the goal.

Once we'd got to 1–0, even though we hadn't played as well as we'd have wanted to, we were never going to let the Swiss back into it like we had the French. They had a player sent off, Wayne scored again just afterwards and then Stevie got onto Gary Neville's cross for 3–0. We played four games at Euro 2004 and had wonderful support from the fans at all of them. That game in Coimbra, though, was a little different. It was the one time I got the feeling our supporters weren't satisfied with what they were seeing. We'd beaten Switzerland and were back in the tournament but the impression I got from our supporters was: *Well, what do you expect? We should beat teams like that every time.*

I can see their point. If we want England to be one of Europe's top teams then we have to be sure we don't slip up against teams like Switzerland. I felt good after the game, though. Better than I had for some time. A couple of months before the end of the season in Madrid, I'd been aware that, since Christmas, I hadn't been at the physical level I'd been at before it. At Manchester United, we'd always done a lot of conditioning and fitness work right through the season. In fact, over Christmas back home, I'd got used to what amounted to another little pre-season burst in training. At Real, that didn't happen: once we were into the La Liga campaign, we were much more focussed on technical work and practising game situations.

I knew before I came to Spain that things would be different at a new club and, when you think about how successful Real have been down the years, it didn't seem it was my place to be questioning the way we prepared. If I felt I was struggling a bit, it was down to me to sort myself out. I joined a gym in Madrid and got into the habit of going there and working with weights every afternoon after I'd trained and had lunch. I worked very hard and the sweat told me I must be doing myself some good.

In fact, I found out later that all those bench presses and the rest were the last thing I needed. While I was working out in the gym, I put on nearly a stone in muscle but all of it in my upper body. I'm not built to be a boxer – I'm not exactly Wayne Rooney, am I? – and my body's just not designed to carry that kind of extra weight around. My natural shape is like a distance runner's. Now, as I put the weight on in muscle, I was losing it elsewhere and my aerobic capacity – the ability to run and keep running – suffered as a result.

Towards the end of the season in Madrid, nothing felt right. I had a lot on my mind and assumed, at the time, that was the reason why. But I've learnt now there was a physical explanation, too, for why I was struggling ten minutes into games, short of breath, heavy-legged and feeling aches and pains, it seemed, from every injury I'd ever had. Stamina is a large part of what my game's all about and I seemed short of it for the first time in my career. Doubts about myself crept in and, because of that, the rest of what I was doing suffered too.

Perhaps the heat in Coimbra slowed the game down a bit. I know I felt better physically. The pass to Michael for our first goal and some other things I did during the game pleased me too. I came off tired and hot like everybody else but feeling confident that I still had time in the tournament to get back to something like myself. More importantly for the team, we'd got ourselves back into a position where we were favourites to go through to the knockout stages.

Anyone who watched Euro 2004 knows we played our best football of the tournament against Croatia. The Estadio Da Luz was heaving with England supporters for another 'home' game in Lisbon. We just needed a draw to go through. Even though the manager never prepares us for anything but winning football matches, knowing that all you have to do is not get beaten can still make you cautious. You're tempted to take the simple option and try to make sure you avoid making any mistakes. That night, 21 June, against Croatia, we got off to the worst possible start but, in hindsight, that maybe did us a favour.

Croatia scored after five minutes when we didn't get a free-kick away but the goal made up our minds for us. We didn't have any choice then but to go after the game. We did to Croatia what France had done to us: kept the ball and pushed on, confident something would happen for us. Just before half-time, it did. I was pleased for Scholesy that he got the equaliser. There's a lot more to Paul than goals but, because he hadn't scored one for England in something like 30 games, I think the attention that was focussed on that didn't help the rest of his game. He's been an automatic choice for England for the past few years. We're going to miss him now he's decided to retire from international football and concentrate on what he still does better than anyone else in the Premiership for United.

Scholesy's goal came five minutes before half-time and we still had time to go in at the break ahead. Wayne Rooney was fantastic for us in every game at Euro 2004. He'd been big trouble for France and Switzerland and Croatia couldn't get anywhere near him. That game, as well, he and Michael seemed to be on absolutely the same wavelength. Michael was involved in the build-up to both Wayne's goals and I thought that made us look as if we could be even more dangerous from then on in the competition. We passed the ball well all game against Croatia and, even when they got a goal back to make it 3–2 we went straight up the other end to get another ourselves.

Frank Lampard had an amazing time at Chelsea in 2003/2004: he probably started the season on the fringe of the England team. By the time we left for Portugal, the manager couldn't really leave him out. He scored that fourth against Croatia; he'd got the goal against France and he went on to score against Portugal too. I looked across our midfield at Euro 2004 and saw Frank, Stevie and Scholesy: three players who are all about getting forward and getting goals. All of them exceptionally talented, too. The way I felt in myself and the way those three were playing – and scoring – meant I was happy to be the one who usually took the responsibility for sitting in while they got forward.

It worked for us against Croatia and afterwards there was a genuine feeling that we were starting to get into our stride. France beat Switzerland the same evening so we went through as runners-up in our group. That meant we would play Portugal in the quarter-final at the Estadio Da Luz – their home ground, maybe, but it felt like ours too – the following Thursday. However confident our fans were back in England, we were even surer than they were that it was a game we could win. I was certain we would. Gary Neville was the one player – he's played more European Championship games than any of us – who tried to hold people back:

'Just remember: every game is a scapegoat game from now on.'

All the lads who'd been at World Cups or European Championships with England in the past knew what he meant. There's always one man, it seems, who has to get the grief if we fail, never mind that football's a team game. Phil Neville, Dave Seaman, David Beckham: we all know what it's like to be the one who gets slaughtered in the weeks after a big defeat. We tried not to think about that possibility, though, in the couple of days we had to prepare to play Portugal. Surely it wouldn't come to that this time, would it?

Whatever anyone else says, I believe this group of England players is good enough to win a major tournament. But no team ever wins anything without a couple of lucky breaks at vital times during games along the way. Plenty's been said and written about our quarter-final in Lisbon but, in amongst all the recriminations, people should remember that when we needed the run of the ball against Portugal – or the run of the officials' decisions – we didn't get them.

It never fails to make me feel like the proudest man in the world. Leading the team out at the Estadio Da Luz was no different. The stadium's fantastic and that night was perfect. There seemed to be at least as many England supporters in the place as there were Portuguese. No question at all, either, who was making the noise. It was odd. The first goal came out of nowhere and our supporters had built up such an atmosphere before kick-off it almost felt as if going ahead so early dampened things down.

It was a perfect start for us, though, wasn't it? One of their midfield players – Costinha, I think – misjudged a header and flicked it backwards beyond his own defenders. I don't know how great strikers know, but they do: Michael had already made his run in behind and the ball fell just right for him to lift it over Ricardo, the Portuguese keeper, who was so surprised he was late getting off his line to close down. Three minutes gone and a goal up against the home nation. We couldn't have asked for better.

It maybe took us a bit by surprise, going ahead before the game had got any shape to it, but for the next twenty minutes it seemed like we had the situation just how we wanted it. The Portuguese are very good technical players and none of them better than Luis Figo. We knew that, if they had the ball, we'd have to work very hard to get it back again. But we pressed them in midfield and it looked as if we'd be more likely to score again than they would be to equalise. Michael got away again and Ricardo, their keeper, made a really good save.

England and England supporters knew all about Wayne Rooney before Euro 2004. Now everybody else does as well. He's still young and he'll get better but what he gives a team already reminds me of what we get from the top man, Ronaldo, at Real. Wayne's got that same ability to make something out of the ordinary happen whenever he gets the ball. He's got the same strength in possession, the same turn of pace to shake off defenders and he scores goals as well. Having him in the team at the tournament was a huge plus for us. Losing him when we did, half an hour in against Portugal, was just as big a knock.

We'd got accustomed to being able to look up and find Wayne. He and Michael were a perfect combination, probably the best at the tournament. One's great at dropping off and then turning to run at defenders and the other's got the pace to play on the last defender's shoulder. In our first games, defenders knew about Michael and were set up to defend against him, which left them open to what Wayne could do. Come the Portugal game, it had switched round. They were so worried about Wayne being on the ball that their plan looked like being to drop Costinha back to keep an eye on him. That only gave us an advantage in midfield and left spaces in behind that Michael could run into.

It looked like a nothing challenge when Wayne and their defender went down together chasing a ball into the area. Wayne got up but we could all see straight away that he'd had it. Before Duscher broke mine, I'd never heard of a metatarsal. Now, breaking it has happened to too many England players: Gary Neville and Danny Murphy before the last World Cup and now Wayne. It's not an excuse but losing him hurt us. There's nobody in England that plays his type of game. We were set up for it at Euro 2004 and now we had to reorganise as best we could.

There was so much that was good in the game. I think the battle between Ashley Cole and Ronaldo down our left was just about the best thing at Euro 2004. Ronaldo's got so much ability and had already made a big impact for Portugal, just as he has at United. But Ashley was amazing that night at the Estadio Da Luz and wouldn't give him an inch. I think Ash won the battle but what made it such a good scrap was that Ronaldo, every time he got taken out by a tackle, just got up and came back for another go. They're two of the best young players in Europe. If I hadn't been playing, I'd have been happy to pay to watch the pair of them at it.

Portugal, like France in the opening game, had more and more of the possession as the game went on. We got pushed back deeper and deeper which meant when we won the ball there wasn't much option but to launch it forward and hope for the best. I couldn't see Portugal getting back, though: they didn't really make a good chance until they scored. I charged down one cross from the left but the winger got it back and, with his right foot, got a cross in that nobody expected. Postiga headed in and suddenly it looked like we'd be hanging on hoping for extra-time.

As it happened, it should never have come to that. We got a corner on the left, bang on the 90 minutes. I wasn't comfortable at all with how I was feeling physically but I still trusted myself to put a dead ball into the right area. Trusted a team-mate to get on to it, too. As Sol got up to score with his header, I was leaning round to look along the touchline to see where my corner had dropped. I've not had the stomach for watching it again on TV but I saw, there and then, that Ricardo had got himself in a terrible position. I didn't see any England player foul him. He just couldn't get past John Terry and Sol to the ball.

Like I say, any team needs some luck along the way to winning a major tournament. If the goal had been allowed, we'd have been looking forward to the semi-finals. Instead, we were looking forward to extra-time. If us having had two days since our last game – as opposed to Portugal's three – was going to make any difference, you'd expect it to be in the added half hour. We were just doing our best to hold a line on the edge of our penalty area but Rui Costa had come on as a sub and scored a great goal which I think the Portuguese thought was going to win the game for them.

I wasn't even thinking about it at the time but, if it had gone to half-time in extra-time at 2–1 we would have been out on a silver goal. But, even though it would have spared us the grief of penalties again if that had happened, I'm proud of the way we got ourselves back in it again that night. People get so involved in criticising individuals they sometimes lose sight of what we've got as an England team. We were out on our feet and, because we'd been under the cosh for so long, looked like being out of the tournament too. I think about the spirit of the best sides. I think about what we had while I was at United: we were never finished. And, against Portugal, England came back too.

We got a corner on the right and, when the ball broke back towards the edge of the area, Frank had got himself a yard and stuck it past Ricardo. We were almost too whacked to celebrate at the time but that moment counts for a lot with me. You can't ask for better from a team that they have the belief, the sense of togetherness and enough ability to make sure you can't ever write them off. Since Sven took over, we've lost just three competitive games: and it was only a break of the ball or one mistake or being on the wrong side of a referee's decision in each one of those that made the difference.

In the second half of extra-time, we had one good chance when Darius Vassell got away but was pulled down. England at major tournaments, though? We're all used to it going to penalties now, I suppose. Even though I'd missed against Turkey and had my last one saved by Fabien Barthez, I didn't think twice about taking the first penalty against Portugal. And I'll still take the next one that comes my way, too. If it comes down to beating a goalkeeper from 12 yards, unless something strange happens, my technique is good enough to make me sure I'll score. Something very strange indeed, though, ambushed me in the shootout that night at the Estadio Da Luz.

We'd trained at the ground the night before and taken some penalties. I'd noticed – a few of us had – that the turf around one of the penalty spots was unstable. We'd told the manager and I think he talked to the stadium people about it. When I walked down from the halfway line to take the first penalty against Portugal, though, I wasn't thinking about that. All I had in my mind was: *Score.*

A lot of people had been criticising me during the tournament, but the people I cared most about, the England supporters in the stadium, were fantastic. '*One David Beckham, there's only one David Beckham.*' The reaction of those supporters means a lot to me. They were on my side then – whether they thought I'd had a good tournament or not – and I hope that they'll be on my side over the next year and a half too while we're trying to qualify for the next World Cup. They're the best supporters in the world and I want to make sure they've got something to celebrate in Germany in 2006.

A penalty shootout is always tense but, like I say, I believed I'd score. Believed the rest of the lads would, too, and that David James, sooner or later, would be the goalkeeper who guessed right and made the save. It seemed to take an age for the whole process to get started but, eventually, I was ready to put the ball down in front of the Portuguese fans at the shaded end of the ground. It seemed as if it sat alright on the penalty spot, so I turned and walked away. One look upwards and a squint against the sun, I tried to put everything else other than where I was going to hit the ball – to Ricardo's left, the opposite side to the one Fabien had got across to – out of my mind.

I ran up and just as my right foot came back to hit the ball, I felt the pitch move sideways underneath my standing foot. I couldn't believe it. In fact, I think I was aware of where the ball had ended up going even before I understood what had happened. My kick flew up over the angle of the post and the bar: *What's happened? I couldn't have hit it there, at that angle, if I'd tried.* It took a split second to take in the cold fact of it. That I'd missed. I stared down at the spot and the turf around it, waiting for it to make sense. It didn't.

I blew out and began walking back towards the halfway line where the rest of the lads were standing. Everything just seemed to have been going wrong for me that possibly could have. I don't know if any of the other England players said anything to me. I was away somewhere else. *Is that going to cost us winning Euro 2004?* And then, almost at the same moment as that thought came into my mind, the realisation what it might mean.

It was different when I was sent off against Argentina at France 98: then, the disappointment was for myself at first, not knowing what might happen in the rest of the game and then after I got back to England. Now, though, I was a husband and a father and I had the experience of having been the villain six years ago behind me. Even before Deco ran up and scored Portugal's first penalty, it was roaring away in my head. *I can't put my family through this now. I can't put Victoria through that all over again.* That was all I could think of while the rest of the shootout unfolded what seemed like miles away down in the penalty area.

After Michael and Frank scored – everybody was trying to stamp down the turf now – Rui Costa, who I bet was as sure he'd score as I'd been, slipped too and missed. For those few minutes afterwards, it seemed possible that what had happened to me wasn't going to matter after all. John Terry, Owen Hargreaves and Ashley Cole all hit great penalties. The Portuguese scored theirs as well, which meant it was all square after the first five apiece. Sudden death: Darius Vassell was first. It even crossed my mind before he took it that we'd come round again and I might have to take another one.

Ricardo saved and then scored himself. He'd made a mess of that corner at the end of normal time but he had enough about him now to be the hero for Portugal. I don't know what Darius was thinking beyond being as disappointed as the rest of us. I just put an arm on his shoulder:

'Don't worry about it. You've done everything you could tonight. Done everything you could every time you've played for England. You'll get another chance at all this.'

At the same time, the thought came to me: *You're a really nice lad. I know what might be around the corner here. It's better if I end up getting the stick for all this than you having to.*

It was very quiet in the dressing room afterwards. Mr Eriksson thanked us for what we'd done at the tournament, and in qualifying for it too. 'I thought that we could win this competition. I thought we would. Now we're out, but I believe that we were very, very close.'

Figo, who'd been taken off by the Portuguese manager Luis Felipé Scolari – the same man who'd been in charge of Brazil two years before – had asked if I'd swap shirts. I could have just headed straight back onto the coach and given it to him back in Madrid but I thought it was a time to be strong. I found my way into their dressing room. I gave the shirt to Luis, shook Scolari's hand and congratulated their players.

'Well played. Good luck in the rest of the competition.'

Back at the hotel we all had a drink together before we went up to our rooms. Victoria and I were alone together for the first time since the game had finished. I didn't really know what to say. Thinking about what tomorrow – and the days after it – might bring:

'I'm sorry.'

'For what? What's there for you to be sorry about?'

Well, there was England being beaten, for a start. And that was bad enough. But it wasn't what I meant, sitting next to Victoria, staring at our reflections coming back to us in the window glass:

'I don't know if it's worth it. I'm sorry for what this'll mean for us and I can't keep putting you, putting my family, through what comes with these big tournaments. I love football. And I think I can play but . . .'

I'm lucky that Brooklyn and Romeo are still young enough that they probably won't have to go through stuff like *It was your dad's fault, he missed the penalty* from friends at school. I knew there was every chance, though, that Victoria would get whatever was coming my way and more.

I don't know why it happened this summer after we've been together for so long. Victoria's always supported what I've been doing as a footballer. During Euro 2004, though, she actually got interested in the game. We've talked about it since and she says that, in the past, she didn't think she could affect my game in any way.

'It never mattered, did it? We could have a huge argument on the phone an hour before a game. I knew you'd go out and play a blinder anyway.'

During the tournament in Portugal, though, she was the one person who knew how I was feeling physically. And, more importantly, how that had left me feeling uncertain about myself as a player before and during Euro 2004. She knew that my state of mind, for the first time in my career, was having a real effect on my performances and started watching the games more closely to try and make sure she could read my mood. And change it, if that was what I needed. In spite of herself, almost, she found herself getting into the football itself. For the first time ever, we were having conversations about other teams and other players: *Don't you think the Czech Republic played well last night?*

What all that meant, in that room at the Solplay in Lisbon on a warm July night, was that Victoria knew exactly what I needed to hear:

'You've lost and we're going home. But you're England captain. Do you know how many people would give their right arm to be able to say that? All that matters now is that you get this out of your system and get onto the next one.'

In the days that followed, she made sure that was what happened. Ever since I'd won the prize of a trip to Barcelona at Bobby Charlton's soccer school, I'd always known, in the back of my mind, that I'd love to set up something like that. I'd had 15 years to dream about it and, during my first year in Madrid, a couple of chance meetings had made it seem like something for now instead of something for away off in the future.

Next summer – 2005 – David Beckham Soccer Schools will open in London and Los Angeles. My plan is to create something that combines coaching for youngsters from all sorts of backgrounds with some of the fun and the spectacle of a theme park. It's the most exciting thing I've ever been involved with in football aside from actually playing the game. And it's something I hope

I'll still be doing long after I've finished pulling boots on myself. What I've had from football, it only seems right to pass a bit of it on.

Before Euro 2004, we'd set everything up for being able to announce the official launch in America and then back home in England during August. It would mean plane rides, public appearances, TV interviews, the lot. I think Victoria decided on the spot, in the hotel after we'd lost to Portugal:

'Look, it's your decision but I think you need to put all that to one side. You're captain of your country. You play football for one of the biggest clubs in the world. We need to do whatever you need to make those things work.'

Over the next few days, she reorganised everything. The launch was put off until Christmas 2004 and, instead, we went off together – the two of us – for a week's holiday in Morocco. Then we took Brooklyn and Romeo to the South of France for ten days. Being with them, the world and the fuss about Euro 2004 rattling on somewhere else altogether, was exactly the right thing to have done. I feel fitter now, a new season with Real waiting to start and a World Cup qualifying campaign to get going in Austria and Poland, than I have for nearly six months. I haven't been near the gym. I made sure I was right, physically, for pre-season with the lads in Madrid and the new coach, José Antonio Camacho. During our two games on tour in Japan in August, I felt like the player who'd started out life at a new club twelve months before.

Even more important, I'm back in the right frame of mind. A month or so on, the frustration and the self-doubt had all ebbed away. You can't ever pretend that what happened to us in Portugal didn't happen. But you can put the headlines to one side and put the thing into some kind of perspective. First of all, I think I now understand why I felt like I did during Euro 2004. And time with the family made me remember that there are things that are more important than football. Victoria and Brooklyn and Romeo are the heartbeat my world turns to. Having them close to me, warm to how much they mean to me every single day, doesn't push my career to one side. The opposite. I can already feel our life together in Madrid setting fire to my passion for the best game in the world all over again. I'm a bit wiser, maybe. Contented with today and excited about tomorrow, I feel as happy right now as I ever have in nearly thirty years. There's a lot of football to be played yet and I'm ready. A lot of living for the four of us Beckhams to do too. I can't wait to find out what the next twist in my story – our story – will be.

Career Record

Compiled by Mark Baber of the Association of Football Statisticians to 1 July 2004

Personal Summary

Full name: David Robert Joseph Beckham

Place and Date of Birth: Leytonstone, 2 May 1975

Parents: Sandra and Ted

Sisters: Joanne and Lynne

Married: 4 July 1999

Wife: Victoria Caroline Adams Beckham

Sons: Brooklyn Joseph Beckham, born 4 March 1999

     Romeo Beckham, born 1 September 2002

Height: 5ft 11in (180 cm)

Weight: 10st 13lb (75kg)

Early Career

- As a junior played for Ridgeway Rovers, winning the Fyfield 5-a-side tournament.
- At 11 years old won the Bobby Charlton Soccer Skills Competition.
- Played for Waltham Forest under-12s.
- Scouted to Manchester United by Malcolm Fidgeon.
- Represented Essex Schools as a schoolboy.
- Attended Tottenham Hotspur's school of excellence.
- 8 July 1991 – joined Manchester United as a trainee.
- Won the 1992 FA Youth cup.
- 23 September 1992 – First team debut in the Coca Cola Cup at Brighton.
- 22 January 1993 – Signed as a professional.

Notable moments

7 December 1994	Scores on his Champions League debut (vs Galatasaray)
19 August 1995	First Premiership goal (vs Aston Villa)
17 August 1996	Lobs Neil Sullivan from the halfway line (vs Wimbledon)
1 September 1996	Full international debut (vs Moldova in Kishinev)
26 June 1998	First goal for England (vs Colombia)
15 November 2000	Captained England for the first time (vs Italy)
July 2001	First Sportsman on front cover of *The Face*
9 May 2002	Meeting with Tony Blair
10 May 2002	Meeting with Her Majesty the Queen
June 2002	First solo male on front cover of *Marie Claire*
21 May 2003	Meeting Nelson Mandela
1 July 2003	Signs for Real Madrid
27 August 2003	First goal for Real Madrid as they win the Spanish Super Cup (vs Mallorca)
30 August 2003	Scores his first Primera Liga goal, 2 minutes into his debut (vs Real Betis)
27 November 2003	Awarded OBE, for his efforts both on and off the pitch

Career Breakdown

Season-by-Season breakdown

Season	Competition	Total Apps	On as sub	Subbed off	Goals	Yellow	Red
1992–93	League Cup	1	1	0	0	0	0
1994–95	Champions League	1	0	0	1	0	0
1994–95	English FA Cup	2	1	1	0	0	0
1994–95	English Premier	4	2	1	0	0	0
1994–95	League Cup	3	0	0	0	0	0
1994–95	Third Division	5	1	0	2	0	0
1995–96	English FA Cup	3	0	1	1	1	0
1995–96	English Premier	33	7	5	7	4	0

Season	Competition	Total Apps	On as sub	Subbed off	Goals	Yellow	Red
1995–96	League Cup	2	0	0	0	2	0
1995–96	UEFA Cup	2	0	1	0	0	0
1996–97	Champions League	10	0	1	2	1	0
1996–97	English Premier	36	3	3	8	6	0
1996–97	FA Community Shield	1	0	0	1	0	0
1996–97	FA Cup	2	0	0	1	0	0
1997–98	Champions League	8	0	1	0	0	0
1997–98	English Premier	37	3	2	9	6	0
1997–98	FA Community Shield	1	1	0	0	0	0
1997–98	FA Cup	4	0	0	2	0	0
1998–99	Champions League	12	0	0	2	2	0
1998–99	English Premier	34	1	6	6	5	0
1998–99	FA Community Shield	1	0	0	0	0	0
1998–99	FA Cup	7	0	0	1	1	0
1998–99	League Cup	1	0	0	0	0	0
1999–00	Champions League	12	0	0	2	5	0
1999–00	English Premier	31	1	7	6	6	0
1999–00	European Super Cup	1	0	0	0	0	0
1999–00	FA Community Shield	1	0	0	1	1	0
1999–00	FIFA World Club Championship	2	0	0	0	0	1
1999–00	Inter Continental Championship	1	0	0	0	0	0
2000–01	Champions League	12	0	3	0	3	0
2000–01	English Premier	31	2	3	9	3	0
2000–01	FA Community Shield	1	0	0	0	0	0
2000–01	FA Cup	2	0	1	0	1	0
2001–02	Champions League	13	0	3	5	0	0
2001–02	English Premier	28	5	4	11	6	0
2001–02	FA Community Shield	1	0	0	0	0	0
2001–02	FA Cup	1	0	0	0	0	0
2002–03	Champions League	13	3	3	3	1	0

Season	Competition	Total Apps	On as sub	Subbed off	Goals	Yellow	Red
2002–03	English Premier	31	4	2	6	5	0
2002–03	FA Cup	3	0	2	1	0	0
2002–03	League Cup	5	0	0	1	1	0
2003–04	Primera Liga	32	0	10	3	7	1
2003–04	Spanish Super Cup	2	0	0	1	0	0
2003–04	Champions League	7	0	0	1	3	0
2003–04	Copa del Rey	5	0	1	2	1	1

Honours

Team

1992	FA Youth Cup
1995–96	FA Premier League
1996	FA Cup
1996	FA Charity Shield
1996–97	FA Premier League
1997	FA Charity Shield
1998–99	FA Premier League
1999	FA Cup
1998–99	European Champions League
1999	Inter-Continental Cup
1999–2000	FA Premier League
2000–01	FA Premier League
2002–03	FA Premier League
2003	Spanish Super Cup

Personal

1996	August Carling Premiership Player of the Month
1996	Sky Sports/Panasonic Young Player of Year
1997	PFA Young Player of the Year

1997	Sir Matt Busby Award 1999
1999	European Player of the Year (2nd place)
2000	World Footballer Of The Year (2nd Place)
2000	Nation Football Awards Player Of The Year
2001	Western Union Most Valuable Player 2000/01
2001	Britain's Sportsman Of The Year 2001
2001	BBC Sports Personality Of The Year
2001	FIFA World Footballer Of The Year (2nd Place)
2001	European Footballer Of The Year (4th Place)

League Milestones

Milestones for Manchester United

No.	Season	Date	Home Team	Home Score	Away Team	Away Score	Goals	Time
1	1994–95	02/04/95	Man Utd	0	Leeds	0	0	
10	1995–96	16/09/95	Man Utd	3	Bolton	0	0	
50	1996–97	16/11/96	Man Utd	1	Arsenal	0	0	
100	1997–98	21/02/98	Man Utd	2	Derby	0	0	
200	2000–01	25/02/01	Man Utd	6	Arsenal	1	0	
250	2002–03	28/12/02	Man Utd	2	Birmingham	0	1	73

Milestones for Real Madrid

No.	Season	Date	Home Team	Home Score	Away Team	Away Score	Goals	Time
1	2003–04	30/08/03	Real Madrid	2	Real Betis	1	1	3
10	2003–04	23/11/03	Real Madrid	2	Albacete	1	1	38
20	2003–04	15/02/04	Real Madrid	1	Valencia	1		
30	2003–04	01/05/04	Deportivo	2	Real Madrid	0		

Club Goals

Season	Team	Competition	Goals
1994–95	Manchester United	Champions League	1
1994–95	Preston North End	Third Division	2
1995–96	Manchester United	Premiership	7
1995–96	Manchester United	FA Cup	1
1996–97	Manchester United	FA Community Shield	1
1996–97	Manchester United	Premiership	8
1996–97	Manchester United	Champions League	2
1996–97	Manchester United	FA Cup	1
1997–98	Manchester United	Premiership	9
1997–98	Manchester United	FA Cup	2
1998–99	Manchester United	Premiership	6
1998–99	Manchester United	Champions League	2
1998–99	Manchester United	FA Cup	1
1999–00	Manchester United	FA Community Shield	1
1999–00	Manchester United	Champions League	2
1999–00	Manchester United	Premiership	6
2000–01	Manchester United	Premiership	9
2001–02	Manchester United	Premiership	11
2001–02	Manchester United	Champions League	5
2002–03	Manchester United	Premiership	6
2002–03	Manchester United	Champions League	3
2002–03	Manchester United	League Cup	1
2002–03	Manchester United	FA Cup	1
2003–04	Real Madrid	Spanish Super Cup	1
2003–04	Real Madrid	Primera Liga	3
2003–04	Real Madrid	Champions League	1
2003–04	Real Madrid	Copa del Rey	2

Total number of domestic goals: 95

England Goals

Date	Competition	Home	Away	Home Score	Away Score	Goal Time
26/06/98	WC XVI Finals gp G	Colombia	England	0	2	29
24/03/01	WC XVII Europe gp 9	England	Finland	2	1	50
25/05/01	Friendly	England	Mexico	4	0	29
06/06/01	WC XVII Europe gp 9	Greece	England	0	2	87
06/10/01	WC XVII Europe gp 9	England	Greece	2	2	90
10/11/01	Friendly	England	Sweden	1	1	28p
07/06/02	WC XVII Finals gp F	Argentina	England	0	1	44p
12/10/02	ENC XIII gp 7	Slovakia	England	1	2	65
16/10/02	ENC XIII gp 7	England	Macedonia	2	2	13
29/03/03	ENC XIII gp 7	Liechtenstein	England	0	2	53
02/04/03	ENC XIII gp 7	England	Turkey	2	0	90p
20/08/03	Friendly	England	Croatia	3	1	10p
06/09/03	ENC XIII gp 7	Macedonia	England	1	2	63p

Total number of international goals: 13

England Playing Record

Cat	Date	Competition	Home	Away	Home Score	Away Score	Goal Time	Goal Type
Y	07/10/1992	UEFA	France	England	2	0		
Y	17/11/1992	U18	England	Switzerland	7	2		
Y	17/02/1993	U18	Spain	England	1	1		
Y	30/03/1993	U18	England	Denmark	4	2		
U	06/06/1995	Toulon U21 XXIII gp B	England	Brazil	0	2		
U	08/06/1995	Toulon U21 XXIII gp B	England	Malaysia	2	0		
U	10/06/1995	Toulon U21 XXIII gp B	England	Angola	1	0		

Cat	Date	Competition	Home	Away	Home Score	Away Score	Goal Time	Goal Type
U	12/06/1995	Toulon U21 XXIII SF	France	England	2	0		
U	02/09/1995	UEFA U21 XIII gp 6	Portugal	England	2	0		
U	14/11/1995	UEFA U21 XIII gp 6	England	Austria	2	1		
U	24/05/1996	Toulon U21 XXIV gp B	England	Belgium	1	0		
U	28/05/1996	Toulon U21 XXIV gp B	England	Angola	0	2		
U	30/05/1996	Toulon U21 XXIV gp B	England	Portugal	1	3		
A	01/09/1996	WC XVI gp 2	Moldova	England	0	3		
A	09/10/1996	WC XVI gp 2	England	Poland	2	1		
A	09/11/1996	WC XVI gp 2	Georgia	England	0	2		
A	12/02/1997	WC XVI gp 2	England	Italy	0	1		
A	30/04/1997	WC XVI gp 2	England	Georgia	2	0		
A	24/05/1997	Friendly	England	South Africa	2	1		
A	31/05/1997	WC XVI gp 2	Poland	England	0	2		
A	04/06/1997	Tournoi de France	Italy	England	0	2		
A	07/06/1997	Tournoi de France	France	England	0	1		
A	10/09/1997	WC XVI gp 2	England	Moldova	4	0		
A	11/10/1997	WC XVI gp 2	Italy	England	0	0		
A	15/11/1997	Friendly	England	Cameroon	2	0		
A	22/04/1998	Friendly	England	Portugal	3	0		
A	23/05/1998	Friendly	England	Saudi Arabia	0	0		
A	29/05/1998	King Hassan II Cup	Belgium	England	0	0		
A	22/06/1998	WC XVI Finals gp G	Romania	England	2	1		

Cat	Date	Competition	Home	Away	Home Score	Away Score	Goal Time	Goal Type
A	26/06/1998	WC XVI Finals gp G	Colombia	England	0	2	29	FK
A	30/06/1998	WC XVI Finals 2nd Rd	Argentina	England	2	2		
A	14/10/1998	ENC XII gp 5	Luxembourg	England	0	3		
A	18/11/1998	Friendly	England	Czech R	2	0		
A	10/02/1999	Friendly	England	France	0	2		
A	27/03/1999	ENC XII gp 5	England	Poland	3	0		
A	05/06/1999	ENC XII gp 5	England	Sweden	0	0		
A	04/09/1999	ENC XII gp 5	England	Luxembourg	6	0		
A	08/09/1999	ENC XII gp 5	Poland	England	0	0		
A	13/11/1999	ENC XII Play off 1st Leg	Scotland	England	0	2		
A	17/11/1999	ENC XII Play off 2nd Leg	England	Scotland	0	1		
A	23/02/2000	Friendly	England	Argentina	0	0		
A	27/05/2000	Friendly	England	Brazil	1	1		
A	31/05/2000	Friendly	England	Ukraine	2	0		
A	03/06/2000	Friendly	Malta	England	1	2		
A	12/06/2000	ENC XII Finals gp A	Portugal	England	3	2		
A	17/06/2000	ENC XII Finals gp A	England	Germany	1	0		
A	20/06/2000	ENC XII Finals gp A	England	Romania	2	3		
A	02/09/2000	Friendly	France	England	1	1		
A	07/10/2000	WC XVII Europe gp 9	England	Germany	0	1		
A	15/11/2000	Friendly	Italy	England	1	0		
A	28/02/2001	Friendly	England	Spain	3	0		

Cat	Date	Competition	Home	Away	Home Score	Away Score	Goal Time	Goal Type
A	24/03/2001	WC XVII Europe gp 9	England	Finland	2	1	50	OP
A	28/03/2001	WC XVII Europe gp 9	Albania	England	1	3		
A	25/05/2001	Friendly	England	Mexico	4	0	29	FK
A	06/06/2001	WC XVII Europe gp 9	Greece	England	0	2	87	FK
A	15/08/2001	Friendly	England	Holland	0	2		
A	01/09/2001	WC XVII Europe gp 9	Germany	England	1	5		
A	05/09/2001	WC XVII Europe gp 9	England	Albania	2	0		
A	06/10/2001	WC XVII Europe gp 9	England	Greece	2	2	90	FK
A	10/11/2001	Friendly	England	Sweden	1	1	28	PEN
A	13/02/2002	Friendly	Holland	England	1	1		
A	27/03/2002	Friendly	England	Italy	1	2		
A	02/06/2002	WC XVII Finals gp F	England	Sweden	1	1		
A	07/06/2002	WC XVII Finals gp F	Argentina	England	0	1	44	PEN
A	12/06/2002	WC XVII Finals gp F	Nigeria	England	0	0		
A	15/06/2002	WC XVII Finals 2nd Rd	Denmark	England	0	3		
A	21/06/2002	WC XVII Finals QF	Brazil	England	2	1		
A	12/10/2002	ENC XIII gp 7	Slovakia	England	1	2	65	FK
A	16/10/2002	ENC XIII gp 7	England	Macedonia	2	2	13	OP
A	12/02/2003	Friendly	England	Australia	1	3		
A	29/03/2003	ENC XIII gp 7	Liechtenstein	England	0	2	53	FK

Cat	Date	Competition	Home	Away	Home Score	Away Score	Goal Time	Goal Type
A	02/04/2003	ENC XIII gp 7	England	Turkey	2	0	90	PEN
A	22/05/2003	Friendly	South Africa	England	1	2		
A	20/08/2003	Friendly	England	Croatia	3	1	10	PEN
A	06/09/2003	ENC XIII gp 7	Macedonia	England	1	2	63	PEN
A	10/09/2003	ENC XIII gp 7	England	Liechtenstein	2	0		
A	11/10/2003	ENC XIII gp 7	Turkey	England	0	0		
A	16/11/2003	Friendly	England	Denmark	2	3		
A	18/02/2004	Friendly	Portugal	England	1	1		
A	01/06/2004	Friendly	England	Japan	1	1		
A	05/06/2004	Friendly	England	Iceland	6	1		
A	13/06/2004	ENC XIII Finals gp B	France	England	2	1		
A	17/06/2004	ENC XIII Finals gp B	England	Switzerland	3	0		
A	21/06/2004	ENC XIII Finals gp B	Croatia	England	2	4		
A	24/06/2004	ENC XIII Finals QF	Portugal	England	2	2		

Games for Real Madrid in 2003/04

Date	Competition	Home Team	Home Score	Away Team	Away Score	DB Goal	Time
24/08/2003	Super Cup	Real Mallorca	2	Real Madrid	1		
27/08/2003	Super Cup	Real Madrid	3	Real Mallorca	0	1	73
30/08/2003	Primera Liga	Real Madrid	2	Real Betis	1	1	3
02/09/2003	Primera Liga	Villarreal	1	Real Madrid	1		
13/09/2003	Primera Liga	Real Madrid	7	Valladolid	2		
16/09/2003	European Cup	Real Madrid	4	Marseille	2		
21/09/2003	Primera Liga	Malaga	1	Real Madrid	3	1	71
27/09/2003	Primera Liga	Valencia	2	Real Madrid	0		
05/10/2003	Primera Liga	Real Madrid	2	Español	1		

Date	Competition	Home Team	Home Score	Away Team	Away Score	DB Goal	Time
18/10/2003	Primera Liga	Celta Vigo	0	Real Madrid	2		
22/10/2003	European Cup	Real Madrid	1	Partizan	0		
01/11/2003	Primera Liga	Real Madrid	3	Athletic Bilbao	0		
04/11/2003	European Cup	Partizan Belgrade	0	Real Madrid	0		
09/11/2003	Primera Liga	Sevilla	4	Real Madrid	1		
23/11/2003	Primera Liga	Real Madrid	2	Albacete	1	1	38
26/11/2003	European Cup	Marseille	1	Real Madrid	2	1	35
29/11/2003	Primera Liga	Osasuna	1	Real Madrid	1		
03/12/2003	Primera Liga	Real Madrid	2	Atlético Madrid	0		
06/12/2003	Primera Liga	Barcelona	1	Real Madrid	2		
14/12/2003	Primera Liga	Real Madrid	2	Deportivo	1		
18/12/2003	Copa del Rey	Leganés	3	Real Madrid	4	1	13
03/01/2004	Primera Liga	Real Madrid	1	Murcia	0		
18/01/2004	Primera Liga	Real Betis	1	Real Madrid	1		
21/01/2004	Copa del Rey	Real Madrid	3	Valencia	0		
24/01/2004	Primera Liga	Real Madrid	2	Villarreal	1		
01/02/2004	Primera Liga	Valladolid	2	Real Madrid	3		
04/02/2004	Copa del Rey	Real Madrid	2	Sevilla	0		
07/02/2004	Primera Liga	Real Madrid	2	Malaga	1		
11/02/2004	Copa del Rey	Sevilla	1	Real Madrid	0		
15/02/2004	Primera Liga	Real Madrid	1	Valencia	1		
24/02/2004	European Cup	Bayern M	1	Real Madrid	1		
29/02/2004	Primera Liga	Real Madrid	4	Celta Vigo	2		
06/03/2004	Primera Liga	Racing	1	Real Madrid	1		
10/03/2004	European Cup	Real Madrid	1	Bayern M	0		
13/03/2004	Primera Liga	Real Madrid	1	Real Zaragoza	1		
17/03/2004	Copa del Rey	Real Madrid	2	Real Zaragoza	3	1	24
20/03/2004	Primera Liga	Athletic Bilbao	4	Real Madrid	2		
24/03/2004	European Cup	Real Madrid	4	AS Monaco	2		
28/03/2004	Primera Liga	Real Madrid	5	Sevilla	1		
03/04/2004	Primera Liga	Albacete	1	Real Madrid	2		

Date	Competition	Home Team	Home Score	Away Team	Away Score	DB Goal	Time
11/04/2004	Primera Liga	Real Madrid	0	Osasuna	3		
17/04/2004	Primera Liga	Atlético Madrid	1	Real Madrid	2		
25/04/2004	Primera Liga	Real Madrid	1	Barcelona	2		
01/05/2004	Primera Liga	Deportivo	2	Real Madrid	0		
08/05/2004	Primera Liga	Real Madrid	2	Real Mallorca	3		
16/05/2004	Primera Liga	Murcia	2	Real Madrid	1		

Total appearances: 46
Total goals: 7

Key

Apps = Appearances

Cat = Category

Gp = Group

FK = Free Kick

OP = Open Play

PEN or p = Penalty

List of Illustrations

Dedication: Boots © Stu Forster/Getty Images: News and Sport

Brooklyn (page 17) © Popperfoto

Wedding thrones (page 18) © Tony Ward/Mirrorpix

Wedding and Reception photographs (pages 18 and 19) © OK! Magazine

Hair styles (pages 20 and 21)

Main photo © Mike Hewitt/Getty Images: News and Sport

Insets (left to right) © Rex Features; © Ben Radford/Getty Images: News and Sport; © Ross Kinnaird/Getty Images: News and Sport; © Laurence Griffiths/Getty Images: News and Sport; © Popperfoto; © David Fisher/Popperfoto; © Sipa Press/Rex Features; © Carlos Alvarez/Getty Images: News and Sport, © Sean Gleason

Romania game (page 22) © Bradley Ormesher/Mirrorpix

Portugal game (page 22) © Bradley Ormesher/Mirrorpix

With Kevin Keegan (page 22) © Bradley Ormesher/Mirrorpix

England Captain (page 22) © Darren Walsh/Action Images

FIFA World Club Championships 2000 (page 23) © Bradley Ormesher/ Mirrorpix

Training at Carrington (page 23) © Bradley Ormesher/Mirrorpix

Lifting FA Cup (page 24) © Action Images

With Sir Alex Ferguson (page 24) © Rui Vieira/PA Photos

With Roy Keane and Alan Shearer (page 24) © Rui Vieira/PA Photos

Completing the Treble (page 24) © John Sibley/Action Images

Made to measure (page 25)

Main photo © Dean Freeman

Cowboy © Clive Brunskill/Getty Images: News and Sport for PepsiCo

Dressing down © John Rogers/Mission Pictures

Made to measure (pages 26 and 27)

Main photo © Dean Freeman

Insets (left to right): © John Rogers/Mission Pictures

Pushing buggy (page 28) © Jason Fraser

Victoria with children (page 28) © Jason Fraser/Eliot Press

Romeo with Dad (page 37) © Rex Features

Corner kick – Portugal 2004 (page 38) © Ross Kinnaird/Getty Images: News and Sport

With Steven Gerrard – Portugal 2004 (page 39) © EPA/PA Photos

Missing penalty – Portugal 2004 (page 39) © EPA/PA Photos

Vassell's penalty miss – Portugal 2004 (page 39) © Giampiero Sposito/ Corbis

Ready for 2004/05 (page 40) © Sean Gleason

All other photographs supplied courtesy of author's family collection.

Index